BLACK MONTANA

BLACK MONTANA

Settler Colonialism and the Erosion of
the Racial Frontier, 1877–1930

ANTHONY W. WOOD

University of Nebraska Press   *Lincoln*

© 2021 by the Board of Regents of the University of Nebraska

Portions of this manuscript originally appeared in "After the West Won" *Montana: The Magazine of Western History* 66, no. 3 (September 2018): 36–50; and "Colonial Erosion: Unearthing African American History in the Settler Colonial West." *Settler Colonial Studies* 9, no. 3 (Summer 2019): 396–417.

All rights reserved. ∞

First Nebraska paperback printing: 2023
Library of Congress Cataloging-in-Publication Data
Names: Wood, Anthony W., author.
Title: Black Montana: settler colonialism and the erosion of the racial frontier, 1877–1930 / Anthony W. Wood.
Other titles: Erosion of the racial frontier. | Settler colonialism and the erosion of the racial frontier, 1877–1930
Description: Lincoln: University of Nebraska Press, 2021. | Revision of the author's thesis. | Includes bibliographical references and index.
Identifiers: LCCN 2020041734 | ISBN 9781496219435 (hardback) | ISBN 9781496237484 (paperback) | ISBN 9781496227713 (epub) | ISBN 9781496227720 (mobi) | ISBN 9781496227737 (pdf)
Subjects: LCSH: African Americans—Montana—History. | African Americans—Montana—Social conditions. | Race discrimination—Montana—History. | Montana—Race relations. | Settler colonialism.
Classification: LCC F740.N4 W66 2021
DDC 978.600496/073—dc23
LC record available at https://lccn.loc.gov/2020041734

Set in Minion Pro by Laura Buis.
Designed by L. Auten.

For my parents, Tom and Mary,
who took us to live in the mountains

Contents

List of Illustrations	ix
List of Tables	x
Preface: Public History and the Birth of an Archive	xi
Acknowledgments	xxi
Note on Terminology	xxvii
Introduction: Colonial Erosion	1
1. The Golden West: Black Settlers to Montana, 1877–1917	27
2. Making Black Settler Space: Confronting the Colonial Color Line	69
3. Great Debates: Black Settler Politics in the New Age	105
4. Thinking with Magpies: Montana's Conservation Movement and the Occlusion of the Black Wilderness Experience	137
5. Colonial Kinships: Sexuality, the Family, and Anti-Miscegenation Law in Montana	169
6. History among the Sediments: On the Entanglements of Race and Region	199
Epilogue: The Endurance of Black Montana	225

Appendix: Montana Homesteader
Displacement Data following 1917   235
Notes   237
Bibliography   291
Index   315

Illustrations

1. Detail of 1892 Helena, Montana, Sanborn Map rendering — xiii
2. Individual Sanborn Sheet, downtown Helena — xiv
3. 1910 Helena census enumerated by J. B. Bass — xvii
4. Official 1910 Helena census — xviii
5. Montana and location of tribal lands, ca. 1864 — 33
6. Black infantrymen at the Yellowstone River — 39
7. The steamboat *DeSmet* in eastern Montana — 40
8. J. P. Ball portrait of African American man — 47
9. J. P. Ball portrait of African American woman — 48
10. Black soldiers at Fort Shaw, Montana — 56
11. J. P. Ball portrait of African American man in military dress — 57
12. Black student in a class photo, Helena, 1910 — 83
13. Howard Crump house, Helena, 1895 — 88
14. Advertisement for the Zanzibar Club in the *Montana Plaindealer*, 1907 — 100
15. A magpie and a ram in Wheatland County, Montana, 1922 — 139
16. Portrait of James P. Beckwourth — 149
17. Ninth Cavalry members at "Beaver Dick's Tepee," 1896 — 151
18. Pleasant Hour Club picnic near Helena, 1926 — 154
19. The *Daily Missoulian* headline about "Whipping Post Law," 1909 — 181
20. "When the Land Belonged to God," hanging in the Montana Club, 1948 — 202

Tables

1. African American population for urban centers in Montana, 1910 — 36
2. African American population for urban centers in Montana, 1930 — 36
3. Interracial marriages recorded in 1910 census — 183
4. Interracial marriages recorded in 1930 census — 184
5. African American population of Montana cities by gender, 1910 — 193
6. African American population of Montana cities by gender, 1930 — 193

Preface
Public History and the Birth of an Archive

My work on the history of the Black community in Montana began in the basement of a converted duplex and office building that housed the Montana State Historic Preservation Office (SHPO) back in the fall of 2014 (I am happy to say that it has since moved to a beautiful historic building elsewhere on the Capitol campus). At the time, I was still over a year away from receiving my undergraduate degree in history from Carroll College, a small liberal arts school perched atop a hill rising from the capital city of Helena. Working as an intern with SHPO, only twenty years old, and without the type of training that one typically receives in graduate school, I can safely say that I had no idea what I was doing. Luckily, my job consisted at first mostly of sorting through census materials, city directories, historic Sanborn Insurance Maps, and Google Earth images as I tried to locate extant buildings that may have had architectural and historical significance. Perhaps the most fortunate event in my life was returning after graduation to begin my first job as historical researcher for Montana's African American Heritage Places Project (MAAHPP).

In the late spring of 2015, my supervisor, Kate Hampton—who has spearheaded the project since it began in the mid-2000s—and I came up with an idea. We envisioned creating maps of all the residences and businesses of the Black community in Helena using several collections of detailed historic insurance maps. If things were done correctly, the aim was to produce a mosaic of turn-of-the-century Helena that would be geographically accurate and then to transpose that map over current satellite imaging. Needless to say, my attempts to stitch together over forty individual sheets of maps using Microsoft Paint both showed my limitations with technology and utterly offended the sensibilities of the

SHPO's new geographic information system (GIS) specialist, who had just moved into the office upstairs from my basement lair. Luckily my transgression prompted her to offer her expertise to create an *actual* map that georectified my data and highlighted all the relevant buildings so as to facilitate effortless interpretation. (Considering this was our first interaction, to this day I remain absolutely amazed that she agreed to marry me a year and a half later.)

That map set me on a trajectory that has informed my professional research and graduate studies ever since. For the project's purposes, the map showed over one hundred buildings and houses that were owned or rented by Helena's African American community between 1880 and 1930. Information from the 1900, 1910, and 1930 censuses, over thirty years of Polk City Directories, and a wealth of local knowledge helped map one of the largest and most vibrant Black communities in Montana and the Rocky Mountain West at the time.[1] It quickly became evident that the map also told a more ominous tale than we had anticipated. In the several distinct Black neighborhoods and the lively downtown business district that held dozens of Black enterprises throughout the years, fewer than 20 percent of all houses, tenements, or storefronts once occupied by Helena's African American community now remain. When we eventually mapped the other major Black communities across the state, we saw similar—and sometimes much higher—percentages of loss.

Urban renewal initiatives in the 1970s and 1980s removed many buildings from Montana's capital. The targets were, as in many cities, areas of poorer housing, or damaged and neglected commercial buildings. This leveling was preceded by the demolition of dozens of historic homes in Helena's shaded residential quarters during the mid-twentieth century. What the Helena map shows, however, is not the evils of thoughtless development on the part of urban renewal officials or private individuals. It is unlikely that city officials, developers, or owners of historic houses had any idea that the piles of debris they created were once the stores and neighborhoods of Montana's historic Black community. For it was that, by the mid-twentieth century, too few Black residents from that era remained in Helena to fight for their cultural heritage. This was what

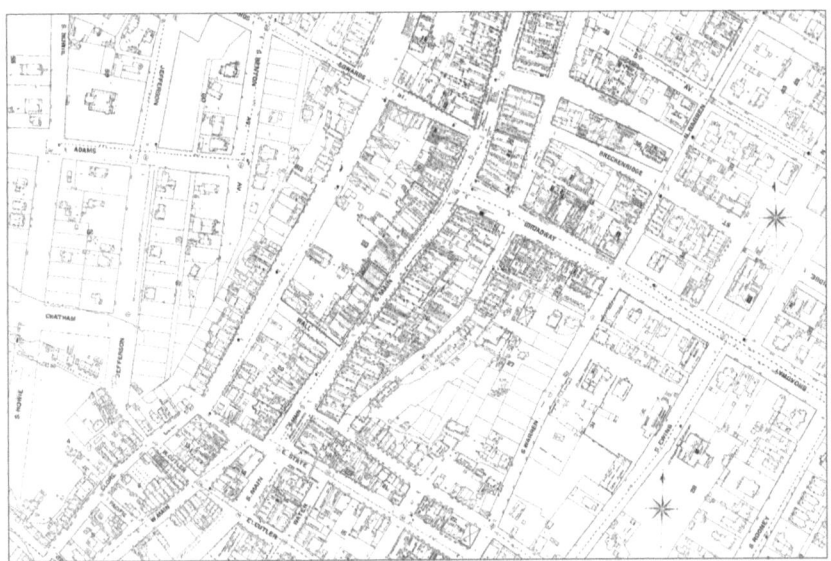

1. Detail of 1892 Helena Sanborn Map rendering. Each map sheet typically includes three to four blocks. The image above is comprised of about twelve separate Sanborn sheets. On file at the Montana State Historic Preservation Office, Helena, Montana. Courtesy of Steffany Wood.

the map so poignantly spoke to—not the physical removal of the Black community per se, but the ongoing, intangible occlusions of the region's colonial history, scouring the heritage of African Americans from the land as well as their experiences and stories from our collective memory.

Even as I relied upon this observation to inform my research and writing for the project and, later, my master's degree at Montana State University, not until I started my PhD at the University of Michigan did I begin to think more critically about the role of public history in the creation of an archive. The goal of the MAAHPP was not just to tell important local and state history, but to very consciously provide a body of primary and secondary sources that academic historians and the public alike could access and use. The birth of this archive came both through the labor of professional historians, researchers, and archivists—that is, members of the community who got paid—and through the donated time and effort of dozens of volunteers, inquisitive citizens

2. Detail from an individual Sanborn Map superimposed over a current aerial photograph of downtown Helena. This cluster of fifteen African American residences inhabited from 1890 to 1930, including several early log cabin dwellings seen near the bottom left, illustrates the extent of the erasure due to twentieth-century urban renewal initiatives in Helena, Montana. Data: ESRI base map. On file at the Montana State Historic Preservation Office, Helena, Montana. Courtesy of Steffany Wood.

who attended numerous public talks and lectures, and descendants of the Black community living across the country. All contributed their knowledge and understanding to the endeavor in incalculable ways that I think a purely academic project could never replicate.

Only some of what the community produced constituted "new" material, like the spatial analysis, historic maps, and several oral histories. Much of what can be found on the website has been cobbled together from older archives established by state entities over the last century and a half. However, in our attempt to bring history to the people and make the past legible in very specific ways—after all, that is the primary job of the public historian—I think a profound subversion took place. Prior to the new archive, Black individuals, whose names appeared infrequently among the names of hundreds of thousands of white settlers from 1870 to 1930, became buried and trivialized as a group of people too small in number to be of any real consequence, easily missed and more easily "forgotten."

One example from the colonial archive of Montana illustrates this with mind-numbing clarity. The Black community of Helena in 1910 was the largest in the state, at just over 420 individuals. For reasons that remain unclear, rather than collect census data house by house, as was standard practice, census officials appointed a prominent member of the community, Joseph Blackburn Bass, the owner and editor of the local Black newspaper, to collect the information of the city's African American residents. It becomes immediately clear to all those who work with this document that his task was an impossible one. It required him to have knowledge of *all* Black citizens in town, including the many transient laborers who rented tenement rooms or lived in other impermanent dwellings. Helena did not have one single Black neighborhood, but rather several different enclaves of as many as a dozen or as few as two or three Black homes spread throughout the city. Bass's census reveals that he likely collected information at large gatherings, such as after church, instead of going door to door. Next-door neighbors sometimes appear over one hundred entries apart. Some households are counted twice, some none at all. My very first job as a college intern on this project amounted to several months of just trying to make sense of it all. Bass's enumeration is also not the "official" census; his copy bears a large X and sometimes even the word "UNOFFICIAL" scrawled in dismissive hand across each page. Department of the Census bureaucrats counted the rest of Helena but, evidently, skipped every Black man, woman, and child they encountered. At the end of each section, it appears that they cross-referenced Bass's count once they had finished and added the information in the remaining spaces. Not only is the Black community absent from their physical space in the census and in the archive, but it also seems that officials transposed Bass's census onto the official copy *in pencil*, almost as if to acknowledge the Black community's presence, but not their permanence. Indeed, many such entries in the official census are so faded that they are all but illegible today; only the original copy offers us any information about the Black residents of Helena in 1910. Of course, I had no idea at the time, but that was my first encounter with the occlusions of the "colonial archive."

Whereas state records such as censuses assert legibility upon a population and are often employed as a form of social control, the 1910 Helena census suggests that something else equally as odious was afoot. The erosive patterns are mirrored by the 1892 map mosaic mentioned above. The task of recreating the physical space of the Black community in Montana was an exceedingly difficult one—by design. Ten years before I started at SHPO, another employee working on the project, Scott Meredith, painstakingly sorted through every page of Montana's 1870, 1910, and 1930 censuses and created spreadsheets of every listed Black Montanan. His actions likewise constituted a deeply subversive act against the distortions of state power. When I pored over that data a decade later and added some of my own; when my wife, Steffany, rendered it in physical form as an easily comprehensible map; and when the Montana Historical Society uploaded all of this for public consumption—this, too, was subversive.

To be clear, the real subversion—an idea I want to emphasize throughout this book—did not come from the gathering together of sources, *but from its purposeful intent to inform public memory*. Snoopy academics could have ferreted out all this knowledge (though very few seem to have attempted it so far) and published their findings in journals and books and then filed away their research in desk drawers and on library shelves. Don't get me wrong; that is a critically important endeavor. After all, you are holding one such book, and I can assure you every extra space in my home holds piles of poorly indexed maps, records, photos, and notepads. It is important that this archive emerged as a form of public history, created through a collective reassessment of the past by and for the community, precisely because the loss of collective,

3. 1910 Helena Census enumerated by J. B. Bass. U.S. Federal Census 1910; Helena, Lewis and Clark, Montana; Roll: T624_833; Page: 10A; Enumeration District: 0153; FHL microfilm: 1374846.

publicly held knowledge about this past was just as purposeful. Unless this type of corrective is offered, the very same racism, oppression, dispossession, and elimination that has curated our history thus far will inevitably reproduce those same forms of violence today even while it falsely absolves those implicated of any culpability in its ongoing duress.

And so, the book you hold, I say with real pride, is almost entirely the product of work in that subversive archive. It informed what secondary literature I chose to engage with and what types of questions I asked of my scholarly predecessors. Because I was not prepared for the depth of occlusions and erasures I would encounter when I first began research nearly seven years ago, I was forced to return to every source and cita-

4. Official 1910 Helena Census. Ten African American individuals appear at the end of the district. U.S. Census 1910; Helena, Lewis and Clark, Montana; Roll: T624_833; Page: 8B; Enumeration District: 0154; FHL microfilm: 1374846.

tion, reread every piece of text, and reconsider every argument multiple times. As archives go, this one is by no means immense, but, as the 1910 census would suggest, it bore certain entanglements and complexities that required continuous examination from new angles and with new tools of inquiry. Therefore, this final product, I deeply hope, will not be "final." If I have the last word on the matter, I will have failed miserably. By gesturing to new questions that scholars might attend to in the future, it is my hope that more critical perspectives and diverse experiences will continue to hone and reshape our understanding of race and society in Montana's past as well as its present.

For all the archive's merits, there can be no doubt that it has suffered a devastating loss of Black voices. The materials that generally offer the clearest perspectives of historical actors—family histories, archived letters and memoirs, and other extensive archival collections—fall victim to a process of *colonial erosion* that I detail in the introduction. Those who have read extensively in the history of the Black West will know that the African American history of the Northern Rocky Mountain region is perhaps the most ignored and understudied in the wider historiography. The erasure of Black communities, along with the memories and voices they harbor, is at least in part why. From written sources, we can detect the imprints of the lives of men and women like Louise Harrison and Walker Browning, whose names appear in these pages, but their own writings, thoughts, and words are absent. Sadly, this is the case for most of the Black Montanans who lived in this era.

This book relies heavily upon those few Black voices that do survive, such as newspaper editors like Joseph Bass, Chris Dorsey, and John Duncan, as well as the various individuals to whom they gave voices in the pages of their papers. Additionally, oral histories conducted in the 1970s by Quintard Taylor provide us with the last recordings of Black settlers who called Montana home in the early twentieth century. Other individuals left extensive biographical sources: census records, addresses, marriage licenses, mentions in local papers, army records, death certificates, and obituaries. These sources, too, can help retrace the lives of Black Montanans across physical space and time despite not containing the voices of the persons themselves. Still others appear for only a brief instant in the archive, but nevertheless provide us with an insightful window into a particular moment or event. To this end, my goal for this book is to subvert these silences by offering the reader with an (admittedly limited) impression of how Black Montanans experienced and understood their world at this time. By taking these sources together and attending to the occluded lives of Black Montanans with no small amount of urgency and analytical weight, we map out the traces and imprints of a history that is subjected to such powerful structures of forgetting and erosion.

This is not solely a book about Black westerners living in what is now called Montana. This book is also the work of a white settler Montanan who wants to understand how the state has become home to fewer Black Americans than any other, and what that history means for our colonial present. My positionality requires an acceptance of certain limitations caused by the blinders of social privilege that I inevitably wear. It also demands a fierce reliance on the perspectives and ideas of other scholars who have come before me and a dedication to the voices of resistance that emerge from the archive. It is my hope that these voices and scholarly antecedents will combine with my own research and framing to speak to some important questions. How does racial ideology inform the way that so many contemporary Montanans understand their home, their values, their collective identity, and even the way they move through their world? To be certain, this book will not exhaust the answers to such questions. It does, however, seek them in a history that few Montanans even know to exist.

Acknowledgments

I am as surprised as anyone that this book exists. From the very first moment I considered submitting a proposal to presses as I waited in a checkout room of the University of Michigan Hospital until its "completion," this project's path was narrow at best, and foolhardy at worst. I am most fortunate that none of my amazing peers, colleagues, or professors who took the time to advise me during this process believed it was the latter, or at least they did not let on. *Black Montana* has been shaped by three great institutions: the Montana Historical Society, Montana State University, and the University of Michigan. Individuals and faculty at each of these places gave me the resources and time I needed to fall in love with the study of the past, to find the questions I wanted to answer, and to grow as a storyteller and writer.

I must endlessly thank Kate Hampton at the Montana State Historic Preservation Office for caring about Black history in Montana and its preservation, such that she has dedicated countless hours in service to this project and the community over the past decade or more. Without her innovative thinking, researching, planning, advocating, and, above all, writing all the grants that paid so many people for their time, including two years of my own, I am hesitant to even think what would have become of so many people's stories. As I do not recall writing a single application for funding during my time at SHPO, that means that Kate is responsible for securing grants and other forms of support from the National Park Service Underrepresented Community Grant Program, the Montana Cultural Trust, the Montana Historical Society, the Montana History Foundation, and the Friends of the Montana Historical Society. As it turned out, her hard work funded my first forays into archival research for this book. Kate, I am overwhelmed by how many beers I need to buy you.

Reflecting on my different graduate school experiences, I count my two years as a master's student in the history department at Montana State in Bozeman among the most formative and productive in my academic journey so far. The intellectual debts I accrued there are profound. Mark Fiege's graduate seminar on the West and settler colonialism remains the most important class I ever took. I learned later that Fiege had only recently himself encountered the new field and its theories shortly before that class. That this eminent scholar of the American West, prodded by curiosity and a willingness to challenge his own ideas, would reshape his seminar of expertise such that he, too, was reading, learning, and processing these questions along with his students, taught me a lesson about humility and teachability that I hope never to forget. Mary Murphy and Billy Smith were likewise amazing scholars to learn from in seminars, and especially, in their undergraduate classrooms where I was lucky enough to student-teach or grade with them both. Their generosity with their time and knowledge cannot be overstated.

The department in Bozeman offered generative space where I was able to present my work at faculty and graduate student colloquiums that were equal parts casual and challenging. I am deeply sorry to my dear friends Jen Dunn, Laurel Angel, and Amanda Hardin, who were unfortunate enough to have to work within earshot of me. In Bozeman, I found a community that loved history and sought to engage with the past in their everyday lives. Thank you to Crystal Alegria and Marsha Fulton at the Extreme History Project for the opportunity to lead walking tours, speak as part of their fantastic lecture series, and generally just be inspired by committed public history professionals making a difference in the world.

The first person who told me I needed to publish my research as a book was Amanda Hendrix-Komoto. After serving on my thesis committee, Amanda waited only about twenty minutes following my defense to tell me that what I had written deserved to be a book someday, and not just a chapter in my future dissertation or a series of academic articles. Her support and friendship helped carry this project well beyond what it was as a thesis. Indeed, more than any other individual, Amanda identified and focused on the bigger questions my project was (slowly) beginning to encounter and encouraged me to tackle them. This type of mentorship takes a great deal of time and a genuine interest in the work. Every graduate student needs someone like her. She has also been a fun and uplifting coconspirator in the publishing process, as we both signed our first book contracts with University of Nebraska Press around the same time. She had a head start on me, but I think I closed the gap.

What Ann Arbor lacks in mountains it makes up for with wonderful scholars who took an interest in a project that was well underway by the time I arrived at the University of Michigan. Conversations over coffee and between meetings with Matt Lassiter, Matthew Countryman, Matthew Spooner, Greg Dowd, Stephen Berrey, Tiya Miles, and Anthony Mora helped me visualize the next phase of the project and think about what impact I wanted my scholarship to have. Seminar discussions with Heather Ann Thompson, Greg Dowd and Deborah Dash-Moore, Matthew Spooner, Stephen Berrey, Sandra Gunning, and Jason Young have enriched and shaped my thinking on so many relevant issues, making their way into these pages in some form or another.

A number of individuals read drafts and chapters and offered helpful comments and critiques. Many thanks to Amanda Hendrix-Komoto, Mark Fiege, Mary Murphy, and Billy Smith, who read this book in its master's thesis form. Matthew Spooner, Dorceta Taylor, Sueann Caulfield, and Han Xu read chapters or other sections. Anthony Mora and Greg Dowd graciously agreed to read and comment on the entire manuscript as I prepared it for submission. At the University of Nebraska Press, Bridget Barry has been supportive of this project since the beginning. She read my endlessly wordy emails and made the processes manageable during a remarkably stressful time. She also found two wonderful reviewers in Herbert Ruffin II and Jason Pierce. Dr. Ruffin's thoughtful critiques pushed me to make a deeper engagement with previous scholarship and to sharpen my analysis of racial ideology in the Black West. Dr. Peirce read the entire manuscript twice and commented on the initial proposal and sample chapters (for which he certainly must have set some kind of record for fastest reviewer). His commitment during this part of the project was incredible, and his recurring calls for more Black voices changed the way I thought about my subjects as I desperately wondered what someone was thinking at a given moment. When the sources were available, I resolved to make the most of their exhortations, intellect, and emotion. In the end this attention opened up new ways of thinking and writing about the lives of Black Montanans of a century or more ago. I hope that readers will register the absences of such sources and pause and contemplate what they say when their voices have managed to outlast the erosion of our colonial past and present. These readers and reviewers have saved me from many errors, lapses in judgment, and countless obfuscations. The faults that remain are my own.

More broadly, numerous scholars, historians, and thinkers have contributed immensely to how I think about the study of the past. The work of Ann Laura Stoler, Patrick Wolfe, Tiya Miles, Cedric Robinson, Robin Kelley, Quintard Taylor, Kelly Lytle Hernández, and Margaret Jacobs continues to challenge, sharpen, and sometimes even upend the types of questions I ask about the past. Getting answers from the archives more often than not was forthcoming with the aid of many amazing archivists and librarians. In Helena, Zoe Ann Stoltz at the MHS Research Center and Jeff Malcomson at the Photo Archives were both immensely helpful tracking down images and other materials from other collections. Kate Hampton and Ellen Baumler consistently managed to uncover information that had eluded me. So many wonderful oral histories allowed me to listen to individuals tell their stories and come to a better understanding of the world I wanted to write about. I must thank Kate Hampton, Alan Thompson, Laurie Mercier, and Quintard Taylor for their skill and dedication to this critical form of history work, and for making such recordings available to future researchers.

I owe a special thank you to Dr. Tycel Phillips, Tera Mayer, and all the nurses and staff at the University of Michigan Cancer Center and the Bone Marrow Transplant and Acute Leukemia Clinic. It is never easy to face such times, but their care and expertise allowed me to stay in classes, work on the book, and maintain something of a normal life while putting difficult things into perspective.

Finally, my family offered endless support and a constant interest in my work even when I am quite positive that they wished I would talk about something else for a change. My sister Amelia, already a thoughtful scholar and writer, provided weekly conversations around topics in environmental studies from science and literature to art and history. She causes me to think deeper and reflect on the way we live in the world. Thank you, Mimi. My dad is far and away the sharpest thinker and most patient writer I have ever met. As an intellectual engaged in numerous conversations in his field of theology, his willingness to consider the different perspectives on a subject in which he is already an expert taught me a great deal about scholarly humility from an incredibly early age. He engaged the arguments of this book as he offered his support, ideas, and, most important, copy edits.

My wife, Steffany, read every chapter multiple times. She pointed to wherever my arguments were unclear and helped me think through sections that needed more work. She is a brilliant cartographer, making beautiful maps for both this book and for the *Montana's African American Heritage Places Project*. Since the day that I first walked into her office asking for help putting together a map of 1892 Helena, she has been my whole world.

Note on Terminology

For this study, I use the disciplinary standard for naming and racial identification. "Black" and "African American" are used interchangeably to facilitate the flow of reading. I have left unchanged all terms used by historical actors when quoting them. Black papers, which offer some of the clearest voices in this history, typically used "Negro" and "colored" following the conventions of their day. Additionally, both Black papers of Montana often referred to the whole Black community as "the race." White papers also used such language, though more often "negro" appeared without the capital "N"—a spelling that frequently conveyed derision or disrespect at the time.

When referring to those peoples whose ancestors called North America home before European invasion, I use "Indigenous," "Indian," or "Native" peoples, as this category covers many nations and tribes. When possible, I use the specific tribal name such as Crow or Northern Cheyenne. Tribes in Montana today often prefer to be called "American Indian," but as much of this book deals with the era before the 1924 Indian Citizen Act, I have chosen to only use "American Indian" or "Native Americans" in reference to individuals *after* that date as a reminder that being "American" was an identity and a form of citizenship denied to most Indians for nearly one hundred and fifty years, an identifier they achieved with great struggle.

Finally, as this work is insistent that settler colonialism is an ongoing project, I frequently refer to both Black and white Montanans as "settlers," whether I am referring to a group of migrants in the 1870s or residents of established communities in the 1920s.

BLACK MONTANA

Introduction *Colonial Erosion*

When Annie Gordon, a former slave, came up the Missouri River onboard a steamboat and disembarked in north central Montana Territory in the 1880s, she was terrified of the Indigenous people she encountered. According to the stories she later told her daughter, Rose, Annie watched in terror as bands of "warriors," in feathers and regalia, lined the banks near Fort Benton while their boat stalled from time to time on sand bars. Clinging tightly to her infant, John, Annie explained to an older Black woman who served as the stewardess how she would be at ease knowing they were not staying here, where so many Indians lived. Throughout their voyage, the stewardess had reassured and comforted Annie as they churned farther and farther up the Missouri and away from the world she had known. The journey west overwhelmed Annie at times. In one fit of tears, the stewardess put her arm around the young woman, saying, "Child, you is goin' to a tough country and you must nerve up."[1] To dispel Annie's fear of Indian peoples who lived in the territory, she told her that there were "lots of those folks [where she was going]," but also that there were "some fine folks among them."[2]

Annie and her daughter Rose Gordon's relationship with the Indigenous peoples of Montana, primarily the Crow, remained a fixture in the ways they retold their origin stories for years after. Like her mother, Rose, too, could claim her beginnings in Montana had been witnessed by the land's aboriginal inhabitants. Indeed, intriguingly, when Rose recounted the story of her birth, she proclaimed more than once that she was the first "white" child born in the camp, as all others were Indian children up until 1883.[3] As she wrote and rewrote that vignette for newspapers, articles, and eventually a draft of her autobiography, she also penned a version of her birth story in which the Indian midwife who delivered her was the one to give her that title. "She did not know that most coulored [sic] children are born a pale-face," she explained. But, as for the other residents of Barker, "the settlers and miners knew differently; they had a great laugh."[4]

In her nearly two-hundred-page unpublished autobiography, nostalgically titled "Gone Are the Days," Gordon recounts her experiences as a Black woman among white settlers in addition to chronicling the history of early pioneers in the territory. She watched the young state of Montana transform from a social space still largely dominated culturally and demographically by Indigenous people, such as those who witnessed her parents' arrival and her own birth, into a space where even her memories as a Black women seemed out of place in a state fast on its way to becoming one of the whitest in the country. This book explores the racial legacy of Montana and the experience of Blackness within and against a settler colonial society. How was Rose Gordon a "white" settler—either in her own estimation or in that of the Indian woman who delivered her—when she was born among Native peoples, but Black among white settlers? Rose Gordon was keenly aware, both as a child, and then as an adult looking back, that her identity as non-Native was significant in the society into which she was born. Her world was split between those being dispossessed and those dispossessing. Beneath the sedimented histories of this superficial binary, however, and what Rose Gordon's story reveals, is that her very presence represented a subversion to any such clean delineations within an ongoing imperial project.

On Black Settler Colonialism

This book begins from a simple, critical premise: the American West is a settler colony. The society that exists today, on all levels, whether it is politics, cultural production, economics, religion, and especially regional place identities, has developed through the governing logics of settler colonialism. While traditional or "franchise" colonial formations might share important genealogical attachments to the rise and spread of global capitalism in the seventeenth and eighteenth centuries, a growing number of scholars define "settler colonialism" as the ongoing process where colonists arrive on a land held by Indigenous peoples with the singular intent on residing there as permanent settlers. This is contrasted with traditional colonists who, empowered by an imported colonial government, remain only long enough to extract resources from the land and labor from the Native inhabitants. Settler colonists, on the other hand, recognize the *land* as the preeminent manifestation of colonial power. Moreover, in time that power translates to a sense of belonging. Settlers who arrived only a generation or two before come to feel that the land is their birthright, and that they are *home*.[5] Going further, some scholars argue that settler colonialism is not merely a different type of imperial formation, but, more precisely, an ongoing imperial project that has failed to secure the permanence of colonial domination.[6]

Settler colonialism's defining characteristic, then, might be found in the anxiety circulating through settler societies: its unease is that it is always failing to rest upon its twin goals of Native elimination and assimilation.[7] This incompleteness of settler domination often produces an anxious settler consciousness that is made ever aware of the illegitimacy of its claims to home and belonging. In spite of this failure, settler colonies are uniquely resistant to any meaningful decolonization. Indeed, the decolonization of settler forms remains difficult to even imagine, let alone bring about. This challenge arises in part because white settlers have inhabited and called the land home for centuries in many places around the globe. Their governments, solidified in their status as nation-states, control the land on which many sovereign Indigenous peoples continue to endure. But among the surest lines of defense of settler states against decolonization is a widespread ignorance (or denial) of their existence and inherent violence, as well as an imprecise understanding of the mechanisms of their durabilities.[8]

Black Montana takes up both concerns. First, its arguments engage, critically at times, with the pioneering scholarship of Patrick Wolfe and others who have theorized the workings of settler colonies around the world.[9] One of the most powerful ideas animating settler colonial studies today is that this social ordering relies upon the *elimination of the Native*, and that "settler invasion is a structure, not an event."[10] Wolfe has referred to this as the "logic of elimination." That logic remains within the social ontology of "the settler" well after the violent phase of elimination and expropriation seems to fade away. The process of elimination, however, does not actually end. Rather, it merely changes form and becomes less visible—continuously negotiating who can gain access to land and power, and who cannot.

Scrutinizing these negotiations of power centers anti-Black racism in discourses on settler colonialism in important ways. As both the product of and the framework onto which colonial regimes are fastened and maintained, race and racialization have animated settler colonial studies and the various critiques leveled against it.[11] For instance, the work of Robin D. G. Kelley, Iyko Day, Lisa Lowe, and others who have engaged Cedric Robinson's theory of racial capitalism and, more recently, Black feminist theorists like Tiffany Lethabo King have challenged what some have called "white settler colonial studies" to decenter white Europeans from the historical narrative of settler colonization.[12] Despite falling back on a somewhat Eurocentric framing, Wolfe's own work nevertheless manages to illustrate the centrality of race to colonial histories.[13] In *Traces of History: Elementary Structures of Race*, Wolfe historicizes his logic of elimination thesis, which has become indelible in the field of settler colonial studies itself. In doing so he contends that "race is colonialism speaking."[14]

Wolfe's tragic and untimely passing in 2016 meant that sustained scholarly engagements with his ideas would carry on without his voice, but it seems not entirely without his perspective. The study of settler colonialism's "racial regimes" has remained, generally speaking, locked in a somewhat one-sided debate around Wolfe's insistence on a binary lens of whiteness and indigeneity. Resultingly, the lion's share of articles and monographs that have been published on the racial regimes of settler colonialism come from the fields of ethnic or Indigenous studies.[15] While such work is and will remain vital in order to make sense of our colonial past and present, there is also a notable absence of Black studies scholars—specifically historical thinkers—in the United States who have taken up the framework of settler colonialism. With a few very recent exceptions, Black studies scholars might recognize settler structures, but they rarely attempt to combine their concepts, theories, and methodologies and produce a detailed account of African American experiences in settler society.[16] As a result, the recalcitrant binary between white colonizers and Indigenous colonized is only reinforced.

Bound by the settler binary, Black history in the West is often resigned to "third spaces" in the colonial encounter—a subjectivity that does not reflect people as either the producers or direct objects of historical actions. Rather than breaking down the settler binary, framing Black western history as taking place in "third spaces" instead risks reproducing the settler myth that Black history is ultimately produced through the ambivalent agency of white settlers. At most, Black migrants to the West can be "contributors" to a narrative that is, ultimately, still about the establishment of white settlers and the ongoing elimination of Native peoples.

Such has been an occluding pattern. Consider the only work that attempts a synthesis history of the United States as a settler colony: Walter Hixon's *American Settler Colonialism* (2013). Though laudable on many fronts, Hixon's approach, like most others in the field, rarely mentions African Americans beyond the condition of slavery or in an "Indianized" form as Black-Indian freedmen living among the Seminole, Creek, Choctaw, Chickasaw, and Cherokee nations. Additionally, such scholarship is emblematic of how a singular focus on white-Indigenous colonization might actually reinscribe the telos of the settler imagination that all but excludes Black experiences from its central focus. Influential works from "white settler colonial studies" and writings from Indigenous perspectives have profoundly shaped and guided many different studies of settler societies, including this one, but they do not yet sufficiently challenge this narrowly prescribed vision of the Black experience within and against American settler colonialism.[17]

Black Montana contributes to the slowly growing body of work by recent historians seeking to unsettle the settler binary in meaningful ways. Two examples bear particular significance for this conversation.

Kendra Field's *Growing Up with the Country* (2018) presents the varied and complicated realities of Black homemaking on Indian lands after the Civil War. In her rich, microhistorical account, Field argues that African Americans migrating to Indian lands faced ever-shifting racial categories as they "moved over time and space" and shows us not only the contingency of such homemaking, but its inherent colonial contradictions. Kelly Lytle Hernandez's *City of Inmates* (2017) powerfully demonstrates the explanatory power of a settler framework to histories focused on race and incarceration in Los Angeles. Her work focuses on the settler logic of elimination as it was employed by the state through an emerging carceral landscape that targeted those people deemed to be "illegitimate" settlers. At times this included transient whites as well as Blacks, Asians, and Chicanos.[18] In effect, these scholars draw our attention to the ambiguities of eliminatory logics and illustrate how the lived realities of those within setter society often defy the settler conceit of a binary world.

As such prominent works would now suggest, most scholars will admit, on a certain level, that Black migrants to the American West contributed to and participated in the settler project. As of yet, however, no body of work directly considers the Black settler colonial experience as opposed to merely the Black experience *under* "white" settler colonialism.[19] This study attempts to do both. As such, I am aware that many in ethnic studies have challenged the idea that people of color can be characterized as settler colonists at all.[20] The history put forward in this book aims, first, to register these challenges. But, in doing so, it also becomes clear that the space to explore and debate these often problematic and complicated histories remains wide open. To be certain, avoiding the prolonged discussion on "what do we do with the 'black settler,'" as historian Tiya Miles recently phrased the impasse, has not been the product of either lack of thought or lack of sources.[21] Since (and perhaps because of) the publication of Wolfe's seminal essay "Settler Colonialism and the Elimination of the Native," the lived experiences of formerly enslaved African Americans who left the South to settle Indian lands to the west have floated uncomfortably in the conceptual ether. Early theorists at times seemed to write off free, and freed, Blacks as merely an inconvenient distraction from the more important structuralist history at hand. "Yes, some Indians were involved in Black slavery," Wolfe admitted, "and yes, some Blacks participated in Indian dispossession, but neither Indians nor Blacks were the originators and collective beneficiaries of these systemic crimes. Rather, both *were caught up* in a system that had been created and was being maintained by others."[22] For years now, Wolfe's obviously passive and temporally inarticulate framing has been easier to merely sidestep than to engage or challenge. But, as the stories of hundreds and thousands of Black Montanans will make clear, Black migration to the West following the Civil War and Reconstruction cannot solely be capitulated to the goals of "white" settler colonialism.[23] Black westerners themselves contested the category of "settler" such that they were at once participants in the wider colonial project while fostering new ideas of *home* and *belonging* that ultimately threatened to expose the racial (il)logics of the settler regime.

Omitting the complicated experiences of Black migrants from our analysis of settler societies has not been without consequences. Indeed, appropriately framing the lives and landscapes of Black newcomers in the broader history of the American West remains a complicated task as historical and contemporary obstacles to our understanding have emerged. Perhaps the greatest barrier that scholars face as they try to come to terms with this historical moment has been erected by the rigidity of meaning—not to mention inherent violence—that now accompanies the term "settler." Tiya Miles has attested to the challenge of writing the history of African Americans and other racial minorities in light of the chasm of meaning that has opened between, on one hand, the language we fall back on in order to categorize people in settler society, and on the other, the lived realities which are "always messier than theoretical concepts."[24] To be Black and to be a settler blur the lines of two identities that we often imagine as incommensurate: colonizer and colonized.

Similarly, historian Justin Leroy acutely identifies the broader impasse surrounding the issue of naming and definitions as each field—Black studies and settler colonial studies—reducing "the other to a variation on the theme of liberal multiculturalism in order to maintain the integrity of its own exceptional claim."[25] Other scholars rely on alternative analytical language to navigate Black and settler colonial histories. Their terms, however, often create other challenges, specifically for the history of the Black West in the nineteenth and twentieth century. In this later context, Jodi Byrd's widely acknowledged conceptual category "arrivants," for example, potentially absolves historical actors from their role in U.S. colonialism. This, in turn, unintentionally severs entire populations from central themes in U.S. history. In other words, by discursively removing non-Native people of color who created and occupied settler space—however compromised and incomplete that space may be—from the colonial project, we ultimately limit our own ability to fully account for the shifting structures of race and power within settler societies.[26]

It is my hope that this book might offer a far more useful point of reference for historians to probe structures of settler power and to explore the all-too-hidden elements of Wolfe's passive assertion that Black settlers *were caught up* in a project not of their making. Rather than being swept along by a historical moment of violence and dispossession in which they held no real power or responsibility—and, ultimately, no future either—the archive suggests Black settlers played active and self-aware, and, at times, contradictory and dissenting roles in settler expansion. This requires historians to account for the Black experience in ways that go beyond what Richard White and Lawrence de Graaf long ago called the "contribution school" and has been more recently articulated by Herbert Ruffin II as the "we were there" frameworks so prevalent in the historiography of the Black West.[27] Black Montanans, for their part, exuded an ideological worldview that claimed robust participation in the ongoing project of Native dispossession would serve as the avenue through which an oppressed people could repossess the self socially, politically, civically, and culturally. It occurred as a new era of oppression descended on Blacks during what Rayford Logan has described as the "nadir" of the Black experience in the United States.[28] Critical to this Black settler ideology was the belief that Black settler colonialism fulfilled the liberal demands of civic and political liberation for Blacks and full incorporation and equal membership in the American social body. Simultaneously, it accomplished this while it championed the accumulation of capital and a material independence that Black conservatives prioritized. Its hybrid quality and new geography made it unique to other race-conscious social ideologies of the day. Black settlers in Montana did not need fear for their life if they criticized a public official, spoke out against racism, voted, ran for office, or sent their child to a white school (or so the promise went). But neither did this progressive posturing mean that Black settlers did not see ownership of the land and the accumulation of wealth as a sign of, and a means to bring about, racial liberation.

Not to be missed in this articulation of a distinct settler form is that, like all settler forms, Black settler colonialism fundamentally relied upon the dispossession of Indigenous lands and engaged a politics that underpinned the elimination of Native peoples. In some cases, like the history of the Buffalo Soldiers and the Black military personnel who directly perpetrated or witnessed the violence of the western Indian Wars of the late nineteenth century, the connection between Black settler colonialism and a political and military structure that worked toward the elimination of the Native is direct and concrete. Many Black soldiers became settlers themselves and later served as semimythical heroes or martyrs for Black settler communities who mobilized the memory of the Buffalo Soldiers to legitimize their own continued presence on the land and to bolster emerging ideas of home and belonging in the West. No less significant is the way that Black settlement in Montana—which, at first glance, appeared to take place long after the bleeding edge of settler violence and far from contemporary Native communities—nevertheless remained joined to the ongoing settler project. To be sure, Black settler colonialism's implication in earlier violence against Indigenous peoples *did* become more abstract in the twentieth century. In fact, references in the Black press of Montana to Native Americans by the early twentieth century are surprisingly rare. Most writings, which generally pertained to the "opening" of Indian reservations, mentioned neither violence nor even Indigenous peoples. And yet, though it may have seemed beyond the purview of a small ethnic community that increasingly struggled to influence their state and local governments, the new politics of settler violence imbued the soils from which can be articulated the establishment, growth, and eventual decline of Black Montana.

Though its history can never be divorced from the attending violence of U.S. colonialism toward Indigenous peoples, the story of Black Montana is about another dynamic as well, one that emerged tenuously between white and Black settlers, and it is the major tension that this book examines.[29] Why was it that, when confronted with the unwanted reality of Black settlers, white settler society seems to have pursued a course of total racial exclusion rather than the far more prevalent racial regimes of oppression and segregation that formed elsewhere in the United States at roughly the same time? In the narrative of Rose Gordon's birth, there is the tension between how the Crow midwife perceives her, as white, and how Rose perceives herself. Yet there is also the tension that arises from the way that Gordon plays with the ambiguity of race as she claims for herself the distinction of settler and the derisive opinions of the white settlers in the camp who "knew differently." In their worldview, this Black child could no more be a legitimate settler than she could be white. The question remains: Why? Indeed, it will take most of this book's arguments to gesture at a possible answer. A simplistic summary might run something like this: if race, as Patrick Wolfe has claimed, "is colonialism speaking," then any attack on the (il)logic of racialist thinking, particularly denying the fundamental logic of white supremacy, becomes an attack on the underlying colonial formation. Though Black settler colonialism cannot be said to have always or often stood in solidarity with Indigenous peoples on issues of land and sovereignty and cannot be absolved of settler violence in all its forms, it nevertheless rejected a fundamental tenet of American settler colonialism's racial regime: that *white* settlers would inherit the earth.[30]

Devoid of these spaces of contestation and compromise, settler colonial theory again becomes almost teleological. Indeed, among the most salient critiques levied against the field is that the relentlessness of settler invasion and the primacy of elimination in historical writing reinscribes the settler myth that Indigenous peoples are resigned to vanishing. Scholars counter with the observation that, despite the seeming dominance of settler regimes around the world, Indigenous peoples, however oppressed, have not disappeared. Accounting for the durability of resistance, therefore, emphasizes the contingencies and overall incompleteness of settler domination. By altering the terms of the settler and Indigenous binary debate slightly and turning our attention to the *historical* construction of the category of "settler," rather than merely its permutations and application for the present, "Black settler colonialism" does not rely upon a totalizing or transhistorical use of the term or a teleological, recalcitrant binary. Instead it points to one of the many moments of contestation over legitimacy that reveal settler colonialism to be an uncertain, incomplete, and narrowly won political form.

Attending to this history of compromised coloniality, this book argues that Black settler colonialism emerged as a unique phenomenon near the end of Greater Reconstruction in 1877 and continued to shape the Black experience in Montana into the early twentieth century. This study focuses intently on Montana, though there are fingerprints of Black settler colonies throughout the American West from the "Black towns" of Oklahoma, to oasis-like communities in Spokane, Denver, or Cheyenne.[31] Black settlers seized upon a political moment and geographic space they believed held unprecedented potential for personal and communal liberation, and they had various names for this and what it would look like. Among those notions articulated were the materialistic promises of the "Golden West," the political possibility of the "New Age," and even the edenic sublime of "God's Garden." But that settler vision was not to be. Even as Black settlers sometimes relied upon or articulated a system of differential racialization to imagine themselves "above" Indians in order to legitimize their role as colonizers, white settler society sought to preserve their own fantasy that, ultimately, settler space would be racially exclusive. White settlers reacted to this vision through the exclusion of African Americans, their communities, and even the erosion of the memory that they once existed.

Colonial Erosion

One goal of this book is to parse out some of the ways that American settler colonialism operates beyond the standard interactions of white colonizers and Indigenous colonized. It is important to begin, then, with the fact that when Euro-Americans invaded and settled the region that now encompasses the state of Montana in the Northern Rockies and Upper Great Plains, these newcomers did not carry out their project of territorial expansion alone. Shaped by the national debate around slavery and the unprecedented racial and ethnic diversity of those Americans already looking to the West for a new life, a struggle to define and restrict who could be a "legitimate" settler emerged. The negotiation of the category "settler" in that time and place led to the establishment of a distinctly *western* racial regime that worked to enshrine a particular vision of a world dominated and defined by white settler society.[32] As discussed earlier, those definitions are potently durable. If our own inherited and narrow language, therefore, forecloses the space for us to see these complicated histories, I would suggest that Black westerners themselves pushed against the boundaries of meaning of "settler" that were hardening around the turn of the century. At the moment of Rose Gordon's birth in 1883, her ambiguous status as a "legitimate" settler—that is, as white—speaks to the unique place where she found herself. Certainly, she would never have called herself "white" in other settler colonial spaces like Alabama, Michigan, or New York in 1883. It also demonstrates that the methods and ideologies that sought to produce a space governed by the logics of white supremacy were still shifting to meet new demands of colonial expansion.

Under this new regime, the "whitening of the West" was thus a structure, not an event.[33] Evolving economies, cultural aspirations, and prevailing attitudes about race and Native elimination led to the West being viewed (at least by Euro-Americans) as a space that would ultimately become the locus of whiteness.[34] Moreover, such aspirations emerged in a region where the cultural origins of white settlers was little more than a sanitized account of Indigenous land appropriation. The legacy of that violence thus continued well after settler communities were established or homesteads plotted. Though generally unspoken, elimination was an understood reality that could not be so easily ignored or forgotten, even with the passage of time. Within this highly racialized settler worldview, the goal was not merely the exploitation or segregation of Black settlers, but their total exclusion.

In much of the West, with the exception of what some historians have called the "Urban Archipelago," it would appear that the settler colonial project and its regime of western racism against Black settlers achieved partial success.[35] By the second decade of the twenty-first century, fourteen of the twenty least Black states by percentage of total population were located in the West.[36] But how was the extent of this exclusion achieved? To those readers more familiar with the racial regimes of slavery or Jim Crow, the history of Montana has a surprising lack of overt anti-Black violence. Hatred and bigotry did lead to the deaths of a small number of Black westerners in the state, but there was no Colfax Massacre; no reign of terror the likes of which gripped Elaine, Arkansas, in 1919; nor were there "race riots" comparable to Tulsa, Oklahoma, in 1921. Still, Montana was not without its own massacres. I argue that the violence of the settler state, which in the 1870s perpetrated the mass murder of untold numbers of Indigenous men, women, and children, continue in the social relationships people build, the stories they tell, the monuments they erect, and the institutions they establish.[37] At a moment when a fantasy of a white settler state was complicated and subverted by the unprecedented ethnic and racial diversity of the peoples of the West, white settlers sought to legitimize a vision of a racially exclusive society. They justified the brutality of such a project using older as well as retooled ideologies of white supremacy.

In the West, perhaps the most lasting form of violence committed under settler colonialism against Black Montanans comes in form of a considerable cultural and institutional forgetting and trivializing of Black history. This is but one aspect of what I refer to as "colonial erosion": the process by which various colonial logics (such as Native elimination, assimilation, appropriation, white supremacy, and anti-Blackness) precipitated the vulnerable conditions that the Black community struggled to overcome in the past. And, in the present, the ongoing course of colonial violence continues to occlude Black history from white settler consciousness.[38] The characters in the West's settler narratives—the pioneer family, the cowboy, the rancher, the homesteader, the one-room schoolteacher, the prospector, the vigilante, the outlaw, the land speculator—are all implicitly white (narratives of criminality and conquest are another matter). Yet when Black westerners are counted among any of those groups, usually as a result of an archival presence that catches people off guard, "their" past never impinges upon the racial consciousness of the white settler. Thus, colonial erosion works to exclude racial "Others" in the present through the stories people tell about the past. Black history in the West has been seen as novel, as unique, as interesting, but not as *essentially western*. In such landscapes of popular memory and scholarly debate, scoured by the settler project and buried deep in the sediments of racial and colonial logics, the West merely functions as a new setting for African American struggle for equality to take place, but remains disengaged from many other western narratives, notably the dispossession of Indigenous peoples and the course of U.S. empire.

The study of erased communities—those most subjected to the erosive logics of U.S. colonialism—is still lacking in Black western studies, even after some scholars answered critiques against the "contribution school" in the late 1980s. In 1998 Quintard Taylor responded with his book *In Search of the Racial Frontier*.[39] It built on the early studies of African American–specific history in the West such as Nell Painter's *Exodusters* (1976) and Lawrence de Graaf's work on African American women.[40] Taylor ambitiously presented a regional history of African Americans from 1528 to 1990, and his work spawned an explosion of historical writings about race and the Black experience across the West.[41] Nevertheless, histories of large contemporary Black western communities like Los Angeles, San Francisco, Denver, Seattle, or Oakland are privileged over those with relatively few people or ones that no longer exist.[42] Books and articles explore the histories of Black Spokane and Black San Francisco, but not Black Cheyenne, Boulder, or Pocatello, despite the fact that such cities were home to comparable numbers of Black residents at different times.⁴³ This trend in western Black historiography could be mediated by ruminating on how settler colonialism shaped the experience of Blackness in the West, especially when it led to forms of social exclusion.⁴⁴

Bearing the past and present trajectories of this erosion in mind, *Black Montana* attempts to plot the course of that exclusion through the colonial archive while at the same time looking elsewhere to recover the occluded voices of African American settlers. It attends to this shallow archive and the falsely presumed banality of Black lives with no small amount of urgency because colonial spaces, as scholars are keen to point out, develop in such a way as to deliberately shroud their very making.⁴⁵ Such occlusions are evident in the failure of many contemporary Montanans to see the vestiges of U.S. colonialism in either their everyday lives or their history. Consequently, race and racism, which form the scaffolding onto which the more exterior expressions of violence and identity is fixed, becomes unmoored from the origins of the settler colony. Present-day readers may look upon the story of Rose Gordon's "white" birth as evidence that westward expansion was a project more or less free from the historical burden of slavery and racial violence. The near-disappearance of Gordon and the Black community she knew as a young woman from settler memory, however, tell us that the opposite is true.

Black Settlers and Racial Regimes in the West

This book posits that the period from the end of Greater Reconstruction in 1877 through the 1930s represented a pivotal moment in the settler colonial project throughout the American West. It largely came after what I have called elsewhere "the bleeding edge of settlement," in which violence and murder were widely accepted methods for white settlers and state agents who carried out the logic of elimination. Prior to 1877 in the West, huge swaths of the region teetered on a razor's edge, threated to be severed from U.S. oversight and authority by expanding Indigenous powers. In addition to ascendant Lakota military might, the prodigious historian of nomadic empires Pekka Hämäläinen has observed that, by the early 1870s, conditions had changed so that burgeoning numbers of Native peoples "were reported to be living in what U.S. maps called the Montana Territory, curbing the ambitions of some of the most vociferous settlers in the American West."[46] American victory over the Lakota and their Indigenous allies in 1877 brought the on-the-ground reality of things marginally closer to the cartographic fictions already in place. This conspicuous development also took place in a somewhat marginalized period and geography when viewed from a more traditional, national perspective. It was part of imperial expansion during a time when the more widely recognized history of the U.S. empire was taking place elsewhere, in far-flung corners of the globe such as Cuba, Panama, China, and the Philippines.

The history of the settler West also appears somewhat removed from the established halls of power and industry, leviathans in the history of the Gilded Age and the rise of Progressivism. The Reconstruction Amendments in the wake of the Civil War provided freedpeople their first (thin) cover of federal protection and membership within the nation. Apart from birthright citizenship, which also benefited Asians and Latinx communities, many protections did not extend to Indigenous peoples, Asian immigrants, and, functionally, many Latinx Americans as well.[47] Still, for African Americans throughout the country, their new rights and freedoms were under constant assault from those working to uphold white supremacy. Southern Blacks felt this colonial racism most acutely. Seeking to defend their claim to territories they had stolen from the Creek, Chickasaw, Choctaw, Cherokee, and Seminole Indians only half a century earlier, white elites severed Black farmers from the land through the institution of sharecropping, limited their mobility with vagrancy laws and a bourgeoning carceral landscape, and passed laws and codes that returned Black laborers to a condition of neoslavery. Each maneuver ensured the continued capital accumulation of white settler elites. At this same moment in the West, Indian dispossession was far from complete. The trajectory of the settler colonial project in places like Montana, therefore, departed markedly from the one ongoing in the South, the Northeast, or even the Midwest. The racial regimes that settler colonialism continuously produces draw upon these divergent histories and thus create different categories of racial exclusion.[48]

We must therefore seek to historicize the exclusionary forces deployed against Black settlers on the part of the white settler community as it established itself throughout the region in the nineteenth century. Historians Gayle Berardi and Thomas Segady argue that "the response on the part of white settlers for the most part took one of two forms: either to deny African Americans their rights . . . or to deny African-Americans entrance into the newly-developing communities in the West entirely."[49] The laws, constitutions, ordinances, newspapers, and other archival materials in the West frequently speak to the developing perception among white settlers that the region could be established as the locus of whiteness—even to the legal exclusion and removal of Blacks, Indians, Asians, and Latinx. As early as 1857 Oregon state legislators wrote an exclusion clause into their first constitution forbidding free Blacks from settling in the new state.[50] In 1893 the town of Liberty, Oregon, resolved that "all black people leave town."[51] Historians have noted that similar resolutions are "scattered throughout the historical record."[52] White and Mexican settlers in California, whose Hispanic-style rancheros prospered for decades using unfree Indian labor, quickly turned an about face after 1846. Eschewing Indian laborers for a track of genocidal erasure, a racially homogenous vision for the future became more widely accepted.[53] San Francisco's major newspaper, the *Californian*, infamously proclaimed on March 15, 1848, "We desire only a white population in California, even the Indians amongst us, as far as we have seen, are more of a nuisance than a benefit to the country; we would like to get rid of them."[54] It was here, in a region of newfangled ethnic complexity, that Blacks were racialized in new ways by racial regimes that attended to ever-shifting colonial contingencies.

The construction of racial categories in the West proceeded according to colonial logics that differed from those of other regions. This occurred in part because the process of settlement required an initial labor force much larger than the number of available white settlers in addition to the types of extractive economies that seemed likely to develop. In turn, racialized labor systems and widespread exploitation accompanied fear and anxiety about the West's unprecedented ethnic diversity.[55] And it was unprecedented: the heterogenic population of the American West stood in sharp contrast (and still does) to the "white West" of the settler colonial imagination. For instance, whites seeking fabled wealth and opportunity were threatened by the role of Chinese immigrants in emerging labor markets of the Pacific coast, often extending into the interior by way of the railroad. The racialization of the Chinese as a threat to the wages of lower-class whites is well documented.[56] In the American West the removal of the larger Black community was stalled by their status as citizens in ways that the Chinese project of removal was not. Negotiating the idea of citizen within settler states itself needs to be examined. Edlie L. Wong's superb study *Racial Reconstruction: Black Inclusion, Chinese Exclusion, and the Fictions of Citizenship* (2015) not only illustrates how race served as the proving ground for the negotiation of who was included in the American political body and who was not, but it also comes closest to probing the shifting racial categories of the settler colonial West. Wong's literary sources are unusually prescient and attentive to the differential racialization that occurred between Blacks, Asians, and Indians in California. Because Indians and Chinese immigrants were classified as "heathens," and, as Wong notes, "[heathenism] racialized both non-Christian Chinese and Native Americans as antagonistic to the nation's manifest destiny," some Black observers endorsed Chinese exclusion expressly because of a nationalistic ideology.[57] That position, as espoused by Philip Alexander Bell's San Francisco paper, the *Elevator*, was met by forceful rebukes from other members of the Black press who readily saw the oppression of Chinese workers and Black workers as one and the same. Nevertheless, Black writers placing themselves within the West's racial and ethnic milieu more often than not leaned on the logics of differential racialization to claim citizenship.[58]

As the issue of Chinese exclusion pressed upon not only the question of citizenship, but ultimately upon the very idea of racial belonging in the West, the big "problems" of race in American—the "Negro problem," the "Indian problem," and the "Chinese problem"—proved inseparable.[59] Fearful that extending social and civil liberties to the newly freed

Blacks might set a precedent for Asians, Mexicans, and Indians, many western states retreated into exclusionary regimes of racial domination in order to secure white settler interests. Many of the resulting measures were symbolic as well as concrete; states like California and Oregon, for instance, did not ratify the Fourteenth and Fifteenth Amendments until the mid-twentieth century.[60]

In addition to the dire conditions American settler colonialism created for Indians, Asians, and Chicana/os as the twentieth century approached, its racial regime also shifted to work on behalf of white settlers to prevent Blacks from entering the ranks of "legitimate" settlers. It did this by cutting off Black laborers from certain middle-class occupations or from enjoying the security of unionized workforces. The fear that white, working-class westerners might lose their higher paying jobs to African Americans, or that their presence alone in the workforce might drive down wages, was certainly overstated, but not entirely unfounded. Railroads across the West from time to time chose to break strikes by bringing on thousands of Black laborers to continue the work.[61] Even more potent for whites were times in which Black soldiers arrived to put down labor conflicts. Organizers of the Western Federation of Miners in Coeur d'Alene, Idaho in 1899 were met with six companies of the Twenty-Fourth U.S. Colored infantry, one of four regiments commonly known as the Buffalo Soldiers, who arrived to enforce martial law in response to an ongoing violent strike in the timber industry.[62] Though the Black men arriving in the area were not there to take their jobs, white laborers increasingly saw the presence of Black settlers and soldiers in the region as an intolerable affront. It was during this critical period that white settlers solidified an imaginary connection between the exclusion of Blacks and their opportunity and access to work, wages, and ultimately, land.

Black Montana is arranged thematically, rather than along a simple chronology. Each theme deals with what might traditionally be called the agency of Black Montanans. Within the context of this study agency might be reframed as a form of *Black settler sovereignty*. This is not an uncomplicated task. At times, Black Montanans chose paths that might be viewed as an obvious subversion of the racial ambitions of the white settler state. Yet, at the very same time, they may have been doing so out of a desire to make Montana their home, even if that process dispossessed a similarly persecuted Indigenous population. Nearly every action, from starting a political newspaper to going on a picnic, might be interpreted as either an act of resistance to white settler supremacy, or simply in step with the social hegemony. This demands analysis that necessarily goes beyond previous methods of the "contribution school."[63]

We should not mistakenly equate the forms of sovereignty that different settler populations "carry with them," as Lorenzo Veracini has articulated. Rarely, if ever, did Black westerners appear to imagine themselves as migrants imbued with "total settler sovereignty," a concept laid out by Wolfe and Veracini and powerfully employed by Jeffery Oster in his sweeping synthesis *Surviving Genocide* (2019).[64] The power to wield judicial, legislative, and military might in order to establish a settler state upon Indigenous lands never fell to Black westerners, even with the founding of Black towns and municipalities from Nicodemus, Kansas, to Deerfield, Colorado. This is not to say that Black westerners did not call upon favorable court rulings, progressive legislation, or the memory of the Black military presence to bolster their own claims to home and belonging. As chapter 1 outlines, Blacks who settled on western Indian lands after the Civil War and well into the twentieth century first manifested their sovereign status through mobility, not unlike the claim made by persons escaping slavery; their assertion of sovereignty largely remained one of individual and collective liberty.[65] Claims made by white settler communities, conversely, asserted their right, and that of their government, to deal with ultimate authority with regards to Native peoples. In this model the force behind such totalizing impunity was the individual and collective logics of white settlers themselves.

Black settlers to Montana and the West confronted and compounded a highly racialized project of Native land dispossession that continued to shift and change course. In 1887, as Black migration to the territory began to rise, Congress passed the Dawes Allotment Act.[66] Indian reservations across the country, including within the borders of Montana, fractured and shrank by astounding margins as the individual tribal members and families received designated acres of land within the reservation, the rest being sold or given to land-hungry settlers. After generations of sustained policies that encouraged physical violence, assimilationist agendas, and even the outright theft of Native children from their families, many tribal populations had collapsed, exacerbating the unprecedented loss of their homelands.[67] This project continued apace well into the twentieth century. Confronted by mounting challenges to their existence in new settler communities across the region during this time, some Black Montanans and especially the Black press saw Indian dispossession as a means to accumulate property and a measure of independence. Some influential voices, ranging from local newspaper editors to Booker T. Washington himself, looked upon the condition of Black settlers in Montana and determined that the only way they could secure a future in the land would be to own it and become productive farmers, ranchers, or miners.[68]

Partially because the capital needed to act upon such advice was exceedingly difficult to come by, and partially because not all Black settlers agreed that the only hope to realize a future in their new home was to adhere to an increasingly conservative ideology of "racial uplift," most Black settlers continued to live, work, and make a home for themselves in Montana's cities and towns. As historians have documented, Black life in western cities centered around the formation of interdependent networks of kinship and community. As traditionally understood, Black churches, clubs, taverns and so on offered a refuge away from the persecution of white supremacist society. Chapter 2 examines those networks of kinship and community. It finds that Black Montanans similarly anchored themselves to Black settler spaces. Yet the racial regime of the settler colonial West reacted to these perceived trespasses much differently than, for instance, the racial regime of the Jim Crow South of the same era. Based upon the needs of the settler state, official racial segregation never fully materialized in Montana. Even in 1909, when the state legislature passed its infamous ban on interracial marriage, both the wording and emphasis of the bill as well as its prolonged effects on the Black community demonstrate that its goal was not merely the segregation of white, Black, and Asian settlers, but the total exclusion of those "unwanted elements" from white settler society.

As Black settler spaces came under sustained and targeted attack, the need to break into exclusively white settler institutions in Montana's cities pressed upon a growing number of Black residents. Some institutions were already open to Black settlers. Black men in early Montana could vote with little trouble and in some cases run for office.[69] Both Republicans and Democrats courted the Black vote at times, representing the starkest difference between the Montana and other parts of the country. Likewise, few places in Montana saw forcibly segregated neighborhoods, often producing multiple effuse Black enclaves in a city.[70] Even still, the ability to secure work in skilled industries proved almost impossible in a state that became famous for its labor activism. The growing presence and political power of whites-only trade unions in the state's more populous cities meant that Black workers were locked out of high-wage and sustainable careers in the early twentieth century. Resultingly, their voices in state and local politics likewise diminished. In chapter 3, which details the saga of the state's first Black-owned and -operated newspaper that began in an election season of great consequence, suggests that the ballot box came to represent the limits of the Black community in their mission to push white settlers to imagine a Montana that included them as well.

The racial regime of the settler state did not subdue the Black community into passive colonial subjects on a path to an eventual exodus. Rather, what emerges from the archive is an adapted, hybrid, Black settler ideology that helped Black Montanans make sense of their lives and imagine new futures. While this ideology informed patterns of home ownership and educational pursuits, it also encouraged political and social activism. Black settlers simultaneously took part in social formations that dispossessed Indians even while they challenged the underlying settler logics of white supremacy that worked to justify Native elimination. This project was not limited to federal Indian policy or the establishment of settler communities and economies. The paradoxical position of Black settlers as colonizers and colonized reached beyond the halls of politics and industry, and, at times, cut deep into foundational settler beliefs about *home* and *belonging*.

Chapter 4 turns to the settler project of "dispossessing the wilderness" in Montana as it reached an apex at the dawn of twentieth century.[71] Unsurprisingly, claiming ownership over vast tracts of forests, prairies, and mountains—as well as dominating the animal and natural resources of those spaces—occupied an outsized role in the settler imagination. Its significance was derived in part from the knowledge that much of the land could never be fully "settled" in the prevailing sense of the term. Under the "Big Sky" of Montana, the racial regime of the settler state also made its indelible mark on human relationships to the land. The views held by conservationists in the early twentieth century in Montana and across the nation were undeniably colored by racialized understandings of the body, the environment, "the nation," and who their movement was intended to benefit. In Montana colonial logics proliferated conservationist approaches about which resources should be preserved and why. The magpie in the early 1900s was both a material example of a Native species slotted for elimination by white conservationists, as well as a serendipitous analogy for how they conceived of the relationship between an unaccounted-for Black settler community and Montana's natural environment. An account of the actual Black environmental experience, however, thoroughly subverted those same misconceptions. Though Black Montanans in many cases pioneered the region's first outdoor exploits and continued to maintain and foster a Black "wilderness ethic" well into the twentieth century, their exclusion from the cultural memory of that aspect of Montana's past is testament to the effectiveness of colonial erosion.

The anxieties that white settlers transposed onto the natural world spoke of a constant desire for social and "natural" simplicity. In the human realm, the antithesis of the simple binary world that settlers imagined is perhaps most embodied by the colonial term "miscegenation."[72] The history surrounding the 1909 prohibition of interracial marriages—the subject of chapter 5—illustrates that the politics and public sentiments of racial sexuality in Montana were contingent upon the absence of a "southern" color line and based on the regional goals of the settler society. Historian Tiya Miles has argued that interracial relationships in Montana and the West might not fall solely within the framework of analysis associated with the sexual violence born of the exploitation of slavery. The agency that Miles and other scholars such as Peggy Pascoe find in the lives of Black men and women within interracial relationships is reflective of African Americans exerting their freedoms within the settler society.[73] The prohibition of such relationships therefore had dramatic and far-reaching effects, despite the fact that only a few dozen Black Montanans took white partners or spouses. Their trials and triumphs for Black Montanans homemaking after 1909 point to how racial legislation targeted not just the future stability of interracial couples, but entire networks of kinship that reached across the state and provided a thin safety net to Black settlers making their way in a volatile and unpredictable landscape.

Black Montana reconstructs and reconsiders this history to offer an understanding of the lives of Black settlers that does not succumb to passive characterizations that they were merely caught up, and then cast away, by settler colonialism. Absent official state policy to remove Black settlers from Montana, such a reductive formulation of the Black western experience cannot account for the out-migration of nearly one-half of Montana's Black residents by the end of the 1930s. Instead, during the early twentieth century, the erosion that this book traces across a wide sweep of state history produced a high degree of social, cultural, and economic precarity. Following a severe drought in 1917–18, the onset of World War I, and a devastating outbreak of Spanish flu, Montana's economy all but collapsed, sending settler society into a tailspin of racial anxiety and xenophobia. The decades that followed are marked by an intensification of white settler identity as Montana became the only state to lose population between the world wars, Blacks accounting for disproportionate number of those who left.[74]

In the space where old markers of settler identity dissolved and fractured under the strain of a state and then global depression, new markers of social and cultural belonging emerged. The end of the homesteading era, the increased presence of the federal government in the resource economy, and the tightening of networks of rural and industrial communities alike shaped the narratives that Montanans would employ to make sense of the chaos of their world and to move toward a better future. Black and white settlers in this turbulent era contested the category of "settler" from a profoundly compromised position. Additionally, though the multilayered forces of erosion taking effect over decades may well indicate the accretion of force that imperial forms harness, it also speaks to how narrow the exclusion of Blacks from settler society proved to be by mid-century. Regardless, these events had a profoundly colonial and racial past. Chapter 6 concludes by calling upon scholars and westerners alike to consider the entanglements of race and regional identity, and thus how colonial formations continue to press upon the history of Montana and the West broadly.

One of the greatest challenges in doing this work remains the way that colonialisms, as Ann Stoler suggests, tend to fold back upon themselves and occlude the nature of their origins.[75] In a strange way this revelation is what drove me to telling the story of Black Montanans from this particular vantage point. In a state that is home to fewer African Americans than any other, the greatest durability of its colonial present may be the categorical loss of its once-vibrant Black cultural resources and heritage places. The erosion of the "racial frontier," as Quintard Taylor famously calls what the West represented to so many Black Americans, has silently become part of the white settler ontology. Largely as a result of this loss, historians still struggle to articulate its genesis, establishment, and exclusion as a distinctly western narrative even a century after the zenith of the African American community in Montana.

1

The Golden West *Black Settlers to Montana, 1877–1917*

After killing *Natisqelix* the "people eater," Coyote threw the monster's body piece by piece across the earth. Finally, the world was fit for humans.[1] Where pieces of flesh landed, the Salish and Pend d'Orielle peoples each emerged from the land. Their origin story, which they share with other Indigenous groups of the Northern Rockies, did not tell of their arrival to the land; they were of it. The Salish, for their part, sprang from the earth in the Bitterroot Valley, and their domain expanded north and east, reaching the smooth pebbled beaches of Flathead Lake, later named after their European misnomer. Ancient forests of ponderosa and fir were made good for foraging and hunting through extensive management and controlled burns. These forests lined the lush summer meadows and the wide glacial valleys that made up the homelands of the Salish and their allies the Kootenai and Pend d'Orielle. It was there that they eventually encountered the first signs of an impending settler invasion. In the 1730s, nearly half a century after the Pueblo Revolt in the high deserts of the Southwest freed up herds of Spanish horses to be bred and traded to neighboring Indian groups, the Shoshonis and Nez Perce swept north and west from where Coyote had placed them long ago in present-day Idaho, Nevada, and Utah. Mounted bands crossed into Montana's western valleys, while new enemies—the Siksika, Blood, and Piegans, commonly known as the Blackfeet, a people hardened and ruthless to their foes—encroached from the northeast.[2]

The Blackfeet tell of their own emergence from the land. After *Napi*, Old Man, walked north making the mountains and the plains, as well as the buttes and the rivers, he rested and made woman and her son out of clay in the land that would be called Saskatchewan. Old Man stayed with the new people and taught them to hunt, fish, and cook with fire. Finally, Old Man taught them how to listen to the spirits, who came in the form of an animal, and how to follow the guidance of spirits who had heard their prayers. With this last wisdom imparted, he continued north.[3] During the early eighteenth century, the Blackfeet followed migrating herds of bison past the subtle outline of the Sweet Grass Hills and across what would be called in the next century the Medicine Line, the border of Montana and Canada. They pushed west to the Rocky Mountain front, attaining horses that were traded up from the central plains, where Arapaho and Northern Cheyenne were already imagining whole new worlds astride the mustang that could traverse and be sustained by the ocean of grasses and prairies stretching east from the Great Basin and Rocky Mountains. By the close of the eighteenth century, Blackfeet, as well as other Indians to the south like the Crow and Lakota Sioux of the Great Plains, had attained more than just horses. Firearms and the other goods became part of tribes' material culture as the fur trade moved west with startling rapidity. Before too long the last great sign of invasion arrived among the various peoples of the land. Smallpox appeared in the Northern Rockies among the Shoshoni and Nez Perce as early as 1780.[4] Plains tribes often owed much of their early westward migration in the sixteenth and seventeenth centuries out of the Ohio River Valley to the utter catastrophe of European contagions that decimated the population of eastern Indian peoples. Though sparser population density spared Montana's Indians similar devastation, disease would continue to weaken and compromise vulnerable groups and individuals.[5] In the midst of these migrations, the Lakota moved northwest into the interior of the continent by the late eighteenth century as part of a social and political reorganization that historian Pekka Hämäläinen has identified as an emerging Indigenous empire stretching from the central Great Plains to the Rocky Mountains of what would become Montana.[6]

Enslaved to the young military captain William Clark, York, the first Black man to see that land, arrived in 1805 with the Corps of Discovery.[7] When the expedition passed back through the region, Clark and

York split from Lewis and half the corps where the Three Forks of the Missouri flowed through some of the most pristine hunting grounds the corps had encountered on their expedition, later named the Gallatin Valley.[8] Blackfeet and Crow warriors displaced more passive tribes out of the lush valley further to the west, after which they only dared reenter it seasonally to hunt. Because the Crow and Blackfeet also used the valley for seasonal game, living primarily on the edges of the high plains, early Anglo trappers and settlers noted that the area did not seem to be claimed by any one tribe.[9] This became the basis for a damaging settler myth that many Montanans continue to hold. The Gallatin Valley, home to some seventy thousand settlers in 2020, was supposedly never truly "home" to any Indians. Rather, the valley was fantasized to be something akin to a neutral ground where no one group laid territorial claim. Nuances of this idea aside, it had the effect of creating a small pocket of terra nullius deep in the Rockies that drew settlers almost immediately upon the return of the Corps of Discovery to the east.[10]

Some two decades later, in the 1820s, the fabled Black mountain man Jim Beckwourth became one of the very first men to follow the Yellowstone River and cross over the pass into the Gallatin Valley since York left in 1805. Beckwourth's own autobiography complicates what can truthfully be said about his many exploits. Yet his time among the Absaroka Crow in south central and western Montana in the 1820s made him a dominant figure in the expansion of the fur trade into the state.[11] Black settlers to Montana would remain sparse and marginal among the overwhelmingly white settler invasion into the Northern Rockies and Far West. Almost all antebellum Blacks lived either as poor or working-class laborers in the North or as enslaved people in the South. They were hardly a group in a position to make a dangerous and expensive exploratory trek beyond the reach of railroads and riverboats lines into a contested wilderness. Regardless of their few numbers, the adventures of early Black westerners like York, Edward Rose, Jim Beckwourth, and even Esteban—the famed Black explorer of the sixteenth century—helped build a new semimythical origin narrative in a region where, myths aside, the nature of one's cultural beginnings would prove to be of profound importance.[12]

To trace the racial logics that animate Montana as a settler colonial space, the Black experience must be considered as central in its history. This chapter analyzes the migration of thousands of Black Americans to Montana as a function of settler colonial expansion. Its framing Black challenges the traditional vision of westward expansion as typified by peaceful white pioneers conquering an immense and untenable natural world. It also disrupts the idea that African Americans played no part in the horrors perpetrated against Native peoples. Make no mistake: Black westward expansion was fraught with paradoxes. This chapter offers a history that suggests that African Americans actively fled oppression, exploitation, and death, only to bolster a society in the West that inflicted many of the same terrors on its Indian inhabitants. It considers Black settler sovereignty and the contradictions such an idea necessarily harbors. Certainly, Black settlers were not merely pawns in an expansive colonial project. African Americans, seeking relief from the injustices of a broken nation, joined the military, claimed homesteads, and boarded trains and steamboats, all to assert their freedom of movement and destiny. Diasporic narratives in Black American history such as this one hearken back to the ultimate assertion of one's liberty: escape from bondage. A study of Black westward expansion and the possible futures many believed awaited them in the "Golden West" must not ignore these challenges and contradictions.[13]

Such a task also acknowledges an extension of Montana's colonial era, though this is by no means a novel assertion. Neither conquest through imperial wars against the Lakota nor the capture of Chief Joseph and the last of the Nez Perce heartbreakingly close to the Canadian border in 1877 closed the book on the region's colonial era. Likewise, the history of Montana as a "postcolonial" state did not commence when the last soldiers of the Fifth and Ninth Cavalries (the Ninth being an all-Black regiment) returned to Fort Keogh outside Miles City after they had put down the Sioux uprising at Pine

Ridge, crushed the new religion and its Ghost Dancers, and packed the frozen earth over trenches that held the remains of 274 Lakota Sioux whom they massacred at Wounded Knee in 1890.[14] Instead, the violent campaigns of land appropriation and the elimination of Native people were merely the bleeding edge of the ensuing settler colonial society. The colonial regime that was established through the arrival of wave upon wave of white settlers on the homelands of American Indians continues long after the memory of its bloody origins fade from collective consciousness.

Today, Montana covers over ninety-four million acres of the American West. At the time of the last official battle between the U.S. cavalry and Indigenous peoples at Pine Ridge in 1891, it was one of the most ethnically diverse states in the union. Indeed, "native-born" white settlers were by no means an overwhelming majority within an overall population that included the second largest foreign-born, naturalized population in the country; thousands of Chinese immigrant laborers and many thousands more Indigenous peoples, both groups not fully eligible for citizenship at the time; and well over a thousand Black residents, whose presence, perhaps more than any of these other groups, caused settler anxieties to churn as they watched Black communities across the state steadily grow in size and prosperity as the first phase of settler invasion faded into memory and myth.[15] It is here that the story of Black Montana truly begins. During the twilight of the nineteenth century, the narrative trajectories of Black settlers to the West—replete with their own ideas about freedom and citizenship—began to accelerate on a collision course with the erosive designs of the colonial state that governed by a deeply racial ideology that marked who was fit to be a settler, and who was not.[16]

Black Migration to the "Golden West"

In their zeal to establish the American West as a locus of whiteness, settler elites—those people, usually men, who came to control the land and its wealth, as well as the those who pulled the levers of power in the emerging political and social institutions that governed settler space—facilitated the unexpected growth of vibrant Black communities both in Montana and throughout the region. Because of the back-breaking labor required, the settler project in the case of Montana was complicated by the fact that settlement could only be achieved by appropriating the bodies of various nonwhite peoples. From the perspective of the white settler, this might have been viewed as an inconvenient, but nevertheless temporary, condition of early western life. From the vantage of the African Americans facing west, however, settler space did not appear to be "for whites only," and they did not view their future as some temporary sojourn in which their role was only to help establish a new society and then leave. The promise of ample land and increased autonomy drew the first of these people to the West, seeking to start their lives anew before the ink had dried on the Emancipation Proclamation. Concurrently, the federal push to continue and secure the removal of Native peoples brought thousands of Black soldiers to the West throughout the 1870s and 1880s, and then to Montana between 1888 and 1907.[17] Shipping and travel lines up the Missouri River and the extension of railroads across the continent in the name of supplying and supporting the settler society likewise relied on hundreds and thousands of Black laborers and their families, many of whom made Montana their home.

While the West pulled Black settlers into its orbit, events also aligned back east to push African American individuals and communities from lands on which they had lived and labored for hundreds of years. Postemancipation settlement of Montana by African Americans began primarily in the social milieu of Radical Reconstruction's implementation and sabotage. The failure to secure the basic liberties of southern Blacks and to ensure their unencumbered civic engagement began what would be nearly a century of out-migration that did not slow until the 1960s. Of the tens of thousands of African Americans who left the South before the Great Migration, only several thousand made their way to the territory, and eventually the state, of Montana. Despite their small numbers, their stories show the incredible diversity of those who made

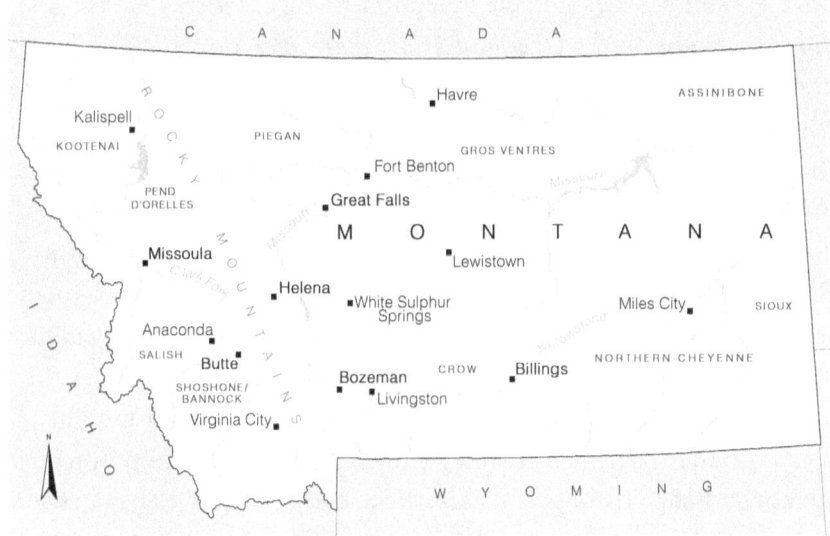

5. Montana cities and towns. Location of tribal lands, ca. 1864, from Ken Egan Jr., *Montana 1864, Indians, Emigrants, and Gold in the Territorial Year* (Helena: Riverbend, 2014). GIS Data: Montana State Library. Map by Steffany Wood, 2019.

the journey. Women like Elizabeth Williams, a business owner and real estate speculator; men such as Jefferson Harrison, a twenty-seven-year veteran of the Twenty-Fourth U.S. Colored Infantry; and Walker Browning, an orphan, refugee, gold miner, railroad worker, and early explorer of Yellowstone National Park, along with thousands of other Black Americans, came to the West in search of the liberties and freedom denied to them in the South and increasingly in the urban North.[18] In doing so, however, Black settlers would take part in a colonial project of removal and elimination that would come to be a defining theme in the experiences of Black communities in Montana and across the American West.

The migration of African Americans to Montana peaked following the end of Greater Reconstruction in 1877 and lasted into the early decades of the twentieth century. Recent scholarship of nineteenth- and twentieth-century Black diaspora, however, mostly neglects the movement of African Americans to the West prior to 1915. Shirley

Ann Wilson Moore's notable exception, *Sweet Freedom's Plains: African Americans on the Overland Trails 1841–1869*, provides a rich and textured account.[19] Even still, Black settler migration to Montana in the nineteenth and early twentieth centuries cannot be solely reduced to the "contribution" of Blacks to the national project of westward expansion. As settlers, African Americans "carried their sovereignty with them," a critical marker in the identification of settler colonial formations.[20] Sometimes that sovereignty precipitated the formation of Black towns and governments from Nicodemus, Kansas, to Allensworth, California. At the very least, sovereignty arrived with Black settlers as they asserted self-possession through exercising their right of mobility, a dynamic that Nell Irvin Painter and Kendra Field have powerfully demonstrated.[21] Through this assertion, early Black settler migration represented the genesis of a distinctly western narrative in the history of African American liberation.

Black diasporic studies emphasize how such movements are manifestations of both the oppression of the places being fled, and the hope that emanated from these new "promised lands." The North during slavery, Kansas and Oklahoma during the Exoduster migration, and, for some, Africa during Reconstruction and the early years of Jim Crow all represented this hope of freedom against the backdrop of southern atrocities.[22] The American West, however, is seldom considered along these other "promised lands." Yet, for nearly half a century, southern Blacks slipped away from the violence of the South and away from the narrow fixation of the nation that had argued, discussed, and postulated the rise or fall of the race in places like New York, Philadelphia, Mississippi, and Liberia, and sought a better life for themselves beneath the Big Sky of Montana. Even still, establishing a new life was not easy, and claiming one's freedom in such conditions often came at a cost. Kendra Field reminds us that African Americans migrating to Indian lands faced ever-shifting racial categories as they "moved over time and space." She writes: "Once in Indian Territory, [Black settlers] gained access to Indian land through purchase and marriage. They simultaneously partook of federal expansion and economic, political and cultural negotiation over land and space with Indians, freedpeople of the Indian Nations, and white settlers and oil speculators. Freedom was not an uncomplicated claim for African-American migrants."[23] Though they settled nearly a thousand miles to the northwest of Indian Territory, Black settlers in Montana likewise encountered a complicated freedom. Even so, their very presence on the land challenged the racial regimes that constructed whiteness, in the words of W. E. B. Du Bois, as the "ownership of the earth, forever, amen."[24]

From a purely quantitative perspective, the scope of Black settlement in Montana and throughout the Northern Rockies can appear underwhelming. In 1880 Montana Territory was home to only 346 African Americans. In 1890 the Black population had risen to 1,490 individuals. In 1910 it peaked at nearly two thousand Black residents, a majority of whom were born in other parts of the United States, primarily the South and Midwest. Considering that the overall population of Montana was 376,000 in 1910, it may well seem that the Black population was inconsequential and thus functionally invisible to white residents.[25] Montana's population was overwhelmingly rural at the turn of the century, before the crash of the homesteading boom sent thousands of poor white farmers into the cities and towns in search of work. The rural population was, however, almost entirely white. In contrast, the Black community, with only a handful of exceptions, lived exclusively in eight or nine cities and towns. The statistical sleight of hand that occurs when Montana is left to be viewed by outsiders as a single monolithic entity of ranchers and miners renders populations of less than two thousand people all but completely obsolete. As a corrective to this elision, consider that, when viewed on their own, Montana's cities in 1910 had a much larger percentage of Black residents than what was represented by the statewide census reports (only half of 1 percent at the state level when compared to as much as 3 percent in the case of Helena in the same year). Anaconda, Billings, Butte, Great Falls, Helena, and Missoula were all home to a Black community of one hundred to four hundred African Americans between 1890 and 1920.[26]

Table 1. African American population for urban centers in Montana, 1910

CITY	AFRICAN AMERICAN POPULATION	TOTAL POPULATION	PERCENTAGE
Anaconda	128	10,134	1.26
Billings	147	10,031	1.47
Bozeman	33	5,107	0.60
Butte	264	39,165	0.67
Great Falls	118	13,948	0.84
Havre	31	3,624	0.85
Helena	425	12,515	3.40
Lewiston	53	N/A	N/A
Livingston	16	N/A	N/A
Miles City	60	N/A	N/A
Missoula	136	12,869	1.00

Source: 1910 census records, populations, and ethnic demographics; see "Montana—Race and Hispanic Origin: 1870 to 1990: Research of the Montana Historical Society," MHPRF.

Table 2. African American population for urban centers in Montana, 1930

CITY	AFRICAN AMERICAN POPULATION	TOTAL POPULATION	PERCENTAGE
Anaconda	106	12,494	0.84
Billings	142	16,380	0.86
Bozeman	21	6,855	0.30
Butte	170	39,532	0.43
Great Falls	208	28,822	0.72
Havre	37	6,372	0.58
Helena	133	11,803	1.10

Lewiston	15	N/A	N/A
Livingston	0	N/A	N/A
Miles City	35	N/A	N/A
Missoula	116	14,657	0.79

Source: 1930 census records, populations, and ethnic demographics; see "Montana—Race and Hispanic Origin: 1870 to 1990: Research of the Montana Historical Society," MHPRF.

The establishment of these communities came about in various ways. Each cause of Black westward expansion to Montana—whether it was mining, military, railroad, or other economic opportunities—can be understood both as a means of Black self-determination and as an agent of settler colonial expansion. The participation of Black settlers in the appropriation of Native lands and the establishment of a settler colonial society was reinforced by several key factors. Most significantly, African American settlers understood the West to be as much their entitlement as it was for Euro-Americans, at least initially. A deeply problematic version of colonial history that has emerged, however, states that this was never the case. Put rather bluntly by two historians: "There is little evidence, on the part of African-Americans, that a change in geographic location brought the promise of increased political freedom and economic opportunity. There is also little evidence that they perceived Horace Greeley's famous shibboleth 'Go West Young Man,' to be intended for them."[27] While the first statement was true in many cities and towns where Blacks settled, the second cannot be so easily defended. Black settlers to the West did not undertake such an arduous endeavor without a hope for better lives or without an understanding that they were part of a national project of expansion.

We might consider the life of Ed Simms, a Black man who came to Fort Benton, Montana, as a steamboat hand before deshipping at the very end of the westward Missouri River line in 1883. By 1886 Simms and his wife Elizabeth had made their way to the famed Great Falls of the Missouri and its namesake city. Finding the new town there so inviting,

Simms promptly wrote several coworkers who labored on the docks and shipping lines as far away as Georgia. He told of the opportunities that the territorial town had to offer African Americans. Several friends and their families took Simms seriously, and by 1887 more than a dozen Black men and women lived in the city after it was connected to the East via the Northern Pacific Railroad.[28] In 1890 the Black community of Great Falls organized the first African Methodist Episcopal Church (AME) in the new state of Montana, which they named Union Bethel. The permanence symbolized by the sturdy gothic church building cemented Great Falls as an ongoing place of opportunity for African Americans for the next fifty years. In line with this sense of permanence, its Black population grew to over three hundred by 1920.[29] Whether it came from Horace Greeley or the growing voice of Black westerners, "Go West!" would prove to be a clarion call for many Blacks elsewhere in the country whose lives of oppression and deprivation gave them little reason to stay.

More than just a place free from the physical and psychological memory of slavery (as the South was for so many), the West promised to be a space of expanded social and political rights. The promise of equitable communities and property ownership continued to attract African Americans until Montana's crippling drought and depression, which began in 1917. Right up until the economic collapse, African American newspapers from cities like Topeka and Kansas City lauded Black communities in the West for their social progress. The *Kansas City Sun* published a series of pieces entitled "The Golden West." Over a dozen columns detailed the travels of an AME bishop to a different western city each week, including four in Montana. The column praised the character of individuals from each city he visited and commented on the financial and social success of each community. The effusive subheading of the column spoke to the thinly veiled mission of the author: "An Interesting Review of the People, Towns and Possibilities of the Great Western Section of Our Country . . . The Colored Americans Making Good in the Far West and a Steady Stream of Desirable Immigration Now Pouring into That Splendid Country with Its Wonderful

6. Black infantrymen and their families cutting ice on the Yellowstone River in eastern Montana near Fort Keogh. Montana Historical Society Research Center Photograph Archives, Helena, Montana. PAC 95-70, box 17.

Possibilities."[30] Like white settler elites, the call for migration to the West from an emerging Black bourgeoisie seemed to target a specific, "desirable" class of Black settlers.

Native Lands, Black Opportunities

The Black press, a voice of racial boosterism in cities across the region, enticed migration to the "Golden West" by parading the region's true wealth, available Indian land, to readers at home and back east. Historian Quintard Taylor provides an extensive account of the rise of dozens of "all-Black" towns in Kansas, Oklahoma, and Colorado. Following the

7. Many black men and women came to Montana on steamboats like the *DeSmet*, pictured here in eastern Montana. Seven black men are seen standing in the grass. Montana Historical Society Research Center Photograph Archives, Helena, Montana. PAC 74-15.5.

Dawes Act, reservation lands within the boundaries of Indian Territory attracted Black settlers. Indeed, "the whole Indian territory," as one Black homesteader noted, "will have been swallowed by the white man, [but] many black men helped in the swallowing."[31] Well after the Exodusters of the 1870s, Indian lands that had been set aside for the Iowa, Sac and Fox, Comanche, Cheyenne, Apache, Kansa, and the "Five Civilized Tribes" became more than just a financial or speculative opportunity for Blacks. "For many African Americans," Taylor states, "[Oklahoma Territory] represented a concerted effort to create towns and colonies where black people would be free to exercise their political rights without interference."[32] In all, Black settlers and boosters founded thirty-two all-Black towns in the Indian and Oklahoma Territories.[33]

Western Black papers voiced their enthusiasm for the allotment of reservation lands and the wealth new property could bring to their community. This even included those Black Indians whose reservations shrunk under the federal policy. The *Denver Star*, for instance, printed a story in 1918 suggesting the possible benefit that Black homesteaders who received only the rugged, unwanted land might sustain in the rapidly modernizing world. When the so-called Five Civilized Tribes' land, in what originally had been constituted as the Indian Territory, fragmented under waves of allotments, several young Creek freedmen found themselves unsuspectingly blessed when their 160 acres yielded surprising wealth. During the allotment process, older and politically established Indians and Black Creeks and Cherokees whom the paper claimed were "practically all . . . full blooded negroes" chose the best land in the fertile river bottoms. The children of these men, the paper suspected, were then left with only broken and mountainous land for their own claims. When oil and gas was discovered on some of the property of these young men and women, and fortunes were made so effortlessly that even a child of fourteen could do it, the implication was that second-rate land in the West was still worth Black investment and emigration.[34]

In 1906 the Black paper in Helena, Montana, extolled the opportunity that a new bill making its way through the Idaho legislature might bring to their Black readers. The Coeur d'Alene Indian Reservation near the northwest corner of Montana (and near the large Black urban population living in Spokane, Washington) was soon to be "opened" for settlement. In reality this meant a further erosion of Native land and sovereignty by the state. Doing so provided white, and potentially Black, settlers with the fruits of dispossession, further engendering the logic of land appropriation in western communities and individuals. The *Montana Plaindealer* justified the dispossession, reporting that only five hundred Coeur d'Alene Indians were living on a capacious, half-million-acre reservation. According to the editor's hopeful calculations, 460,000 acres would be allowed for purchase, homesteading, and settlement after allotment.[35] When that allotment process concluded in the summer of 1909, despite outrage and disbelief on the part of the tribal leaders who had only nineteen years earlier been promised the whole of their already reduced reservation land in perpetuity by the secretary of Indian affairs, 200,000 acres of "excess" was sold.[36]

Even though African Americans fared poorly in attaining good land through the allotment or homestead acts, the opening of the Coeur d'Alene Reservation engendered somewhat surprising levels of fervor on the part of the *Montana Plaindealer* in early 1909. Down the entire left-hand column of the regional and state news page of the paper, the editor printed detailed instructions for how Blacks might apply for and receive valuable land in the Northwest. Tellingly, the secretary of Indian affairs reserved the first ballots for veterans or their widows—especially significant to Black readers in Helena, as the city was home to the largest population of former Buffalo Soldiers anywhere in the state. The paper's vocal conservative editor, Joseph Bass, went out of his way to explain that those who fought in the "Spanish war or the Philippine insurrection" (the conflicts of which dozens of his readers were veterans) could claim prime sections of land.[37] The real excitement, however, came from the selection process itself. Applicants mailed envelopes to the office of the reservation superintendent, James Witten, in Coeur d'Alene, Idaho. The mailing was to contain no signature or the sender's name, only the name of the reservation on which the mailer wished to apply for the land lottery. Immediately upon receipt such mail would be placed in a special canister that prevented any letters from being removed before the lottery date. At random, later in the summer, applications were drawn for each section of available land until all two hundred thousand acres had been claimed.[38]

Whereas homesteading on Montana's vast prairies in the eastern half of the state received no such special attention from this same Black paper, the cause for excitement in June 1909 was clear enough to all who read it. The selection process was color-blind. At no point could one's race be used to formally or informally disqualify them from receiving Indian land.[39] Like Joseph Bass, columnists and editors at national Black journals back east looked to the allotment process of the early twentieth century as an opportunity that carried overt promises of racial destiny. These were opportunities that Black farmers and settlers could not afford to miss. The *Chicago Defender*'s increasingly urgent coverage of Black settlement in the West, and Montana specifically, suggests that the region continued to grow in the imagination of some influential African American circles well into the new century.

One early opinion penned in 1910 by a Black farmer in South Dakota entitled "Where the Negro Fails" admonished Black farmers for not rushing the western portion of the country and its limitless land.[40] The next year the *Defender* publicized the allotment of the Pine Ridge and Rosebud Reservations in South Dakota, exclaiming in the subheading, "The Defender Wants All the Young Men and Women Who Have Trades and Professions to Get Some of This Land . . . BEAT THE FOREIGNER TO THIS LAND."[41] No doubt the editors' brand of Black nativism was aimed at northern European and Scandinavian immigrants who made up the bulk of new arrivals to the northern sections of the interior. But, where the *Defender* saw "foreigners," many white Americans saw ideal settlers.[42]

Two years later a correspondent for the *Defender* living in Butte, Montana, called upon Black farmers in the East to "follow the sage advice of Horace Greely to the young men of his generation and go west and grow up with the country." Again, the occasion was the breaking of Sioux and Assiniboine control of their reservation lands in northeast Montana following a federal act of Congress in 1908, which led to the dispossession of 1.3 million acres, about one-third of the total reservation land.[43] The readers of the *Defender* did not encounter an examination of this process. Instead the writer urged them, "You are an American citizen and you should have some of this land—Do not let the European peasantry get all of it." Further down in a second long heading the standard American settler colonial justification appeared in full force: "It does not matter whether you live in the South or in China, your fathers died in all the battles of America, and you and yours should get the land."[44] Juxtaposing these different encounters between Black settlers and the system that redistributed reservation land and resources suggests that, even when the opportunities that drew millions of white Americans west often failed to materialize for African Americans, the hope that the region might yet prove to be the Golden West endured. Though no Black paper operated in Montana past 1912, Black Montanans corresponded with the national Black press as late as 1928 and 1930, continuing their call for more Black settlers to claim Indian lands.[45]

Still, a lingering question remains: To what extent did Black settlers understand and grapple with their positions as colonizers within a racial project of Native elimination? As part of American society, awash in many of the same anti-Indian sentiments circulating throughout the country, it is hard to imagine that most new Black settlers to the West felt much differently toward Indians than their white counterparts. We cannot, therefore, readily assume that most Black settlers felt the irony of their position as colonizers. Some, such as the more conservative Joseph Bass and those editors at the *Chicago Defender*, seemed rather unapologetic about Black settlement on former reservation lands in the West. Instead, they highlighted the virtue of Black soldiers in their campaigns against Indigenous peoples in the Southwest. Indeed, in the context of Black soldiers, the answer is much more clearly defined. The professional and social identity of the Buffalo Soldiers is difficult to separate from the violence against Native peoples. It is telling, then, that in the whole of the archive of Black Montana, not a single negative word is written or spoken regarding Black soldiers. As will be discussed later in this chapter, it was the most valorized group of Black settlers who were the closest to, and most directly implicated in, the initial phase of violence in the settler project.

The *implicit* violence in purchasing or claiming allotments, however, is far more abstracted than the campaigns of the U.S. military. Very often discussions about homesteading or the breaking of reservations—such as the column by the Black South Dakota farmer in the *Defender*—took place without ever even referencing the Native people being dispossessed. This is itself a form of Native elimination. Nevertheless, the "Indian question," as it came to be called, likely kept the association between western Indian lands and settlement alive in many circles of American intellectual debate. The range of backgrounds of those who migrated would indicate that, as in most other matters, Black Montanans did not form unified opinions on the issue. As the coming sections and chapters will demonstrate, debate and contention were almost the entertainment of the day. Lively meetings and late-night dinner conversations concerning numerous issues of Black life frequently made their way into local papers, continuing the discourse so that all could partake.

Here the archive of Black Montana shows some of its limits. We readily see Bass's opinion on Native dispossession in the pages of the *Montana Plaindealer*, which ran from 1906 to 1912. But the issues that dominated the coverage of the other Black papers, the *New Age* (1902–3) and the *Colored Citizen* (1894), were more centered on electoral politics. Likewise, both those journals had short runs and provide only a brief glimpse into Black life at those moments. Had another community-oriented paper such as the *New Age* been able to stay afloat over the next decade, it would be readily visible how the matter of colonization played out in the Black community. This is even more true seeing that its editor, John Duncan, was of a decidedly different political persuasion than Bass.[46] Such speculations, of course, are merely the historian's stand-in for a lack of evidence, although it seems unlikely that a community of people so eager to debate ignored the questions of Indian dispossession. Still, we are left to imagine what justifications or critiques Black Montanans brought to that discussion.

Cedric Robinson draws our attention to yet another important factor that undoubtedly influenced Black migration and participation in the colonial project. The rise of a Black middle class during the waning decades of the nineteenth century was indelibly shaped by the more conservative teachings of a Black intelligentsia, notably the historian George Washington Williams and other academics from the American Negro Academy under the tutelage of Alexander Crummell.[47] Such thinkers developed a program stressing racial "uplift" through the ownership of capital. Thus, a Black petite bourgeoisie emerged as a formidable social force by the end of Reconstruction. Numerous scholars of the Black working class have noted the recalcitrance of the

Black business elites who "jealously guarded" the franchise against poorer Blacks as they sought to preserve their tenuous alliance with the white southerners. This further entrenched the many barriers to Black voting rights in the South.[48] Black capitalists and cultural elites engaged in a concerted effort to take part in the foundational myths of American exceptionalism. These newly self-ordained race leaders thus believed that only they "could realize the task of Negro resurrection." Throwing themselves headlong into these "Americanizing" projects no doubt contributed to, in Robinson's estimation, "the tendency of the Black intelligentsia toward an elitist consciousness of race—a synthesis of Eurocentric racism and a preoccupation with imperial political forms."[49] In short, the guiding ideology of the ascendant Black middle class dovetailed neatly with many of the imperialist impulses of western expansion.

Despite their efforts, well-to-do Blacks still found the various myths of national history, from the egalitarianism of the Revolution to the openness of the frontier, firmly beyond their ability to claim as their own cultural capital. Moreover, few of the new Black settlers to Montana hailed from the Black middle class. Still, their migration and therefore their latent participation in settler colonialism may have come, circuitously, from the far-reaching influence of the Black bourgeoisie. Uplift ideology had expanded well beyond the halls of Black colleges after the 1890s, when Booker T. Washington rose to national prominence. Like other conservative Black southerners, Washington publicly discouraged agitating for social equality. His message was rigidly enforced by many Black business and commercial power brokers who formed together under Washington's Negro Business League, which opened chapters throughout the country, including Montana.[50] From the end of Reconstruction and into the new century, a primary emphasis of this program was to keep Black laborers in the South, a mission that led to tremendous support for Washington from white political and industrial leaders. Despite his personal success, life for working Blacks frequently became untenable under such "leadership," and migration became a form of social resistance and a rejection of accommodation-

8. Acclaimed photographer J. P. Ball of Helena ran a successful studio. Dress and furnishings showcased the trappings of Victorian and Gilded Age ideas of class mobility. Montana Historical Society Research Center Photograph Archives, Helena, Montana. #957-602.

9. J. P. Ball took portraits of many of the city's black residents. Montana Historical Society Research Center Photograph Archives, Helena, Montana. #957-382.

ist leaders. In an ironic turn, many who left the South for Montana as former slaves or sharecroppers became the first African Americans in their new home. With considerable fortitude and no small amount of vision, their early arrival to the West afforded a small group the ability to hold considerable sway in growing Black enclaves. Thus, it was not always the Black bourgeoisie, but its mobile critics, who shaped the future of the Golden West.

In light of this, the varied forms of dissent, resistance, and subversion available to working-class Black settlers should not be neglected. Robin Kelley has argued forcefully that hidden transcripts of African Americans' resistance to white supremacy during Jim Crow forms an important archive with which histories of duress and the struggle for Black liberation must engage.[51] Under the current approach in settler colonial studies, insurgency against settler forms generally follows the overarching concerns of Indigenous land and sovereignty. Though it may well be that unnamed and unrecorded Black Montanans stood in solidarity with Indians in their right to exist, I suggest that the most prescient defiance to settler formations grew from African Americans attesting to the illegitimacy of the white racial regime. White settlers made this fanciful claim to the land not only through the overt reign of violence against Indigenous peoples, but through the establishment of their institutions of government, education, and industry, as well as through the molding of cultural and regional identities. Thus, trespassing into these "white spaces" by Indians, Blacks, Asians, Latinos, and those poor whites deemed not "fit" to be settlers, amount to a vast archive of hidden resistance to the settler state.[52] Important expansions to our understanding of anticolonial resistance have taken place in recent years. Scholars have become more attuned to the colonial dimensions of Indigenous political activism from antinuclear movements to the protection of water rights and recognition of spiritual and sacred space.[53] These movements, in turn, have expanded the domain of the political to include the fundamental right to call a place home. In Montana's Black community, claiming that right took many forms.

Pillars of the Community

Even before the Golden West was penned for an African American audience or Joseph Bass urged his readers to appropriate Native lands to create Black property, Black men and women knew of the promise that Montana held. Often these individuals, such as Ed Simms of Great Falls, were the instigators of what would become steady migration and vibrant communities, literally calling on others to follow. Billings's Black community owes much of its longevity to Walker and Ruth Browning. After his father died during the Civil War and his mother soon after that, teenager Walker Browning was left to care for two infant siblings in the city of Paris, Missouri. In 1872 he moved his family, who were still quite young, to Omaha, where he met and married the young Ruth Merriweather. The next year he moved his family farther west, to Fort Laramie, Wyoming. Working as a cook, Walker joined a government survey coinciding with the opening of Yellowstone National Park. Like York and Jim Beckwourth before him, Browning ventured into one of the strangest and most beautiful lands in North America as a settler-explorer. Following the conclusion of the historic survey of America's first National Park, the Browning family moved to Deadwood, South Dakota. For several years Walker tried his hand at gold mining. When the gold rush in Deadwood subsided in 1880, Browning took whatever gold dust he had secured and moved west again, to Billings, a burgeoning railroad town in south central Montana. After working and saving for two years, the Browning family built their home among the labor encampment on the south side of the rail yard in 1883.[54] It was around the Browning residence, Ruth's famous hospitality, Walker's magnanimous personality, and the weight of their remarkable, profoundly western, origin story that the Black community of Billings grew in the 1880s and 1890s.[55]

Black Montanans played a decisive role in the creation of a viable society in the West even before the presence of a sizable Black community. Likely born a slave in Kentucky, Elizabeth Williams made her way to Montana Territory shortly after emancipation. A shrewd businesswoman and entrepreneur, Williams came to fill one of the most important roles in fledging Montana communities. Lizzie, as she was known, arrived in Bozeman in 1870, at a time when the success of the cow town and stop along the Bozeman trail to the gold fields of Virginia City was anything but certain. The lifeblood of many Montana towns, the railroad, would not reach the Gallatin Valley until 1883. Until that point, when much-needed resources and products could be affordably transferred across the vast prairies to the inhospitable Rockies, towns like Bozeman needed courageous investors to ensure its survival.[56] Together with a Black Haitian-Ojibwa businessman named Samuel Lewis, Lizzie Williams speculated in commercial property and real estate in the early 1870s. Capital investment in homes and businesses as provided by Williams and Lewis was similar to that of white magnates like Nelson Story and Leander Black, among other famed pioneers of early Bozeman who built fortunes and prestige speculating in land and obtaining lucrative government contracts with the nearby Fort Parker. The small Black community there developed only after Williams and Lewis had died. The contribution of Bozeman's earliest and most successful Black residents benefited the white community at large, a community that mostly forgot them. The streets, buildings, and city parks of Bozeman now bear the names of Story, Black, Cooper, Beall, and Lamme, but not their contemporaries, such as Elizabeth Williams or Samuel Lewis.[57]

Black Women in the Settler Imagination

Though Williams's life remains largely absent from the local memory of Bozeman and the state generally, she is actually somewhat emblematic of the group of African Americans who are perhaps most represented in the various historical writings about Montana. Successful businesswomen, very often single or widowed, are the most well-known individuals from the early years of Black settler migration. Sarah Gammon Bickford of Virginia City, Rose Gordon of White Sulphur Springs, Mary Fields of Cascade, and Mattie Bell Castner of Belt take up a sizable portion of the historical scholarship on Black Montanans to date.[58] While it could be argued that the lives of these women have been more thoroughly scrutinized on account of their extensive archival presence (which is undoubtedly part of their prominence), I would suggest that their significance is also founded in their role within a gendered settler ideology.

Margaret Jacobs, who has attended to the variations of gendered power within the settler projects of North America and Australia, identifies the central role that white women played in the expansion of settler populations and politics through both the recuperation of white settler families through marriage and child-rearing, as well as the policing of nonwhites through the guise of the protection of white womanhood. Within this system white women were key to the next stage in the colonial project, which shifted its focus from exterior physical violence toward the colonization of intimate spaces. As Jacobs argues, white maternalism was foundational to the practice and justification of the removal of Indigenous children from their families on both continents. Whether on the "frontier" or in the "outback," gendered ideals facilitated both the expansion of settler colonialism as well as the solidification of whiteness as a prerequisite for one to claim to be a legitimate settler.[59]

As will be shown in the coming section on the Buffalo Soldiers, whose rugged masculinity would serve as a recognizable motif for the precarious project of legitimatizing Black claims to the land, Black women, too, occupied an important place in the Black settler imagination. The prominence of autonomous, successful Black women in the contemporary scholarship also speaks to the durability of their stories as figures brimming with potentiality for Black communities in the years that followed their many notable exploits. As scholars have noted, there can be no settlement without women. In 1870, before the predominant era of Black migration, Black men outnumbered Black women in Montana Territory a little more than 2:1. By 1910, that ratio had evened out considerably, to 1.4:1.[60] These prominent women, living in the 1870s and 1880s, therefore represented more than just curious historical notes and should be considered in the context of the increased migration of Black women and families. Often pictured in front of mining equipment or brandishing a shotgun, women like Mary "Stagecoach" Fields of Cascade and Sarah Gammon Bickford of Virginia City were proof that Black women who wanted to come west could not only achieve a measure of autonomy from a male provider if they desired, but could also accumulate considerable personal wealth and power. Well known in the subsequent Black community were those women "pioneers" who came to hold important governmental office, like Fields, as a mail carrier, or Bickford, who owned and operated the former territorial capital of Virginia City's water utilities.[61] Unattached to a male breadwinner, the paradigm of Montana's Black pioneer woman promised a renewed life for Black women looking west.

This is no more apparent than in the persistence of Montana's most widespread Black settler origin myth. Searching the newspapers and family albums for the stories of Black women, one invariably stumbles upon some version of a long-held family history that a mother, grandmother, or great-grandmother arrived in the territory as a cook for General George Armstrong Custer. According to Elizabeth "Libbie" Custer's 1885 memoir, *Boots and Saddles*, the infamous cavalry commander did employ an African American woman as a personal cook. Though Libbie Custer and subsequent scholars have identified the woman as Eliza Brown Davidson, numerous claims to that title appear throughout the archive of Black Montanans.[62] Annie Morgan, who later settled in an idyllic cabin in the Rock Creek valley outside the small mining town of Philipsburg, and Mary Adams, who was related to one of the founding Black families of the community in Great Falls, were both well known for this distinction.[63] Likewise, Ruth and Mary Mundy Driver, the daughters of a Black rancher living outside Helena, also claimed their grandmother Susan Mundy cooked for Custer and were later photographed and featured in the Anaconda-Butte paper looking through one of her cookbooks.[64] While the ubiquity of this story might cause one to chuckle a bit, imagining that far more than Custer's famous ego was being overfed, the historicity of these claims matters less than what they collectively represent. Long before Black soldiers patrolled the plains and mountains to secure Montana for settlement, Black women held tightly to a version of the past in which Black womanhood helped "win the West."

The Buffalo Soldier Era

The Golden West that attracted both steamboat porters like Ed Simms and railroad workers like Walker Browning to Montana became a viable settler society in part because of the participation, and, in the case of Elizabeth Williams, the capital investment, of African Americans. Yet many other Black men came to Montana not as civilian-settlers, but as soldiers in a war of Native elimination.[65] In 1888 a young Black man with an easygoing name from Tennessee signed enlistment papers for service in the Twenty-Fifth U.S. Colored Infantry.[66] The military took Lee Pleasant Driver first to Texas, then to Montana. Like most of the Black infantry and cavalry units, the Twenty-Fifth moved north from the deserts of the Southwest to wide expanses of North Dakota and Montana in 1891. Following the Pine Ridge Campaign in the wake of the massacre at Wounded Knee, most Buffalo Soldiers were stationed at forts across Montana. Driver mustered out of the army in 1891 while the Twenty-Fifth was stationed at Fort Missoula. Though Missoula had a promising timber economy, Driver sensed the real opportunity lay farther upriver. At the headwaters of the Clark Fork, which ran through the center of Missoula, the newly built smelter city of Anaconda turned raw mineral ore into pure copper as it attracted thousands of laborers, including Driver, in 1895.[67] Regiments or companies of Black soldiers were common in nearly all of the state's forts for the next several decades, even after the Spanish American and Philippines conflicts at the turn of the century.[68] By the 1890s and early 1900s, Black military families, like that of Lee Pleasant Driver, made Montana's urban cities and towns their homes. It is important to recognize that the core of many Black communities across the state—cities and towns that by the twentieth century were mostly removed from Native populations living on more remote reservations—were made up of men and their families whose connection to settler violence was direct and inescapable.

Popular notions of the West also likely played a role in the largest influx of African Americans. In line with ideological principles of bettering oneself and earning a salary, the army presented thousands of African American men the opportunity to make a living wage and escape slavery-like living conditions of sharecropping and the stench of Jim Crow. The African American military tradition reaches back to colonial times. As a matter of official recognition, however, the first detachment of all-Black soldiers fought for the Union Army during the latter years of the Civil War. Between 1866 and 1869, the newly constituted U.S. Army reconfigured the original companies into four military units: the Ninth and Tenth Cavalries and the Twenty-Fourth and Twenty-Fifth Colored Infantry Regiments. Soon afterward they began their deployment in the American Southwest protecting westward-moving settlers. Throughout the 1870s and 1880s, in addition to their regular duties of manning forts and defending military outposts and frontier towns, the two infantry regiments performed public service work such as stringing telegraph wire across the vast expanse of Texas, New Mexico, and Arizona. In contrast, the Ninth and Tenth Cavalry Regiments led far more dangerous lives, fighting various Native peoples in all-out campaigns and brief skirmishes, earning them not only the name "Buffalo Soldiers" from Plains Indians, but also renown among recently established African American and white communities in the western territories.[69]

Beginning in the late 1880s, the Twenty-Fourth and Twenty-Fifth Infantry Regiments gradually redeployed north to the Dakotas and the Montana Territory. Over the next decade Forts Shaw, Maginnis, Custer, Keogh, Assiniboine, Harrison, and Missoula became temporary homes for the Buffalo Soldiers. It was during this time that the Twenty-Fifth captured the American public's imagination as an experimental bicycle division. Seeking to replace expensive horses with cheaper forms of transportation, the military personnel of the Twenty-Fifth performed patrols and other duties on two wheels. The experiment gained national attention when, in 1897, these African American cyclists embarked upon a remarkable journey from Missoula to St. Louis.[70] Albeit an entertaining and fascinating piece of western and outdoor recreational history, a fixation on Montana's Black bicycle soldiers somewhat obscures their role as federal agents forcing tribes onto reservations across the state and then patrolling their borders.

10. Soldiers of the Twenty-Fifth Infantry, Fort Shaw, 1890. Montana Historical Society Research Center Photograph Archives, Helena, Montana. #947-375.

In 1898 the Spanish-American War on the island of Cuba, where conflict had been mounting for some time, forced a temporary end to the western deployment of the Buffalo Soldiers. All four regiments were redeployed to active combat duty. The Tenth Cavalry became renowned for its gallant charge up San Juan Hill alongside Theodore Roosevelt's Rough Riders, while the other regiments equally distinguished themselves in less celebrated clashes with the enemy. In fact, both the Tenth Cavalry and the Twenty-Fourth Regiment played a significant role in the capture of San Juan Hill as well as in the battle for El Caney. In the immediate aftermath of America's success in Cuba, the Buffalo Soldiers were sent to repress guerilla fighters in the Philippines, a highly controversial campaign that would last for years.[71] The wars in Cuba and the Philippines had a lasting impact on the shape of Montana's Afri-

11. A black man in Helena, 1890, wearing a military-style jacket. Many of Ball's portraits feature subjects in military dress, suggesting the status of soldiers in their community. Montana Historical Society Research Center Photograph Archives, Helena, Montana. #957-605.

can American communities between 1904 and 1910. During this time several companies were stationed in Montana forts between the first and second conflicts in the Philippines, the later taking place in 1906–7. Not a few returned home from the harsh tropical conditions weary of both a war that was not their own and a government that required of them such great sacrifices. For these reasons many Black soldiers chose not to reenlist and returned to civilian life. A sizable number of those Black men in Montana from 1905 to 1910 decided to make the Big Sky their permanent home following the Spanish American and Philippines conflicts.[72]

Miles City and Havre both became home to modest Black populations due to their close proximity to Fort Keogh and Fort Assiniboine, respectively. These communities slowly faded away as the Black units were removed from the northern frontier at the onset of the Great War. However, Missoula and Helena both enjoyed lasting communities due to a high number of veterans who took up permanent residence there. In 1906 the *Montana Plaindealer* recorded the names of twenty-seven men identified as former Buffalo Soldiers living in Helena, asking for their attendance at a meeting.[73] Three years later nearly twenty additional African American men appeared in the federal census of Helena's permanent residents that were previously listed as members of the Twenty-Fourth Infantry Regiment in the 1903 and 1904 directories of Helena that included nearby Fort Harrison. From these sources, as well as tracking individuals year by year in city directories, we know upward of thirty-five to forty men left the Twenty-Fourth during the time that it was stationed at Fort Harrison, between the first and second Philippines wars (1902–5) and continued to live and work in Helena up until 1910. Nearly all of these men were married, and a majority had two or more children. Consequently, as much as one-quarter of the population of African Americans living in Helena during this five-year period were directly connected to a Buffalo Soldier.[74]

Considering the importance of this highly visible group, it is somewhat surprising that African American soldiers have been largely disregarded in the scholarship of settler colonial expansion. Roxanne Dunbar-Ortiz is among the few scholars who place Black military men at the fore of Indigenous land appropriation and genocide. Even so, in *An Indigenous Peoples' History of the United States*, Dunbar-Ortiz recognizes the role of the Buffalo Soldiers only insofar as they were used by the white settler state to dispossess the land of Native peoples.[75] While it is certainly the case that the campaigns of the Buffalo Soldiers were beyond their control (especially without the leadership of Black officers), the history that follows highlights how their role as colonizers anchored Black settler communities to the land and legitimized the creation of Black settler space.

The "Negro Problem" Comes to Montana

It is difficult to compare this movement of only a few thousand people over a thirty-year span to the tens of thousands of freedpeople who fled the Deep South for Kansas, Missouri, and Oklahoma during the Exoduster period, much less with the millions who migrated north from 1915 to 1965. Yet migration is not about mere numbers. Migrations elicit a sense of purpose and direction.[76] As millions of people left the South after 1915, scholars have rightly expounded upon the many contributing factors leading to the Great Migration as well as the incredible new world that event created.[77] An important part of the newness that emerged throughout the country can be seen in the public response of those whites who felt threatened by the possibility of a seismic geographic shift of the Black population.

Historian James Gregory notes that, during the early years of the Great Migration, northern white newspapers published an array of pieces that dealt with the new influx of southern Blacks. Northern journals and magazines from Chicago to New York wrote of the impending pressures that the new populations were sure to bring. Questions of social and cultural mixing were pondered in public in editorials with titles like "The Negro Problem," "The Race Problem in Schools," and "The Negro Influx Proves Burden."[78] Such sentiments reflected weekly in print were manifestations of systemic and personal racism targeting African Americans' assertion of sovereignty through mobility. This interpretation carries special significance for our understanding of Black migration to the West in the late nineteenth century. Indicative of the attitudes of the greater public, newspapers reflected and intensified social fears and anxieties. Like the northern papers in 1916 and 1917, western papers in the 1890s and 1900s also exhibited similar anxieties about African Americans.[79]

The *Anaconda Standard*'s Sunday morning paper of November 19, 1899, commented at length on the "Fading of the Negro Race." Its authors claimed that, due to the supposedly incorrect results of the 1870 federal census, African Americans had lost, not gained, population in the preceding decade. They conjectured that those losses were proof that African Americans were not suited for their new place in a more equitable society and were doomed to die out.[80] This article, and the many like it, responded to the fear that many southern whites and their northern sympathizers held that the Black population during Reconstruction was set to dominate aspects of American society—namely, industry and politics.[81] The 1890 census garnered an excitement far beyond the way that census enumerations are now received. It was the one-hundredth anniversary of the first national count in 1790, and, as historian Louis Warren notes, "Americans were preoccupied with the [1890] census because they fully expected it to confirm their power and success."[82] But, as the story printed in the *Anaconda Standard* shows, another issue pressed on the minds of Americans. The previous two censuses—the first two that enumerated millions of freedpeople—were the fodder for an enlarging national discourse around the future of Black Americans and the "Negro Question." Du Bois noted in his widely read study *The Philadelphia Negro*, "A census that which gives a slight indication of the utter disappearance of the American Negro from the earth is greeted with ill-concerned delight."[83] Such delight stemmed first from an undercounted Black population in the 1870 census. The following decade, however, saw a more accurate count and showed Black population growth outpacing that of whites, leading to frivolous speculation of white race suicide.[84] Thus the 1890s were anxiously awaited by all. Michele Mitchell writes, "[In 1890] another undercount resuscitated extinction theories. If the 1890 census was partially responsible for the last decade of the nineteenth century witnessing 'an unparalleled outburst of racist speculation on the impending disappearance of the American Negro,' that speculation continued into the first decade of the next century."[85]

Articles like the one appearing for readers in Butte and Anaconda were more than sensationalized diatribes against African Americans. Rather, they attempted to soothe the anxieties of many white Montanans. The fact that such pieces would run in the corporate paper of mining towns, each home to a modest Black population at the time, suggests that the Anaconda Company's employees and their families were contending with the cultural and social realities of their new neighbors on a daily basis.[86] In 1901 the *Butte Inter-Mountain* spelled out a similar position in a piece on the same subject, written by a reporter in Butte, Montana, specifically for publishing in the daily:

> There were many who affected to see danger in the steady Increase [sic] of the negro population. It was pointed out that in time the colored race would increase until the problem now being dealt with in the South would become more difficult of solution and the Southern states be the home of such a large black population that the white inhabitants would be in a hopeless minority. The report of the census bureau in completed form dissipates these fears. It is seen that not-withstanding the Increase [sic] in the negro population the percentage of blacks In the South is lowered.[87]

Again, the response of the white community suggests that Montanans engaged in and contributed to the national dialogue that consumed the country's press. Outside of publishing articles and editorials of similar persuasions from 1880 to 1910 (one appearing in the Virginia City paper as early as 1865), both Democratic and Republican newspapers across the state lent their voices to the issue of race and the societal role of African Americans in other ways.[88]

Most notably, many Democratic papers printed reports from the South, where terrorist groups kidnapped and lynched Black men for supposedly heinous crimes. Articles appeared in Montana papers with headlines like "Henry Salzner the Wife Murderer Is Lynched" and "Was Burned at the Stake: Negro Murderer Paid a Frightful Penalty for a Most Horrible Crime."[89] Clearly, these types of editorial provocations were not aimed to inform their readership. Rather, they sought to influence the opinion on the race question and African Americans within their own community. Fanning the flames of the so-called race war occurring in far-removed locales had the effect of bringing the conflict to a head in their own cities. As historian Khalil Muhamad has forcefully argued, this era of racialized journalism functioned as part of a larger project to criminalize entire populations of Black Americans as they opted out of the neoslavery that emerged after Reconstruction. In the urban North, the question of "what to do with black migration" spawned a sad series of programs that criminalized Black culture, called for more policing of emerging Black neighborhoods, and led eventually the rise of America's new racial regime, mass incarceration and the carceral state.[90]

Likewise, as northern papers in the 1910s decried an impending "burden" caused by Black migration, especially on public facilities and institutions like schools, Montana's press did so in the 1880s. Amid a debate over whether Montana would segregate its schools by race, some imagined what would become of the institution of the white settler family with the increase of Black children. "Were all race distinctions abolished," the *Helena Independent* hypothesized in 1882, "amalgamation would inevitably result in the end. It would begin first among the poorer whites, who would intermarry with the wealthier Negroes, and would afterwards extend among all classes."[91] Montanans were still over two decades away from passing prohibitions on interracial marriage when the settler anxieties about "miscegenation" began to appear in the 1880s. From 1870 to 1890 the Black population of the state quadrupled. And, with sustained growth, the "Negro problem" pressed more and more on the minds of white settlers who had supposedly left the racial messiness of the old America behind them.[92]

Important similarities—and some even more important differences—surface in the portrayal of the "Indian problem" in the white press at this time. One particularly illustrative article detailed a new program of the Bureau of Indian Affairs to educate children of the Flathead Tribe in northwestern Montana in public schools alongside whites.[93] During a public meeting in Polson, a city that had been carved from the southern portion of the Flathead Reservation after a series of allotments, the Indian education supervisor, Mr. Baker, assuaged the anxieties of the white audience. He reminded them that the land on which their schools stood had been Indian land specifically sold to them for the purpose of establishing a public school system. It would only be logical, therefore, that Indian children living within that district could attend.[94] While this certainly represented a more progressive opinion in 1911 when compared to the segregationist impulses that laced writings on the influx of Black students in schools decades earlier, Baker's rationale for why settlers should support the measure carried the classic markers of colonial logics of elimination. "It seems to me," Baker reasoned, "that the people who come to settle on an Indian reservation should take a broad-minded view of this problem of the education of the Indian children. . . . If denied schooling, the Indian would grow up to be a vicious element in the community." As he continued, the eliminatory persuasions of Baker's progressivism became more pronounced: "The Indian, as a distinct race, is fast disappearing and he is becoming just a component part of our body politic. The sun is setting on the Indian as a member of a nomadic race, but rising for him as an American citizen."[95] Continuing the colonial project of Native elimination through assimilation required breaking down all distinctions between white and Native, beginning with education.[96]

Conversations in the white press on the "Negro problem" and the "Indian problem" point to the persistence of settler anxieties about the continued presence of racial "others" in settler spaces like the workplace or public schools. These "problems" moved in opposite directions, according to settler logics. Though articles appearing after censuses in the late nineteenth century labored to depict the disappearance of African Americans as a race, the observable reality was that Black settlers in Montana were increasing in number at the turn of the century.

Ideologically, principles such as the "one-drop rule" ensured that Blackness was an ever-expanding category.[97] Conversely, to the eyes of early settlers, there could be no doubt that the elimination of the Native was being waged with vigor. Black children posed a threat in public schools through "amalgamation," but Indian children, if educated with whites, might cease being Indian altogether and disappear. Yet neither African Americans nor Indians were "disappearing."

Conclusion

The inherent paradoxes between Black settler migration and American settler expansion is evident both in the lives and aspirations of those African Americans who moved to Montana, as well as in the white community's varied responses to their arrival. The dialogue that engaged Montanans around the turn of the century represented more than a latent interest in issues of race in the national arena. Within their colonial context, white newspapers expressed the anxieties of the "Negro problem" or the "race question" because it promised to present itself within their own community. Similarly, the Black press portrayed the West, and the availability of land there, as a golden opportunity for the oppressed people of African descent. As far back as the Exoduster migration of 1878, Black communities sprang up in as diverse places as Kansas, Oklahoma, or Colorado. In these locales the beginning of the "Black West" rested solidly upon the colonial project of land appropriation. Little changed as more and more African Americans turned their ambitions to the West over the decades that followed. Black settlers accounted for individuals and families, all with unique lives and circumstances. Despite the wide array of backgrounds and personal motivations, the migration out of the South between 1877 and 1917 speaks to a collective project that emanated from hope and assertion of Black settler sovereignty as manifested through physical and social mobility. The avenues by which African Americans reached Montana, be it the railroad, riverboat, or military, all fit within the emerging beliefs that southern Blacks needed to cast off the slavery-like social conditions that they were expected to bear. Yet the same causes of the Black community's initial growth were intimately connected to the appropriation of Indigenous land and the attempt to eliminate the Native population.

We should consider the implications of Mahmood Mamdani's famous observation that settlers are made by conquest, not just immigration.[98] The beginning of Black migration to Montana Territory in the 1870s and 1880s occurred in the immediate aftermath of Indian removal in the region. Following the garrisoning of Montana's forts during the Civil War, settlers and Native tribes came into increasingly contentious contact. From 1855 and the first treaties spearheaded by governor Isaac Stevens until 1891 and the last Sioux conflict following Wounded Knee, the federal and territorial government consistently reduced the size and range of reservations and hunting grounds. Over the course of the nineteenth century, the settler project shifted from military campaigns against foreign combatants to forcing the Sioux, Flathead, Northern Cheyenne, Blackfeet, Nez Perce, and several smaller tribes onto impoverished and compromised lands as "domestic, dependent nations."[99]

The vision of the Golden West put forward by both African Americans living in Montana around the turn of the century and by those living elsewhere looking in cannot be divorced from the challenging relationship between settler colonial structures and the narratives of western Black diaspora. Black settlers in Lewistown, Livingston, and especially White Sulphur Springs—populations that boomed in the 1880s and 1890s—only moved into central Montana and the Judith Basin area after the 1870 Baker Massacre on the Marias River in which the Second Cavalry murdered 173 Blackfeet, including 53 women and children.[100] By the mid-1870s the Blackfeet, Gros Ventres, Assiniboine, and Sioux mostly fled the Judith Basin and the surrounding area to ever-decreasing reservation lands north of the Missouri River.[101]

Black men like Walker Browning waited in anticipation for the continued success of the settler project. From 1880 to 1882 the Crow relinquished the right of way for the path of the Northern Pacific Railroad, which Browning and hundreds of others immediately helped build through the southeastern part of the territory from the Dakotas to Billings.[102] The erosion of Native sovereignty was the necessary precursor to the economic opportunity that allowed the growth of Black enclaves in Havre, Miles City, and Billings. Likewise, following the disastrous winter of 1883 that crippled the health and vitality of many Native peoples living on Montana's severely underresourced reservations, white settlers inexplicably continued the frantic call for federal military support.[103] Even as the ability of many Indian tribes to resist white expansion withered, the army chose to place the four Black regiments, stationed up until that point in the Southwest, at forts across the state to preside over the final erosion of Native power. The mission of the Buffalo Soldiers in this respect was informed entirely by the logic of settlement.

As this book continues to place the history of the Black community in Montana within a broader framework of analysis of the settler colonial West, it is necessary to bear in mind the participation of African Americans in the "bleeding edge" processes of land appropriation and settlement. The westward expansion of America projected and solidified the power of the nation-state. Moreover, it was a project in which the oppressed Black community could participate and thus become equal citizens in the nation, at least in their estimations. Many African American leaders commonly emphasized certain occupations and practices as ways that Black citizens could be accepted as Americans. Service in the military, education, and property ownership all conveyed a sense of belonging. The West served as a conduit for many of these same "Americanizing" projects.[104]

Yet, to the white settler colonial elite, the dominant relationship between colonizers and colonized in the West would be erected upon a foundation of appropriation, not exploitation. As such, the process of appropriation encouraged removal, erasure, and even genocide. This process depended upon the initial establishment of a settler state by any means necessary. Ultimately, its proponents desired a state of whiteness.[105] Many communities of varying degrees of whiteness participated in the settlement of the American West. Mormons, Jews, Irish Catholics, Asian, and various eastern European peoples also came as settlers. They were compelled to conform to the region's whiteness or be forced out.[106] Black and Asian communities faced similar fates. Unlike the others, who could eventually conform to the standards of the white West, Black westerners remained, in perpetuity, nonwhite and thus faced acute exclusion from the society in which they made their home.[107] Certainly, as Kendra Field has reminded us, freedom was not an uncomplicated claim for Black settlers.[108]

By 1917, when a drought, intense labor unrest, and a devastating outbreak of the Spanish flu crippled the state's society and economy, several thousand Black men and women had come to Montana, and, at its peak in 1910, nearly two thousand remained as permanent settlers.[109] The sometimes vitriolic response of the white community against the possibility of new Black neighbors could be seen as foreshadowing the trials ahead. African Americans across the state nevertheless established growing, thriving, and vibrant communities that seemed to be on the brink of the success. The Golden West, in its most idealized form, promised the opportunity for community growth and various forms of property ownership that conservative Black leaders like Booker T. Washington felt were central to economic and, eventually, social equality. Given its ties to uplift ideology, it is no wonder that the Black community created its own road map for life in Montana. This Black settler ideology addressed the unique challenges presented within the colonial society. Yet the racial regime of Montana's settler society was unlike that which had become almost standardized during Jim Crow. In this temporal and geographic phase of the settler project in Montana, the color line that emerged, and that the Black community would struggle against, would not produce official segregation, but the erosion of Black settler space.

2

Making Black
Settler Space   *Confronting the Colonial Color Line*

On a September day in 1881, one of the most unexpected and illustrative events pertaining to the unique political and social experience of Blackness in western settler society began inside a restaurant in Butte, Montana.[1] William Woodcock followed closely as his employer, the U.S. marshal Alexander C. Botkin, carefully made his way into the Virginia Chop House. Botkin suffered from an ailment that, according to one Butte paper, required his Black valet to assist him with many daily tasks. Woodcock and Botkin were accompanied by Botkin's brother, a well-known lawyer in Butte. Together, the two men helped Marshal Botkin through the door and to the nearest table available, one just right of the entrance. The Botkin brothers took their seats while another man, Sterrett Higgins of Deer Lodge, joined the dignitaries, leaving no place for Woodcock at the marshal's table. William looked around the dingy uptown establishment, filled with the typical hodgepodge of prospectors, mine workers, and common laborers. He chose a table near the door where heat and smell of the chop house mixed with the crisp September air filtering in from outside. He sat down to take his lunch by himself, but still near enough to the marshal to assist him if the need arose. Almost immediately, one of the other diners removed himself from Woodcock's table, mumbling angrily as he retreated further into the restaurant. Another man, identified as Mr. Fiske, having observed the events of the past several minutes, grabbed a passing waiter by the arm and demanded that he inform Woodcock that "he must leave the table and that he could not get a meal in the house." Marshal Botkin stepped in, suggesting that room be made at his own table as to avoid further offense to Mr. Fiske. Woodcock would have none of it, declined to eat, and waited for his employer to finish his meal.[2]

Local papers later reported a slight variation on Woodcock's reaction—additionally suggesting that the waiter only asked him to move tables, not leave the chop house—claiming he erupted in indignation announcing loudly to the witnesses that "he would not eat in the damned house if he could not sit where he pleased."[3] Regardless of what transpired that day, Woodcock brought suit against the owner of the Virginia Chop House under the Civil Rights Act of 1875.[4] Perhaps it was the stature of his employer and the great insult such a request brought to a man connected to a high federal office that caused Woodcock to seek redress. Or perhaps it was his new western environs, a place so far geographically and culturally from the South, where the color line was already becoming an impassable barrier to Blacks living in the freshly shattered ruins of Radical Reconstruction. Or maybe simply it was a matter of personal dignity. Whatever the cause, the result comes as a shock for many twenty-first-century Americans. After two years of languished adjudication, the Territorial Court in Deer Lodge ruled in Woodcock's favor in 1883, awarding him $500 in damages to be paid by the restaurant owner.[5]

Such a decision already would have been unthinkable in the South, as well as much of the urban North, but in Montana the defendant and his lawyers declined even to appeal the case to the Territorial Supreme Court, or, ideally, the U.S. Supreme Court, to establish precedent either way. Nine years later, in 1892, Homer Plessy took his seat in a first-class train car in Louisiana, though he was of one-eighth African descent, in order to challenge the state's 1890 statute that public transportation required "separate but equal" accommodations. Plessy challenged the ruling, hoping to set a precedent that separate but equal clauses were unconstitutional. The two cases bear important differences—notably, that Montana lacked the legal segregation of the South. However, if Montana's courts, legislature, and settler elites desired the type of segregated society that would eventually defeat challenges to white supremacy like Plessy, then appealing the Woodcock ruling would have been a logical place to start. What, then, should be made of both the territorial court's apparent progressivism and the ambivalent response of the defendant? The eminent Montana historian J. W. Smurr would presciently suggest almost sixty years ago that the case was not appealed or even lavished with attention by the local press precisely because such a low-profile ruling emanating from the far-flung reaches of a western territory was unlikely to hold widespread authority. As it played out, the larger white community in Butte and Montana Territory escaped the possible implications of such a ruling with only a $500 fine to one of its members.[6]

The Woodcock case reveals several entangled themes underlying Montana's racial and colonial history. Firstly, as an employee of a high federal officer charged with overseeing the entrenchment of settler society in the western territories, Woodcock embodied Black participation in, and personal advancement through, the colonial project. Unlike in the South, racist legislation and policies akin to the Black codes had not passed into law in Montana. Woodcock's challenge to the color line in the courts, therefore, had the distinct advantage of carrying the weight of federal law, which governed the territories prior to statehood. Secondly, his very time and place in the long narrative of American settler colonialism and racial oppression afforded him the space to confront injustice. Finally, Woodcock also exhibited a defiance that at once conveys an awareness of his advantageous position and gave voice to an emerging ideological worldview that pushed against the racial regime of the settler state even while he attempted to benefit from it.

This chapter pulls at the threads of several central developments in Montana's past: the creation of Black settler space, the colonial state's rejection of the Jim Crow color line in favor a more absolute—but less direct— form of social exclusion, and the rise of a Black settler ideology. These developments cannot be viewed in isolation. This task is critical in order to understand what became of the world that Black Montanans made for themselves, and how they fought to preserve it. White settler society, operating under the colonial logics of elimination and anti-Blackness, struggled to negotiate the exclusion of African American settlers who established themselves on the land and in their communities. These new migrants, who had already imagined the land as their Golden West, set about making it so. Black settler space came under attack from the white political and social elite, who imposed their own rendering of the color line. Within settler society Black Montanans could access some public and community institutions like schools, unsegregated neighborhoods, and the ranks of business and property owners, while also being denied the ability to freely establish permanent spaces of Black place identity where they could cultivate their own sense of social and cultural belonging and foster new ideas of home. In this fashion, by not challenging the Woodcock ruling, settler courts ensured that a legal basis for the establishment of separate Black settler space, however unequal, would remain an intolerable affront to settler sensibilities. In response to those who sought to limit and exert social control over Black settler space, Black Montanans forged a new language and social theory that contested their ongoing social exclusion.

Jim Crow and the Color Line in Colonial Perspective

According to W. E. B. Du Bois, the problem of the twentieth century, throughout the entire world, would be the problem of the color line.[7] Whether one looks to the rise of southern segregation, residential redlining in postwar suburbs, the decolonization of Africa in the 1960s, or the end of apartheid in 1994, his prediction seems to have sprung from a deep well of understanding. The division of physical space and the enforcement of "managed mobilities" have defined imperial forms, whether they existed in Durban, South Africa, or Birmingham, Alabama.[8] The concept of the "color line" bears special consideration for those scholars who attend to the history of settler colonies. The settler elite employed different manifestations of the color line during a time and geography that managed both the citizenship of African Americans in law and the continued violent elimination of Indigenous people in policy. The expansion and collapsing of physical, social, and cultural space flows like a current beneath settler projects wherever they occur.[9] The U.S. West is no exception. At stake for Black Montanans was the establishment and continuation of Black settler space; at stake for white settlers was nothing less than the legitimacy of their racial project to dispossess Native peoples and the realization of the foundational settler fantasy of a white West. As such, the racial regime that took hold in the Jim Crow South needed to be stripped of some of its most recognizable mechanisms of oppression and retooled to counter a new kind of resistance.

Understanding Jim Crow has proved instructive for challenging racist systems the world over, and the American West is no exception. Jim Crow was more than just the archetype of American anti-Black racism; it was a specific type of racial regime that upheld the ideology of white supremacy that rose from the rubble of the reconstructed South. It sought to dehumanize Black people by creating conditions wherein untold physical, sexual, and psychological violence could be perpetrated within the realm of social and cultural acceptability. Recourse to its violence was beyond the purview of legal recourse or other democratic processes. Southern elites as well as many northern sympathizers employed the Jim Crow regime to maintain rigid structures of power and domination that recreated the colonial logics of antebellum America: Black labor on stolen Indian lands continued to produce white wealth. It is imperative to remember that the racism of Jim Crow was doing a specific type of labor in the service of white supremacy. The reign of terror it employed lasted the better part of a century. During that time, its methods and technologies of violence spread throughout the rest of the country and to various spaces across the world.[10]

The archive of Black Montana at times speaks to this insidious relocation. Helena's nominally first Black newspaper, the *Colored Citizen*, once carried a short message to the editor from a "bourbon Democrat" who complained, "A Lot of Democrats have ordered your paper stopped. You are on too high a plane. Why don't you come down and give us some Jim Crow? Be sure to scratch my name off. Oh, you have already done so."[11] It is almost certain that this snippet was written by the editor, J. P. Ball, and not a "bourbon Democrat," as a means to laud his own tract as the kind of paper southerners would detest. More subtly, it also insinuated what was at stake if the paper failed to achieve its mission, falling back into the clutches of "bourbon Democrats" and Jim Crow. Though this might have been somewhat disingenuous, as the *Colored Citizen* was funded by Democrat copper baron William A. Clark in order to help Helena, his choice for the new state capital, defeat Marcus Daly's company town of Anaconda. Ball claimed that "there are no strings on us. We are running a paper devoted to the interests and welfare of our people," but most likely this was not entirely the case. Even though the paper was incredibly well written and touched on various community issues, its content was overwhelmingly Clark's propaganda and boosterism, merely with a Black spin. The *Colored Citizen* terminated the week of the election, successfully seeing Helena chosen as the capital. The fact that it did not continue publication suggests that it was never intended to be the type of paper that the community in Helena needed.[12]

Some fifteen years later, the conditions for a Black paper to thrive in Helena had changed. What had not changed, however, was the looming prospect of slipping backward into a society dominated by the privation of a Jim Crow regime. The *Montana Plaindealer* lamented the passage of the 1909 ban on interracial marriages by stating that "Montana has joined the Jim Crow colony alongside of Mississippi, South Carolina, Texas, and Arkansas."[13] Yet even as the editor's implication here was that the reign of Jim Crow did not reach all parts of the country, its infamy as the paradigm of oppression was well known. However, there could be little doubt for someone such as the author of these words, Joseph Bass, that the racial regime that defined his society was different than that of the Jim Crow in the South. In true form for a nineteenth-century journalist, Bass's editorializing mixed dry humor with healthy doses of purple prose or downright venom that could exalt or flay his subject as needed. From his downtown storefront office, he railed against city, state, and national Democrats, but could just as easily seethe as he set the type for headlines that denounced his own party. His boisterous opining and dissent in all political matters in Montana moved in lockstep with his personal civic engagement. His vote was actively courted by both political parties in the state, though he had remained an avid

Republican since his early experience as a congressional page in the Kansas legislature during the 1870s.[14] As he openly criticized various members of the settler political elite at every level of government, he also loudly championed his city as a bastion of Black working- and middle-class prosperity. Though Bass was clearly wary of a turn toward the despotic that such a law might foreshadow, the racism he experienced on a daily basis was doing a very different type of work than what was accomplished for a true Jim Crow colony.[15]

In many states, "anti-miscegenation" laws, for instance, were employed in the service of racial segregation. It was merely one aspect of what came to be known as the "color line." The color line was a social technology that produced the conditions of official segregation and upheld the inequities of power between Black and white, colonized and colonizers. This and the next chapter seek to understand the manifestations of the color line beyond the Jim Crow South or "James Crow North," and how and for what purposes was it employed by the racial regime of Montana's settler colonial society.[16] Robin D. G. Kelley has remarked that "Jim Crow ordinances ensured that churches, bars, social clubs, barbershops, beauty salons, even alleys, remained 'black' space."[17] But what of Black space beyond the reach of Jim Crow? Very much by design, no such assurances materialized for Black Montanans. Though Montana had Black churches, bars, social clubs, barbershops, beauty salons, and alleys, seldom was Black use of these spaces' white counterparts prohibited (control, of course, was another matter). Even churches, the most segregated spaces in the state, existed in a state of precarity, and many Black Montanans worshiped as part of white congregations. Indeed, fewer than a dozen Black churches were ever established to serve the Black community in a state with a landmass larger than that of Germany.[18]

What concerns me here is not solely the fact that the color line appeared in a slightly different variation than Jim Crow regimes elsewhere, though that is critical to understanding the workings of settler formations. It is more that the permutations of dissent that formed as a result of these differences should be registered. Struggle against the color line and segregation in the South (and North) during this era famously produced several contrasting ideological agendas, some of which were discussed in the last chapter. Under the banners of household names like Booker T. Washington, W. E. B. Du Bois, and Ida B. Wells, programs of racial advancement and the struggle for equality and justice permeated most parts of Black American life, including in the U.S. West and Montana. How these social ideologies were adapted by Black Montanans in the struggle against colonial erosion tells us a great deal about their everyday lives and the durability of a settler color line. What is more, the aspirations of Black settlers amounted to more than just rhetorical arguments or sternly voiced demands to far-off powers. The struggle against the racial regime of the settler state was not merely ideological; it was also a physical struggle over the creation and durability of Black settler space.

Radicals, Accommodationists, and a Black Settler Ideology

The ideological fingerprints of Booker T. Washington are not difficult to find in Montana's history. One does not need to read into events or actions to see that Washington was influential. He was one of the most dominant thinkers of his day. He made sure of it. Though many disagreed with him, the "Wizard of Tuskegee" became a force in American society and politics after Reconstruction. His influence was compounded by a tight control of much of the country's Black press, as well as a good deal of promotion by white Republican journals. He preached a gospel of Black capitalism in which African Americans could only ever be truly free through economic equality and independence. The path to this freedom for Washington lay clearly in a life of industrial education and property ownership. In time, he believed, civil equality would follow the long process of self-betterment. This image of Washington as the bearer of an "uplift" message, accompanied by a widely espoused "politics of respectability," was among his most popular depictions at the turn of the century. However, there were many other, less admiring opinions of the "Great Educator." Within the southern Black community especially, his message often appeared to be compromising at best and bordering on submissive to white supremacy at the very worst. One historian characterized Washington as the "white-appointed accommodationist leader of the race."[19] Moreover, his dismissal of agitating for civil rights in favor of accommodation won him many critics, both past and present.[20]

Accommodation, as historian Bernadette Pruitt has written, was a "compromise of practicality that originated in slavery." In practice, "the willingness of subservient caste (slaves and freed Blacks) to acquiesce to the philosophies and actions of a dominant group (slaveholding and nonslaveholding whites) incongruously aided and hindered African-origin peoples."[21] Accommodationists like Washington utilized public deference to whites to lend a veneer of security and legitimacy to their own capitalist agenda. Though only middle- and upper-class African Americans seemed to have anything to gain from accommodation—at least materially—its practice nevertheless had a toxic effect on lower-class Blacks, who often internalized those sentiments of inferiority and self-hatred. This, according to Pruitt, became a lasting element in the afterlife of slavery.[22] Because, or perhaps in spite of this condition, poor and working-class freedmen and freedwomen after slavery also came to use and rely on aspects of accommodation to survive after emancipation. Or, as Tiffany Lethabo King has put it, "the conditions of surviving under conquest is never clean."[23] Maneuvering in a profoundly compromised and ambiguous moment, Washington drew followers from all classes of Black Americans after Reconstruction.

Washington's ascent to prominence as a social commentator who championed Black capitalism and accommodation, however, did not take place in an unformed Black political climate. Years before his infamous 1896 Atlanta speech, or the publication of his autobiography, *Up from Slavery*, reformers like Ida B. Wells had been writing, speaking, and laying the necessary groundwork for a sustained critique of Washington's accommodationist program that would later be most commonly associated with the sociologist W. E. B. Du Bois.[24] Well's 1892 pamphlet *Southern Horrors: Lynch Law in All its Phases* not only condemned racial violence in the South, but also drew several important lines that connected racialist thinking to issues concerning home and region in the United States. Her critique of the New South that used physical and sexual violence against Black men and women to produce "a white man's country"—an epigram all too familiar to westerners in the late nineteenth century—precipitated her departure from the South for Chicago.[25] Drawing on this dislocation, Wells authored the *New York Age* article that led to the publishing of *Southern Horrors* under the pen name "Exiled," highlighting her own displacement from the security of home in the South.[26]

Ida B. Wells fit the "Talented Tenth" paradigm that Du Bois laid out in his 1903 collection of essays, *The Souls of Black Folk*, though the education of Black female writers and reformers like Wells, Amanda Smith, Gertrude Mossell, and Anna Julia Cooper did not seem to factor into Du Bois's thinking.[27] As one historian notes, the religious and affective undercurrents in many Black women's work directly challenged the "secularism and reactionary politics of the turn of the century" that eventually propelled Washington to social prominence by the late 1890s.[28] Despite this omission, the work of such women did not fade from Black political and social discourse. We can see shadows of Well's "Exile"—a form that reflected the "double bind" of Black womanhood being excluded from programs of Black self-determination and singled out for discrimination by white supremacist society—in *Darkwater* when Du Bois notes, "All womanhood is hampered today because the world on which it is emerging is a world that tries to worship both virgins and mothers and in the end despises motherhood and despoils virgins."[29] The radicalness in Du Bois had been nurtured by others like Wells and William Monroe Trotter who were actively dissenting from Washington's program by the turn of the century.[30]

William Trotter, a Black Harvard graduate whose Boston newspaper, the *Guardian*, began publishing powerful tracts in 1901 that called for the end of segregation and voting restrictions and promoted racial equality, was also a catalyst in the growing opposition to Washington.[31] After an event in 1903 in which Trotter planned to confront Washington at a lecture that quickly devolved into what was termed the "Boston Riot," any illusion among the African American public that a consensus existed between Black reformers was shattered. Du Bois, who had had close relationships with both Trotter and Washington's Tuskegee Institute, emerged from this volatile moment as nascent voice for radical change, publishing *The Souls of Black Folk* in the months after the events in Boston.[32] In the years that followed, Washington had no greater intellectual rival than Du Bois. While maintaining a semblance of cordiality in public, the two sharply disagreed on the accommodationist undertones of Washington's ideology.[33] Du Bois saw the decades of Washingtonian practices degrading not only the civil liberties of Black southerners, but also the foundation of Washington's own beliefs. "As result of the tender of the palm branch, what has been the return?" Du Bois questioned in *The Souls of Black Folk*. "The steady withdraw of aid from institutions for the higher education of the Negro."[34] The young sociologist saw utter foolishness in many of Washington's educational practices: "He advocates common-school and industrial training, and depreciates institutions of higher learning; but neither the Negro common-school, nor Tuskegee itself, could remain open a day were it not for teachers trained in Negro colleges, or trained by their graduates."[35]

Besides dissatisfaction with Washington's educational premises, Du Bois lamented his unwillingness to challenge white Americans on issues of civil liberties.[36] Washington placed a higher value on the education of Black children and the accumulation of wealth than all other means of advancement. For Du Bois it was intolerable that Washington called for this curriculum to be carried out at the expense of voting rights and civil justice. It must also be said, though, that Washington spent a great deal of his later life working behind the scenes to secure civil rights legislation across the country. On occasion, he made these feelings public in speeches that certainly carried more Du Boisian radicalness than his typical style.[37] During his storied career, spanning from his rise to national prominence after the Atlanta speech in 1896 until his death in 1915, Washington rose above Du Bois, if not in intellect or scholarliness, then certainly in public exposure. Even Du Bois could not deny Washington's keen ability to use both the Black and white press to further his mission. Writing in *The Souls of Black Folk*, Du Bois admitted that Washington was a man of unrelenting energy whose singularly focused program earned him "unquestioning followers." Even as he rejected his methods, Du Bois commended his rival, saying, "His work prospered, his friends are legion, and his enemies are confounded."[38]

As citizens under the settler government, the political lives of African Americans living in Montana straddled the ideological divide of this great debate. Self-ascribed followers of Washington championed the public-school educational opportunities of Montana and boasted of Black business and home ownership, all Washingtonian aspirations. Yet there was also a tone and muted radical demeanor much closer to Wells, Trotter, and Du Bois. Visions of the Golden West promised not only property and opportunity, but also unaccommodating political and civil liberation upon arrival. As discussed in the last chapter, Black middle-class race consciousness grafted onto many of Washington's accommodationist and materialist programs. Cedric Robinson has argued that, infused with a more Eurocentric, racialist ideology, the worldview of the Black elite of the 1880s and 1890s was also shaped by a healthy dose of imperial political dogma, ready-made for the ongoing settler colonial project.[39] If the whole of Black settlers in Montana had arrived under these auspices, then our task would be an easy one, and the emergence of Black settler ideological thought could simply be attributed to the misplaced aspirations of the Black bourgeoisie. Of course, the reality is far messier than that. Though Black newspapers and social clubs proudly waved the flag of Washington, they simultaneously agitated for political inclusion of all Blacks (not just those who had been "elevated" by capital accumulation) and called for an end to lynching and racial oppression in the South. On major issues, such as exercising the franchise, Black Montanans engaged en masse, working and middle class alike. Even this was due in large part to their positionality vis-à-vis the rest of settler society. White political elites no doubt viewed Black voters as an ostensibly unified base of potential (and unthreatening) support to be exploited by state Republicans *and* Democrats.[40] Thus, when it came to demanding the right to vote, Black Montanans could remain avid practitioners of Washington's uplift methods without having to compromise within their own community on these divisive matters.

Similarly, Black Montanans exercised a great deal more autonomy than their southern and northern countrymen because of their geography. The crux of Washington's power lay in his connections to white political elite and thus the tremendous weight his opinion came to carry. Nearing the end of his life, Du Bois wrote that it was this arrangement that had concerned him the most about Washington. A Black man or woman seeking access to the very limited openings of privilege and power in post-Reconstruction America without Washington's consent faced an almost impossible task. But the levers of power that Washington had fought so long to control did not reach far beyond the system of emerging Black colleges or the halls of eastern industry.[41] Removed as they were from the influence of Black elite like Washington, Black settlers in Montana moved between a conservative rhetoric of property ownership and capital accumulation and a more radical posturing that demanded immediate civil and social equality for the masses of Black Americans.[42]

The budding of this Black settler ideology occurred alongside the growth of the state's Black community. While each city where a sizeable population of African Americans lived varied somewhat in the percentage of home ownership or the success of their Black businesses, each community eventually became home to a small Black working middle class. This in turn led to the continued success of Black groceries, saloons, clubs, drugstores, and any number of other small businesses. In addition to the success of the smaller number of slightly more affluent Black Montanans, laboring African Americans also managed to accumulate enough wealth or collateral to purchase a home, oftentimes establishing Black neighborhoods.[43] With a steady job and residence, Black community members in Anaconda, Butte, Billings, Great Falls, Helena, and Missoula enjoyed a measure of security in their lives, built stable families, and raised children who could then receive a public education.

African American Education in Montana

In spite of the liberating promises of the Golden West, Black Montanans by no means enjoyed full equality. Prior to 1871 the Montana Territory had passed no law segregating the education of Black and white children. However, the territorial legislature of that year approved article 34 of the general education statutes, stating that children of "African descent" were to be educated in separate facilities. The establishment of those facilities would follow the application of at least ten Black children to a school board of trustees. The law lasted until 1895, straddling six years of statehood. In that time, Montana had by the best estimates only a few dozen children of "African descent" who sought to attend public schools.[44] In cases like that of the son of America Turner, a Black woman living in southwest Montana in 1873, the school board of Deer Lodge refused to admit the child under the new law. Conversely, in Fort Benton in 1881, the school board granted admission to a Black student, inciting an outcry from segregation's proponents. Meanwhile, White Sulphur Springs saw as many as one-third of white parents threaten to remove their own children if a Black boy was allowed to attend.[45] Though the number of Black children seeking entrance to public schools prior to 1895 in many towns and counties never even approached ten, many still were turned away entirely. Thus, it is impossible to determine the number of Black children who were denied their education prior to 1895 in Montana's more rural cities.

The question of school segregation played itself out during the early stages of Black migration. At the time the law was penned in 1871, only 346 African Americans lived in the territory, only a few dozen or so children among them.[46] By 1880 the bill had been upheld several times, being met with both criticism and support.[47] In the 1890s, as the Black population exceeded a thousand individuals, the weight of segregation had already been noted on the finances of the more populous districts.[48] Helena, as early as 1877, experienced budget shortfalls and depleted its school fund when South School was filled with only twelve Black children. In March 1882 (significantly, as William Woodcock's case was making its way through the territorial courts), Helena voted to reject the segregated school system and to allow five Black children to attend. That same year Montana schools ended the practice of officially labeling students of being "of African descent."[49] The process actually began in

12. A group of classmates pose for a photo in Helena, 1910. A single black student can be seen third row left. Montana Historical Society Research Center Photograph Archives, Helena, Montana. PAC 74-104.50GP.

the territorial legislature of 1883, when the general education bill was amended to read "no child shall be refused admission to any public school on account of race or color." However, by 1887 the original language of section 34 reappeared in legislative statutes. As historian J. W. Smurr notes in his insightful essay "Jim Crow Out West," the old law had lost much of its weight. Montana slowly moved to officially desegregate all schools after 1895.[50]

As the first generation of Black Montanans grew up under the Big Sky, their engagement with their wider community often came first in a small classroom, where they learned alongside white children. The few reminiscences of Black childhood from the early twentieth century speak mostly of a life unencumbered by type of challenges endured by their parents. Attending school, playing sports, or participating in other extracurricular activities was recalled idealistically by many.[51] Still, such voices cannot speak so generally to an experience that may have varied greatly across Montana. The school-age years of those living in Helena or Butte, where dozens of their classmates were also Black, must have been very different from that of Rose Gordon and her brother Taylor from White Sulphur Springs, where the intense protest against allowing Black students just years prior to their own schooling were still fresh memories. Despite the challenges that Black children faced, many, like Rose and Taylor Gordon, excelled. When Rose finished her secondary school education, her graduation speech extolled to the nearly all-white audience the great leaps taken by Black folk toward equality since emancipation. Her own position as valedictorian lent authority to her narrative of racial uplift.[52] Some decades later in Helena, two Black students also graduated at the top of their class and used their platform to espouse elements of uplift ideology.

On an early June day in 1902, William Gordon delivered a speech on the life and teachings of Booker T. Washington to his fellow students and their parents. Though there can be no doubt that some amount of pressure was placed on Gordon to select a racially informed topic, it is telling that the Black newspaper from Butte (located some ninety miles to the south) reprinted larges sections of his speech. It held up the young people as testaments to the community. According to the *New Age*, Gordon's address began by offering a sketch of Washington's life, his struggle to educate himself in the South, and his rise to national prominence as the principal of the Tuskegee Institute. The new graduate then outlined Washington's program of uplift ideology in no uncertain terms. "Mr. Washington's one aim," he stated, "and the purpose of the institution which he has established at Tuskegee is to teach the young negro the worth and importance of knowing some trade rather than the mere knowledge of books."[53] Though it may seem strange that such a gifted young man would stand before his school peers and denigrate Black scholarliness, there is much to suggest that such Washingtonian statements were meant to assuage white anxieties. The emphasis of William Gordon's speech was that African Americans would achieve equal footing on "the higher vantage ground upon which the Caucasian now stands," through working to enrich their new society, two centuries of unfree labor apparently notwithstanding.[54] He continued:

> The Negro must become a skilled workman, a master in the work of the farm, the factory and the shop, and be able to stand side by side with the white man in work of the same kind. . . . His manufactured products will add as much wealth to the country, his foodstuffs will build the same tissues for the body as the same products of his white brethren do now. He will then become a power in the commercial world and as such recognized and respected by all. To agitate the question of social equality is at present mere nonsense. If we are to enjoy the progress and privileges of the other race, this enjoyment must come to us as the result of constant struggle rather than by legislation or other arbitrary means. . . . Upon this foundation of labor and worth Mr. Washington is seeking to raise up noble characters.[55]

Nowhere else does Montana's historical record offer a version of uplift ideology that encapsulates the myriad and, at times, blatant racism of Washington's accommodationist impulses as young William Gordon's graduation address.[56] Though similar opinions appeared with regularity in the pages of the state's two Black newspapers, most only chose to highlight Washington's principle of wealth accumulation through industrial education while they simultaneously called for social equality.[57]

Though the *New Age* did not record the words of the other top Black graduate that day, it is quite likely that her thoughts on the matter departed from young Mr. Gordon on a number of points. As he delivered his speech, Jessie Woodcock sat by, knowing that her father, who had passed away earlier that same year, would strongly disagree with the idea that courts doled out justice "by arbitrary means" or that agitating for social equality was "mere nonsense." A decade earlier he had challenged racial discrimination in the courts of Montana Territory and won, using his settlement to help establish himself and start a family in Helena. The irony created by William Woodcock's connection to the speech perhaps speaks to the nuanced ways in which the hybridization of Washington's materialism and progressives' emphasis on political struggle manifested in an emergent Black settler ideology out west. It also directs our attention to a possible displaced and hidden transcript of dissent. Black voices are notably absent—or erased—from the archive that maps the crooked road leading to the end of school segregation in Montana, leaving the ambivalent agency of white lawmakers as the only driver of change. We risk portraying Black students and parents as passive nonactors in their own story if it remains disengaged from other struggles against and within settler society. Jesse Woodcock and her father, William, reveal the intimacy of these histories. We should not be so quick to dismiss the idea that William Woodcock may have chosen to challenge racial discrimination when he met it in Butte so that he might one day be able to sit and watch his own daughter become a top graduate of an integrated public high school.[58]

Possessing Black Montana

Taking advantage of Montana's unique educational position vis-à-vis the settler color line typically followed the stability of family life—the most recognizable representation of that being home ownership. While a majority of Black families in Montana rented their homes or rooms around the turn of the century, there was a sizable population of Black homeowners across the state. In 1910, when the community was at its peak, one hundred homes were owned by African Americans in the seven major urban centers: Anaconda, Billings, Bozeman, Butte, Great Falls, Helena, and Missoula. Bozeman's small Black community overwhelmingly owned their own homes, with only twelve of the thirty-four people having to rent in 1910. Billings and Great Falls each boasted home ownership rates of 31 and 42 percent, respectively. The Black communities of these two cities persisted well into the 1940s and 1950s, longer than any other in the state. Helena, Butte, and Missoula had home ownership rates between 20 and 26 percent. Anaconda fell behind all others in 1910, with only Frank Walker owning his home in that year. That number rose to ten African American–owned homes by 1930, even with the Black population falling in Anaconda by about 10 percent over those two decades.[59]

These figures vary slightly throughout the years, trending toward more homeownership by 1930 in the midst of dwindling populations, suggesting that poorer residents who rented homes were the first to leave. In the context of the state's relatively compact Black neighborhoods, even these modest numbers of Black homes created a sense of cohesion and community. Moreover, home ownership elicited a tangible pride. As the accumulation of property was a tenet of Washingtonian beliefs, it is completely understandable that pride in Black property consistently paired with discussions on the "progress of the Negro" and other ideological axioms.[60]

Joseph Bass, the *Montana Plaindealer*, and its various contributors from Helena frequently printed pieces expounding the material virtues of the Black community. Included in their praises of character and spiritual fortitude, was inevitably a section on business and property ownership:

> Brother J. J. Baker very kindly gathered for us a list of the property owners in Helena. They follow with their valuation: G.W. Alexander, $6000, B.F. Hooper, $6500, Mrs. R.C. Dorsey, $8000, James Crump $4000, J.E.W. Clark $3000, Geo. W. Lee $3000, Henry J. Baker $3500, Mrs. E.G. Cole $5000, Miles York $4000, Nathaniel Ford $4000, Jefferson Harrison $3000, C.C. Mathis $1500, Nathan Walker $1500, L.C. Foreman $1500, Arthur Palmer $1500, Logan Smith, $1500, Sergeant Robinson $1200, Sergeant Smith $1000, L.C. Mathis $1500, Robert Brown $1200, W.C. Rose $4500, Mrs. Annie Marshall $2000, Alonzo Leatherbury $1000, Spencer Smith $300, Mr. William Miner $1000, Robert Lucas $1500, One AME Church $15000. This showing ought to be reassuring to all members of the race everywhere. Full of encouragement for the betterment of the race, the party left the hospitable gates of Helena.[61]

As a fervent supporter of Washington, Bass used his paper, the circulation of which remained fairly regular for over five years, to impress upon his readers the social value that property ownership brought to

13. The home of African American Norman Howard Crump at 1003 9th Avenue, Helena, 1895. Montana Historical Society Research Center Photograph Archives, Helena, Montana PAC 79-53.

Helena's African American community. For men and women like Bass, and many of those individuals mentioned in his manifest, the accumulation of wealth stood as the outward expression of civil progress for all African Americans. For Black settlers the $108,400 of combined property values of twenty-nine homes (not including the value of businesses) was a product and, more important, a promise of future social and civil equality.

Across the state homeownership rates remained high, considering that a majority of Black homeowners earned meager wages. With property even a waiter or porter like Jefferson Harrison of Helena could pride themselves as members of the Black middle class.[62] The middle class radiated with the promise of Washingtonian advancements. Writing for Bass's paper, Mahala Ann Walton, a prominent member of the Black community and leader within various women's clubs and societies, stated the goals of home ownership and the accumulation of wealth in unequivocal terms: "Our people make enough money to support not only retail stores, but wholesale houses as well. With the race patronage alone we would soon have rich merchants and capitalists carrying on large business enterprises in every section of the country, that would demand the respect and recognition of the world and then prejudices against the colored race would cease and every unjust law would be wiped out."[63] In Helena the *Montana Plaindealer* pressed upon its readers, both Black and white, that the success seen in their city would be the path toward the elimination of "prejudices against the colored race." Across the state Washingtonians and Black settlers held fast to the promise of their property and their enterprises.

Such assumptions, however, were flawed in several ways, not least of which being a complete underestimation of some people's blind capacity for harboring their own prejudices. Insofar as Montana was concerned, the promise of material uplift rested upon a simple miscalculation. Black Montanans were not yet numerous enough, and most did not in fact make enough money to support every enterprising member of their community. Helena's nightclub, the Zanzibar, a Black barbershop run by a pair of retired soldiers, and various tailoring parlors in the city were among the meager number of Black businesses in the state—including the Ozark Jazz club in Great Falls—that could be sustained by a (nearly) all-Black patronage. Even so, many of these still enjoyed white customers as well. The fact remained, regardless of what individuals like Bass or Walton wished to believe, that most Black businessmen and women placed their trust in the acceptance and patronage of the white community in the absence of other African Americans.[64] Even Booker T. Washington recognized this in letter he wrote after visiting Butte and Helena. "There are not enough colored people in any one community," he decried, "to support any large business, and the white man here has not accustomed himself to trade with the Negro. The result is that he is practically out of the commercial world."[65] Though this was no doubt something of an overstatement made by a man who had only spent a few days in Montana, the essence of Washington's assessment was true enough.

Perhaps Washington's visit in 1913 had been a little late. Many Black businesses enjoyed their most profitable years between 1900 and 1910. Among other economic factors, the presence of former Buffalo Soldiers had a dramatic impact on the ability of Black men and women to open and operate a variety of enterprises. The promise of business ownership, however, was not limited to only those towns near large Black military populations.[66] A number of medium-sized rural towns provided small numbers of African Americans who had the initiative and ability to open a variety of service operations. Diners and restaurants owned and operated by Black women and men could be found in Miles City, Havre, Bozeman, White Sulphur Springs, Butte, Anaconda, and elsewhere. There were Black-owned clubs and saloons in nearly every major urban center. The gold, silver, and copper booms between 1870 and 1900 provided the ability for many Black men and women to move into predominantly white cities and open a business or shop and experience relative success; Elizabeth Williams of Bozeman, Rose Gordon of White Sulphur Springs, and Lee Pleasant Driver of Anaconda are all prime examples. These businesses, however, lasted only one generation. White patronage often faded after the death or retirement of the Black business owner who had come to be viewed as a staple in the business community, but not one to be replaced by other enterprising Black Montanans.

Where many onlookers, including W. E. B. Du Bois, saw the promise of widespread Black business and property ownership as impossible in the South, given the oppression of Jim Crow and the rigidness of southern white culture, circumstances were different in Montana and the West. Washingtonian "uplift" ideologies at times appeared to be made for the settler colonial West and its small, concentrated populations of African Americans. In addition to the opportunity for education and entrepreneurship, Republicans relied upon Black voters during local and city elections to propel them into office. African Americans were even the target of many Democratic campaigns on the state level, notably the vote for the location of the new state capital in 1894.[67] Likewise, a handful of Black men rose to offices like constables and clerks in the 1890s, and dozens were selected for political conventions around the state.⁶⁸ As such, because Montana and the West was not the same political and social climate as the South or urban North, African Americans could embrace the more admirable positions of Washingtonianism without having to bear the full burden of accommodation and submission that caused many progressives to reject his uplift message and politics of respectability.

The circumstances engendering this hybridization might be contrasted with the efforts during roughly the same era to restrict the voting rights and civic inclusion of American Indians in Montana following the 1924 Indian Citizen Act. Just three years (only one full legislative cycle) after the U.S. Congress extended the full protections of the Fourteenth and Fifteenth Amendments to all Indigenous peoples born in the United States, Montana passed a law that required all county commissioners and school board officials to be elected through an at large selection process. Senate Bill 17, in effect, made it impossible for localities like Big Horn County with a large minority Indian population to elect their own representatives. This process, which historian Orlan Svingen details in his essay, "Jim Crow, Indian Style," continued and expanded the means of disenfranchisement well into the 1980s.⁶⁹ By drawing on the work of historian Natalia Molina, the interplay between Black and Indian disenfranchisement as the relational workings of what she calls "racial scripts" becomes understandable.⁷⁰ In Montana the logic of elimination operated in relation to similar methods of the Jim Crow South as voter registration, participation, even civic dignity was systemically denied to American Indians in Montana. Moreover, colonial logics permeated the government as well as the opinions of the voters. Svingen notes one encounter that Gail Small, an American Indian attorney from Lame Deer, Montana, and candidate for the legislature, had with a local rancher when campaigning in 1984. After she introduced herself to him, the rancher "pointed off in the distance where the ruins lay of a blockhouse fortress used in the so-called 'Cheyenne Outbreak' of 1897. 'It was just yesterday we were fighting you off,' he replied to Small, 'and now you want me to vote for you?'"⁷¹

According to Small, encounters like the one with the local rancher who effortlessly collapsed time and space to make his point characterized many of the meetings she had with non-Indians. Settlers in 1984 continued to obliquely draw upon the land and settlement as their point of reference. No matter how outdated and depopularized racial scripts from a century or more ago may appear, Molina tells us, they are always available for "use in new rounds of dehumanization and demonization in the next generation or even the next debate."[72] After 1924, intensified racial categories of anti-Blackness also contributed to the continued erosion of Native sovereignty and civic participation. The logic of settlement could still be seen, as American Indians living off the reservations, supposedly assimilating into white culture, were not the primary targets of the 1927 legislation. The goal was to politically shackle Indians living in large numbers on reservations from translating their large voter base into any kind of minority representation and, thus, political control over local and county lands. It is no great leap to suggest that if Black Montanans had posed such a threat to the white political structure, similar actions would have been levied against them as well. In this hypothetical environment—which was very much the reality for Montana's Indigenous peoples—it is not a given that the hybridization of Wellsian and Du Boisian resistance with the Washingtonian principle of accumulation would have so readily occurred.

The blending of contrasting social ideologies in Montana's Black community thus rose from a need to voice dissent while still engaging the political system. Many uplift programs like education and property ownership eventually died on the vine; they produced little fruit when confronted by the exclusion of the white settler society. At only sixteen years old, the incompatibility of uplift for Black life in the West was already clear to one young man named Jess Lee Brooks. As he walked the halls of Great Falls High School in 1910, Brooks already surveyed his future prospects in Montana with measured skepticism. Many of the older Black men of his community that he knew were well suited to careers in the mining, smelting, or other commercial industries that turned the economic wheels in Great Falls, but too often they spent their days searching for odd jobs and wages. This greatly discouraged Brooks. Moreover, he feared what would become of these men, and maybe himself in such an environment. "Idleness is a great hindrance to any race or class of people," he lamented in the pages of his high school journal, "yet, if employment is cut off on all sides by prejudiced beings who refuse to work with a man because he is of a little darker color, the result is the idleness of the oppressed."[73]

In his opinion total social exclusion of African Americans, not potential demographic upheavals, was the real "race problem in the West." Jess Lee Brooks had thought hard on its possible solution, hoping that national "leaders of the race" were "trying to eliminate [it]." But he also questioned whether either side could deliver on their own. "This is the predicament that the negroes in the West are in today," Brooks suggested to his (nearly all-white) readers. "It is almost impossible for an educated negro to use his education for his support. . . . What we must have are highly educated leaders. We hear many criticisms of higher education of the negro, and many say that university education is only time wasted. I do not agree with these critics. Not that industrial education should be minimized, but that higher education should be emphasized."[74] What good was learning an industrial trade for Black Montanans like himself if former sharecroppers and Tuskegee graduates sat together outside the downtown stores waiting for menial labor that never materialized? Brooks was a young man when he penned his thoughts on race in the West, but his homegrown politics reflected the intellectual milieu of more radical community leaders and newspapermen like John Duncan and Chris Dorsey—both of whom worked in the mining city of Butte and self-published the *New Age* several years prior. Yet it was also conditioned by a more conservative Black politics such as Joseph Bass's (who had known Jess's mother for many years and republished the young man's essay in his paper) that most clearly reflected the hybridization of Black settler ideology.

Brooks recognized the value of industrial education elsewhere in the country, but noted that, in the West, labor unions and state legislation undermined the key tenet of Washingtonian ideology. Therefore, with "employment cut off on all sides," and little opportunity for the higher education he desired, young Jess Lee Brooks chose to leave Montana the next year. He attended Western University in Kansas—a Black industrial college—where he studied music before moving to Los Angeles. There the Montanan found work playing sheriffs and doctors in the Black western films of Richard Kahn, such as *Two Gun Man from Harlem* (1938).[75] Like many westerners, both Black and white, he brought authenticity to many of his roles, which resonated with the moviegoers of Los Angeles, Chicago, and Harlem, eventually becoming one of the great Black actors of his generation.[76]

Perhaps surprisingly, only three years after Brooks's essay appeared, Booker T. Washington felt compelled to partially agree with the young man's assessment of the future of Black folk in Montana. In a letter written from his hotel in Helena and later published in the pages of the nationally circulated Black paper the *Chicago Defender*, Washington observed, "[The Negro in Montana] is an 'odd job' man, and the white people, it seems, do not expect him to occupy any other position. . . . The trades [sic] unions seem to have made up their mind to keep the Negro out. The result is that he is continually pushed to the outer edges of the industrial world, and this fact naturally hurts him in the estimation of the white man, who grows into the habit of naturally associating all black faces with odd jobs of a menial character."[77] Departing from Brooks, however, Washington did not see the ultimate problem in the West as being one of labor, but of accumulation. In his mind only a few individuals seemed to have accumulated enough property and wealth to rise above the great difficulties life in Montana posed for African Americans. Because of this, Washington believed that "those who mean to live in this country [must] accumulate something that may be handed down to their children."[78]

Though both Washington and Brooks agreed that unions held an iron grip on the political arena in many towns—and an even tighter hold on their membership rolls—Black Montanans such as the young Brooks often did not acquiesce to Washington's program. Instead many people recognized the need to agitate politically and engage the various unions, and the political parties they controlled, in industrial centers like Butte, Anaconda, and Great Falls, in order to secure the right to work.[79] Successes were sparse. Often those Black laborers who managed to secure jobs in refineries or other mining-related operations did so without the support of the union in the lowliest jobs, for the lowest wages.[80] Even these gains, however, were not achieved without prolonged struggle.

Political agitation on the part of the Black community took on two primary forms. In one sphere Black Montanans attempted to pull their community together to create a unified body of votes to leverage their political power and affect positive change in the everyday lives of citizens; they sought to integrate African Americans into the political fabric of the state, thus fulfilling the hopes of many Black liberals through collective action. The other form of political agitation, however, was far more individualistic. It emanated from the handful of vocal politicos within the press whose voices were the loudest throughout the archive of Black Montana in the shifting discourse of "race" politics taking place at the state and national level. Though Republican Party politics was a common theme of Black papers across the nation, including those controlled by Washington and his interests, race men and women in Montana went to lengths not only to call out politicians in far-removed places like Mississippi and Washington, DC, but also voiced virulent criticism of politicians in their own state, cities, and neighborhoods. Narratives of political agitation in the South, where African Americans levied complaints against their local leaders, often, sadly, ended in violence and the reassertion of the color line.[81] For this reason civic participation carried strikingly different consequences. Moreover, though many Black Montanans voted the Republican ticket, it did not mean the community at large always toed the party line. In the ambiguous space between a white settler state and a small Black community, Black voters could not afford to submit to the policies of their party's leaders as even representatives who they elected at times took decisive steps toward the erosion of the Black community.

Joseph Bass and the *Montana Plaindealer* chastised politicians and city officials for pushing for racist policies. He did so even if he had previously supported many of those same candidates. In March 1906 the *Montana Plaindealer* ran a piece encouraging its readers to vote the Republican ticket for city officials in Helena, including the mayoral candidate, Frank Lindsay. In a lengthy editorial, Bass elaborated on his position: "Let's endorse the principles of Republicanism as advocated by Theodore Roosevelt, and elect a Republican Mayor in Helena. The election of a Democratic Mayor is an indirect rebuke to President Roosevelt. As executive officers we want Republicans on guard."[82] Lindsay managed to win the office, perhaps (if Bass's endorsement carried much weight) with the help of the city's substantial Black vote. However, as strong a proponent of Republicanism as Bass was, his ire could quickly turn on those he felt had forsaken their principles. In November of that same year, following an incident known as the "Brownsville Affair," President Roosevelt's character and moral scruples were called into question by Bass on the front page of the *Montana Plaindealer*. Allegedly, several members of the Twenty-Fifth Colored Infantry, along with other non-military personnel, fired shots in the town of Brownsville, Texas, killing a white man. Though it was reported that all the Black soldiers of the Twenty-Fifth were in their barracks at the time of the shooting, accusations against them persisted.[83] President Roosevelt's hurried and callous response was to dishonorably discharge the entire company after the presumed shooters would not step forward or be identified, citing their discharge on the grounds of participating in a conspiracy of silence.[84]

Bass's headline read: "Sentiment So Strong Against Dismissal Order of President Roosevelt."[85] The issues that followed in the months after were filled with the belief that Roosevelt had rebuked his own party and forgotten the nobility and courage of Black soldiers generally. Bass summed up his feelings on a man in whom he once placed the hope of his race: "President Roosevelt has lowered his dignity as a soldier and a statesman in the estimation of thousands of loyal Americans citizens." Indeed, earlier issues of the paper held Roosevelt in high regard. Bass searched for possible reasons for this shift: "We cannot understand his attitude on the Negro question at this time. It seems that since his trip south he has joined hands with Southern rebels to continue the outrages on the Negro."[86] Not only Bass and the *Montana Plaindealer*, but many Black papers across the country, condemned Roosevelt's decision in similar fashion. Yet, for Bass, the willingness to voice outrage against his own party was not an outlying event, nor was it reserved for politicians far removed from the streets of Helena. Eventually Mayor Frank Lindsay, too, would be the target of Bass's political contempt during the legal saga of Helena's famed Black social club the Zanzibar.

The Zanzibar and the Struggle for Settler Space

For three years starting in 1903, Lloyd Vernon Graye rose to unparalleled heights as a Black businessman in Montana's capital city of Helena. He owned a tailoring shop from which he offered a variety of services including cleaning, hemming, and shoe shining. Yet his coffers also benefited from a bevy of somewhat more illicit and lucrative enterprises such as gambling and prostitution. Though he was certainly a fixture in city life across Helena, the crowning jewel of Gray's empire hunkered its brick walls against the steep slope of Last Chance Gulch, where Clore Street snaked along the western side of downtown. He named the establishment the Zanzibar after the East African island. In its broadest definition, the Zanzibar was a social club. Owned and operated by Graye and his partner, Aaron Gordon, its doors were open to everyone for its many functions. Graye's establishment not only offered saloon services, but also included a dance hall, live bands, café and diner, gymnasium, billiards, library, and an "oriental parlor."[87]

To clearly see the erosive attack on Black settler space in the Zanzibar saga, the story must begin a year before a city alderman, Jake Lisner, and Police Chief Bailey drummed up the charges that eventually led to the closing of the famed Black social club. In 1904 and 1905 a full-page insert ran in several eastern African American papers. It included a photo series of the Zanzibar, showcasing its many amenities. In each frame Black men and women posed for the camera looking modern, well dressed, and very much at home. As Bass noted of the insert, it showed "the possibilities in store for a young man with hustling qualities, and what the owner [Graye] had at that time accomplished in the line of business."⁸⁸ The message this conveyed to readers, both Black and white, was that Helena was upholding the promise of the West that had been espoused throughout the rest of the country. The Zanzibar opened in this context, in conjunction with the arrival of several hundred Black infantry men, stationed three miles to the west of downtown at Fort Harrison in 1903.⁸⁹ The soldiers, along with nearly every other grouping of the Black community, converged on the Zanzibar for entertainment and romance. Young men could spend the day or evening dancing and listening to music with local women. As for those men who tended to have more money than charm, apparently options abounded for them as well. Though the Zanzibar was not a brothel, Bass alluded to Graye's connection to the Queen City's booming prostitution scene.⁹⁰ Even the more conservative citizens found reasons to patronize Graye's establishment. Reading clubs, society groups, and even a men's quartet used the Zanzibar as their home base.⁹¹

Historian William Lang, who chronicled the first account of the unhappy story of the Zanzibar, emphasizes the club's location among an infamous grouping of hovels and hangouts that sprouted along a stretch of Clore Street. It was known as the base of many of the city's "Chinese elements," long seen as the center of the city's opium scene. It also encompassed part of Helena's red-light district and was home to several of the city's seedier establishments. White city officials uncritically imagined the Zanzibar as the fulcrum of the unruly part of town. It was under these pretenses that city alderman Jake Lisner began his campaign in 1906 to "clean up Clore Street."⁹²

At first glance the history of the Zanzibar and its demise might be seen as a product of Lisner's greed and racism against its flamboyant Black owner. Surely Lloyd Vernon Graye was a rough and abrasive character. Joseph Bass made his feelings for Graye clear by calling him a "hustler" and a man of "loose morals."⁹³ While prohibitionists and staunch Methodists such as Bass might have decried his character, men such as Jake Lisner, Police Chief Bailey, and mayor Frank Lindsey found other faults with Graye. His business, Bass noted, was virtually the same as the clubs owned by Lisner only a few blocks away. Graye, in fact, was the competitor of several prominent white "gentlemen" within the city administration. Thus, it would be simple enough to assume that the Zanzibar saga was merely that of a racially fueled business vendetta. However, several other factors should also be considered.

Lloyd Vernon Graye had created three important unifiers for the Black population of Helena and Montana. First, he provided leisure: dancing, music, drink, relaxation, and sex. While such forms of recreation were open to Black customers at various establishments across the city, none provided them in a setting that fully allowed, let alone encouraged, the flourishing of one's cultural identity as Black. Second, he made a hub for Black community identity outside the church. St. James AME in Helena and the half-dozen other Black churches in Montana were often the first places where new settlers gathered and formed community in the West. These spaces served many functions, but churches typically hosted social activities that emphasized a limited and more conservative notion of Black respectability. As such the Zanzibar serviced Helena in other ways, supporting a more vibrant and dynamic community. Finally, the Zanzibar cultivated a sense of place for the Black community. The club was a physical location where being Black and being a Montanan were one and the same. Much like the Ozark Jazz Club that would later form in Great Falls, the very name "Zanzibar" (and its reference to the East African island) asserted that this was an unapologetically Black space that enjoyed social prominence in a majority-white city. These realities were not lost on the leaders of Helena and the city council. The Zanzibar took on even more place-based qualities to white men like Alderman Lisner, Police Chief Bailey, and Mayor Lindsey. From their vantage Clore Street not only represented the establishment of Blacks in Helena, but also of all unwanted ethnicities. While Lisner might have campaigned against the Zanzibar for personal reasons—Graye's inroads into the city's realm of white prostitution threatened his own business prospects—the Zanzibar had come to represent more than Graye's personal success.[94] It threatened white settler sensibilities by symbolizing the vitality of the Black and other minority communities.

14. Advertisement for the Zanzibar that ran in several eastern black newspapers. *Montana Plaindealer*, January 4, 1907, 4. Image from chroniclingamerica.loc.gov.

Lisner, Lindsay, and Bailey began a crusade of vitriol against Graye and the Zanzibar in 1906. At one point the *Helena Independent*, operating as the mouthpiece of the city officials, even printed crime statistics that suggested upward of 70 percent of the city's illegal activities spawned from the Zanzibar and Clore Street.[95] Those numbers were laughable and baseless. Nevertheless, they served their purposes to cast the social club and the area as a scourge to the decency of white middle-class Montanans. When two murders involving prostitutes from the club occurred in 1906, Lisner and Bailey moved quickly to revoke the business license of Graye and Gordon. However, since the partners had committed no crime, the Zanzibar reopened, seemingly a sign of a great victory for African American liberties.[96] Sadly, the campaign to deprive Graye of his property—and, more important, the community of their place identity—rebounded. In a year charges would be brought against Graye for selling alcohol to minors.[97] In January 1907 the courts ruled against the proprietors. As Bass lamented in one of his more colorful statements, "The maledictions of a coterie of pothouse politicians and veritable negro-haters used an ungrateful and acrobatic city administration as a cat's paw to throttle L. V. Graye."[98] Those "veritable negro-haters" now also included the mayor, whom he had once supported. Bass did not shy away from conflict, an approach that would have likely led to repercussions had he lived in the South. However, as the saga of Zanzibar suggests, the color line in the West was not necessarily operating explicitly in politics, business, housing, or any of the typical social spheres divided by the color line of Jim Crow.

The clear anxieties over Black settler space shifts the significance of this history away from the personal and toward a community and place-centered narrative. Framing the Zanzibar saga as a purely vindictive act is complicated by the fact that Graye was not "throttled," and those "veritable negro-haters" clearly were not using the city administration to displace one "overly bumptious" Black man. Rather they sought to destroy the sense of place for the entire community.[99] As sinister as Lisner's personal intentions against Graye may well have been, the underlying meaning of his actions embodied something far more odious. Graye was not run out of town—or, in the vigilante tradition of the Queen City, forcibly led to the infamous hanging tree. Instead Graye maintained his prosperous tailor parlor and presumably continued on in his other pursuits as an "object of admiration of the damsels of the silk-stocking district of prostitution."[100] Though a deep blow to his fortunes, Graye was able to keep his feet and thrive for several more years in Helena. His former business partner, Aaron Gordon, found a less contentious compatriot in the city's first Black constable, William Irvin. Together the two men opened a bar across the street from Jake Lisner's club on

West Main Street. Their club kept its doors open for a year, but it never seemed to replicate what the Zanzibar had been able to become during its brief tenure.[101] Other places in the capital city remained for a while as other bastions of Black place identity, such as Dorsey's Grocery on 8th Avenue, St. James African Methodist Episcopal Church, and, in an intellectual sense, the pages of the *Montana Plaindealer*. Unlike the rest, however, the Zanzibar seemed to provide something for everyone, even those who might have decried some of its functions. The *Montana Plaindealer* and Dorsey's Grocery were deeply dependent on a community of nearly all Black patrons to stay afloat. As the 1910s came and went, fewer African Americans could provide that income.[102] Why this occurred is the subject of later chapters. The promise of the Zanzibar had been unique: it existed for years as a business model that simultaneously prospered financially and encouraged the continued establishment of Black settler spaces.

Conclusion

The history of the color line in Montana was characterized by the struggle over the creation, viability, and eventual erosion of Black settler spaces. Against such forces of erosion, Black Montanans like Joseph Bass, L. V. Graye, Jess Lee Brooks, and William Woodcock dissented in a distinctly western fashion. We should not be surprised by such resistance. As anthropologist Ann Laura Stoler reminds us, structures and systems of ruin and ruination do not create passive populations; instead they manifest an active struggle.[103] The Black settler ideology that was forged by the struggle against a distinctly settler colonial color line exposed the subversive place that African Americans held in their new world. Westward expansion opened possibilities to Black Americans that equated directly to several tenets of Booker T. Washington's teachings. The historical record shows that home ownership and education rates remained high in Black Montana in the late nineteenth and early twentieth centuries. Yet, at the same time, the level of political agitation from members of the Black community illustrate to what degree the promises of uplift ideology were under siege from the rest of society. The social ideology of Black Montana was therefore not solely representative of either Black conservatives or Black radicals, but a hybrid ideology that formed to meet new challenges. This, too, did not constitute a uniformly held position and was seldom expressed as a conscious political form by Black Montanans at the time.

The African American community mobilized its political agency through various means, methods, and party platforms in the early twentieth century. Strict Republicans and followers of Booker T. Washington like Joseph Bass not only engaged in political discourses in ways that Washington consistently warned against, but Black Republicans also publicly voiced their disdain for party representatives whom they viewed to be no better than the malicious racists of the Jim Crow South. These political dissentions were often voiced in response to the conditions of life in Montana. However, it would be wrong to assume that Black politics were reactionary. On the contrary—the very presence of African Americans in the region and the establishment of Black spaces forced settler elites to respond.

The active quality of Black political life at the dawn of the century provides the critical background for an inquiry into the meaning of home and belonging for Black settlers in Montana and throughout the West. Some Black Montanans sought to carve out a realm of political influence even as they recognized the limitations of being a small and trivialized political voice. As the next chapter examines more closely, some chose to eschew Republican politicians who consistently acted against their interests and pushed to break into the fractious and fickle world of industrial politics. They hoped that the fruit of such struggle might be the best defense against the violation of the most basic right: the ability to call a place home. The history of Black Montana now turns to just such a moment of political activism and its fight against the erosion of freedom's frontier.

3

Great Debates   *Black Settler Politics in the New Age*

Armeta Elizabeth Smith caught a glimpse of the tall, dark man amid the normal hustle and bustle of Butte one day in 1905. She asked her friend who he was, motioning in the man's direction. "That's John Duncan," her friend replied. Without missing a beat Armeta declared, "I'm going to marry that man." Though she recalled that day seven decades later, there is little reason to doubt her assertiveness. She also decided something else about her future when she saw John for the first time. She had been traveling with a wealthy white woman throughout the U.S. West and Canada for most of 1904. Armeta began working for her in Delaware, where she started a career as a schoolteacher after graduating from Ingleside Seminary in Virginia. She had seen much of North America in the previous year; on a street corner in Butte, Montana, Armeta decided that she had seen enough. Despite the fact that her friend quickly informed her that John "was not the marrying type," Armeta was resolute. She informed her employer that she would be remaining in Butte.[1]

It took two years, but Armeta proved correct. After the two married in 1907, John and Armeta Duncan modeled the experiences of a successful "progressive" African American family in the early twentieth century.[2] Armeta's own history of education and public service merged well with John's. Two years before her arrival in Butte, John had been the coeditor of the *New Age*, Montana's first African American weekly published by and "in the interests of Colored people," which ran from May 1902 until February 1903.[3] When John set out in journalism, the relentless requirements on his time—soliciting advertisers and subscribers, not to mention writing columns and even setting the type—meant that he had to forgo his professional career as a barber.[4] After the paper ended cir-

105

culation, Duncan returned to his tonsorial enterprise, eventually buying his own barber shop. In October 1919, after more than two decades in Butte, John Duncan made a drastic career move and began studying at the University of Massachusetts School of Podiatry and Orthopedics at Emerson College in Boston. After two years, and with a degree in hand, Duncan returned to his family home and opened his own practice.[5]

Duncan's podiatry clinic treated the weary and broken feet of Butte's Black laborers and white copper miners alike until just before his death in 1958. During that same time, his wife organized and engaged the Black community on numerous issues. In 1923 Armeta became a founding member and president of the Montana State Federation of Colored Women's Clubs, reflecting the Duncans' lives of service to their community. In 1928 the couple purchased their second home, located at 715 West Park Avenue, on Butte's west side.[6] From their new vantage the Duncans could look across the ever-expanding "Mining City." All around them headframes marked the entrance to Butte's mine tunnels, which splintered and forked beneath the city for thousands of miles. Only a flew blocks to the south, the Emma Mine neighborhood on the east side of Montana Avenue and the Shaffer's Chapel neighborhood to the west were home to many of Butte's Black residents.[7] West Park Street climbed the hill westward from the Duncan home to the entrance of the Mining College, where today the Copper King Marcus Daly, captured in bronze, stands watch over his domain.

Their spacious new residence, as well as their second home nearby, stood as testaments to John and Armeta's fortitude and business acumen. This pattern of business initiative and home ownership likely would have been met with praise by Booker T. Washington for the manner in which it was believed to bring about racial uplift and self-betterment. It is quite possible John and Armeta had a chance to discuss that subject with Washington during a lecture tour stop in Butte in 1913, after which he was entertained with a reception at Shaffer's Chapel, where John and Armeta were prominent members and that served as the offices of the *New Age* during its short run a decade earlier.[8] We can only speculate whether the subjects of the Duncan's avid and unique political lives or the *New Age* were ever broached. It seems more likely that the political activism of the Black community would have been of interest to W. E. B. Du Bois, who likewise met with Butte's most established Black family, even visiting the Duncan residence when he lectured to audiences in Butte some years later.[9]

Indeed, one of two letters written by Washington regarding his time in Butte suggests he found something unexpected, and perhaps even disconcerting, about the Black community of Butte as opposed to Helena. On the whole he found the people of Helena to be more "industrious," "intelligent," and surprisingly "cultured."[10] Though he spent only a few days with Montana's two largest Black communities, his hasty judgments are nevertheless curious, considering that Butte and Helena were relatively well matched in many of the ways that Washington would have seen as important, such as business and home ownership. The two cities also boasted comparable social establishments (e.g., churches, fraternal and women's auxiliary associations, reading clubs). Though he stated that African Americans in Montana fell far behind what he would have desired in all these categories, he nevertheless felt that Helena was the more "progressive" city. This begs the question: What did Washington encounter in Butte that lowered its citizens in his estimation?

The story of the *New Age*, Butte's first and only Black newspaper, offers us a possible answer. Considering that many of the leading Black citizens in the city organized and directed social clubs and business league chapters that adhered to Washington's own national programs, it would have been most surprising for the visiting dignitary to learn that many of these same men and women were Democrats. In national politics the Democratic party, which was still the enemy of Roosevelt's progressives, vehemently fought against civil rights legislation. Many African Americans at the dawn of the twentieth century, including Washington, were still fervent defenders of the party of Lincoln. A Black Democrats Club such as the type that had existed in Butte for a full decade at the time of Washington's visit in 1913 must have been regarded as almost sacrilege to the nation's most famous Black Republican. We will likely never know if Washington was told by his hosts how and why such a political development came to be. Based upon his long career advocating industrial pursuits over political agitation and, specifically, his advice for Black Montanans to continue accumulating land and property rather than attempt to break into labor circles and secure jobs as professional and skilled workers, one can conclude that the mission of editors John Duncan and Chris Dorsey, as well as a handful of other Black citizens of the Mining City, would not have earned his blessing.

Why Black settlers living in Butte at the turn of the century would venture to engage with Democratic Party politics at the local level despite the national party's hostility to equality and openly racist political positions has much to do with their geographic, industrial, and economic circumstances. The important role that the city of Butte and its powerful mining capitalist class played in the settler domination of Montana and the Northern Rockies is critical to understanding the history of the *New Age*. Settler logics of white supremacy and anti-Blackness dominated the city's powerful labor and trade unions. Only by breaking such logics could Black settlers hope to carve out a future in the region.

The previous chapter outlined how and why a Black settler ideology took root in Montana. Actively subverting—as well as responding to—a number of new challenges posed by settler society, Black Montanans pulled from and adapted the social programs of various national Black leaders. Though much of this ideology, one might argue, was reactionary to some degree (particularly the underlying aspects of Booker T. Washington's materialism), still other parts of the African American experience in Montana took on a robust activist, even opportunist, quality. What unfolded during the publication of the *New Age* from the spring of 1902 until early 1903 between the editors, their readers, and other politically active Black residents in Butte reveals a moment of unprecedented potential. How that moment developed tells us that individuals like Duncan and Dorsey understood what was at stake in their activism: a better future and a more fully realized idea of "home." Probing the limits of their success therefore unveils the types of erosive methods the settler society would exploit in order to counter such Black activism.

This chapter focuses on the election season of 1902 both in Butte and the rest of Montana and the grassroots political action taken by members of the state's Black community.[11] It offers various openings for us to more fully consider the discourse of the "Negro question," which already shadowed the history of Black migration to Montana and the establishment of a unique racial regime in the West.[12] Not only did the paper report on the types of discourses that engaged Black Montanans—particularly issues debating the merits of industrial versus higher education or the primacy of wealth accumulation and property ownership over the legislative victories for equality—but, as a political tract, the paper also served as a physical illustration of what some Montanans clearly believed to be the right side of such debates. Yet the story of the *New Age* also requires one to account for the history of white Montanans, their politics, and their struggles to survive. Without it, an important part of this story is lost. Black Montanans weighed their political options carefully between national party affiliations, the possibility of creating local and statewide solidarities with white working-class Montanans, and their own moral reasoning in an era of unprecedented political corruption. As such, their commitment and concern for the wider politics of their city and state should not be overlooked. Ultimately, this short-lived grassroots movement failed to bring about the desired results stated by the paper's editors, who themselves disagreed on the appropriate path forward. It would be more than two decades until an economic recession and one of the nation's most bitter labor disputes in Butte laid bare the consequences of Black Montanans' continued political exclusion.

Colonial Butte

Montana senator Burton K. Wheeler famously said of Butte, "It is safe to say that no one who has ever been there has forgotten it."[13] As true as this statement is for everyday people, it is perhaps truer for historians. Over the years Butte has commanded the attention of historically minded thinkers at the local, state, regional, national, and even global level.[14] One might be forgiven for thinking of Butte as Montana's shining star of relevance to world history. The material resources that electrified the

American imperial machine from the Spanish-American War through both world wars were pulled from what came to be known as the "richest hill on earth." The significance of Butte extends far beyond its role in the ascension of the United States to a global capitalist superpower. Even as its mines produced a vast majority of the nation's copper ore, which was necessary for the next stage in industrialization, Butte and its people furthered the entrenchment of U.S. settler colonialism across a five-state region. Thus, another moniker for Butte might be added to the "richest hill on earth" and the "Gibraltar of Unionism": the colonial metropole of the Northern Rockies.

Very nearly straddling the continental divide in southwestern Montana, Butte (and its buried wealth) fortuitously sat along ancient north-south and east-west corridors. Only some forty miles to the east of the city, the three forks of the Missouri River converge near the famous Bozeman Trail. Within Butte's city limits, Silver Bow Creek empties to the west and, less than twenty miles away, meets with other tributaries to form the Clark Fork River, running to the northwest, emptying into the Columbia, and, eventually, the Pacific. Wide glacial valleys stretch south on either side of the spine of the continent leading to both the Great Basin and Rocky Mountain Front and the metropolises of Denver and Salt Lake City.

Prospectors rushed a second time to Butte City around 1875, when silver was discovered in the tapped-out gold mines that had been dug and abandoned a decade earlier.[15] Custer's defeat at the Battle of the Little Bighorn a year later signaled that the newly organized Territory of Montana controlled and governed only a tiny archipelago of mining encampments and river towns spread precariously thin across ninety-four million acres of land. On the ground, Butte was a speck of settler-miners in a vast sea controlled culturally and politically by Indigenous peoples.[16] Historian Richard White argues that encounters between the worlds of the white colonists and Native peoples facilitated the creation of a middle ground where both groups would traffic in cultural hybridization and accommodation in order to make their own experiences and desires legible to the other. In places like the Great Lakes region and French Canada, the middle ground appeared to have survived much of the sixteenth and seventeenth centuries. The erosion of the Algonquin middle ground, according to White, came quickly, though not unexpectedly.[17]

If a social form akin to a middle ground ever took shape in nineteenth-century Montana, when Indians still occupied the position of political and demographic power over white traders, trappers, miners, and settlers, then its erosion might best be visualized as the product of a massive and terrible flood, washing away new potentials and imagined futures seemingly in a blink of an eye. Historian Elliott West has chronicled the rapid breakdown of the old social order that bound and made legible the worlds of the Plains Indians and white fur trappers of Rocky Mountain Front after gold was discovered in hills above Denver in 1858. In a span of a few years, entire communities of Métis people as well as their white and Native kin suddenly found themselves outside the world of the white settler, a world they themselves helped bring about.[18] As rapidly as this took place in Colorado, the erosion of Native sovereignty in Montana seems to have been even more ephemeral. The dispossession of Native lands had already begun even as much of the physical space remained unoccupied by Anglo-Americans.[19] Violent clashes throughout the region, broken treaties, and reneged reservation contracts put Indian tribes into an increasingly precarious position over the second half of the nineteenth century.[20]

Typical histories usually discuss the "subduing" of Montana's Indigenous population through a handful of key "battles" like those against the Blackfeet on the Marias River in 1870 or against the Nez Perce in the Big Hole Valley in 1877. Following such grisly episodes, these histories typically shift to take place in reservation offices, or in correspondence between Bureau of Indian Affairs (BIA) officials and the federal government. This narrative focus keeps the significance of the "Indian problem" safely away from the lives of people settling in places like Butte.[21] Even Montana's most prominent state historians remarked that "in contrast to the camps in Colorado, Arizona, or the Black Hills, Montana's gold camps were distant from Native American Lands."[22] Despite the fact that many early mining camps absolutely shared space with Indians, the only distance that truly existed between white miners' claims to the land and Native sovereignties was temporal. To sink a mine shaft into ground that had *not* been claimed by Indigenous peoples quite recently would have proved to be an impossible task anywhere in nineteenth-century Montana. Even still, in understanding how the state could be demographically and geographically dominated by Native peoples when Montana Territory was founded in 1864, and how that reality had been all but completely reversed by statehood in 1889, Butte becomes one of the central figures in this drama of dispossession.

As mentioned earlier, Butte began as a tiny island of settler-miners in a vast sea of land unoccupied by Anglo-Americans. The settler expansion into that territory was in part predicated on the material and economic success of Butte and other places like it. Montana's white population in 1870 was roughly 20,000 people. In the first census after its reestablishment in the mid-1870s, Butte's population was a modest 3,363—still, a bustling mining community. By the next census in 1890, Butte had drawn nearly 11,000 residents to the wealth of its mines. Again, during the next ten years its population would over double to more than 30,000 by the close of the century. The state population would likewise balloon from only 20,000 in 1870 to a quarter-million by 1900. However, by almost any metric, Montana remained a seemingly "empty" place. Settler expansion, therefore, continued apace as the twentieth century dawned. By World War I Butte's population reached 90,000, making it the largest city in the region, integral to the state's economy, and a source of capital for many of its far-flung homesteaders and agricultural towns.[23] The wealth that overflowed from the ground as well as from the pockets of early capitalists gave Butte a name known around the world as one of the greatest places of opportunity anywhere in the country. As a result Butte pulled new settlers into its orbit from elsewhere in the West as well as Chicago, New York, the South, and, especially, Europe.[24]

The local geography of the Black residents of Butte and southwestern Montana is telling in light of its colonial condition. It was impossible to move from spaces of Black identity in Butte such as Shaffer's Chapel or

Bethel Baptist Church, or from the homes and flats of Black workers, without confronting the reality that the lives of Black Montanans constantly intersected with some of the most wealthy and powerful men in the world and one of the most active union strongholds in the country. African Americans imagined their future in this world through more than just the symbolism of tunnels and veins of copper ore creeping under the foundations of Black homes, churches, and businesses, but also as partially informed by the volatile thrashing back and forth between workers and management, wealthy and poor, empowered and oppressed that defined the social and political life of Montana at the time. Perhaps no piece of Montana's Black history shows this intertwining with more clarity and nuance than the story of John Duncan and his friend Chris Dorsey's foray into the hotly contested world of journalism and mining politics. At the dawn of the new century, a new configuration of political power—and, as the two men hoped, a new age of equality and engagement for their community—seemed possible.

To make sense of why a small group of Black barbers, porters, and valets would commit their time and resources to start a political paper in a town where every other piece of print media served as a mouthpiece for some wealthy corporate interest or another, it is necessary to take a step back and survey the turbulent world of Montana mining politics around the turn of the century. Several excellent books have detailed the political turmoil that unfolded between the rivals William A. Clark, Marcus Daly, F. Augustus Heinze, and East Coast corporate entities, so that terrain will not be fully revisited; just a brief sketch of the various plotting, maneuvering, corruption, and treachery will suffice.[25]

The ambition of young William A. Clark held no small amount of sorrow for the people of Montana, past and present. Clark arrived during the gold rush of 1863 as a sprite and beady-eyed twenty-four-year-old. One historian notes that "he longed, according to those who knew him, to be Montana's richest man and its most prestigious statesman."[26] The political side to this goal overshadowed his accumulation of one of the great American fortunes of the Gilded Age. He became so desperate to reach the U.S. Senate that, when he was eventually able to buy enough votes in Montana's legislature, congressional leadership refused to seat him until he resigned in disgrace. Though he eventually managed to reach the Senate chambers in 1901, Clark's belligerent use of bribes and other forms of corruption partially spurred lawmakers to propose the Seventeenth Amendment, which called for the direct elections of senators. Throughout all of this, the barrier to Clark's success at home took the form of a likable Irishman named Marcus Daly, who arrived in Butte the same year that Clark acquired his first silver mines in the city.[27] Already having earned fame and a modest fortune as a mine manager and hard-rock specialist during the Comstock silver rush in Nevada, Daly fortuitously purchased a near-worthless claim called the "Anaconda." Daly's miners quietly dug down until they hit the largest and purest vein of copper ore ever discovered on earth. In secret Daly began buying up all the mines around the Anaconda, investing tens of millions, and cemented his mining empire and status as Butte's "Copper King."[28]

With Clark's and Daly's interests opposed, a bitter rivalry ensued from 1880 until 1900. Twice Daly undermined Clark's bids for Congress: first in 1889 for Montana's lone House seat, and then again in 1899.[29] Even as Clark sustained loss after loss, the tide was turning. Daly took ill in 1899. His company, which he managed with San Francisco investor James Ben Ali Haggin, came into the crosshairs of the world's largest corporate trust, Standard Oil. Prior to this Daly and Haggin had managed their Anaconda Company under the principle that contented workers were better for business. Although this form of corporate paternalism left much to be desired by workers, such an outlook dovetailed with a burgeoning labor movement in the Butte mines. Organizations grew and flourished leading to Butte being known as the "Gibraltar of Unionism." But Daly was dying. When his company went public in 1899, it was bought by a division of Rockefeller's Standard Oil, Amalgamated Copper. After this the elections of 1900 and 1902 took place in a new political reality: one without Daly at the helm, and thus one where local interests threatened to be stamped out.[30]

William A. Clark's new enemy was now a formidable corporate behemoth. To counter this threat, Clark turned to the third and lesser-known

Copper King, "Fritz" Augustus Heinze, a young German immigrant capitalist who made his fortune running independent smelters operating in Butte at reduced prices. Heinze was a likable man who quickly gathered around him the remnants of Montana's short-lived, but consequential, experiment with populism. Together the Clark-Heinze ticket in 1900 positioned itself as a stalwart against "foreign" corporate trusts that sought to disband labor unions and run roughshod over Montana. The tactic worked. Heinze gained what he desperately desired: control of judges and the local governments of Silver Bow County and the City of Butte. Clark, for his part, finally conquered his "white whale." A Democratic legislature at last sent the sixty-year-old Copper King to the Senate without the cloud of (as much) corruption. Clark could gloat over his old nemesis for only a few weeks. Just after the election, Marcus Daly died, leaving his Anaconda Company, which had become one of the most profitable on earth, solely in the hands of Rockefeller and Standard Oil. Perhaps under threat from such forces (who could easily have seen to it that Clark would again face an investigation and be refused his Senate seat), Clark immediately abandoned Heinze and made a tentative peace with the new Anaconda Copper Mining Company. Shortly following the 1900 election season, dubious mining practices earned Heinze both the acute need of judicial patronage and protection, but also undying enemies, including Clark and his new allies at "the Company."[31] Recalling her early years in Butte, Armeta Duncan noted that her future husband began his paper during the "great feud" between Clark and Heinze—a moment of reckoning that impacted all citizens of the city.[32]

What came to be known as the Battle for Butte hopelessly scattered and confused any semblance of party lines or affiliations among the city's voters. This confusion cannot be overstated. Some trade unionists backed Clark, a Democrat, though his interests were now with a nominally Republican and corporate force in the Anaconda Company. Other union voters stayed with their man Heinze, whom they viewed as fighting the good fight by battling the scourge of Eastern monopoly. Republicans in the state also reluctantly split allegiances between the two men, as Heinze was more closely tied to the reviled populist hero and Democrat William Jennings Bryan. But equally aversive to Republicans was Clark, a racist, conservative bulwark who spent his six years in the Senate battling Roosevelt's antitrust and conservation policies. To further muddy the waters, Heinze, in order to offer different candidates for offices than those backed by Clark, began running men as Republicans after 1901 though he himself remained—or, rather, returned to being—a Democrat. Tellingly, local papers generally ceased identifying candidates by party altogether; instead they advocated for either the "Clark ticket" or the "Heinze ticket."

In the vacuum created by Marcus Daly's death, a battle raged for the copper of Butte's Hill, the labor of its workers, and the votes of its residents. At this moment of chaos and intrigue, the role of Black Montanans was hopelessly lost, blotted out from our historical memory. And yet it was precisely at this juncture that a handful of individuals saw a moment of great potential, which they believed would be the dawning of a "New Age."

Great Debates and the *New Age*

The historical record reveals little regarding what kinds of financing, labor, and organizing efforts went into the publishing of the *New Age*. When its inaugural issue rolled off the presses on May 30, 1902, it was the first of its kind seen anywhere in Montana. Its front page featured three dominant columns: one supporting the career of Booker T. Washington; another detailing the ongoing affairs of the city's very active Black women's clubs and associations; and the last looking abroad to deliberate the possible annexation of the Danish West Indies. If incorporated, the paper noted, the majority Black population would change the face of the raging national debate about the "Negro problem."[33] In these three articles alone, the range of opinions on several pertinent matters of African American life in the post-Reconstruction era is telling. To call upon the life and work of a figure like Washington, as previously shown, was to make certain connections between the goals of Black liberation and equality and which program of uplift they should follow. For Washington, it was industrial education—that is, agricultural and service sector training opposed to pursuing professional jobs and higher education—and property ownership that would eventually secure racial harmony.

The declaration made by the Black women's club of Butte nodded to Washington's program of uplift and his politics of respectability, stating, "We are accumulating property, building characters, getting education, wealth and culture." However, they also qualified their support: "But with all our progress we have in America today a race problem. The representatives of the people sit in Washington, its marble halls, and make a football out of the constitutional rights of ten millions of American citizens and freemen."[34] The progress of working Black men, no matter how much wealth they attained, would never be enough. The women concluded, "The destiny of America today sits in the lap of American womanhood." The editors of the paper likewise looked toward the blatantly imperial destiny of the United States when they considered what a proposal before the Senate to annex certain islands from the Danish West Indies—especially Saint Martin and St. Croix—would mean for the demographic breakdown of the United States, given that a majority of the potential new citizens would be productive Black West Indians. Despite accommodationist leaders like Washington warning Blacks against looking to voting majorities to affect change, the editors of the *New Age* editors nevertheless saw great promise.

The event unfolding in the halls of Congress, however, was much farther afield than the one taking shape in their own city and state. Opening the paper in 1902, the editors voiced an even more plain-faced rebuke of certain Washingtonian beliefs in an editorial entitled "Our Position." They rejected in unequivocal terms the notion that Black people would attain racial equality simply by means of accumulating wealth or staying out of the social and political fray, as Washington advocated. In the center of the page, they began:

> One of the chief aims and purposes of our journal which we shall endeavor to carry out to the best of our meager ability will be to

at all times and in every conceivable way work and labor for the greatest political and legal rights which our race is guaranteed under the Constitution of the United States and the State of Montana, and to by every means bring the race in this State to a compact union, a fraternal spirit, free from all petty jealousies and dissensions—a perfectly united machine, adjusted in every part—in order that these rights may be attained.[35]

Fittingly, they imagined their paper as a ship launching into stormy seas as it undertook its maiden voyage. They explained that their aim was to foster political unity and, through that unity, wield their democratic powers as effectively as possible. Their ambition came with the recognition that accomplishing this task would neither be straightforward nor easy. How, exactly, does one create a "compact union" and "fraternal spirit" among a group of people, connected by racial identity, but living in small towns and cities spread out across the third largest state (at the time) in the country? For their part, the editors saw the path to a perfectly united machine laid out quite clearly ahead of them. Their paper would report on issues and stories that Black Montanans would want to read. Dorsey, Duncan, and Smith (the third editor, whose name left the masthead early on) acknowledged it would be a challenge to fill their four-page tract each week with new and engaging material, much of which they would reprint from eastern Black newspapers.[36]

They also thought about their readers' regional identity as westerners and Montanans, including a fair amount of regional news seemingly taken from white papers that spoke on matters such as mining, agricultural technology, trade, and western politics. At least one of the paper's editors or contributors seems to have been an avid hunter and outdoorsman, as the paper made frequent references to Black hunters and anglers living in cities beyond Butte.[37] Creating a common intellectual community among Black Montanans (whom census records indicate were on average mostly literate and well educated) provided a platform of knowledge from which they might debate current affairs, articulate informed positions, and, ideally, come to a common consensus on the most pressing issues.[38]

And debate they did.[39] Public meetings and reading clubs that erupted into lively arguments and long orations about the "race question" made headlines in the *New Age*. The Silver Bow Literary Society, one of several Black social clubs in the city, struck up "no little amount of enthusiasm" when the topic of conversation turned to one of the great debates of the early Progressive Era: "Which is, or would be, the greatest advantage to the Negro—'education or wealth?'"[40] In their retelling of the meeting that took place in November 1902, the authors remarked that both sides of the issue were well represented, with eloquent points and rebuttals. Not to be silent on the matter, however, the editors responded, "It is a clear conclusion in our minds that education will never solve the great race problem alone."[41] Education, they reasoned, did not deliver on the promise of racial equality. This was evident *in the South* where they claimed Black men and women were more learned than their white counterparts but remained hopelessly oppressed. It did not have to be so, they argued. Calling for industrial pursuits to be carried out with vigor, the editors reasoned that "if a negro presents the proceeds of his mine or the produce of his farm to the market; the broker does not take into account that he is a negro."[42]

It is worth pausing to consider the editors' first reference: to the Black mine owner. We know from census records and several mentions in Helena's Black paper that there were, in fact, several Black men and women who owned mining claims in Montana at the turn of the century, and even earlier.[43] But this statement carried other layers of meaning for readers in Butte, as well as those participating in the Silver Bow Literary Society debate. First was the column's implicit contrasting of South and West. If Black mine ownership was rare in the West, where ample land and a vigorous extraction economy prevailed, then Black mine ownership provided no relief for Black southerners. Even if we think regionally and consider Black farm ownership, more common in the South, that property-owning minority still faced acute racism and inequality despite (and often because of) their accumulated material wealth. Another layer to their argument was equally as odd. It would not have been lost on readers that widespread engagement in the gold, silver, or copper markets would be putting the cart before the horse, so to speak. The election season had just finished in November, and the Black working class was still no closer to laboring in Butte's mines.[44] The editors' argument for the accumulation of wealth over education rang hollow. To be sure, it was not even convincing to those in attendance that day. The column begrudgingly continued, "We are sorry to note that the results of the decision of the debate was decided in favor of education, when we see around us the great necessity of commercial industry."[45] Not to come down too harshly on education, the editors admitted that it would also be foolish to turn from intellectual pursuits entirely (as one might expect coming from a clearly educated journalist), and that a hybrid of wealth accumulation and educational training for Black folk was needed.[46]

The level of contention on display in public meetings carried a significant gendered component as well. In a community of only a few hundred, the voices of Black women could not be so easily silenced or ignored. Indeed, due to the challenging circumstances in which laboring Black men found themselves, Black women emerged as equal, if not the loudest, participants in such debates. The Silver Bow Literary Society had both male and female branches and officers, so one can assume that women were present at the meeting in question.[47] Furthermore, several articles in the paper alluded to the independence of women's auxiliaries and their political discourse. John Duncan detailed a visit he and Chris Dorsey made to listen in on a women's club meeting in the summer of 1902: after blithely remarking, with casual sexism, that they were skeptical that a group of women could organize and carry out a meeting without the oversight of male leaders, both men admitted that the level of argumentation surprised them, and that the Black women of Butte were aware of the issues and equipped to debate the many issues affecting the race in their community.[48]

Recalling the position of Butte's women's clubs on the inadequacy of wealth accumulation to secure equality in the opening issue of the *New Age*, it is likely that among the voices rejecting the conservative program of industrial education were many of Butte's leading Black women. The unequal coverage of male political engagement by men should not distort the reality that women clearly saw their lives and futures as full of potential and radical possibilities as the male editors of the *New Age*. We can never know the full extent to which women pushed the men of their community toward the edges of "respectable" Republican party politics. It is clear, however, that they also believed the conditions of life in the West demanded something new. For the women's clubs in May 1902, that included holding politicians in Helena and Washington accountable for making the issue of racial equality a "football" to be punted at the first inconvenient moment. They also demanded that steps be taken to secure benefits and social services such as childcare for working women.[49]

Debates like those in the Silver Bow Literary Society and others reported on in the pages of the *New Age* throughout 1902 and early 1903 depict a self-reflective community regarding their own unique condition vis-à-vis the racism exhibited by local Republicans and Democrats alike. There would be no mention of accommodating white supremacist demands that Black southerners give up their hope of the franchise, no discussion of segregating the races in Montana or working "as separate as fingers, yet on one hand," as Washington infamously said during a nationally circulated speech in Atlanta in 1896.[50] And, of course, there could be no talk of staying out of the political fray. After all, throwing their hat into the political ring was the purpose of the paper in the first place. The conditions of life for Blacks who the *New Age* tried to bring together were just that: new.

The Battle for Black Butte

If one thing can be said for certain, it is that Black Montanans needed very little prompting from John Duncan or his coeditor, Chris Dorsey, to foster a coherent sense of community identity. As part of their mission to keep their readers informed of the various goings-on around Montana, the *New Age* faithfully published a state and local news and gossip column each week. From this wealth of historical knowledge, it is apparent that Black residents of Butte and nearby Anaconda visited each other with great frequency. Not only did the editors receive news of the activities of Black Montanans who lived hundreds of miles from Butte, but they assumed that their local customers were eager to read it. These types of local gossip columns—the same that later appeared in Helena's the *Montana Plaindealer*—reveal that Black Montanans made and maintained connections to families and friends throughout the state. Indeed, the paper relied upon these networks of friends and kin to spread their political message in Butte and beyond.

On the matter of creating a "perfectly united machine, adjusted in every part" for the purposes of political engagement, however, things did not unfold as planned. In its first several months, the paper gave readers a steady stream of materials and news that the editors believed illustrated Black Montanans' need for meaningful civic engagement. The paper lamented that in the past Black Montanans had traded their votes for a few positions at the capital, where Black men were given the "privilege" of opening the doors for white legislators.[51] This was what happened when their community blindly toed the party line for Republican leaders in Helena and Washington. Party loyalties, the *New Age* suggested, needed to be put aside if they wanted to force white politicians into making more meaningful concessions on issues affecting the Black community. The paper made no mention of the Black public servants who had been voted into office or onto the police forces in Great Falls and Helena during the preceding decade.[52] Perhaps calling for Black representation in a government whose course was almost solely dictated by the whim of wealthy capitalists dampened similar ambitions in 1902. Instead their focus turned to securing the ability of working-class Blacks to make a fair living and enjoy the full protection of the law. Prefiguring the national shift of Black voters into the camp of FDR's labor-oriented Democratic Party in the 1930s, some of the paper's staff pushed to align Black interests with Butte's unions, but not unanimously.

Chris Dorsey was a wild card. Unlike John Duncan, about whom a trove of biographical information is available, Dorsey's life beyond what was written in the *New Age* remains largely unknown. He moved to Montana sometime after the enumeration of the 1900 census, in which he does not appear. He left Montana in December 1902, making his sojourn in the Treasure State very brief indeed. Nevertheless, during his short time in the city, he became a well-known man of great political charisma, very highly connected in the world of Montana mining politics. He was, after all, Augustus Heinze's personal assistant. Heinze had come to Butte in 1889 and built his empire by refining the ore of smaller and privately owned mining operations at discounted prices. For this business model—which stood in stark contrast to the cutthroat methods of William Clark, as well as the corporate nature of Marcus Daly's Anaconda Company—Heinze became a favorite of the common people. Historians Michael Malone and Richard Roeder note that "his talents included a fine oratorical ability, a shrewd sense of politics, and, so valuable to him in Butte, a glaring lack of moral scruples."[53] Dorsey's employment by the magnate elicited a certain amount of pride that one of the paper's editors was so well connected with one of the state's most important moneyed interests. The relationship between employer and employee proved consequential in Dorsey and Duncan's mission to unite the political factions of Black Montanans.

Even before political tensions started to pull the two apart, Duncan engaged in his share of friendly ribbing at his partner's expense. Numerous jokes and barbs reveal aspects of their prior relationship as well as their respective roles at the paper. "Anyone going out of town and never coming back," Duncan wrote in June, "who wishes to borrow some money a short time before train time will be readily accommodated by calling on Mr. Chris Dorsey. It is his latest hobby, so we understand."[54] Apparently undiscriminating about to whom he lent money, Dorsey was gently mocked in the pages of his own paper. Other mentions might suggest a possible reason. "Mr. Chris Dorsey leaves Wednesday for Helena. Again!" one issue lamented. "We fail to understand these constant trips to the capital. Our esteemed colleague avers that it is always on business for the copper Napoleon [Heinze], but we are rather inclined to the opinion that he is endeavoring to get a lease and bond on something in Helena himself."[55] Duncan, left behind to manage and edit the paper, seemed to grow tired of his partner's frequent absences from Butte. Dorsey, for his part, appears to have operated as a traveling political reporter and correspondent during his touring with Heinze, which took him to Helena, Bozeman, and even as far away as the Yukon and Alaska.[56]

The first column on Heinze published in the pages of the *New Age* came from Dorsey's reporting on one such trip to Helena. He accompanied both his employer and several other politically minded Black men from Butte to witness the ribbon-cutting of the newly constructed state capitol building. On hand were not only thousands of Montanans, but the two remaining Copper Kings. Clark and Heinze gave the official dedication of the new statehouse as well as its immense dome cast from the same mineral that had turned them into two of the richest men in America and the most powerful individuals in the Rocky Mountain West. Observing the festivities firsthand, Chris Dorsey reported that during a dinner that evening Heinze took a bold political step, declaring that he would become a Democrat, officially changing his party affiliations. The move came as a surprise to many for a number of reasons. Dorsey noted that "he had been considered a Republican up to the present time, although as a matter of fact, his strength has been largely in labor circles."[57] This reorientation, Dorsey speculated, "will probably play an important part in future political campaigns of this state."[58] His employer signaled that he would again return his interests to his dominant political base, one that historians have noted rose largely from Montana's failed populist movement of the 1890s. Moreover, it uncovered the stakes that Heinze must have felt were highest during the upcoming campaign. His former affiliation as a Republican could have gained him votes elsewhere in the state, but his sights were still firmly set on Butte and Silver Bow County, where he desperately needed to maintain a tight control on the city government and a healthy patronage with the local courts; in that city, labor Democrats reigned supreme. Heinze also saw a vital opening. His rival, William Clark, had ceded important ground among labor camps by his recent peace with the antilabor corporate trusts of Standard Oil. Thus, it became politically prudent to show support for Butte's large majority of Democratic voters.

John Duncan doubted Heinze's sincerity, going as far as to claim his representatives were "the so-called Heinze democrats, who try to shield their dishonest purpose under the cloak of the pure party."[59] On one hand, Duncan might well have understood Heinze's political maneuverings during 1902. His actions were largely predicated on certain dubious activities taking place beneath the feet of Butte's residents. Over the previous several years, questions about how to discern the underground boundaries of mining claims—and, more precisely, which mine owner had rights, exclusive or partial, to a vein of copper ore that ran between competing claims—were hotly contested. While litigation commenced above the surface in local and state courts, Heinze's miners dug horizontally to extract copper from areas directly below and adjacent to shafts owned by the Anaconda Company, as well as those of William Clark. Under such conditions it seems true enough that Heinze's cozying up to labor rang hollow to Butte's residents. His antics were not only damaging to his rival mine owners, but they also posed a real danger to unionized miners on both sides who were compelled by their bosses as well as their own interests to defend their precious subterranean riches.[60]

On the other hand, the intensifying schism between the coeditors suggests a trace of meddling in the political affairs of Black Montanans from the highest ranks of Montana's settler capitalist elite. As Chris Dorsey campaigned around the state for candidates backed by his employer, John Duncan noted with increasing agitation that his unscrupulous partner was bent under the will of power and money to work against the real interests of Black Montanans. Duncan, however, was not free from all speculation that his political positions, too, were at least partially influenced by moneyed men. The previous year William Clark donated funds and a city lot to the AME congregation of Butte, which used his gifts to build a new church building and outfit it with impressive furnishings and stained-glass windows.[61] Not to mention that the *New Age* used the church building as the newspaper's main office. This act of generosity, like all things with Clark, was politically calculated. As noted in the previous chapter, Clark had funded the first Black paper in Montana to act as his mouthpiece during the state election for the permanent capital. Even as early as 1894, Clark recognized that Black voters, nationally consolidated under his rival Republican Party, were faced with an open ticket, as Marcus Daly also represented a Democratic force in the state. Neither copper baron allowed Black men to work underground in Butte, though this had as much to do with union racism as with management.[62] And so, leading up to the vote on the location of the state capital, about a thousand Black votes seemed up for grabs in what promised to be a contest determined by razor thin margins. In 1901, when Clark made his contribution to the Black churchgoers of Butte, it seems evident that his desire to scrape together any and all possible supporters would be pursued at any cost (other than offering paying jobs in the mines of Butte, of course). How much Clark's actions influenced the burgeoning rise of Black Democrats in Butte cannot be known. Well after Clark passed away, and mining politics became even more fraught during the interwar years, John Duncan's son, Walter, noted that his father, and most Blacks he knew, had always been Democrats.[63]

The first major shift to take place after Heinze's announcement and the breaking of party alliances between the editors of the *New Age* during the late summer months came in the news that Chris Dorsey would be leaving the staff of the paper that he helped found. Sometime after their return from a trip to Bozeman in late September, Dorsey and Duncan split company.[64] At the height of campaign season the political disagreement between the two turned ugly. In one meeting of a Black social club in Butte only a few days after the state African American convention in Bozeman, the *New Age* reported on a public debate between the merits of Clark and Heinze: "The Clark representation through the best points showed and the fairness of the campaign was given the most attention." Incredulously, the columnist (likely Duncan) turned to the opposition: "Chris Dorsey, who always has a lot to say, made a flowery speech for the Heinze side, but like Heinze himself failed to show the audience that his words had any significance." Had the editor ended the column here, this quarrel might have accounted for one of the tamer excoriations of Dorsey and Heinze that appeared in the paper regularly from that point on. But he continued, "Chris Dorsey has made himself very unpopular among the colored people by daring to invade their confidence with the Heinze method of campaign (rule or ruin)." And, finally, commenting on Dorsey's impending trip to canvas Black voters around the state, the columnist warned, "Our advice to him . . . is never go to any town where he cannot have protection of the soldiers. If he does we are of the opinion that Mr. Heinze will be looking for another valet."[65] Black Montana was by no means insulated or detached from the divisive world wrought by King Copper.

In the very same issue that openly threatened physical violence against its former coeditor, the tone of the *New Age* shifted decidedly. For months the paper had only advocated that Black voters in Montana needed to come together as a political force, "free from all petty jealousies and dissentions," and never actually pointed to one party or the other to support. On October 4, however, columns and editorials suddenly started endorsing various Democratic candidates for congress and the courts. Under the column heading "Our Candidates . . . Who Is the Friend of the Negro?," the paper made its position clear.[66] Duncan filled the paper until the election in November with short biographies and testimonials of various local Democrats while condemning Republicans. More than blindly endorsing Clark's men, the *New Age* detailed a level of Black activism around Democratic Party politics that had not been documented until that moment. In the fall Aaron Webb joined John Duncan, along with several other members of the community, to start the Colored Democrats Club. The group held meetings and even hosted stump speeches from white Democratic candidates who, likely, had never spoken before an all-Black gathering. On these occasions the *New Age* reported the supposed good intentions of their white guests. "Hon. M. P. Gilchrist," running for a state senate seat, "was immediately requested by the chairman to make a little talk in behalf of the club, to which he responded, and in his discourse, which was ably delivered, he mentioned of his life-long acquaintance and integrity to the colored race." Duncan further opined that "Mr. Gilchrist is a man of pure conscience and holds no malice or grievance against any race on account of color or previous servitude. He will receive the hearty support of the colored boys in this election, and if the colored vote of Silver Bow County can elect him, he is as good as state senator now."[67]

At the same meetings, it was made clear to readers that many of the anxieties swirling around the 1902 election had a uniquely racialized valence among African Americans that it did not hold for white settlers and miners living in Butte. The organizer of the Colored Democrats Club and a close associate of John Duncan, Aaron Webb, stood before a room of some fifty or so Black men (it is unclear if any women were present) and "impressed upon the audience the great necessity of a pure judiciary wherein prejudice against the colored man may not be known."[68] Webb's position echoed a lengthy piece that appeared a week earlier under the headline "For an Untampered Judiciary." Regardless of the obvious party bias, the treatise exposed some positions familiar to Black citizens, as well as some that spoke in defense of a working-class solidarity: "One corrupt judge, we all know, can do more to break down the material interest of a state than famine or plague. The honest laborer of toil suffers with all other persons and all other interests."[69] In Butte—which was famous among Black Montanans as the city rebuked by the court as it upheld the legal rights of William Woodcock, who had sued for discrimination at a restaurant some ten years prior—a single man such as Heinze who sought so openly to control Republican judges and attorneys for his own purposes must surely have evoked deep apprehension within the Black community. Additionally, by opposing Heinze's judicial takeover, Black residents sought to align themselves with white workers whose livelihoods also rested upon the just application of law.

There were other impediments to building working-class solidarities, however. Targeted racism emerged from the white press during the campaign. John Duncan published a series of scathing indictments of the journalistic integrity of the *Butte Inter Mountain* after one of the paper's writers continuously mocked the Black community by penning pieces in a racist "negro dialect."[70] Duncan demanded that the reporter, whom he labeled a "would-be humorist, or rather idiot," be fired. In the weeks and months that followed, Duncan kept his readers up-to-date with the progress of several petitions that were being passed around the Black community calling for action.⁷¹ Certainly, the *Butte Inter Mountain* editorialized in offensive language. One piece focused on a Black man in Butte who ostensibly accosted a white woman alone in her millinery shop, where he attempted to sell her potatoes. According to the reporter, the woman declined, but the man persisted, walking toward her while holding out the spuds.⁷² The paper included several garbled sentences meant to reflect the broken "dialect" speech of the Black man and claimed the woman produced a revolver that sent him running through the streets of Butte.

Beyond the racist dialect, John Duncan could have found much distasteful about the *Butte Inter Mountain*. By 1902 the daily journal had already been purchased away from the future Republican mayor of Butte and U.S. senator Lee Mantle, though it continued to espouse Republican Party politics until 1912.⁷³ During the 1902 elections, the *Butte Inter Mountain* advocated for Heinze's Republican candidates. Racist rhetoric and fearmongering laced their political coverage as well as general commentary about Montana and U.S. society. They reported breathlessly on "black crime" and made every effort to paint Black citizens of Butte as violent and lustful.⁷⁴ Though Butte's union Democrat-controlled papers also engaged in similar race baiting, the *Butte Inter Mountain* remained unmatched in their bigotry during this period.

The vitriol and racism that came locally from Republicans and nationally from Democrats, as well as the manipulations on the part of wealthy men, played an undeniable role in the battle for Black Butte. Regardless of what settler elites like Heinze or Clark may have had in mind for the politics of Black Montana, however, it is also clear that something else emerged. Unable to garner enough votes to truly hold politicians accountable or to propel their own candidates into office, Black Montanans sought to carve out their political niche within existing institutions. They courted and supported local politicians and the unions that backed them even if that meant lending their voices and votes to Democrats. This contradiction between local and national politics was not lost on Black Democrats. At another meeting of the Colored Democrats Club, Aaron Webb acknowledged that "nationally, I am a Republican, but the local issues are the ones that concern us most, and I deem it quite essential that we look forward to the protection of our home industry, for this reason I am a Democrat."[75] If the goal was to secure a political voice for the Black community of Butte at the turn of the century, embroilment in labor politics was essential. To disengage from local industrial or union politics in Montana was to resign one's employment fate to the designs of the white community. The decision of Webb, Dorsey, and other African Americans in Butte to support the party most closely associated with racist and nativist policies additionally shows the uncharted environment in which Black Montanans found themselves around the turn of the century.

When November arrived the *New Age* anxiously awaited the outcome of the general elections for offices ranging from local posts, to judicial benches, to state legislators. But, to the dismay of Duncan, the returns showed that Heinze had, more or less, been victorious in maintaining his vice-grip on the government of Butte. Statewide, also, Republicans backed by the Copper Napoleon gained seats in both the state house and senate. Heinze's victory revealed both the limits of Black Montanans to affect the political landscape of their home, and the fact that the *New Age* had likely not made good on its "plot" to unite all the Black voters under a single front.

Along with John Duncan and his cohorts, we are left to imagine what was at stake for Black Montanans in the fall of 1902. What had been the costs of their continued political exclusion? Had they been able to propel Democrats to victory that year, when the Black population was near its apex, could circumstances for Black workers have improved? Could they have leveraged their newfound relevance in local politics to secure coveted jobs in the mines and smelters, or, more important, obtain union membership? Certainly, Black Democrats' failure in 1902 did not directly lead to their continued political isolation. Being ignored by the city's politicians was a condition that they likely contested with each new election cycle in the decades that followed. Success in 1902, however, might have had long-lasting effects. Some four decades later, the labor shortages of World War II would illustrate that little had changed regarding the racial inclusion of the miner's unions. Remembering those years, John Duncan's son, Walter, would note that Black workers did not enter the Butte mines until there was virtually no other option available for management and unions alike. Those who did go underground, he said, "were terribly not wanted. There was a crying demand for miners during the War. Anybody and everybody who wanted to come and make a nickel in the mines could do so . . ." He took a long pause before continuing: ". . . As long as there was no pigment in their skin."[76]

Like his mother and sister, who had been interviewed by the historian Quintard Taylor the day before in the spring of 1974, Walter Duncan imagined that most African Americans who left Butte in the intervening years made their way to the West Coast, where jobs in the shipyards could be obtained, and a racially sympathetic Democratic-labor party was successfully fighting for the abolition of discriminatory pay scales throughout the 1930s and 1940s.[77] Here appears a sad irony. For Black Montanans, the promise of working-class solidarity was not realized during FDR's New Deal as it was in other states like Washington and Oregon. No such solidarity existed between the working classes of Black and white Montanans, at least not on a large scale. In the mines of Butte; in the smelters of Anaconda, Great Falls, and East Helena; and, later, in the oil refineries and livestock markets of Billings and the eastern portion of the state, the possibility of those connections, which served as a lifeline to Black workers elsewhere in the country, had already eroded away when the Great Depression hit. Just as those solidarities that never took shape, the vision that John Duncan and others had once harbored for their home slipped away.

Had he read his father's paper (none of the surviving Duncan family had, it seems), the reasoning behind the name John Duncan and Chris Dorsey gave their journal would have given Walter Duncan a clear distinction between the city that his father knew at the turn of the century and the one he had grown up in during the 1930s and 1940s.[78]

As it happened, an (understandable) case of intellectual property theft occasioned the editors to explain the logic behind the title they had inadvertently lifted from another Black paper, the Portland *New Age*. Engaging the metaphor of their journal as a ship setting sail in stormy seas, the editors explained:

> In selecting a name for our paper, it was our aim to spring something new on the public in the way of names and set sail to the ports of public sentiment under the guidance of the New Age. We have weighed anchor, blew our fog horn, hoisted our signals and have received answer from a vessel sailing under the same name as ours. . . . We fire a salute to our namesake and wish them bon voyage. . . . We, unfortunately, did not know of the existence of the New Age in Portland, therefore we kindly ask them to pardon us. . . . Two souls with but a single thought, two hearts, that beat as one.[79]

An imagined community, a single mission, and promise and hope connected the people of Butte to another Black community in the Northwest. Even across great distances, an idea of the Black West took shape. Where John Duncan had foreseen connection between Blacks across the region, his son knew only isolation.

John Duncan folded the paper the in February the following year. According to the last issue that survives, he was away from Butte, traveling across Montana, unsuccessfully seeking new subscribers and advertisers. He returned to the far more profitable business he had known before, as a barber.[80] Still, not all things went back to the way they had been. It seems that the ordeal of the *New Age* took a heavy toll on Chris Dorsey. Perhaps because he was so ostracized in the final months of the election, Dorsey resigned his position with Augustus Heinze. In a city with only a few hundred Black residents, and with racial strife and prejudice raging in its halls of industry, perhaps Butte seemed better a place to be left behind. In December 1902 Chris Dorsey was again looking forward, this time much farther west, to Hawaii. He planned to join his uncle's successful law practice, which was located in downtown Honolulu, and he hoped to one day become a lawyer as well.⁸¹ On board a steamer bound from San Francisco, Chris Dorsey slipped into the mists of time, and into some yet undiscovered fold of the historical record.⁸²

It is likely that their parting did not sit well with John Duncan either. Though he wished Dorsey the best in the final issues of the paper and remarked upon the young man's bright future ahead, both his relationship with his partner and to the *New Age* itself was something John Duncan did not want to take with him. After a nineteen year-long career as a barber, and then an even more successful practice as Butte's first podiatrist and its first Black doctor—a life full of family, property, wealth, and opportunity—the ship that he once imagined the *New Age* to be had also disappeared over the horizon. Despite growing up in a home furnished with Black newspapers and magazines delivered from across the United States, neither his wife, Armeta, his daughter, Perdita, nor his son, Walter, ever recalled him mentioning his time as Montanan's first independent Black newsman.⁸³

Conclusion

The political discord between the once-close friends and former coeditors of the *New Age* developed amid the challenging political environment of Montanan's settler society. They met these challenges largely by straddling the ideological chasm that divided racial thinking following Reconstruction. Newspaper editors as well as everyday citizens who lent their opinions to such issues gave a voice to an emerging Black settler ideology in the West by demanding full inclusion in the American body politic. But the story of the story of the *New Age* is not solely one of an unrealized grassroots political movement. In so many ways, what Duncan and Dorsey were able to accomplish runs much deeper in the history of Montana. In print they preserved the vibrancy of their community during an incredible moment in time. They detailed networks of friendship and kin that extended far and wide, revealing to us that "Black Montana" contained dimensions that would have been legible to the people a hundred years ago and thus should be as significant for our study of Montana's past.

Perhaps most significantly, the *New Age* revealed a story that had the potential to undermine the threadbare legitimacy of the settler state to claim the lands they knew as Montana from its original inhabitants. Viewed another way, the *New Age* told of a community that challenged settler logics through the available and practical avenues. We find a remarkable trace of this history in the pages of the paper, taking place far from the heated rhetoric of the day. Hundreds of Black men and women, old and young, crowded onto a platform, waiting to board a day train bound for the picturesque little river town of Basin, Montana, located some thirty miles north of Butte. Carrying picnic lunches, blankets, and fishing poles, the jubilant convoy of Butte's African Americans rumbled deeper into the mountains. Disembarking, they took to an open meadow and set about readying a truly unique August 4 celebration: Emancipation Day. The commemoration did not mark the emancipation of those held in bondage in 1863, but rather marked the full incorporation of African-Creek freedpeople as full members into the Creek Nation in 1865.[84] Indeed, unity carried the day, and "petty jealousies and dissentions" were settled best by foot races and fishing competitions. Young Roy Parsons edged out his challengers in the children's sack race, which secured him the prize of a baseball bat. Twenty-four-year-old Ida Willis took the honors in the women's division. Meanwhile the speedy Geo Simington won the men's race, for his effort (and apparently to temper his chances at victory the next year) he received a box of cigars. The paper reported that "the ball game between the fat and the lean men was 8 to 1, in favor of the lean."[85] And the festivities were punctuated by an address on emancipation given by Reverend Jordan Allen of Shaffer's Chapel. Though Booker T. Washington later suggested that a community as small as the one he met in Butte suffered from a type of social and cultural loneliness—claiming there were not the large church gatherings and picnics to which the Black southerner was accustomed—it seems, rather, that Black Montanans looked to forge new cultural unifiers.[86]

The image of hundreds of African Americans traveling by rail to frolic and fish in the mountain streams of Montana—children playing at the edge of the pine forests, and parents lounging on picnic blankets taking in a foot race or ball game—would be hard for many present-day Montanans to conjure. Those enjoying the fresh Montana air in 1902 were the very same individuals who were locked in a bitter struggle to civically engage each other and the wider community on a host of issues. As the next chapter explores, many Black Montanans continued to search for activities that ordained their newfound place identity with a deep sense of cultural and social belonging. Convening with Nature (with a capital "N") under the Big Sky carried almost spiritual connotations for many. Black Montanans, too, were intent on entering the most sacred of cultural altars: the wilderness.

4

Thinking with Magpies

Montana's Conservation Movement and the Occlusion of the Black Wilderness Experience

In the early twentieth century, ornithologists in Montana began noticing a significant change in the behavior of the black-billed magpie (*Pica pica hudsonia*). The black-and-white bird had usually fed on insects, small mammals, eggs, and carrion. A biologist named Sherlin Stillman Berry, however, observed a series of fatal attacks on newly sheared sheep in Wheatland County, Montana, during the summer of 1912. His article published in *Condor*, the journal of the American Ornithological Society, recounted the tortured demise of several rams. With shearing scars fresh on their back, the white sheep unexpectedly attracted flocks of magpies that began tearing and pecking at the docile livestock until loss of blood and shock overcame them. Berry's anxiety mounted as he surveyed the assault, noting that this behavior was unlike anything "old timers" in the area had ever seen. In his article, published a decade later but with details still vivid in his memory, the biologist made several claims. He suggested that the onslaught was being led and initiated by several individual birds that exhibited increasingly aggressive and opportunistic behavior. He also maintained that this "unfortunate new chapter in avian depredations" against livestock had continued in the intervening decade from 1912 until in 1922, when his article was published. In short, magpies had changed from something commonplace and familiar in the landscape into a terrorizing, unpredictable force of nature, no longer compatible with the sensibilities and envisioned order of white settler modernity.[1]

What makes this piece of ornithology so significant in Montana's natural and social history is the unexpected clarity with which it also articulated several ready-made formulations about race and colonization that would have been available to white settlers living in the Northern Rockies and Great Plains at the dawn of the century. Berry begins his essay by stating, "Civilized man extends his domain into a hitherto unoccupied region, as he has done in the case of much of the territory of our western states." Already operating under the settler premise that land is free and for the taking, Berry then shifts his attention to the paradoxical fact that many species already occupy this "unoccupied" land.[2] In his estimation the inferior inhabitants had but a handful of paths to take in the face of the unrelenting conquest of the white settler. "Some of these," he writes of the plants and animals, "never recover from their first reverses and sink rapidly into extinction." Others, he supposes, are only in the process of an ultimately hopeless battle for survival, while some would manage to cohabitate with humans without having to change much at all. But it is the way that Berry defines the fourth category of animal that illustrates what role the magpie, and all magpie-like creatures, would play in this new world. These animals might counteradapt to the environment of the white settler and hold their own, to the great displeasure of the "omnipotent man."[3] To a certain extent, Berry understood that magpies were in the process of carving out an environmental niche for themselves in a human environment in early twentieth-century Montana.[4]

The author's prefacing paragraph is disquieting in light of a settler colonial framing of westward expansion.[5] On a foundational level, Berry's perspective reinforces Patrick Wolfe's assertion that, in addition to being a violent force in the world, settler invasion is also an ontological condition.[6] We see this in both Berry's fantasy of the American West as terra nullius and, more important, in the way the ideological trappings of expansion and conquest still colored his description of his world in 1912 and again in 1922, decades after settlers and the U.S. government dispossessed Montana's Indigenous peoples of much of their ancestral homelands.[7] Yet beneath Berry's expansionistic rhetoric and scien-

15. A magpie and a ram in Wheatland County, Montana. Image from *Condor*, journal of the American Ornithological Society, 1922.

tific prose also lies an anxiety about an unwanted disruption to settler ontology. Present was a reality that all settler colonists have confronted throughout the process of expansion. The human world, as well as the natural one, did not reflect their fantastical visions of "new lands" filled with passive barriers that would either fade away or be overcome. This innocuous piece of scientific writing speaks to a complexity inherent in settler formations, a complexity that should challenge our telescoping focus of racial binaries in settler colonial history.

Using plain language, early white westerners seldom reckoned with all the ways that the reality of the American West differed from the world elucidated by the nineteenth-century settler imagination. By the early twentieth century, however, farmers, sportsman, conservationists, and scientists such as Berry transposed the anxieties and ills of their human world onto the natural one.[8] During what was supposed to be a triumphant conquest over untamed nature, unwanted poachers and scavengers subverted the establishment of productive land and labor.[9]

In this instance the human analogue of the magpie—at least in the minds of white settlers—did not cleanly map onto Native peoples as one might expect. In fact Berry mimicked the traditional settler belief regarding Indians in passing when he noted that some creatures "linger on, continuing a losing battle in the face of ultimate defeat until perhaps man himself rouses in interested admiration to temper the odds against them."[10] Especially by the Progressive Era in which Berry was writing, it was widely believed that Indian peoples risked total extinction if they remained "Indian"; their only salvation was to assimilate with white "civilization." Richard Pratt's now infamous epitaph "Kill the Indian in him and save the man" spoke to a range of programs and policies that eroded Indigenous culture, sovereignty, and self.[11] Rather than being at the mercy of "man's" interference, magpie populations increased despite their supposed obsolescence in the new world of the settler. By framing his observations of magpie behavior in such an explicitly colonial context, Berry not only highlights the extent to which "the idea of Nature contains, though often unnoticed, an extraordinary amount of human history," but also exposes that the history of the magpie in Montana is profoundly racial.[12]

Lamentably, this chapter will not be an environmental history of Black Montana. Instead, it maintains a focus on the social relations between Black and White settlers as tensions arose when the environment became a key battleground over the negotiation of race and the question of who was eligible to be a "legitimate" settler. That being said, a brief environmental history of the magpie and the anxieties that swirled around this common western bird, oddly, offer us a small opening through which to enter one of the many occluded corners of Montana's settler colonial past. Discussions of magpie behavior were couched in racial ideologies that sought to rationalize and simplify a *particular version* of the natural world that Euro-Americans sought to preserve for the benefit of a *particular kind* of settler. As the first decades of the twentieth century passed, early conservationists looked to the West as a font of natural resources to be guarded and used by settler governments. By the time that elites of the early twentieth century openly encouraged and fostered a conservationist ethos throughout America, people living in places like Montana and the Northern Rockies already drew upon long traditions of both Indigenous—and, later, nineteenth-century colonial—exploration, labor, and leisure in the outdoors. Despite this precolonial heritage, white settlers and naturalists of the twentieth century often imagined themselves as the sole heirs to the mantle of stewardship over the natural world in the face of the (ill-perceived) fading Indian epoch. For white settlers, the seeking-out of a "wilderness experience" or a fierce advocacy for the establishment of public lands and a clean environment became powerful markers of cultural belonging that were already wed to pseudoscientific tropes of racialist dogma. "Whiteness" laid claim to the natural world as its assumed domain. In such colonial environs, convening with Nature could accompany a strange form of racial religiosity. As this chapter will show, Black Montanans, too, were intent on entering the most sacred of cultural altars. In doing so, they subverted a profound settler myth.

Attending to those histories that racist and colonial ideologies have attempted to erase from cultural memory and thus render novel, unexpected, and banal adds to a growing body of work that asks how racial thinking informed and intertwined with conservationism.[13] It is not sufficient, therefore, to "rescue" the history of Black Montanans as they encountered the man-made ideas of Nature and wilderness during the nineteenth and early twentieth centuries, though that is by no means an easy task. Nor is the goal here merely to assert that Black history in this context has been "forgotten"—an all-too-passive reflection that provides undue comfort for some present-day readers. Instead, this history probes at domains such as "home" and "belonging" and reconstructs the overlapping and conflicting claims to the natural world made by Black and white Montanans within the settler colonial society.

Here, the seemingly irreconcilable histories of both colonizer and colonized must be read alongside and against one another. Unfortunately, the archive of Black Montana cannot speak to the fullness and complexity of Black conservationism or iterate commonly held ideas about Nature as it once might have. Its voices are too few, too scattered, and much of their context and cultural references eroded away by the racial regimes of colonial memory. What is left is an archival imprint, a history in relief. When considered in isolation of the attending colonial project of occlusion it offers only a sterile, banal, and threadbare account of a history long dead. This chapter attempts to reanimate that history within the context of American settler colonialism. William Cronon and Marsha Weisiger have reminded us that any number of things "are good to think with."[14] By thinking with magpies, a material creature whose history represents the indices of racial, settler colonial, and conservationist historical narratives, our task might be made a little easier.

Racializing Nature

In 1921 another conservationist, Myron S. Carpenter, also gave voice to the racialized settler mindset in Montana.[15] As secretary of the State Sportsmen Association, he made his plea regarding the dilemma of the magpie to Montanans in the pages of several state papers. "Mr. Carpenter," wrote the *Powder River Country Examiner*, "is urging the sportsmen of the state to carry on an energetic campaign for the destruction of the common enemies of game birds and animals. It is well known that the magpie, so numerous in Montana, is very destructive to the game, song and insectivorous birds."[16] With this call to arms, Carpenter and the various "gun and rod" clubs under the umbrella of the State Sportsman Association cast the black-and-white bird as a pest and nuisance, and, moreover, a poor steward to its environment. Given that magpies were native to the region and had been coexisting with Native peoples for thousands of years and with early white settlers for almost a century, Carpenter thus draws our attention to the fact that the birds behaved as they did not merely because "civilization," as Berry declared, had encroached on their habitat. Rather, magpies and other members of the corvid family were actually exceedingly well suited to the new, human environment in which they would compete with ranchers and sportsmen for the resources of the landscape. This relationship did not fit the schema of a settler colonial ontology.[17] The violence that came to characterize the magpie-human relationship suggests colonial logics of elimination *and* anti-Blackness continued to press upon both the social and natural environment of the West in the early twentieth century.

Historian Justin Leroy has argued that settler colonial projects not only expand by making victims Native—as one can see from Berry's positioning of the magpie against the white settler—but also by making them, in effect, Black.[18] Instructive histories have been written on this type of displacement of racial thinking onto the environment broadly, and birds specifically. Earlier in the nineteenth century, after surveying the wholesale destruction of desired bird species across the country, not unlike the debate in Montana, eastern elites cast blame for the widespread extinction on several ethnic and racial groups, including poorer Blacks. In her study *The Rise of the American Conservation Movement*, Dorceta Taylor chronicles the gendered and upper-class ire directed toward women and minorities for the destruction of birds for purposes of both millinery fashion and subsistence hunting. Unscrupulous populations of Italians, Eastern Europeans, and African Americans ostensibly hunted various desirable birds to extinction across the South.[19] Conservationists, together with middle- and upper-class white women especially, blamed both African Americans *and* magpies, crows, and jays for the loss of specific species of desired birds. Through the prevailing racialist thinking of the day, these elites affixed the behaviors and racial classification of one population onto the other.

In the decades that followed, magpies and crows took on new meanings across the United States as tricksters, thieves, chatty hoodlums, even in unambiguously racialized cartoons in the 1940s. Appearing in film as the duo "Heckle and Jeckle," the opportunistic magpies lounged about the landscape of the South, tormenting hardworking creatures with their antics. Airing in the age of racial apartheid, such programming emerged from the racist cultural milieu that perpetuated the world of "Sambo" and other minstrel-inspired stereotypes of supposedly lazy southern Blacks for American audiences, which included the original blackface character Jim "Crow." As observed in chapter 2, this was part of a racial regime that labored in conscious ways to bolster white supremacist agendas and, in this case, very directly dehumanize African Americans.[20] Though Montanans were by no means removed from these types of cultural productions that emerged decades later, magpies and other birds that subsisted by scavenging and "stealing" the eggs of others were subtly racialized in the bourgeoning conservation movement of the early twentieth century.

Just as white newspapers voiced anxieties about the growing stream of Black migration to the state by breathlessly printing columns and stories about racial violence, crime, and other social ills elsewhere in the country, Montana's media during early years of the conservation movement likewise drew parallels to various accounts of environmental degradation in exotic and far-flung locations. Perhaps not surprisingly, such accounts were, on occasion, laced with racial language and perpetuated damaging stereotypes. One illustrative piece appeared in Stevensville, Montana's *Western News* in 1907: "The West Indian Negro is a born poacher," the journal declared.[21] The article explained the devious and unsporting ways that Black West Indians allegedly snared their prey. Their tactics included putting cayenne pepper in birdbaths so that they could catch the animals when they went blind, or blasting fish from streams with dynamite. The reference to Black poaching likely carried a double meaning for Montana readers: it condemned a type of subsistence lifestyle rather than merely a "criminal" activity, and it no doubt intended to draw a line between such practices and law as sportsman in the state and around the nation fought for legal prosecution of such actions.[22] The *Western News* article depicted those of African descent as biologically predetermined to be wasteful poachers, tricksters, and poor stewards of their natural world. A stark similarity appears in the ongoing discourse in Montana where settlers viewed magpies as antithetical to the colonial project of raising crops, livestock, and using the natural world as they saw fit.

In one sense magpies aid us in thinking through a material and environmental history. Its story is the struggle between biological adaptation and a human way of thinking that drew heavily on an image of the world as one dominated by the laws and logic of settlement. In another sense white settlers were not just discussing a bird as they fretted over and postulated the total annihilation of an unwanted species. Racializing the natural world and the animals within it as they did, white settlers and conservationists direct our attention to the environment as a critical battleground in the formation and maintenance of racial categories in the West and as powerful cultural unifiers in the project to consolidate whiteness and exclude all racial others.

The Black population in Montana had experienced continued growth during the time when Theodore Roosevelt's policies and programs, aimed to conserve the nation's natural resources and scenic beauty, were debated in the press and in Congress before shaping numerous federal institutions. Roosevelt's conservationism, as historian Ian Tyrell argues, stemmed in part from a deep and visceral anxiety about the future prospects of national vitality and the sustainability of U.S. imperialism at home and abroad.[23] Not only did imperial anxieties manifest in Cuba, Panama, and the Philippines—places where many Black Montanans had previously served as agents of empire—but they also emanated from questions about the ability of the environment to sustain the ongoing project of settlement. However, American conservationism contained a more spiritual element as well. The writings of naturalists such as Henry David Thoreau and John Muir encouraged a new generation of settlers to seek their own natural or wilderness experience in the newly emptied landscapes of the West's mountains and forests. Such endeavors were not only good for one's body and soul, they argued, but were profoundly American activities which promised to rejuvenate a sickly and wasteful body and nation.[24] Such activities were critical for settlers to claim possession of newly expanded federal lands that were likely to remain "unsettled." Indeed, we should not neglect one of Patrick Wolfe's more profound, if somewhat pithy, aphorisms: "There is no such thing as wilderness, only depopulation."[25]

The deliberate forgetting of African Americans in the outdoors lays bare the significance of race and racial ideology in the origins of early conservationism, a topic well covered by historians in recent years.[26]

The flurry of debate around national resource conservation further dislodged fears among white settlers that corrupting elements challenged the purity of their emerging racial state. In response this colonial project of occlusion intentionally withheld a vital marker of social belonging—Montana's wilderness and conservation ethic—from its Black citizens through the racialization of nature and its conservation. Attesting to this history aims to challenge the settler myths of white possession and a white wilderness. Black Montanans, looking to remake the region into their Golden West, likewise seized upon the cultural and social significance of Nature and wilderness in settler society. Their participation in *every* stage of the human-nature experience—from mythic origin stories to environmental writings—during the most formative years of a racially conscious movement to protect and conserve the natural environment and its resources actively complicated the settler colonial narrative of the "omnipotent" and "civilized" man who extended "his domain into a hitherto unoccupied region, as he has done in the case of much of the territory of our western states."[27]

Labor and Leisure in an Unsegregated Wilderness

Conservationists' understandings of Nature—be it the mountains, rivers, plants, or animals, including the magpie—were wedded to the violent process of appropriation that had only recently (and incompletely) deprived the Native peoples of Montana of those mountains, rivers, plants, and animals. Scholars such as Dorceta Taylor, Louis Warren, Karl Jacoby, and Ian Tyrrell argue that conservationism was, at its core, a white, middle- and upper-class phenomenon that in part worked to separate those classes from the "lower sorts." This much is clear. Yet, as Richard White also argues, the origins of both conservationism and environmentalism are firmly rooted in the original labor of these "lower sorts" in the natural world.[28] Montanans have long held up their ties to the land and self-appointed role as wardens to their natural surroundings as an intrinsic characteristic of what it means to be a Montanan. At the turn of the century, nearly half of all Montanans lived in the state's cities and towns.[29] Nevertheless, the abundance of public, easily accessible land fostered an intense relationship between humans and Nature in Montana even within the urban community.

In this vein another set of distorting assumptions can be addressed. Much scholarship on the Black West suffers from the afterlives of this colonial erosion. Just as Quintard Taylor suggests that Black western history was dismissed by the rest of the field because it took place in largely urban spaces against the prevailing images of the West's rugged and rural backdrop, it seems clear, also, that those scholars of the West who have written extensively on both the environment and the surrounding social and cultural movements have likewise excluded Black urban communities from consideration. While urban history in the East, as Dorceta Taylor has shown, included numerous moments of intense environmental concern, most accounts of westerners engaging with the natural world during the Progressive Era take place beyond the boundaries of the West's major cities. Somehow, Black westerners living in cities and towns have been problematically sequestered to those spaces by historians, never venturing out into the forests, rivers, mountains, and plains.[30]

In exploring the archive of Black Montana, something unexpected becomes clear: Black Montanans were present and helped shape the rise of a conservation ethic in their state. This did not take place simply because there were Black settlers living in Montana who went into the great outdoors out for leisure as well as labor. Nor was it merely that Black Montanans, through their labor, helped bolster a society as it wielded new federal mandates and conservation reforms in order to "dispossess the wilderness," as historian Mark Spence argues. African Americans offered their own origin stories of Black explorers, frontiersmen and women, pioneers, and prospectors who first toiled in the wild. Through use and reverence, their community elevated natural spaces to that of sublime and edenic creation. Some even saw in nature's diversity the evidence that human's "natural" state was one of racial equality. Such themes contributed to the belief that the beauty, resources, and access to this world should be preserved for their future generations as well. Even while such actions can be viewed as an effort by African Americans to insert themselves into national logics that underlined U.S. colonialism, a Black wilderness experience simultaneously represented a type of sedition buried in the colonial archive. By going out into the wilderness of Montana to hunt, fish, hike, camp, or even merely to rejuvenate one's soul by gazing upon the wildflowers of a meadow, African Americans laid claim to a powerful motif of settler identity and threatened to divorce that experience from its racialized foundations.

The myth that the first white settlers supposedly labored in a pristine wilderness untouched by humans until that moment heavily influenced subsequent generations cultural construction of Nature.[31] Of course, virtually no place where the first settlers toiled in North America was truly untouched by Indigenous game or resource management processes. In Montana, for example, George Bird Grinnell, in his 1891 surveys of what would become Glacier National Park, recounted how the Flathead and Blackfeet continued their traditional practice of burning tracks of land to facilitate hunting and food collection.[32] Likewise, the first non-Native explorers in a given area were not always white.[33] For early Black residents in Montana, their first wilderness experience, concurrent with the first white residents, was not one of leisure, but of labor. York, the slave of William Clark, was the first Black man to see the world that would be called "Montana" in its precolonial state, though his very presence there initiated the first movement toward the later settler society. The "first white man" as epitomized in state lore by Jim Bridger, who trapped beaver in the Rocky Mountains starting in the 1830s, heavily informed white adventurers and outdoorsmen. Yet fewer people recall Bridger's Black partner and friend, Jim Beckwourth, whose run-ins with various Native tribes in western Montana are just as mythic and fantastic in scope.[34] The two men's escapades, which have since informed the generic ideal of the western frontiersmen of the northern Rockies, were the model for later sportsmen seeking that "authentic" masculine frontier experience.[35] From the earliest era of non-Indigenous habitation of Montana, African Americans, too, played a role in the construction of the bond between humans and Nature.

16. James P. Beckwourth. A black fur trapper and "frontiersman" who spent time among Montana's Crow tribe in the early nineteenth century. Wikimedia Commons.

As the use of Nature shifted toward hunting, camping, or other such pursuits for leisure, Black Montanans looked to their own community for examples of wilderness savvy. During the Buffalo Soldier era, Black troops spent a great deal of time beyond the compounds of forts, out on the high line and Rocky Mountain front. Their wilderness acumen and ability to rough it in service roles have long stood as a challenge to the contemporary stereotype of Black urbanism. The Buffalo Soldiers specifically have been the topic of interest to those studying the history of the national parks, representing a rare accounting for Black experiences.[36] The Tenth Cavalry took on the mantel as the first rangers of Yosemite National Park in the early days of federal management. Likewise, in Montana, where the presence of the Buffalo Soldier at the turn of the century was strongest, Glacier and Yellowstone National Parks hosted Black troops in various circumstances.[37] Black soldiers and civilians alike were often among the first non-Natives to venture into vast tracks of federal land in Montana and the West. General Wesley Merritt and his company were led deep into what later was designated Glacier National Park by members of the Tenth Cavalry who were stationed nearby at Fort Assiniboine. Images of the soldiers camping along the banks of St. Mary's Lake are among the only pieces of evidence of Merritt's expedition in 1894.[38] In 1897 twenty-four members of the Ninth Cavalry accompanied the conservationist William Seward Webb's excursion into Yellowstone and what would become Grand Teton National Park. Webb had been a part of an 1879 expedition to survey possible expansions of Yellowstone and continued to travel west to hunt in the years following. While Webb hired the famed trapper "Beaver Dick" Leigh to lead the foray, the expertise of the Black scouts and outdoorsmen were vital.[39]

The founding of Yellowstone in 1872, nearly two decades before the deployment of Black troops to Montana, led to several government surveys of the vast parkland. At least one of the early explorers for the federal government was a Black man named Walker Browning. Browning, who had lived and prospected in Deadwood, South Dakota, and worked the rails in Fort Laramie, Wyoming, continued his life in the wilds of the West after he took part in an expedition of Yellowstone in 1873. Likely

17. Several soldiers of the Ninth Cavalry and other W. S. Webb Teton excursion members at "Beaver Dick's" tepee, 1896. Montana Historical Society Research Center Photograph Archives, Helena, Montana. H-3715.

the only Black man in the expeditionary force, Browning worked as a cook for Hayden's company throughout the summer. Following his time in the park, Browning moved his family to the fledging town of Billings, where the Black community grew around his residence at 106 South 26th Street. In the decades that followed, Browning's home not only became the geographic center of the Black community—which came to include several Buffalo Soldiers and their families, including the renowned cavalry captain Horace Bivens—but he was also revered as a pillar and pioneer of the Billings community by whites and Blacks alike. Though confined to low-wage service jobs by prevailing unspoken racial codes, Browning nevertheless served in various religious, civic, and political leadership positions. The local Republican committee selected him multiple times to be a member of the Republican convention in Billings alongside prominent white men such as the wealthy rancher and land developer Peter Yegan. Browning's life in so many ways exemplified the ideal of the Black westerner, an image that translated into social prominence, if not acceptance. At the time of his death, his time spent as a gold miner, rail worker, and wilderness explorer had become a central point of pride for the entire Black community of Billings.[40]

As the settler project in the West proceeded, and the wild spaces shifted from the unknown into destinations of recreation and leisure, the memory of Black settlers laboring in the wilderness of the American West did a certain kind of political work. As this book will later discuss, the racialization of Nature as a space that cultivated and renewed the white body threatened to sever a Black wilderness experience from its emancipatory and rejuvenating promises. By calling upon the memory of Black mythic figures in the past, however, Black Montanans were able to reject the segregation of the wilderness.

When examining the Black leisure experience in the wild, it is important to remember the toiling of York, Jim Beckwourth, and the Buffalo Soldiers. Stories of Black Montanans venturing into the backcountry—some of which, local newspapers reported, lasted weeks—suggest the possibility that such outings mimicked Jim Beckwourth's or the Buffalo Soldiers' wilderness escapades, and not those of Lewis and Clark, Jim Bridger, or John Bozeman.[41] Further, not only did African Americans enjoy the outdoors, but they also expended substantial time and resources to do so. In one notable case, the Black newspaper in Butte, Montana, reported on a two-week camping trip taken by two Black residents. This would have counted as a most ambitious outing in 1902—or in any era, for that matter. Such trips necessarily required material infrastructure such as tents, packs, horses, mules, and other implements to accomplish safely. The continued presence of such expeditions as well as single-day excursions and longer fishing trips in the pages of Black newspapers highlighted the importance of Nature in the everyday lives of Black Montanans.[42]

Frequently, outdoor activities converged with the formation of social and community bonds. In one instance, as reported in the same paper, a fishing trip on the renowned Gallatin River near the city of Bozeman offered the chance for a young Black man to woo a newly arrived female companion. "Mr. Sam Hall, a popular young farmer of Gallatin valley," the reporter commented, "is arranging a fishing party in honor of Miss Margaret Sutter, formerly of Chicago. That a good time will be in order can readily be vouched for by the many who have partaken of the hospitality of the amiable young man." The writer concluded reassuringly, "Mrs. Phelps and daughter will accompany Miss Sutter."[43] At other times one's wilderness acumen, or apparent lack thereof, would playfully be called to the attention of readers. Short blurbs such as "Mr. Chas. Davis and Mr. Alfred Davis were deer hunting in the mountains Sunday. They found two" accompanied several humorous jabs as well.[44] In September 1902 the editor of the *New Age* satirically mentioned that "it is rumored that the game warden was hurriedly seen leaving Helena the first of the week. On inquiry into the excited state of his feeling elected the reply that he had an injunction against Bob Lawrence's [a local Black resident] hunting party—as it was exterminating totally all the game of the mountains."[45] The placement of such a piece in the paper's "Dope Book" column—which frequently lampooned members of the community with jokes or sultry gossip—leads one to believe Bob Lawrence's hunting exploits were somewhat less than remarkable and that the game of the mountains was under no real threat.

Moving past masculinist images of men hunting, fishing, and camping in the wilderness, some of the most frequent modes of outdoor recreation suggest that nature played an important role for the entire community, not just men. In a photograph taken in 1926, a dozen Black women in white sundresses posed for the camera at the Pleasant Hour Club's picnic in Colorado Gulch near Helena.[46] Images such as this attest to the unexpected ways in which Montana's natural environment intertwined with African American cultural life. Often because the

18. Members of Helena's African American women's Pleasant Hour Club at a picnic in Colorado Gulch, near Helena, 1926. Montana Historical Society Research Center Photograph Archives, Helena, Montana. Pac 2002-36.10.

community had few buildings big enough to hold large group meetings (which were a frequent occurrence), many society, fraternal, and literary clubs chose to meet in public picnic areas, pavilions, or campgrounds. This intersection of the natural and the social within the larger American experience is indicative in part of what led to the beginnings of the national conservation movement across America broadly. By contributing to and shaping such origins, African Americans both participated in prevailing cultural motifs about exploration and adventure, as well as forging their own.

The Myth of the White Wilderness

As numerous scholars argue, the goals and methods of natural resource conservation, wilderness preservation, and wildlife management fit a similar continuum of methods for programs of "race betterment" that flourished during this same era.[47] Led by a subset of individuals who propagated both the tenets of conservation and eugenics—most notably New York banker Madison Grant, U.S. chief forester Gifford Pinchot, and California businessman Charles Goethe—conservationists called for (white) people to commune with unadulterated Nature in order to refresh and rehabilitate a deteriorating race.[48] According to their philosophy, the wilderness served as the proving ground in which whiteness would be refined, both physically and spiritually. Gerald Allen writes that, "for both Grant and Goethe, Nature (with a capital 'N') had moral lessons to teach."[49] Nature was the ultimate arbitrator of the moral laws of the universe. The "truth" of that morality would be exposed through the refinement of the superior and the elimination of the inferior.[50] Therefore, the participation in the wilderness or nature experience was not only a refinement of one's (usually a man's) moral and physical self, but also an activity that laid claim to moral and racial superiority. In addition to imbuing their own conservation efforts with "moral" lessons about the future, eugenicists also "interwove hereditarian and evolutionary tenets and motifs into the narrative they crafted" about the history of West and white settler expansion.[51] Whitewashing the "first" wilderness experiences affirmed the connection this small but influential group made between race and Nature, and thus, their assumed racial superiority.[52] This ideology began as the musings of social Darwinists who metaphorically considered themselves the equivalent of the mighty but dwindling Redwoods. Meanwhile, they conceived of "debased" races and nationalities that were more akin to "invasive" or dangerous species like weeds, wolves, and rats—and, one might add, magpies.[53] Perched as they were atop the intellectual ladder of the day, this way of thinking inevitably trickled down into the broader public perception of the relationship between different racialized peoples and the environment.[54]

A close attention to the archive challenges whether such racialist perceptions similarly infiltrated the Black self-image to the same degree. Though much less frequently, the Black press in Montana also commented on issues related to the preservation of natural resources. Both the Black papers in Montana during the early twentieth century self-identified as "race journals," and they were concerned with the issues affecting their small working-class readership. It is notable that pieces on conservation policy were among them. In 1907 Joseph Bass, the editor of Helena's Black paper, included a front-page center column commending the virtues of the newly established national forests. After enumerating the various industries and livelihoods that benefited from the careful management of timber, the piece added that the forests serve as "great public playgrounds, and as breeding places and refuge for game."[55] The column, tellingly, was situated between a published letter of a visiting Black reverend to Butte (who fondly remarked, "This is great country. I live 7,767 feet above the sea. I am up among the stars") and an article in which Joseph Bass ruthlessly attacked the conservationist President Roosevelt for his hand in unscrupulously dismissing members of the Twenty-Fourth Infantry following the Brownsville Affair.[56] Such intersections of the natural and the social within the larger American experience in Montana were indicative of a similar type of cultural milieu that nurtured the beginnings of the national conservation movements. One's ability to consider the spiritual quality of Nature in the mountains of Montana or contemplate the future of resources and recreation were not separate from issues that pertained directly to the experience of Blackness in society. Despite this, to look upon the wild spaces and natural world of Montana as their "possession" was not an uncomplicated claim for Black settlers.

Moses in the Wilderness, or Adam in the Garden?

Despite the fragmented evidence of a Black conservation ethos in the West, a fundamental disconnect still exists in the minds of many Black and white Americans living outside the western reaches of the country concerning the complicated relationship between African Americans and Nature.[57] Compounding this incongruence, American settler colonial society has largely dispossessed Black communities of the land. Historian Mark Stoll contemplates Black environmentalism from the perspective of the eastern and southern experience: "Africa has come to represent the Promised Land for African Americans. This view results from an alienation of a landless race from the land, and therefore from the land-myths that have animated European Americans from Jamestown and Plymouth Rock to the modern environmental movement." Due to their exclusion from the promise of the American dream, Stoll suggests that nowhere in America have African Americans "felt a pride . . . of mythic origins tied to the soil, of confidence in a divine destiny manifest in the land itself, such as is symbolized for whites by Plymouth Rock, Yosemite Valley, or even Stone Mountain."[58] Stoll acknowledges that, for a moment, the "Promised Land had other metaphorical meanings for African Americans," such as Kansas and Oklahoma as free states for the Exodusters.[59] While it would be difficult to argue that Black Montanans truly enjoyed what he calls full possession, it cannot be denied that they did enjoy fuller participation and engaged in an experience that drew on both Black and white mythic characters and origin stories in the West. Why, then, given its history, did the Black wilderness experience fade from public memory? On this valence Stoll suggests that "the great monuments of Black sacred history are human, not natural, and the dominant metaphor has been Moses in the wilderness, not Adam in the garden."[60] Yet the historical account of Black Montanans in Nature does not always fit a narrative of outright absence and alienation. The legacy of the conservation movement is not one that *prohibited* Blacks from partaking of the wilderness experience. Rather, the legacy of white upper-class narratives, mythic origins, and racist undercurrents eroded the memory of Black men and women from the foundations of the conservation movement.

The history of African Americans going out into the natural environment of Montana is not rare, unique, or even unexpected. No legal or social exceptions were in place to keep African Americans from enjoying Nature. Yet this history is likely new for many readers. The reason for this reflects the circumstances of a settler state that held whiteness up as a required marker of social and cultural belonging. Thinking around the edges of this occlusion, we might consider a different, but intimately related, context. Here the environmental historian Mark Fiege contemplates the absence of Black voices in the syllabi of environmental literature courses.[61] Why, he asks, is W. E. B. Du Bois's *Darkwater* not considered a great piece of nature writing? Fiege's confrontation with racial regimes in the halls of academia is an acute exercise in identifying how imperial formations continue to have meaning in our present.

Du Bois's writings offer an answer to Fiege's question. When asked to define whiteness, Du Bois famously answered, "[It] is ownership of the earth forever and ever, amen."[62] For one to be a steward of the land, one must have some *claim*—individually or communally—to it. The nature of that claim, however, needed to fit within those same racial parameters. Indeed, in many scenes of environmental history, especially in the South, African Americans' relationship to the land was not of this particular sort. Instead, it was one of knowing the land as well as knowing one's labor, and one's deep connections to the source of subsistence in spite of a lack of property rights. It was not good enough to prove a relationship with the earth; to be a nature writer, one must be in a *particular kind* of relationship with a *particular kind* of nature. That is not to suggest that racism has blocked Black writers from an entire genre—quite the opposite. To venture into the world of African American nature writing is to recognize that it can and does exist on a divergent trajectory from the world of Muir or Thoreau. Such men removed themselves from those environments, often to the highest peaks, where one is closest to God and farthest from human toil. Yet even when Du Bois or Langston Hughes come remarkably close to what might be considered "classic" types of nature writings about the wild and sublime, still this work is dismissed.

The absence of Du Bois and other Black voices from environmental literature courses is the occlusion born of the same colonial history that eroded the memory of the relationship between Black Montanans and their natural world. It did so by excluding the Black community from subsequent conservation and environmentalist movements and peddling policies and reform on the national level that used eugenics and pseudoscience to fight for the conservation of natural resources at the same time they sought to conserve whiteness. Scholars such as Du

Bois, Cheryl Harris, and George Lipsitz argue that whiteness is foundationally a religion of sorts, and its principal tenet is the sacralization of ownership.[63] Just as these labor scholars conceive of the religion of whiteness with its temples (factories) and worshippers (laborers), might one also consider the granite walls of Yosemite or the alluvial valleys of Glacier as cathedrals to whiteness, and Madison Grant, Irving Fisher, and Gifford Pinchot their priests? In this way a legacy of federal and state control becomes one of ownership of such places. Montana's public lands and wild spaces—appropriated from Indigenous peoples and subsequently set aside for the "nation"—become places of worship within this property-oriented system of belief. The history of Black Montanans claiming their own possession of the wilderness experience is therefore not only destabilizing to the settler fantasy that painted public wild spaces as property, but also its conservation as unspoken but intrinsically "white" project.[64]

The settler myth of the "white wilderness" did not mean that Black people across the nation did not also look to Nature as a source of potential spiritual and national healing. Indeed, Du Bois laments in *Darkwater* that Jim Crow segregation limited Blacks from traveling to witness the natural beauty of Acadia National Park or the Grand Canyon, places where he contemplated the promise of true liberty in America. In turn, the natural world took on the ethereal *potentiality* of freedom. "I believe in the liberty for all men," he writes, "the space to stretch their arms and their souls, the right to breathe and the right to vote, the freedom to choose their friends, enjoy the sunshine, and ride on the railroads, uncursed by color; thinking, dreaming, and working in a kingdom of beauty and love."[65] Du Bois observes that access to the natural world was limited by racism. Yet for those Black Americans who lived on the edges of such awe-inducing places, it was not their physical access to Nature that was limited; rather, it was their engagement in the national discourse of its conservation.

Recall the Emancipation Day picnic of the Black community of Butte from the previous chapter as it appeared in the pages of the *New Age*. What must certainly have been a majority of the Black community crowded onto a platform and boarded the day train en route to the picturesque little river town of Basin, Montana, located some thirty miles north of the city. By 1902 the Mining City certainly lived up to its reputation as not only prosperous, but as dirty, smoky, and often foul-smelling. Only the city's famed Columbia Gardens seemed to offer citizens a reprieve from the pollution of the copper industry. Perhaps their planned gathering was too large for the gardens, or, more likely, a celebration of Black citizens would simply not have been accommodated by the city. Within the steep forested slopes and canyon walls of the Boulder River valley, however, they found space to both stretch their legs in footraces and baseball games and to breathe the fresh air as they fished or prepared food. They also, as Du Bois might have put it, found the space to stretch their souls as they sang hymns and prayed before Reverend Allen of Shafer's Chapel gave a short sermon on the meaning of their most conspicuous gathering.[66]

Frustratingly, we do not know if Reverend Allen illuminated the Black picnickers that day about the actual origins of August Fourth. The event did not commemorate the emancipation of those held in bondage in 1863, but rather marked the incorporation of African-Creek freedpeople as full members into the Creek Nation in 1865. Assuming that the picnickers knew this history, then why the Black community of Butte almost forty years later continued to recognize the holiday is one of the more intriguing mysteries in Montana history. It is possible that some residents were themselves African-Creeks or Black Indians—unfortunately, the census is unhelpful here. It is also possible that some Black citizens of Butte were recent transplants from Indian Territory and Oklahoma, outside of which scholars claim August Fourth celebrations were rare and had largely faded from popularity by the twentieth century.[67] Newspaper records from Helena and other cities throughout the West, however, suggest that African-Creek emancipation remained part of these celebrations only through the specific day of commemoration. Before Juneteenth became the most widespread summertime emancipatory celebration, various dates in early August were marked to acknowledge the end of slavery in the British West Indies, which took effect August 1, 1838. Well into the 1920s, Black papers from Albuquerque to Seattle told readers to "keep off the Fourth" despite, at times, curiously noting their regional custom of observing a different day than Blacks elsewhere in the country. Several years later Joseph Bass felt compelled to offer his thoughts on the annual celebration for which his paper was running advertisements at the time, exclaiming that "no day in August has any significance to the abolition of American Slavery. But applies only to the gradual emancipation of slaves in the West Indies. The only days that are really Emancipation Days for the American Negro are September 22 and January 1." In many respects it is odd that Bass, having lived and cut his journalistic teeth in Kansas City, so near many of the communities that pioneered the holiday, could not speak to its history. He even noted the distinction, commenting that "back east" the emancipation season stretched anywhere from August 1 to August 10.[68]

Understanding the cause of this selective forgetting is another matter that spills beyond the edges of the current project into more regional questions of Blackness and memory in the West. Suffice to say it seems most likely that, following the 1887 Dawes Allotment Act, tensions mounted between African-Creek freedmen and newly arrived Black settlers to Indian Territory as unresolved issues surrounding the right of Blacks on the Dawes Rolls to claim Indian lands exposed the complicated colonial logics at play. In the decades that followed, August Fourth celebrations may have grown alienated from their original meaning of full inclusion within the Creek Nation. As Black settlers continued their push west into the twentieth century, and as they increasingly looked to claim and make homes on Indian lands, it is plausible that pervasive ideologies of Native elimination redirected the collective memory of Black settlers away from a shared Indian heritage toward other emancipatory narratives. In Butte, Montana, the August Fourth picnic in 1902 was more than just a vaguely conceived connection to the past, or an opportunity to enjoy the summer weather, though it was these things, too: it was a series of performances of home and belonging rooted in the emancipatory potential of wilderness and Nature. Black celebrants in the early twentieth century looked to the West as space where they might realize the hope of earlier generations who first "carried their sovereignty with them" as they left for western lands.

Perhaps Reverend Allen knew the origins of the holiday. Like many AME ministers of his day, he had traveled and worked extensively throughout the American West and Great Plains, meeting all kinds of people and hearing their stories. But the fact that the paper did not record any of his words that day might suggest that the shared Black-Indian heritage of August Fourth remained buried. Whatever was understood about the holiday, the ensuing footraces, baseball games, fishing competitions, and cook-offs fused Black Montanans' veneration for the outdoors to a celebration of a historical moment that represented everything antithetical to the prevailing racial regime in the settler colonial West.

The history of Montana's Black wilderness experience—as well as the radically subversive ideas of home and belonging that such experiences fostered—suggests that the wild spaces of the country did not monolithically represent the continued political and social isolation acutely felt by African Americans. Literary examples of Black Montanans and their soliloquies to Nature instead reflect upon the natural world as evidence of racial equality. Rose Gordon—the older sister of Emmanuel Taylor Gordon, the well-known tenor, author of *Born to Be*, and an important figure in Harlem Renaissance literature—wrote prolifically of her life in the Smith River Valley of central Montana where she was born and made her home.[69] Even early on in its history, the town where she moved to as a young child of freedpeople held the Smith River Valley up as a collective "possession." Gordon grew up not only as a Black girl listening to her mother and older Black neighbors speak about a dark past in places like Missouri and Alabama, but as a member, however complex and fractional, of a community that placed cultural and social significance on a specific natural feature in central Montana. Rose's later writings later speak to this in poetic and nostalgic terms. Her thoughts on the land clearly hold spiritual and social value. She reminisces in her autobiography:

When I was a girl, I would go to church picnics. We would roam the hills and pick flowers and behold Nature in all her gorgeous splendor, see beautiful birds, and hear them sing. We would sit on the high, rocky points and see how perfect the trees were made, as if someone had taken great care in placing them. I said to myself, "These things all belong to God, and it is such a privilege for me to be permitted to enjoy them." I saw the flowers of many colors bowing and nodding to each other. I thought of them as the people of all Nations. And that, dear people, is why I am not prejudice [sic]. This is all God's world and the people regardless of race, color, or creed are his people.[70]

Such lines hearken back to the language of liberty employed by Du Bois, realizing his hope that African Americans might convene with Nature, "thinking, dreaming, and working in a kingdom of beauty and love."[71]

Rose Gordon's writings, as well as her brother's bestselling autobiography, contain numerous references to wild spaces of Montana and Gordon's home in the Smith River Valley.[72] One such passage speaks to the complexity with which one should view her Nature experience. At the beginning of her life story, Gordon writes, "I had always thought of it [the Smith River Valley] as God's garden."[73] Although one of only a few Black residents of White Sulphur Springs, Gordon was by no means isolated from her ethnic community or insulated from the prevailing racism. Juxtaposed to the challenges of the human world, Nature represented a promise of equality; her closeness to Nature became a means to experience that promise. By rendering her natural world as "God's garden," Rose Gordon's words elevated it to the sublime of edenic creation. Her writings qualify Stoll's assertion that while "the dominant metaphor [for African Americans in Nature] has been Moses in the wilderness, not Adam in the garden," it is not the exclusive metaphor.[74]

The purpose of including this fragment of Black Nature writing in Montana is not an attempt to disprove Stoll's thesis, as such an incomplete archive could hardly do. Indeed, placing contemporary scholarly discourses about race and the environment alongside a (seemingly) far-removed history of Black naturalism, as I have done here, risks distorting the original context of the scholarly argument. But that dislocation is precisely the point. On what grounds have some scholars segregated such histories or ranked the importance of one racialized engagement with Nature over another? Against such occluding inclinations, the writings of Rose Gordon and the lives of Black Montanans unearth a shared cultural and social meaning that formed around Nature and wilderness by the early twentieth century.[75] They augment the accounts of the Black wilderness experience in such a way that forces historians to not only reconsider Black participation and contributions, but that also encourages us to ponder their omission from the state and national discourse on conservation—a movement that in part grew from the very same cultural soil.

The rich history of Montana's Black community throughout the early conservation movement is one of culturally rooted engagement. It suggests that Black Montanans' exclusion from a state-wide movement headed by men such as Myron Carpenter and Sherlin Stillman Berry is more acutely synthesized as one that intentionally ignored the ongoing Black presence in the landscape. In doing so, white settlers promulgated the prevailing national discourse that African Americans remained disengaged from the outdoors in any real sense. In Montana the occlusion of Black history from a central social unifier in settler states, the collective ownership of land, continued a project of colonial erosion.

Conclusion

For all the value and contribution that scholars of conservation in the national context bring to Black environmental history generally, their studies often neglect the experiences of individuals like Rose Gordon or other Black westerners who convened with and engaged the natural world in ways far beyond the framework proposed in national conservation and racial discourses. This does not deny that Black Montanans may also have seen the vestige of lynchings in the trees of Montana's forests or the river bottoms as places of mourning where so many Black men and women's bodies were discovered throughout the nation. Nevertheless, what the archive of the Black wilderness experience says about the community's connection to those painful and ongoing memories in the wild spaces of Montana must be considered and has important lessons to impart.

The history of Montana's Black wilderness experience, as well as the writings that contemplate Black Montanans' place within nature, affirm that the connection between race and the environment is—as in all things—a construct, and a historically contingent one at that. White conservationists may well have made temples to whiteness out of mountains and rivers, but it they were not successful in removing African Americans from such places—only the memory of their presence. To be clear, all of this is not to somehow suggest that, because of the unseemly role racial ideology historically played in the building of America's early conservation movement, we should throw out or degrade the many great advances made to preserve the Earth's natural environment that find their origin in this complicated colonial moment. Rather, we should commit ourselves to understanding how categories like race and whiteness inform such histories; it may yet have meaning for our current, precarious moment of environmental action.

Under the racial regimes of the colonial state, Black Montanans, though now missing from historical memory and settler narratives of conservationism, consistently challenged the myth of whiteness that became attached to natural spaces. The racialized ideologies that lay at the foundation of the movement, evident in several key figures on the national level who espoused the simultaneous and connected goals of conservation of Nature and the conservation of whiteness, made that process of forgetting almost total. Conservationism played an important, if uncomfortable, role in the settler colonial project. Especially with regard to the setting aside of land for "public" use, conservation worked hand in hand with various projects of land appropriation and racial exclusion. As readers might well have noted, historical discourses about conservation in the twentieth century disappeared Indigenous communities. This is true both in the sense that settlers ignored what Indians had to say about the preservation of the natural world, and also in that white conservationists crafted a language and dialogue about nature that became less and less referential to Indian history. In a similar fashion, the history of the Black wilderness experience came to suffer the occluding sedimentation of the settler colonial project.

To conclude, let us return to our task of thinking with magpies. In Montana the members of the corvid family, such as crows, jays, and magpies, began to weigh upon the thoughts of the area's human residents in the early twentieth century as settler populations rose. Magpies and other related species are remarkable for their ability to adapt to and thrive in urban and human environments. Certainly this was not lost on Sherlin Stillmen Berry when he classified them as the fourth creature who, "with trickery and adaptation, meets invasive man half-way."[76]

It is important to note under what conditions, exactly, the magpie seemed to be most intensely targeted by settlers. In Berry's account the expansion of industrial and corporate capitalism through large farms and stock ranches ushered in these new relationships between humans and animals. Magpies did not suddenly attack sheep and crops because white settlers had encroached on their habitat; rather, white settlers fostered the ideal habitat for such birds. At the same time, the rise of American conservationism and the desire to preserve certain game and songbirds led to the slaughter of the magpie as an unwanted and dangerous element in the natural world. But this begs the question: Why was elimination chosen as the remedy? The presence of man alone would not inevitably spell the end for the magpie; instead, its end needed to be manufactured. The magpie, when considered in the social milieu of settler colonialism, did not fit the binary fantasy of expanding civilization and the elimination of the Native.

Bearing in mind the timing and conditions that magpies were faced with threats of elimination and biological ruin helps us recognize what settler ideologies of elimination and whiteness actually looked like in the everyday lives of many Montanans. There are striking parallels between the natural and social history. African American communities thrived in Montana during the foremost stages of settler expansion. Despite their success, Black Montanans occupied a paradoxical role as both settlers and refugees. Their efforts enhanced the colonial project, helping to establish a state whose goal was whiteness even as the establishment of Black communities threatened to undermine the legitimacy of white settlers' racialized claims to sovereignty. When industrial capitalism was established in the region, and the uncertainty of Indigenous elimination and early state formation gave way to the realities of market whims (as in 1917), economically and socially successful Black Montanans became out of place in settler society. Moreover, as Black Montanans ventured out to have their own wilderness experiences on the state's public lands, they threatened to encroach on the most sacred of settler altars: the realization of the ownership of the land through participation.

It is precisely at this moment in history that the Black population faced its most dire challenges. Between 1910 and 1930, the number of Black Montanans dropped by over 50 percent. The desire for a white man's West was not only real, but the residents of Montana operated by the logic that argued for this very end. The magpie that "terrorized" livestock, or "poached" the eggs of songbirds existed on the very landscape that these same settlers had already taken from Indigenous peoples at gunpoint, and often by way of massacre. In much the same way, the land on which the houses of working- and middle-class Black Montanans were built was once the site of the bleeding edge of the settler colonial project. The social history of the magpie, therefore, tells of an ideology that fueled westward expansion. By thinking with these creatures, and through their history in the human and natural worlds, the response of white settler colonists to a Black community that did not fit their pattern of ontological development can be more fully understood.

The connective histories of the magpie, the Black wilderness experience, and the conservation movement allude to an unspoken desire for social and natural simplicity within the settler state. Recall Sherman Stillman Berry's suggestion in 1922 that, to address the agitation caused by magpies on livestock, only the selective removal of individual birds was needed. In his estimation not *all* magpies were incompatible with civilization. But the stance that the State Sportsman Association eventually took rejected the complexity that Berry's solution would require. Complexity, mixing, and cohabitation were all concepts that grated against the sensibilities of white settler colonists. The colonial term for this in the human dominion, "miscegenation" (and thus the implicit creation of a complex Métis caste, as the next chapter shows) was likewise just as untenable for many white Montanans.

5

Colonial Kinships

Sexuality, the Family, and Anti-Miscegenation Law in Montana

Joseph Bass, the fiery editor of the *Montana Plaindealer*, worked late into the night of March 4, 1909, seething as he prepared the next issue of his journal. His ire was directed at a familiar enemy, which was making new advances across much of the West in the early twentieth century. Bass's contempt translated clearly into print: "Montana has joined the Jim Crow colony alongside of Mississippi, South Carolina, Texas, and Arkansas." Not fearing reprisals, he identified the villain in the story for his readers. "Muffly, of Jim Crow fame," he wrote, "can now go back to Broadwater and say to his constituency, 'I have saved our race from being devoured.'"[1] Bass lamented the passage of Montana's anti-miscegenation bill. It made interracial marriage illegal, nullified existing unions, and rejected those from other states. Ostensibly speaking for African Americans, he further explained, "This people frown on miscegenation, but object to being singled out for class legislation."[2] Bass died in 1934, not living long enough to record his thoughts on the repeal of Montana's or other western states' marriage bans in the late 1940s and early 1950s. His future wife's newspaper, the *California Eagle*, greeted the news of the *Perez v. Sharp* decision by the California Supreme Court in 1948 and Los Angeles's first interracial marriage as a great victory for progressive personal liberties.[3] Charlotta Bass, who was in no uncertain terms the more famous journalist in the marriage, held decidedly more liberal views than those espoused by Joseph in 1909. The California Interracial Committee, which she helped establish, worked tirelessly against racially discriminatory policies and laws by building and mobilizing solidarities across ethnic and racial lines. Most famously, Bass fought the illegal deportation of Mexican and

Mexican American Angelenos during the Eisenhauer raids known as "Operation Wetback," as well as the internment of Japanese Americans during World War II.[4] Operating on a much reduced scale and using less obvious tactics of racial exclusion, the language of Montana's law in 1909 prescribed "an act prohibiting marriage between white persons and negroes, persons of negro blood, and between white persons, Chinese, and Japanese, and making such marriages void, and prescribing punishment for solemnizing such unions."[5] Though the conservative Bass "frowned" upon interracial marriage, many others in Montana embraced a more progressive position.[6] Beyond the doors of his downtown office, many Black men and women—even some of his own readers—had taken white, Asian, or Native spouses prior to this law's passage. Some would continue to risk security and acceptance by steadfastly declaring their unions well after 1909.

As this chapter will demonstrate, such legislation cannot and should not be emptied of its significance simply because Black Montanans were so few relative to the white population of the state at this time. White settlers and lawmakers like Senator Charles Muffly of Broadwater County may well have acted in sincerity when they proposed legislation based upon a racist belief that, as Bass claimed, the white race was being "devoured" by widespread "miscegenation." As shown in the previous chapter, concerns of "racial purity" and white race suicide saw an upswell in the Progressive Era. Though a looming demographic upheaval such as the kind anxiously imagined by Muffly was simply not a reality, powerful ideological currents about race and sex nevertheless informed settler politics. Despite the fact that the Black population grew from only a few hundred individuals in the 1880s to a vibrant community of nearly 2000 by 1910, perhaps only between 100 and 200 persons, both Black and white, were a part of an interracial marriage or union within a state of some 250,000 residents.[7]

What, then, should be made of this piece of legislation in light of the ways that settler society continuously draws upon racial logics of exclusion? In the eyes of Joseph Bass, proponents of the bill, like Muffly, ham-handedly attempted to employ the segregationist methods of the

Jim Crow South within Montanan society. Certainly, the 1909 law should not be entirely dissociated from its close antecedents, which were passed in the post–Reconstruction era South. Laws like Montana's 1909 antimiscegenation bill (as well as those passed in other western states at this time) engendered both opposition and support that frequently referred to the racial regime of Jim Crow. But settler societies were already replete with operative "racial scripts" and shifting ideas regarding the mixing of white settlers and racialized others.[8] As such, reinscribing another southern paradigm of racialization onto the West can only gesture to part of the story and, in fact, distorts the whole. The task at hand, then, is to explore what this moment and its various social and legal developments looked like from the perspective of Black Montanans who were already entrenched in a silent struggle against the racial regime of the settler state.

Because of the small number of Black Montanans and their fierce reliance on the support of community structures and networks of kinship, the prohibition of interracial marriage carried some distinctly western consequences. Again, the contingencies of shifting historical moments should be kept in mind. These consequences arose precisely at a time in which the consolidation of power by the settler state was at its zenith. The expansion of the mining and timber economies; the establishments of the railroads for both personal and freight travel by 1900; the organization of the state political structure, which for almost a decade had been a broken, ineffective body divided by various interests; and the cultural connections between whiteness and the natural world all point to a consolidation of social power by white settlers.[9] The law passed by the state legislature banning interracial marriage in 1909 stood as an emblematic moment in this ongoing project. Such laws, in effect, moved to consolidate whiteness as both a social and political concept that worked for the benefit of white settlers in Montana through the exclusion of racialized Others.

Race, Sex, and the Transit of Colonial Power

This book has highlighted throughout the shifting nature of racial inclusion or exclusion based on the needs of the settler colonial project at a given geographic location or moment in history. A discussion of racial categories and sexuality, likewise, follows a similar trajectory. However, unlike economicstability or political inclusion, the domain of sexuality—specifically interracial sex and marriage—provides the most direct vantage from which to see the shift from a society in Montana that offered a future for a Black community into one that, increasingly, did not. Ann Laura Stoler reminds us that racialized sexuality lay at the crux of colonial power. Colonizers, be they the French in Southeast Asia or white settlers in Montana, relied on race to function as the primary marker of difference. For this reason, Stoler says, the point through which all colonial power is transferred is sex: power is either retained through the prohibition of interracial sex, or it is diffused and complicated by the emergence of a Métis social caste. Consequently, racialized sexuality should be a central focus of analysis within colonial histories.[10] In a settler state, land functions as the preeminent manifestation of colonial power; the role of race and sexuality within the system of land appropriation is prescribed in the codex of legislation, federal and state Indian policy, and the ideology of whiteness.

Settler colonial concepts such as the "one-drop rule" or Indian "blood quantum" are premised on ideas that interracial progeny could be placed in taxonomies.[11] At times blood quantum delineated the right of an Indigenous person to qualify for tribal membership, and thus a small amount of federal protection or aid. In the nineteenth and twentieth centuries, tribal membership often meant access to reservation lands.[12] Even prior to the Dawes Act of 1887, allotment, and the theft of Native lands accompanied by the erosion of Native sovereignty, white men frequently married Native women in order to make farming, hunting, or mineral claims on tribal lands or reservations.[13] Children of these interracial couples were then subject to the official and deeply complicated system of blood quantum used to determine the amount of Indian ancestry for each generation. While, in some cases, allotment broke the ownership of plots of reservation lands into infinitesimally small portions for each tribal heir—rendering the practical ownership of Native lands by Native people almost impossible in some cases—blood quantum policy eroded the legal status of Indigenous peoples with every generation of white intermarriage and new mixed-race children.[14]

Many historians of the American West note that, prior to the proliferation of white settlement, and particularly the arrival of white women, intermarriage played an instrumental role in western society. Both Anne Hyde and Elliott West, for instance, show that early white-Native marriages served as important conduits of trade, kinship, protection, and political engagement between white trappers and the people of their wives. Elliott West argues that settlement, such as in Denver, was the product of a new vision of what the West was to look like—a vision that no longer included the continued existence of the nomadic Cheyenne, Arapahoe, or any other Plains tribes. Therefore, the relationships that had been forged between the various white and Indigenous communities became anachronistic. With this shift the "squaw men," their Native wives, and, especially, their Métis children were driven from the new communities along the Front Range and on the high plains.[15]

Perhaps the swift Métis exclusion from the new western community should not simply be characterized as the result of a disillusionment with an older structure that had become obsolete. Rather, mixed-race peoples represented a substantial threat to the continuous colonial vision for the region. Connected to the Plains tribes through strong ties of kinship, intermarriage offered a legitimate avenue through which Indigenous peoples might engage with this new society without erasing their Native past and identity. Among the many implications of such an ethnic and cultural mixing—one that especially weighed upon the minds of white settlers—was the potential that Native peoples might retain access to land through ranches, homesteads, farms, mining claims, or other real estate that settlers desperately coveted.

Allotment, "Indian brides," and blood quantum policy all worked to wrest the power and potential of territorial possession away from Native peoples. The central mechanism of the appropriation of tribal land and sovereignty operated on the premise that each generation would have less power, autonomy, or Indianness than the previous. It is telling, then, that Muffly's first iteration of the anti-miscegenation law was roundly defeated in 1907, primarily because it would have outlawed marriages between whites and Natives.[16] With the passing of such legislation, white men seeking to enrich themselves through the further plunder of Native lands and resources would lose the most widely utilized means of doing so. That settler logics underpinned the defeat of the 1907 bill in Montana's state legislature suggests several points of interest. For instance, it reveals that, as Joseph Bass claimed, the subsequent 1909 legislation at least in some part reflected Muffly's white supremacist beliefs.[17] Perhaps the fact that his original language included white-Native marriages shows the extent to which Muffly was not operating under the logic of settlement. Moreover, it shows the extent to which the state legislature, at large, did. The 1907 session illustrates the limited sway of prevailing ideologies regarding racial purity in the face of a more pressing project of land appropriation. Whiteness and white supremacy in the West operated in different economies of power, and toward different ends than they did elsewhere. While Muffly and, to some extent, Bass were not aware of this reality, the power of the state attested to the nuanced ways that racial categories, including Blackness, were being formed and cemented in the region even as late as 1909. Whiteness and white supremacy claimed political and social authority through the ownership of the land. Settler logics informed a legal system in Montana, as well as in many other western states that passed similar laws at the same time, that worked to render Black settlers unable to rely upon the many legal and social safety nets needed in order to claim the right to call land—be it a homestead or a neighborhood—home.[18]

Under the guiding principles of blood quantum, the intermarriage of white Montanans with Native peoples did not threaten whiteness in the same way as did unions between Blacks and whites, or between whites and Asians. Within racist ideologies Indianness supposedly existed on a path to extinction. Like the mindset of white settler colonists in Australia during the same period, indigeneity could be "bred out."[19] The opposite was thought of the relationship between Blackness and whiteness. Based on capitalist market principles, the need to expand commodities and the labor force—both categories that defined enslaved Blacks in the first centuries of white settler colonization on the continent—the one-drop rule created a category of Blackness forever moving away from whiteness in which Blackness expands while indigeneity decreases. Attentive to both beliefs, the goal of the 1909 anti-miscegenation bill was thus to consolidate settler power and whiteness in Montana as a new century dawned.

The Professor and the Kitchen Maid

In the years leading up to 1909, Black and white interracial marriage seemed to occupy the imaginations of white Montanans in ways that shifted and bent over time. Particularly when it involved the marriage of a Black man to white woman, settler anxiety about "miscegenation" produced an archival record that traces an important contour of racial history in the West. Nearly two decades before Bass decried the actions of the Montana legislature, Z. A. Coleman, a Black man, married Mary Laughlin, a white woman, in Helena on January 13, 1891. A copy of their marriage license lists Coleman as Black and Laughlin as white. No legal barrier impeded their union. The white minister, Reverend William Rollins, made no objection as he performed the ceremony in his home with his own family as witnesses.[20] Coleman and Laughlin met in the kitchen of the Merchants Hotel, where they worked as kitchen staff and musical entertainment.[21]

This is all that can be known for certain about the couple.[22] However, adding a layer of complexity to their union and offering insight into interracial marriages in Montana, the local paper, the *Helena Independent*, also provided their readers with an account of the Coleman nuptials. The *Independent* headline read: "A Case of Miscegenation ... A Colored Professor Wins the Heart of a Fair White Maiden."[23] According to the paper, the couple presented their marriage license to the Methodist Episcopal minister. Upon seeing that *both* parties were listed as "colored," he noted that Mary appeared to be white. The paper later defended the minister by claiming that many Black women he had seen were actually of a lighter complexion than the bride.[24] Thus, the paper suggested, Coleman and his new wife, whom they misidentified as a Mary Leonard (not Laughlin), had successfully duped the minister into marrying a Black man and a white woman. It went on to claim that "Coleman is a rather distinguished looking man in appearance, is quite dressy and seeks only the company of white folk for which he is very unpopular with his own race."[25] The piece ends with the reassurance to the paper's white readers that not only had Coleman left the hotel and moved to Great Falls to escape the ire of his own people, but also that the community of Helena was better off without both of them, including Laughlin. The author clumsily ended the article by stating, "The girl is uneducated and unable to write her own name."[26]

What can be made of this newspaper account—given so many discrepancies between Coleman and Laughlin's legal marriage documentation and the fictitious story about the midnight nuptials of Professor Coleman and the base Mary "Leonard," as the paper referred to her—reprinted by the *Independent*? The differences, in light of the kind of message the paper wished to convey to its readers, say a great deal about Montana society's general feeling toward interracial relationships. The *Independent*'s reaction to the union showed that, while still steeped in prejudice, it did not intend to elicit rage from the white community or call for the complete separation of the races. In fact, in every way, the author attempted to highlight the "whiteness" of Z. A. Coleman while subsequently showing the racially marked deprivation of Mary "Leonard."[27] The need to make character judgments about each party to justify the legitimacy of the union, as well as the erroneous claim that the marriage license listed both parties as Black, thus duping the minister, speaks to the deep insecurity of white Montanans about this issue and seeks a justification for it.[28]

In this case, as with many others, no small amount of unease existed within the white community about how to react to a Black man marrying a white woman. The perceived threat that Black men poised to idealized white womanhood in the above account was rather muted and concealed by standards of the South during Jim Crow. Significantly, the Coleman-Laughlin episode represents a transitional view of interracial sexuality from reluctant compromise to recalcitrant exclusion. Though the newspaper claimed it was likely the first interracial marriage to take place in Helena, it was not.[29] At least fifteen years before, Mattie Bost Bell, a former slave, married John Castner, a white man, around 1876.[30] This was likely not the first of such unions either; when the Castners returned to Fort Benton, they were one of five Black and white couples already living there. Notably, the public ire that would be directed toward interracial couples in the early and mid-twentieth centuries was, for the most part, nonexistent.[31]

In her landmark history *What Comes Naturally: Miscegenation Law and the Making of Race in America* (2009), Peggy Pascoe documents how sensationalized "miscegenation dramas" began appearing in papers across the American West around the turn of the century in order to whip up public fervor and opposition to intermarriage.[32] As an early example, the Coleman wedding fit the general mold. The paper caricatured each individual while tracking the developments of a "scandalous" story that supposedly had "moral" lessons to teach or warnings to impart to its readers. The paper's story, however, lacked any explicit condemnation of the couple's actions. Rather, the *Independent* vaguely justified the marriage by casting Coleman as nearly "white" even as they degraded his Irish American wife as almost "black."[33] This proved not to be the consensus attitude taken by whites as the state moved to erase such unions over the next two decades. Instead, Helena in 1891 offers us a window into a kind of transitional period that straddled two distinct moments: one that required the labor of a Black community to further the project of settlement, and one that understood the promise of the region would necessarily exclude Coleman and any future nonwhite children he may have.[34]

White settlers' willingness to compromise on their rigid social "norms" regarding a Black man marrying a white woman diminished as the settler regime came to rely less on Black men's labor. A series of articles in the *Butte Inter Mountain* in 1902 affords us yet another opportunity to examine a middle ground between the nearly unspoken judgment on display in 1891 and legal nullification of interracial marriages in 1909. In early November (in fact, during the same week of the consequential election ongoing in Butte that galvanized the Black voters to form a political newspaper in that city) police discovered the body of Jennie Madison, a white woman, in an alley behind the Washoe Saloon in downtown Anaconda. Injuries to her throat suggested that her assailant strangled her to death. This evidence did not stop the paper from speculating on whether Madison had been addicted to drugs.[35] Coverage of the sensationalized case ran for several weeks in local papers and kept readers in suspense as the main witness and possible suspect, Martin Schuely, lay first in jail and then in the hospital in a comatose state as the result of a head wound. From its first mention on November 4, the paper painted the events as a gruesome murder-suicide: Jennie Madison's husband, Robert, a Black man, had taken his own life in a manner that drew comparisons to demon possession, stabbing and sawing at his own throat with a pocketknife when police came to arrest him the following day. The police and the *Butte Inter Mountain* concurred that Robert likely found his estranged wife in the company of Martin Schuely, a white man, on the night of November 2, at which point he delivered the blow to the man's head and then strangled his wife before killing himself the following evening.[36]

The white newspaper unproblematically presented the disturbing events as a story about a "degraded" white woman meeting her untimely end because of the uncontrollable passions of her Black partner. And yet the only witness in the case, Martin Schuely, provided only conflicting accounts of the events as he faded in and out of consciousness over the following days and weeks. He never described an assailant or named Robert as his attacker in his fragmented testimony. Instead, he claimed that he had fallen on the sidewalk and injured *himself*. What is more, the paper also reported that, upon hearing of the discovery of his wife's body, Robert Madison became inconsolable, crying for a quarter of an hour, exclaiming, "That poor girl!" over and over again. He remained distraught until he began drinking that evening, at which point his friends noted that he became depressed and suicidal. Around this time the chief of police, learning the name and whereabouts of Jennie's husband—and, presumably, his race—sent an officer to arrest (not question) Robert in his room. At the arrival of the police, Madison, drunk and clearly in shock, took his life.[37]

Though this account described the troubled end of a marriage, rather than the beginning of one, it nevertheless fit the model of a "miscegenation drama." It contained multiple layers of racial and sexual anxieties that circulated in turn-of-the-century Montana. Until the final mention of the ordeal, when the couple was laid to rest together, the *Butte Inter Mountain* speculated that Robert Madison murdered his white wife.[38] This was in spite of the fact that the far more obvious interpretation was that Martin Schuely and Jennie Madison had an altercation, and that she hit him with some sharp object before he killed her. Robert's suicide might also be read through the racialized history of violence and lack of justice given to Black men in relationships with white women throughout the United States at the time. While the police and the *Butte Inter Mountain* interpreted his suicide as an admission of guilt—or, at least, evidence of some other troubling character flaw—looking back we cannot be so quick to pass the same judgment.

That Robert Madison died before entering into police custody and that Z. A. Coleman removed himself from the confines of his city and the concern of its white citizens proved to be something of a perverse convenience for settler officials. Before 1909 legal and extralegal recourse to Black and white unions was restricted to a narrow set of relationships or circumstances. Recalling the life of Lloyd Vernon Graye of Helena, his partnership, either professional or personal, with white prostitutes in part drew the ire of the city administration and precipitated the eventual closing of his club, the *Zanzibar*, in 1907.[39] Several months before the Madison case, Sam Harding of Butte engaged the services of a white prostitute on Galena Street, one of the West's most notorious red-light districts. In his actions Harding, who was described by the local paper as "a neatly dressed negro who passes as swell among his colored brethren," transgressed a social, but not yet a clearly legal, boundary. This distinction apparently mattered little to police, who sought to "make an example of the negro" and hauled him before Judge Boyle's bench. However, as the "complaint against him was defective," Boyle reluctantly released Harding.⁴⁰ What exactly constituted the "defect" of the charge is unknown; it could have been any number of loopholes, up to and possibly including the fact that prostitution in Butte survived due to intentional ambiguity with regard to its legality. A common arrangement would have been for police to solicit fines or taxes from brothels, bordellos, and their proprietors rather than those who bought their services. In 1902 it would not have been widely accepted that Harding had done anything illegal according to prevailing cultural expectations. Not to be thwarted by the letter of the law (or anything else, for that matter), the police arrested Harding again the following morning, presumably on similar, but more airtight, charges. Whatever transpired, the local paper and Judge Boyle were clear in their intended resolve: to "impose such a heavy fine on the negro when the case is called that the negro will leave Butte."⁴¹

Given the uncertainties, ambiguities, and compromises exhibited by whites during this time as far as forming any consensus around the perceived threat of Black male sexuality, still Montana was by no means a space removed from prevailing racial discourses that painted Black men as predators. One needs to look no further than the immediate legislative context of the law that passed in 1909. Indeed, most people of the state—at least, according to some newspaper editors—did not even know of the marriage restrictions. Only a select few white papers commented directly on the marriage ban, one being Helena's *Treasure State*, which blithely affirmed that "the black man is not equal to his white contemporary" and dismissed Jim Crow laws as inoffensive to Blacks, saying, "They won't hold him down if he deserves to rise."⁴² While the bill passed narrowly in the legislature, the legislation's other provisions drew much attention. Primarily billed as the "whipping post law," it sought the punishment of public lashings for any man found to have beaten his wife.⁴³ The bill, which garnered popularity as a response to domestic violence, thus contained a thinly veiled association between the exclusion of all interracial marriages and the protection of domestic white womanhood. "Dressy" Black men, as every man who engaged in interracial relations seemed to have been described by the white press, were not beyond suspicion of violence simply because of their

19. Headline announcing the "whipping post law" from the front page of the *Daily Missoulian*, 1909. Compared to other aspects of the bill, the ban on interracial marriages received far less attention, even from politically sympathetic papers such as the progressive *Daily Missoulian*. Image from chroniclingamerica.loc.gov.

outwardly "cultured" appearances. By embedding the marriage debate within a discourse of domestic violence, the 1909 law thus served as a circuitous attack on a particular type of Black man. Economic stability and employment, as well as upward class and social mobility, were therefore just as important to proponents of the marriage ban as was preserving racial categories. In such cases matters of colonial intimacy laid bare unspoken elements of white settlers' exclusionary impulses.

Montana Marriage Laws between the Nation- and Settler-States

The relatively few numbers of interracial unions between Black and white Montanans poses a formidable challenge to re-creating this history in terms other than those curated by white racist journalists. Because of the extensive archival and scholarly accounts of interracial relationships and their significance to broader regional and national narratives, legislation that affected so few people tends to be viewed as largely symbolic rather than purposeful.[44] In Montana the fact that less than two thousand African Americans lived in the state when the legislation passed could suggest that so few people were affected by the bill that it is hardly worth further consideration. This perspective is wrong on two fronts: no number of prohibited or nullified unions is insignificant when placed with the broader context, and interracial marriage between whites and Blacks in Montana, even numerically, was far more substantial than it may first appear.

Nationally, statistics on interracial marriage vary based on available sample sizes. The most accurate numbers come from the 1880 census. Researchers at Columbia University used the full census sample of the United States to determine that Blacks married white partners at a rate of about 1 percent: 3,932 Black and white couples between twenty and forty years of age out of 3,808,334 Black Americans of the same age range.[45] This has consistently grown at an exponential rate since the Civil Rights era, but had remained at comparable levels from 1880 until after World War II. Montana, with its small population, offers its best data on Black and white interracial marriage in 1910, for which the most comprehensive census information is available, and at the peak of the

Black population during the early twentieth century. 1910 was also the first year the anti-miscegenation law took effect.[46]

For any host of reasons—the low number of potential Black partners, small communities separated by large distances, or the perceived progressivism of the new region—Black Montanans married whites at a rate of 7 percent, or 20 interracial couples out of 263 married couples with at least 1 spouse listed as Black. The fact that Black Montanans married whites at a substantially higher rate than the national average of the same period is somewhat beside the point. Rather, the numbers of interracial marriages, let alone cohabitation, in Montana are substantive enough to warrant serious consideration of a bill that outlawed marriages regardless of national averages. In the two decades *after* 1909, 28 couples still openly listed themselves on a government document as in an interracial marriage despite it being illegal. The drop in the number of unions between 1910, when the law had only just taken effect, and 1930 is notable and suggests that the law's implementation had some tangible consequences.[47]

Table 3. Interracial marriages recorded in 1910 census

CITY	NAMES
Anaconda	George (Black) and Elizabeth (white) Ellis
	Joseph A. (white) and Lillie (Black) Roy
	William (Black) and Betty (white) Simmons
Billings	Wafford (white) and Susan (Black) Dakan
	Chas (Chinese) and Gertrude (Black) Tong
	William (white) and Ester (Black) McIntire
Butte	Cornelius P. (white) and Anna (Black) Coughlin
	Harry W. (Black) and Hannah J. (white) Johnson
Missoula	Jordan (Black) and Mary (white) Binga
	Edward (Black) and Etta (white) Haynes
	Edward (Black) and Mary (white) Mack
	Frank (Black) and Alice (white) Benson
	Solomon (Black) and Sarah (white) Dorsey
	Kallilis (Black) and Teresa (white) Johnson
	John (Black) and Annie (white) Williams

Miles City	Levi (Black) and Mary (white) Simpson
	V.B. (white) and Sadie (Black) Thomas
Livingston	William (white) and Willie (Black) Donahue

Source: 1910 census records, populations, and ethnic demographics; see "Montana—Race and Hispanic Origin: 1870 to 1990: Research of the Montana Historical Society," MHPRF.

Table 4. Interracial marriages recorded in 1930 census

CITY	NAMES
Butte	John Rasmussen (white) and Jessie (Black) Cole
	Albert (white) and Ann Lee (Black) Marshall
	Richard E. (white) and Zoila (Black) Randall
Great Falls	Chris (white) and Christine (Black) Peterson
	Cassius (white) and Cecile (Black) Tucker
Helena	James H. (Black) and Mary (white) Howard
	Joseph P. (white) and Pearl (Black) Lacey
Havre	Sam (white) and Ida (Black) Ross

Source: 1930 census records, populations, and ethnic demographics; see "Montana—Race and Hispanic Origin: 1870 to 1990: Research of the Montana Historical Society," MHPRF.

Precise numbers of interracial marriages before 1900 are obscured both by the variances of state record keeping and by the control often exercised over such information. Sketching out even the broadest data requires an analysis of the census. Yet, even for 1910 and 1930, years for which there is a relatively comprehensive accounting of all African Americans living in Montana, censuses omit couples who do not list themselves as married, cohabitating, or same-sex (and possibly interracial), as well as those who moved to and lived in Montana but left or separated before the next census, or, most commonly, instances in which one partner simply chose to identify themselves as white or Black to match the race of their spouse. All of this, compounded by Montana's fraught early censuses—including the total loss of the 1890 enumeration in a fire in Washington DC, in the 1920s—makes it nearly impossible to claim that intermarriage was so rare an occurrence that the 1909 law should be seen as largely symbolic.[48] Instead, the passing of racist legislation at that moment in the historical life of the settler state of Montana was the exemplary manifestation of racialized sexuality at the heart of colonial power.

To understand what effects anti-miscegenation legislation had on the stability of the Black community it is first necessary to consider and contextualize the timing. Two narratives, one national and the other regional, run parallel, and each one illustrates unique circumstances that informed the other. In the national narrative, the early Progressive Era ushered in new-fangled, pseudoscientific beliefs about race, the environment, and biology.[49] Widely known men like Madison Grant and Irving Fisher imbued the discourses of national vitality with their own ideas about public health, eugenics, and race. Grant's *The Passing of the Great Race* and Fisher's report to the National Conservation Commission in 1909 extolling the threat of "race suicide" were the high-water marks of a fervent national discourse about the preservation of whiteness in all aspects of life. Not to be overlooked is the connection between the country's resurgent obsession with whiteness and the dramatic expansion of the United States' imperial power in Cuba, the Philippines, Hawaii, and Panama. The model of imperial presidents, Theodore Roosevelt, endorsed many of the same ideological doctrines regarding race and health as Grant, Pinchot, Fisher, and other conservationists whom he welcomed into to his administration or inner circle.[50]

The national narrative surrounding miscegenation law can also be understood as part of a retaliation of white supremacists to a decade of relative gains made by African Americans. The last decade of the nineteenth century saw a renewed focus on race with the rise of a Black intelligentsia and activists like W. E. B. Du Bois, Ida B. Wells, and William Trotter. The emergence of a widely celebrated Black intellectual class at the turn of the century threatened spheres of influence that had long been the stronghold of white supremacist thinkers. "When the sense of social order is threatened," writes Nancy Scheper-Hughes and Margaret M. Lock, "the symbols of self-control become intensified along with those of social control. Boundaries between the individual and political bodies becomes blurred, and there is a strong concern with matters of ritual and sexual purity, often expressed in a vigilance over social and bodily boundaries."[51] The challenging of social order that took place within the halls of Black colleges and universities and within the pages of the *Crisis* or the *Guardian* of Boston transferred to politics of the body and sexuality, and thereby onto interracial marriages.

The connection between bodily control and the perceived transgression of social boundaries extended beyond those conversations in the South and urban North. It also played out in the ongoing settler colonial projects of the West. The regional and state narratives surrounding miscegenation laws mirrored these national contours, but in distinctly western circumstances. Many western states passed similar legislation as Montana throughout the first two decades of the twentieth century.[52] The preceding decades marked the apex not only of the settler project, but of Black participation and social establishment in the West. The social "transgression" in this sense was the very presence of Black westerners at all.

Marriage bans in the early part of the century preceded an assortment of federal and state legislation aimed at or emanating from the West. The 1882 Chinese Exclusion Act was followed by a spate of other immigration laws, notably the 1924 National Origins Act.[53] As many immigration scholars have noted, the consolidation of whiteness through international politics also worked to legitimize and solidify the real and racial boundaries of the nation-state. Alexandra Stern notes the close association and communication between California eugenicists and the authors of the 1924 National Origins Act as one way of seeing the maintenance of the categories of race working alongside the category of citizen.[54] Likewise, Kornel Chang observes the hardening of the U.S.-Canadian border through protection and transgression of the northern borderlands by Asian workers and immigrants between exclusion and World War I.[55] Following in this western lineage, anti-miscegenation laws in Montana and surrounding areas patrolled the legitimacy of both the nation- and the settler state.[56] Production of the latter can be identified through new formulations of power that were created through marriage legislation intended to police these boundaries. Peggy Pascoe has brilliantly illustrated how locals working in clerk and recorder offices across the West became "agents of the state" infused with a legal mandate. The fact that so many western states passed statutes limiting marriage in this era has much to do with the porous nature of the borders with Mexico, Canada, and the Pacific. Passing marriage bans called for the strengthening of institutional governments in a region where "the state" was still quite new and ill-formed.[57]

One of the central features of laws passed by settler states is that they are often byproducts of the society at large and thus somewhat obscured by the utter complexity of the historical moment, which means they can be divorced and portioned off from their own colonial origins. They are not typically manufactured for the direct purpose to further the goals of settlement—an intentionality apparent in countless treaties with Native tribes or even the Dawes Act of 1887—and thus are rarely taken up by historians of settler colonialism.[58] Anti-miscegenation laws, especially in the West, originated somewhere in between the overt policies of appropriation and, say, the illegal closing of Black businesses, which is not itself colonial, but does stem from and furthers the goals of the settler state.

Some westerners might have been completely oblivious that the project of colonial settlement in places like Montana had reached a critical juncture at the end of the nineteenth century. With the last campaign against the once ascendant Lakota Sioux seemingly complete, the final phase of the reservation system nearly entrenched, and the dominance of extractive capitalism secured, the American people did, however, understand that a new era was on the horizon. Consider that in 1893 Fredrick Jackson Turner made one of the most important (and deeply misleading) statements on the future of the American West. In his famous address "The Importance of the Frontier in American History," Turner declared the frontier "closed." The great expanses of land, he argued, had fueled the growth of democracy. With those lands settled, anxiety about an uncertain future permeated Turner's frontier thesis as well as the public's reaction to it. In a certain sense, Turner had clued the nation in to what might have been an obscure moment in history and created a regional and national debate about the implications of a "settled" West.[59]

The nineteenth-century West had been marked by unprecedented changes and overwhelming uncertainty. The bleeding edge of settler colonialism cut through the region, producing environments of fear, violence, and genocide. The economy of the early settler state was dominated by no-holds-barred unfettered capitalism. Life in the West was, as one historian has put it, required all hands on deck. As such, there was, at least for a time, a place for Black hands as well. As discussed in chapter 1, the Buffalo Soldiers, Black rail workers, Black entrepreneurs, and the majority of Black workers who labored in the hospitality, restaurant, retail, and domestic industries all serviced the early needs of the settler state in some fashion. The excitement around western cities like Butte, Helena, Billings, and Great Falls arose as a result of the thirst for available land, the profit of mining or timber claims, and the availability of jobs surrounding the settler project. The question that Turner indirectly posed to many white westerners at the dawn of the new century was how to maintain settler society, and the democratic ideals it ostensibly produced, when access to the preeminent resource, land, disappeared.

On the one-hundredth anniversary of Turner's address, historians from various disciplines and backgrounds weighed in on the legacy of the frontier thesis. Historian Margaret Washington pondered the lack of Black westerners in Turner's subsequent work. Like many since, she aptly addressed the fact that Turner's histories turned a blind eye to the reality that Blacks as well as whites occupied and settled the frontier at the time of his famous address. Moreover, Washington delved into the concept of "frontier" within African American history. She noted that, in his famous study *Black Majority*, Peter Wood argued that minimal social barriers and an expansion of individual liberty for Blacks marked the frontier of early Carolina. However, Wood suggests, "the large slave importations necessary for developing rice cultivation coupled with black assertion led to mounting white anxiety, creating a more firmly entrenched bondage system and repressive slave codes. As the South Carolina frontier was transformed into a settled region, black autonomy and initiative was stifled."[60] Wood, prefiguring the discourse of settler colonialism by almost thirty years, argued that a shift in racial policies and social acceptance followed the process of a region actively *being* settled, into a region that *was* settled. Just as "mounting white anxiety" caused a tightening of racial control on the shifting frontier of the Carolinas in the eighteenth century, similar processes were underway on the "frontier" of the American West in the late nineteenth and early twentieth centuries.[61]

It is no coincidence that Montana was among the most ethnically diverse states in the country in 1890 when the frontier ostensibly closed. It is no coincidence, either, that the "whitening of the West" began at a moment—roughly the last few decades of the nineteenth century—when public perception of the region shifted from it as an open space where American individualism reigned to a space dominated by federal and state control. And it is no coincidence that white westerners responded to these and other anxieties by tightening state control on issues like the body and sex. The results of Montana's 1909 anti-miscegenation law show that it furthered the exclusionary policies meant to harden the "borders" of the settler state, even if men like state senator Charles Muffly were operating under different, and more nationally informed, beliefs.[62]

Fractured Kinships

From wherever the law took shape and however it was operating in the world, Joseph Roy, his wife, Lillie, and their three sons, James, John, and Joe Jr., faced daunting prospects starting in 1909. The Roy family had lived in Anaconda for about five years, where Joseph worked a variety of jobs on the "Hill" of the Washoe smelter. Joseph was white, born in West Virginia to an English father and a Canadian mother. Lillie was Black. The couple had married twenty-four years earlier in Lillie's home state of Missouri. Like many white men in western Montana, Joseph came to enjoy job security at the Anaconda Company through union membership. Even with this protection, "the Company," one of the largest enterprises in the world, in no uncertain terms held Joseph and his family's future in its calloused hands. That may likely have been the reason that the Roy family moved to Washington shortly after.[63] At forty-four years old, Joseph Roy entered a phase of life in which many people begin thinking about their family's future prospects. In 1909 Joseph was the father of two sons in their late teens and a son who was five years old. Lillie kept and maintained the family home on Spruce Street, which Joseph had bought a few years before and owned free and clear. This suggests that Joseph was a man of at least some means, firmly established in Anaconda's more affluent working middle class. The three Roy brothers grew up in the city's white, Italian neighborhood, though they were still close to the majority of other Black children who lived downtown and on the north side of the tracks along the banks of Washoe Creek.[64] Upon the passing of the state's ban and nullification of interracial marriages, the future of Lillie Roy and her sons was suddenly in question.

Had Joseph Sr. died while the family lived in Anaconda—plausible, considering the dangerous nature of his work—the Anaconda Company, which held his pension and all other benefits, might have had a legal basis to refuse to compensate his widow or sons on the grounds that the couple's union was not binding in the state of Montana. Likewise, insurance companies could refuse to honor the policy, given the state law. The family home might be held by the state as his wife and children were no longer acceptable heirs. In short, the bill that passed in 1909 occluded the Roy family's ability to see a future for themselves in Montana. Later that year Joseph and Lillie sold the family home and moved their sons to several places around the West before settling in Washington, the only state in the Northwest that had no restrictions on interracial marriage.[65]

Interracial couples like the Roys—a Black wife and white husband—offer another important point to consider. Historian Tiya Miles writes on the gender dynamic of interracial couples in the West, and in Montana specifically. Recall the marriage of John and Mattie Bost Bell Castner of Belt, Montana: Miles singles out the Castners as an example of the limits of southern frameworks of analysis in the American West. Bringing with her an expert understanding of the racialized sexual violence that so often weighed heavily upon the relationships of Black women and white men in the nineteenth century, Miles expected to uncover a story in which John, an older white man of means, occupied a position of disproportional power over Mattie, mirroring the age-old southern archetype of sexual violence against women of color. Miles found instead that Mattie's life was not one marked by this unequal power dynamic as much as it was a narrative of Mattie's own agency and self-determination in her new environment. Miles questions if these regional historic truths might not reach as far as we think—that there may, after all, be something distinctly *western* about the Castners' marriage.[66]

In a similar fashion, the fact that Joseph Roy chose to move to Washington, a decision that secured a better future for his Black wife and mixed-race children, suggests something similar. The Roys' interaction with the settler state via the anti-miscegenation law shows that Joseph and Lillie's relationship might very well have more closely resembled a consensual partnership built on mutual love and respect rather than a southern paradigm of sexual violence. The Roys were, of course, only one of over a dozen couples of Black wives and white husbands living in Montana during the decades following the passage of the marriage ban.[67] But their story has, I think, important lessons to teach us about the racial logics of colonial erosion.

Roughly around the time that the anti-miscegenation law was passed, three interracial couples were living in Anaconda, with ten children between the Roy, Daly, and Ellis families.[68] In Missoula all seven of the marriages recorded in 1910 featured Black men and white women. Billings, Butte, Miles City, Havre, and Livingston all had several interracial couples. Again, less than one in ten Black Montanans took white spouses. However, each of these individuals' stories presents the possibility of expanding the richness and texture of the history of family, gender, and race in Montana. Some, like the elderly John and Annie Williams of Missoula, seemed to outlast the assault on their union, as they remained together in Missoula until Annie's death shortly before 1930. John was nearly ninety years old when Annie, an Irish immigrant and his wife of sixty-nine years, passed away.[69]

It is difficult to find the erosive impacts of a law that nullified a union that began in 1871 and continued in the face of legal reprisal for another twenty years. Rather, the Williamses' story seems to be one of resistance under extreme duress. Not all stories follow this path. In Missoula Solomon Dorsey, the younger brother of Ephraim Dorsey, the most prominent member of the Black community of that city, had been married to his wife, Sarah, a white woman, for nine years when the marriage ban was passed. The next year, sometime after the 1910 census was taken, they divorced. These are the details from the archive that challenge us to place deeply personal histories in a broader social context. The cause of Solomon's and Sarah's divorce is unknown. However, even if their marriage was already strained, the cloud of legal prohibition certainly did not make matters easier. The fact remains that while some couples like John and Annie Williams maintained their marriage after 1909, many others did not. Several couples divorced between 1910 and 1930; three of the couples in Missoula divorced, or separated, after 1910 (only John and Annie remained married). Moreover, seventeen interracial couples who were listed as married in 1910 no longer resided in Montana by the next census. It would be impossible to maintain that the law was largely symbolic for these families.

Not only was this law far more than a symbol to the few Black Montanans that married whites, it also shaped a harsh new reality for thousands of Black children and single young adults. In 1910, just after Senator Muffly's miscegenation bill passed, the percentage of single African Americans between the ages of fifteen and forty in the major cities was, on average, 30 percent. Two decades later, in 1930, that figure had dropped to 18 percent. This, taken in account with the 30-percent drop of those cities' overall Black population, meant that unmarried men and women found their marriage prospects severely constricted simply because so few single Blacks remained in the state.[70] Black Montanans living in rural towns across the state additionally faced the reality that they could no longer view the white boy or girl next door or at school as possible spouses. Further, the practice of finding partners from other Black communities became increasingly difficult as the Black population slowly began to decrease. Belle Ward, the granddaughter of Richard and Mary McDonald, Bozeman's earliest Black settlers, traveled eighty miles to Helena to marry a young Black man named Richard Fisher in 1925.[71] Even as late as 1942, sisters Mary and Ruth Mundy, daughters of a Black rancher outside of Helena, married brothers Woodrow and Felix Driver of Anaconda (some one hundred miles away).[72]

Table 5. African American population of Montana cities by gender, 1910

CITY	FEMALE RESIDENTS	MALE RESIDENTS
Anaconda	53	73
Billings	67	79
Bozeman	16	14
Butte	109	154
Great Falls	58	59
Helena	176	237
Missoula	66	71

Source: 1930 census records, populations, and ethnic demographics; see "Montana—Race and Hispanic Origin: 1870 to 1990: Research of the Montana Historical Society," MHPRF.

Table 6. African American population of Montana cities by gender, 1930

CITY	FEMALE RESIDENTS	MALE RESIDENTS
Anaconda	46	59
Billings	67	74
Bozeman	10	11
Butte	78	91
Great Falls	96	112
Helena	67	67
Missoula	56	60

Source: 1910 census records, populations, and ethnic demographics; see "Montana—Race and Hispanic Origin: 1870 to 1990: Research of the Montana Historical Society," MHPRF.

Helena had long been the center for young single African Americans. Through the mid-twentieth century, this necessity of finding spouses from other towns often was the only way Black Montanans could legally marry. The Driver Brothers and Mundy sisters were fortunate in this respect. In 1910 nearly one hundred Helena residents—32 percent of the Black population—were single and between fifteen and forty years of age. Over the next twenty years, that population declined by an astonishing 78 percent.[73] To be sure, these figures do not indicate that the number of marriages increased in the Black community so much as they highlight the shocking percentage of single Black Montanans who left the state at a young age. When considering what could have brought about the erosion of this demographic group, one so important to the longevity of any community, the fact that legislative measures were taken to restrict that very group's ability to find partners and build families should not be overlooked. Precisely at a time when the dismantling of Black settler space and exclusionary employment practices threatened the livelihoods of Black Montanans, the future security of family structures also came under attack. For a half century, until the law's repeal in 1953, it compounded the vulnerability of Black communities, driving many young African Americans to seek their future elsewhere.[74]

There is an inverse side to this discussion as well. Rose Gordon of White Sulphur Springs came to be viewed by the community and the Judith Basin area as a whole as one of their most celebrated residents. Though she frequently suffered indignities in various social spheres for her race, Rose became deeply ingrained in white settler society. She catered to the residents of White Sulphur Springs as a restaurant owner and physiotherapist, performing acts of community maternalism as a caregiver and healer. She also became something of a historian, writing numerous articles for the local paper chronicling the history of white settlers in addition to that of her own family.[75] One must question how Rose managed to so fully incorporate her life into a settler community that otherwise had no Black residents. The broader context of anti-miscegenation laws suggests that a deeply gendered logic imbued settler sensibilities. Rose Gordon was able to become a maternal figure in

White Sulphur Springs in part because she was *not* a mother. We might contrast Gordon's experience to the Black mothers of Butte in 1902 who acutely felt the challenge of participating in the settler society of their city without reliable access to childcare. Though they articulated the connection between material success, racial uplift, and their own establishment of Black daycare centers and kindergartens, the Black women's clubs of Butte nevertheless articulated an economic, political, and social exclusion unique to their lives as Black mothers.[76] Rose Gordon remained single her entire life, and in her autobiography she never alludes to any romantic interests. Therefore, in the eyes of white settlers, Rose Gordon's Blackness remained unthreatening to the future whiteness of their community. Gendered perceptions of Blackness coming from the white community may have functioned in the male sphere as well. Jim Jackson, a retired soldier who lived and worked in Helena from 1903 until his death in 1960, also never married. Unlike many other Black men in Helena, Jackson found steady labor and housing with white working-class men throughout the interwar period. As a single man without a family, Jackson's wages were sufficient. His acceptance by other working-class men both as a boarder in their homes and as a coworker may have depended equally upon his Blackness not extending beyond his labor into a role as a father or husband in the community.[77]

Conclusion

The history of the miscegenation law illuminates a particularly potent force of settler colonial erosion in Montana. In every town with a Black community, or in those towns with even just one single Black family, the passage of the marriage ban in 1909 marked the beginning of a period in which *every* member of those communities, Black and white, became increasingly enmeshed in the politics of the settler state. That is not to say, of course, that they were apart from it before. Peggy Pascoe tells us that, in the case of miscegenation laws, more often than not the real power rested in the hands of city and county officials and community members at large to support or denounce those officials' decisions.[78] Even when white Montanans chose to ignore the law and look beyond bureaucratic declarations to recognize interracial marriages, as they did in some instances, their latent participation in the democratic process that made intermarriage illegal in the first place had far-reaching consequences.

Colonial logics informed the curation of marriage laws and public sexual mores in Montana around the turn of the century. The timing of these legal measures came at a moment when the national discourse on a host of issues including intellectualism, science and health, the expansion of American empire in the Pacific and Latin America, and immigration, all of them swirling anxiously around questions of race. At the same moment, uncertainties also fermented in the American West and Montana as one phase of the settler colonial project gave way to the next. In public parlance this was the "closing" of the frontier and the dawning age of a new West. The old West's cast of characters had (ostensibly) exited the stage. In the mind of the settler, the subjugation of Native people seemed secure, and the theft of their lands was nearly complete. Whiteness no longer would be measured solely against indigeneity but also against Blackness, brownness, or Asianness. The passage of laws that tightened state control over the domains of sexuality and the body must be seen as part of the effort to "whiten" the West.

The whitening did not merely affect the lives of Black Montanans already in an interracial marriage or the children of one. It compounded the precarity of Blackness and destabilized the community across the state. In 1918 Fred and Emily Harris and their son Fred Jr. moved to Tacoma, Washington, from their home in Bozeman, Montana. The couple had worked as chefs in the area for a decade. Fred Sr. managed a theater kitchen in the nearby town of Livingston. Despite the security of their steady employment, as well as the home they owned on South 4th Street in Bozeman, much was still uncertain. As the next chapter will show, Black life in Montana became increasingly precarious. In the case of Fred Jr.'s parents, Fred Sr. traveled over a pass to Livingston each day, a treacherous commute in winter months, and Emily's health was poor; she would pass away a few years later, in 1924.[79] These and many other factors may have eventually played into the Harrises' decision to leave their home in Bozeman. But I would suggest that young Fred Jr.'s life also faced certain challenges imposed by the colonial logics of the settler state. It would be wrong assume that, at the age of eight, Fred Jr. experienced the forces of colonial erosion only vicariously through his parents. From a bird's-eye view, however, his future prospects were most challenging of all. Like his parents, he would face acute economic, political, and social hardships, but the future in the place he was born and knew as home was also bleak in another way.[80] At the time when he left, and throughout most of the following decade, there was not one single person living in Bozeman that Fred Jr. might one day legally marry. This demographic anomaly proved to be only temporary, but, for years, no young unmarried Black, Asian, or Indian women appeared to live in Bozeman.[81] It was a type of isolation that even ten years before would have been unimaginable, but, during the interwar period, the types of questions about one's future that Fred Jr. or his parents likely had to make in 1918 became more and more common.

6

History among
the Sediments   *On the Entanglements of Race and Region*

In 1909, on the hazy docks of the Dram River in eastern Norway, eighteen-year-old Sven Bauste boarded the *Kristiania*, bound for Ellis Island. He had spent his entire life in the port city of Drammen before migrating to America, where it took seven years for his naturalization to be approved. In that year, 1916, Sven applied for ownership of 160 acres in Choteau County, Montana.[1] The land had a quality of exposure that was likely unfamiliar to him. Bauste's new home offered stunning vistas of the upper reaches of the Great Plains. There, the breaks of the Missouri River, buttes, and even the faint snowcapped outlines of the Rocky Mountain Front to the West appeared as dynamic intrusions upon the landscape that captivated the aging "cowboy artist" Charlie Russell, who lived in nearby Great Falls. Russell's 1914 painting *When the Land Belonged to God*, considered by many to be his masterpiece, depicts an immense herd of bison fording the Missouri not far from where Bauste eventually sought to make a go of it as a farmer a few years after Russell added the final brushstrokes. Evident in both its title and its human-less landscape, *When the Land* is the paradigm of Russell's shift away from depictions of white settler conquest and Indian life in Montana toward subject matters that more closely reflected his growing disdain for modern life and white settlement in the West.[2] Russell's work attempted to return the land to a state of the sacred and sublime. In February 1917 the young Norwegian American "proved up" on part of that world in north central Montana and earned his patent.[3] The land belonged to Sven Bauste now, but he would not keep it.

That same year the rain stopped falling from Montana's Big Sky.⁴ Along with Sven thousands of families fled their rural homes and started fresh in new places. These movements of white homesteaders were part of a churning mosaic of concurrent population shifts that took place between 1917 and World War II. Suddenly, a state that had been steadily growing for decades—even booming in certain cities—experienced an overall population loss during this period. Yet, at the same time, the largest cities in Montana maintained modest growth. Moreover, a number of medium-sized towns that typically had served more rural areas also grew by 10 percent, making this demographic the fastest-growing in the state. Thus, the greatest losses were suffered by rural residents, a population that had accounted for about 65 percent of all Montanans in 1910, but had declined by 10 percent by 1945.⁵ By one estimate just under 40 percent of failed homesteaders like Sven Bauste contributed to the swelling of Montana's urban areas during a time of dire economic straits, by leaving their land and reestablishing themselves in places like Helena, Bozeman, Butte, or Great Falls.⁶

After losing his farm in 1921, the thirty-year-old newly minted "white settler" searched for work in the growing city of Great Falls, the largest urban area in north central Montana. Bauste found employment in another industry that had suffered during the period of agricultural tumult—the Park Hotel in downtown Great Falls hired him as a porter.⁷ Hotels across the state derived a large portion of their business from agricultural agents who frequently traveled to grain and cattle regions, where they made and renewed contracts with farmers, ranchers, and local distributors. Though not all or even a majority of white homesteaders entered the hospitality industry, the fact that many men like Sven Bauste did find work in the struggling service sector is quite telling. The arc of Bauste's early time in Montana can help us make partial sense of how the growth of the Black community stalled and contracted during a decade when the cities and towns in which they lived were actually growing despite the economic uncertainty and the withering of a white rural population base.

Some agricultural areas, especially around Great Falls and Billings, experienced significant economic recoveries in the late 1920s that stemmed from good rains, fertile crops, and record yields, even as infamous dust bowl conditions worsened in other regions of the country. Yet tumultuous labor strife in mining and timber industries continued to have lasting effects on Montana's industrial cities, where a majority of African Americans in the region lived.[8] During this time of drought and social unrest, some Black Montanans began relocating from towns like Helena, Missoula, Butte, and Anaconda to the established Black neighborhoods in Great Falls and Billings. Even so, most towns saw a vastly disproportionate loss of their Black population. In those cities the types of exclusion that this book has highlighted, combined with the crash of the homesteading boom, created intensely precarious conditions for African Americans during the third and fourth decades of the century.

Returning to Black Montana in 1917, it's worth considering Sven Bauste alongside another man, Jefferson Harrison. Harrison—encountered briefly in chapter 1—retired to Helena after twenty-seven years in the Twenty-Fourth U.S. Colored Infantry, where he served in the Southwest, Cuba, and the Philippines. As a veteran in his mid-forties, Harrison began working as a porter at the Montana Club under the head bartender, Julian Anderson, one of Helena's most established and widely respected Black residents. Though these positions lacked the security of other professions largely unavailable to Black men and women, employers like the Montana Club did seem to offer some of their employees enough money to purchase homes throughout the city. Along with a handful of other former soldiers, Harrison had steady work at the Montana Club starting in 1908 that he may have augmented with jobs at other downtown hotels.[9] It is possible that Harrison had been on hand as staff in 1915 when Russell's masterpiece, *When the Land Belonged to God*, was at long last unveiled and hung in the reading room of the Montana Club, for which it was originally commissioned.[10] After 1917 the economy worsened, and many laborers in such industries faced uncertain employment, including Jefferson Harrison. Along with another Black veteran, Charles Matthews, who was also his next-door neighbor, the former soldier returned to Fort William Henry Harrison, outside of town, seeking any work that could allow him to keep his home on the

20. "When the Land Belonged to God," hanging in the Montana Club, 1948. Montana Historical Society Research Center Photograph Archives, Helena, Montana. #953-303.

west side of Helena a few blocks from the campus of Carroll College. For several more years, until 1921, Jefferson and his wife Louise made ends meet. Within a year of Sven Bauste's move to the city where he would work as a hotel porter throughout Montana's hard times, Jefferson and Louise would board a train bound for Washington State.[11]

Wallace Stegner's now-famous dialectic between "stickers" and "boomers"—the former referring to those Montanans who outlasted the population losses of the interwar years and the latter being those who did not—is an apt description of the way Black settlers in the Rocky Mountain West have often been portrayed.[12] If the lives of those like Jefferson and Louise Harrison are included at all in the canon of early western history, it often places them within the latter category. Black men, and Black women less so, arrived to perform the lowliest forms of labor in the booming economies of the mid- to late nineteenth century, only to quickly disappear as "booms" inevitably turned to "busts." This version of history, of course, fails on a number of counts. In addition to the reality that some Black Montanans would become "stickers," it further obscures the undercurrents of racism that were present and suggests the decline of Black western communities was somehow predestined.

Against these occlusions, the final chapter of *Black Montana* begins with the meandering, intersecting accounts of Bauste, Harrison, and a famous painting of the American West to illustrate its central theme. The erosion of the racial frontier was a process intertwined with many aspects of life in Montana. Just as small things connected Black and white Montanans—a familiar view, a fanciful lament, a collection of oily pigments—momentous changes would connect them as well. Uncertainty about the future of home and belonging would throw Black settlers into shifting assemblages that sought to provide a measure of stability. Though many African Americans outlasted the hard times, the vision of what Montana could be for Black settlers would not. In this way white Montanans cannot look back to an era in which so many established Black families left and resign it to "their" history. Recognizing these entanglements also challenges the standard ways Black Montanans are perceived to have disappeared. Contrary to this narrative, small enclaves of Black residents endured in several towns across the state, notably Great Falls and Billings. Black Montanans refused, and still refuse, to be erased. But the remarkable character of the "Black Montana" of a century ago, a dynamic group bound by collective origins, self-awareness, activism and dissent, social and cultural distinctions, and networks of kinship and communication, is gone.

Precarity in Black Montana, 1917–1930

This book has sought to historicize the Black community in Montana from 1877 to 1930. In doing so it has retold a story of Montana itself. By way of an open-ended conclusion, this chapter also addresses a lingering question frequently posed to the small number of local historians who work on Montana's African American past. Whether it is asked during a historic walking tour or after a talk given at the public library, we frequently struggle to provide a satisfying answer. It is simply: Where did early Black Montanans go, and why did they leave? Each of the preceding chapters has offered partial insight into these issues. Truly, though, it is the basis from which people have asked that question that begs attention. Though many in this community did migrate to other places, the more pressing question is: Why did Montana cease to be understood as a space of Black settler potential? This chapter returns to the sites of colonial erosion from the 1920s to the mid-twentieth century in order to arrive at a more satisfactory conclusion. Synthesizing the effects of personal and structural racism is challenging, as the lives of an educated doctor, pharmacist, or lawyer were, of course, not identical, nor were they subject to the exact same processes as laborers, porters, bellhops, or waiters. Moreover, those experiences were not necessarily transferable to many Black women in a variety of other occupations and classes. Circumstances also differed significantly based on geography and the types of communities in which people lived. Yet, to one degree or another, all people encountered the erosive designs of settler colonialism. Consequently, the history of that place—where Native elimination and anti-Black racism functioned as the underlying colonial logics—is entangled with the history of all peoples who continue to live there as well as those whom the settler society purposefully excluded.

By the very fact of its subtle ubiquity, the erosion of the racial frontier is a defining characteristic of state and regional history. When the framework of the "racial frontier" first appeared in the scholarship, it was not articulated as simply a place west of the Mississippi; instead, it spoke of the potential of the West as a region where the possibility for liberation remained "open" to Blacks. The erosion of the racial frontier, then, refers, in part, to the closing off of that potentiality—it is not the end of Black western history or Black history in Montana. Even in 2020, when the total Black population constituted less than 1 percent of the 1 million total Montanans, those few people, like all others, continue to have a history. Theirs is a history yet to be written. The final chapter of *Black Montana* looks to the layers of colonial sediment from which that new history must emerge.[13]

Mining and Labor Strife

In 1998 Quintard Taylor devoted several paragraphs to the urban Black communities of Montana in his magisterial survey of African Americans in the West. He discussed Joseph Bass and the *Montana Plaindealer*, a vibrant Black middle class, and a nonaccommodationist yet still Washingtonian political climate. Montana's part in the story ended in two sentences: "By 1910 Helena's prosperous mining days had passed. The town's population declined by five hundred ... but the African American community shrank by half and fell sharply again during the decade of the 1920s."[14] But African Americans struggled with circumstances beyond the mere volatility of the mining economy. What Anna Tsing has called precarity—"the condition of being vulnerable to others" that throws individuals and communities into "shifting assemblages"—is almost deceptively obvious in the context of Black exclusion from the halls of the labor unions that fought for the protection of workers against railroad, timber, and mining corporations like the Anaconda Company.[15] Yet even that exclusion is not as straightforward as it might first appear.

Industrial capitalism, over a century, transformed the land, water, and air of Montana. An economy devoted to resource extraction felled forests, dammed rivers, pulled the minerals from the earth, and returned to the environment a never-ending supply of pollutants.[16] The working-class cities and towns that provided the labor for capitalist expansion across the West often bore the brunt of the damage to both the land and to human bodies. The task of mitigating the risks posed by overwork or dangerous working conditions fell to the various labor unions, who used the solidarity of their members to bargain for better pay, hours, and conditions, as well as for continued union recognition. Individual miners, loggers, smeltermen, and railroad workers were subsumed into the union and thus abstracted into one of the most recognizable kinds of social bodies in the history of the modern era.[17]

How this "body" was constituted and whose interests it served would change dramatically. In Montana, especially from statehood in 1889 until the interwar period, the population was among the most ethnically diverse in the nation. Though much of its diversity came in the form of its new European immigrants, unions were still forced to contend with the racial difference among their members in the process of creating solidarity. The result was a heavily "raced" social body that often openly held up whiteness as a qualifying attribute, one that formed the dominant hierarchy.[18] The varieties of racial inclusion and exclusion ranged from the total omission of Black and Asian workers to European countrymen being either marginalized or elevated to leadership based on ethnicity. Similarly, the potential threats to one's health corresponded to the level of danger inherent in the job—a risk often linked to status within the union.[19]

The cities of Butte and Anaconda stood as models for the struggle for dominance between the unions and the Company. Anaconda was conceived of and built as the company town of the namesake copper producer. From 1883 and the town's founding until smelting operations ceased at the Washoe Smelter in 1980, the two major social forces remained the Anaconda Company and the various unions that represented a majority of workers—unions that denied African Americans membership for several decades. However, unlike the Irish-controlled locals in Butte that prohibited Blacks outright from working in the mines, Anaconda unions did not fight for the total exclusion of Black smeltermen.[20] In 1910 twenty-seven African American men were employed by the Company in various positions.[21] Because they labored outside of the union, their welfare was not the concern of those in union leadership.

During an interview conducted by the historian Laurie Mercier in 1982, one retired white smelter worker recalled the interwar years, in which he understood the Black smeltermen would work only the jobs that whites did not want.[22] These positions were undesirable precisely because the work was dirty and dangerous. Working on the airline in the reduction facilities was grueling and left the laborer vulnerable to physical injury as well as to airborne pollutants that could lead to silicosis. Remarkably, prevailing racist conceptions of health often led many white smeltermen to believe that Black workers were less at risk to health hazards. Blackness, in their minds, constituted an inherent dirtiness that supposedly protected Black bodies from the risks that many whites were unwilling to take.[23] Black men in the smelters of Anaconda and Great Falls, for instance, faced the full force of corporate disregard for their safety. In this way, a precarity manifested itself in the very bodies of Black Montanans working in these industries in the early decades of the twentieth century. The data as to the exact extent of harm inflicted on Black smelter workers is unknown, but the early 1950s study by W. C. Hueper of the National Cancer Institute "revealed that Deer Lodge County had the greatest death rate in the state from lung cancer, more than thirteen times higher than the national average, and one of the highest rates in the nation."[24] The Black Montanans who worked for the Anaconda Company almost exclusively occupied the unhealthiest positions within this system.[25] In this way white unions not only excluded Black workers as a means of reserving better-paying jobs for whites, but they also positioned Black workers and their bodies between themselves and the most potent dangers posed by the expansion of industrial capitalism throughout the settler colonial West.

Eroding the Neighborhood

Historians have recognized the importance of the collapse of the mining economy as it related to the disappearance of early Black communities such as Helena. But the reverberations of this economic decline can be detected much farther afield.. Some cities saw a gradual decrease in the Black population despite decades of steady growth. In Billings Blacks lived almost exclusively in the triangular Southside neighborhood.[26] The story of that city's Black community is also entangled with the turbulent history of industrial capitalism; the establishment, growth, stability, and eventual decline of Black Billings occurred as south central Montana experienced the steady expansion of the railroad, mining, and eventually oil production industries.

Along the Yellowstone River, Billings grew in anticipation of the arrival of the transcontinental railroad in 1882. The railroad camp that stood between the town and the river was little more than a shantytown of mud paths and tents. When Walker Browning, a Black man from Missouri, arrived with railroad laborers, he became one of the first of the city's residents to make the area between the Billings and the river his permanent home. Browning had moved his wife, children, and young siblings from Missouri to Omaha, then to Laramie, then to Deadwood, and finally to Miles City, with the Northern Pacific. By 1882 Browning had decided to end his travels in Billings.[27] Unable to secure land in an overpriced market under the influence of western speculators, Browning instead began building his one-and-a-half-story wood frame home amid the laborers' tents south of the tracks.[28] By the time the Browning home was finished, in 1883, and the rest of the family had finally moved in, other Black rail workers also began building homes in the same area.[29]

The early Black community of Billings, joined by Mexican, Chinese, and Japanese workers, along with poorer whites, established the Southside neighborhood as the railroad continued its westward march toward the cities of Livingston and Bozeman. The importance of this neighborhood as a center of nonwhite place identity in Montana cannot be overstated. Though it is likely that racist housing practices existed within the Billings real estate market that prevented Black families from establishing themselves in other parts of town, the Southside nevertheless took on real significance for the cultural life of African Americans. As the community grew in the early 1910s, Black worshippers decided that they should establish a neighborhood church. Most of the Black community at the time attended the Methodist Episcopal Church downtown. Though the denomination nationwide tended to be far more open to Black participation, certain leadership roles in a white church body were still segregated. The AME Church, whose roots went deep into the heart of the Old South and the legacy of slavery and slave agency, became the most prominent Black church in the West around the turn of the century.[30]

Several prominent Black families in Billings—including those of William McCabe and Horace Bivins, famed cavalry officers of the Spanish-American War—led the push for a new AME Church in Billings.[31] Plans were made to construct a new building, even going as far as to draft blueprints of a stunning neogothic sanctuary, images of which still hang in the Montana State Historic Preservation Offices. Funds were low, however. The congregational leadership, including the aging patriarch of Billings, Walker Browning, sought instead to purchase a church. A large, salt box–style warehouse building was secured in 1917, with plans to convert it into a new sanctuary. However, at the time it stood some seventeen blocks north of the railroad tracks, more than a mile from every member of its future congregation. In one of the most stirring yet rarely recalled moments in Montana history, the Black community moved the building, intact, on what was most likely log rollers, south across the Northern Pacific Railroad to its final location at 402 South 25th Street, in the heart of the Southside neighborhood.[32]

Despite the community's symbolic defiance in 1917 against the spatial division of their world, as well as the de facto segregation that produced it, the challenges facing African Americans in Billings community continued, and indeed intensified, toward mid-century. The railroad, which had brought so many of the early Black residents to the area, quickly became a formidable barrier to everyday life. During this time no school operated on the Southside. There were schools not far north of the tracks, but no overpass existed between the two neighborhoods. Southside residents, both Black and white, frequently complained of the morning trains blocking the way to the rest of Billings, as well as the inherent dangers of making young children walk across the rail yards each day. This issue (reminiscent of Linda Brown's neighborhood in Topeka, Kansas, in 1954) animated much of the neighborhood's local politics, often pushed by Southside aldermen and often ignored by the rest of Billings.[33] What is more, leading up to a pedestrian overpass being built late in 1939, local papers increasingly published sensationalized pieces on racialized crime, presenting the Southside as a section of town where "Mexican criminals" attempted to rob vagrant Black residents who in turn proved to be as armed and dangerous as their assailants, or as a space where Asian physicians operated a front for dope smuggling.[34] In addition to illustrating the twentieth-century turn to carceral logics and the policing of nonwhite neighborhoods, the situation on the south side of Billings suggested that race was a partially conscious element in the original division of the city's residents. Billings is the only example of de facto housing segregation in a city with a substantial Black community, whose members mostly labored in the white neighborhoods and downtown in the service, domestic, and hospitality industries. Though the Black community largely embraced a sense of neighborhood pride, the industries that fueled the growth of the city at large detracted from the health and safety of Black Billings precisely because of geography.[35]

One development in particular came to endanger the Black community in Billings more than any other. By the 1920s another product was making use of the transcontinental lines that had first transported settlers, then mineral ore, grain, and foodstuffs from Montana's emerging agricultural centers: rich oil deposits from across central and eastern Montana needed to be refined and transported to booming markets throughout the country. The first refinery opened in Billings in 1921 directly adjacent to the Southside neighborhood.[36] For the next century, oil companies would continue to expand their operations within blocks of the Black community. For decades pollutants leached into the Yegan Ditch, which ran from nearby fields to the Yellowstone River and, in the early years, provided a water source for some Southside residents.[37] The air, already defiled by the railroad yard upwind, now absorbed black smoke from the huge oil refineries. Despite such environmental racism, the Black community in Billings remained in place longer than any other city in Montana, save Great Falls, whose proximity to Malstrom Air Force base provided a steady stream of Black airmen and their families throughout the twentieth century. By mid-century, however, Black Billings largely went the way of other African American neighborhoods, its population slowly draining away, with few new arrivals to revitalize the community.

The Realm of Montana

Something else toxic and odious took hold in central Montana in the 1920s. Perhaps readers have been surprised thus far not to have encountered the white supremacist terrorist organizations so ubiquitous to the history of race in the South. But, indeed, the Ku Klux Klan established a foothold in the state during its national resurgence in the early 1920s. By 1924 forty Klaverns boasted a statewide membership that outnumbered Montana's entire Black population five to one. Anne Sturdevant has written that, following the drought of 1917, "prairie society unraveled." Faced with the collapse of banks and other social institutions foreshadowing the Great Depression, "thousands of the white Montanans . . . found the Klan ready to salve their wounds and to identify the supposed annihilators of their traditional lifestyle."[38] White supremacists not only worked to deny Blacks access to the social safety net by nullifying ties of kinship in 1909, but a decade later organized to support white settlers who themselves faced the unknowns of a precarious future. Historian Christine Erickson characterized Klan activity in Harlowton, where the Klan first organized in central Montana, as being more "concerned with creating a prosperous and thriving community," as the tiny town and rural county was home to almost no Catholics and even fewer African Americans.[39]

As one might imagine, the settler colonial dimensions of Montana's Klan activity manifested in some striking ways. In addition to its overall goal of holding together reeling settler communities across the state, the way Klan members chose to exert their power directly hearkened back to the days when their forbears began the campaign to eradicate the state's Indian population. The Laurel, Montana, newspaper wrote in September 1925, "From out of the gloom, a flaming cross bloomed forth on the top of Square Butte, four miles west of Laurel. . . . Not since the days when the Indians held ceremonies on the Butte has there been the spectacle of burning fires and moving figures such as were seen Thursday night."[40] With their focused message of nativism, the Klan in Montana took to dispossessed spaces as a new symbol of their "nativeness."

As it happens, one of the only accounts of Klan violence that resulted in the death of a Black man took place on the Crow Agency near Hardin, Montana, where Bureau of Indian Affairs officials were among the most active Klan members. After defending himself in a shootout with sheriff's deputies and Klansmen who attempted to burn him out of his barricaded home, James Belden, the *Hardin Tribune-Herald* noted, was taken by the crowd—which included white men and Indians—and thrown back into his burning cabin, where the flames consumed him.⁴¹ The whole affair had begun when Belden, who had recently moved to the agency from Butte, was wrongfully accused of petty theft, and the local Klan agitated to have him run out of town. Belden's armed resistance resulted in the death of several of his attackers, including John MacLeod, a former special officer on the Crow Reservation. The same event also made headlines in the national Black press, but no mention of the Klan appeared in the editorial. Rather, the front-page headline of the *Chicago Defender* declared in bold print: "MONTANA INDIANS LYNCH MAN." Though the Black paper did claim that MacLeod had instigated the racist killing, the writer opined that, when presented with the opportunity, "the descendants of barbarians worked to show Uncle Sam that the crude Indian could really take on the ways of America's boasted civilization and stage lynchings as effectively as the most cultured Georgian."⁴² The paper went on to highlight the senselessness of the Crow's actions in assisting and perhaps even directing Belden's killing.

The author's use of anti-Indian epitaphs marks perhaps the most negative way in which the Black press portrayed American Indians in their sparse coverage of Montana. Several years earlier, during the passage of the 1924 Indian Citizenship Act, representations of Indian affairs in the Black press were mostly positive.⁴³ However, following the events in Montana, at least some African American observers felt justified placing American Indians in the company of the rest of racist America, sarcastically writing in the following week's issue, "They are full-fledged 100% American citizens now—they are civilized!"⁴⁴ Though it seems likely that reporters at the *Defender* were unaware of the federal Indian agents' KKK association, the tone of their article nevertheless reveals that tensions between colonized peoples—Black and Indian—continued. Left unspoken or unknown by the Black press, the Klan was able to disappear into the background of the tragic story. In its place, American Indians appeared to take on the mantle of colonizers and thus quickly became the fuel for Black writers to denigrate Indians as "barbaric," "crude," and "savage" in the finest settler colonial tradition.

The murder of James Belden aside, historians have tried to argue that the Montana Klan did not focus on anti-Black terror because the Black community was so small during the 1920s. This, of course, makes sense only if the long and complex history of Black Montana is conveniently forgotten. The rise of the Klan and the breaking of the Black community come at the same moment and due to many of the same social and economic conditions. Among the hotbeds of early Klan activity were Lewiston and Livingston, both of which were home to several dozen African Americans during the 1910s. By 1930 virtually every Black resident had left those infected cities.[45] In a more direct account of KKK intimidation, it seems that no offence, real or imagined, against white supremacy was needed to justify spreading terror. The *Anaconda Standard* in 1923 worriedly reported that M. A. Clements, the wife of Anaconda's AME minister, received a letter from the Klan threatening to tar and feather her if the couple did not leave town. The paper expressed a certain regret that the harassment took place, likely because of the prevalence of labor Democrats and Irish Catholics in the city, who also faced down KKK violence.[46]

Because of the Klan's attack on Catholics and Communists and others on the left, the organization found it difficult to break into many of the larger industrial cities, where Irish Catholics and Labor Unions held considerable social and political power. The Klan's decline in Montana after 1930 for lack of clearly defined enemies, as most historians have argued, might be more indicative of its withering rural base than anything else. Certainly Catholics and leftist radicals abounded in Montana's urban industrial centers, and African Americans, though much fewer in number than just a decade before, still called many Montana towns home. Despite this most scholars assume that the Klan faced obsolescence in a racially homogenous state. We are left, then, with the astonishing fact that, even in our histories of the most infamous anti-Black terrorist organization, the Black community is only considered relevant in its supposed absence.

Precarity in the New Deal Era and Beyond

The fact that Black settlement in Montana did not continue and become part of the Great Migration suggests something remarkable about the society that the settler project created in Montana by the 1920s and 1930s. In reaction to the unbearable oppression of the Jim Crow South, the Great Migration was in full swing by October 1929. While northern industrial cities like New York and Chicago reeled from the crash of the stock market and the Great Depression, Black southerners—at least those who could afford it—increasingly looked west, especially to California, Oregon, and Washington.[47] Why was it that the promise of the New Deal existed in other places throughout the West, but did not lead to new streams of Black immigrants to Montana?

It is important to remember that the settler project was not a uniform, homogeneous, or predestined event. At best it was fragmented and uneven. For this reason, by the third and fourth decades of the twentieth century, migrating Black southerners, and Black Montanans themselves, undeniably saw a better future for themselves in Los Angeles, San Francisco, Oakland, Portland, Tacoma, Spokane, and Seattle than in any city in Montana. Just as the state recovered from its most severe drought in decades, and the future of Black Montana struggled beneath compounding layers of colonial racism, these same circumstances deterred the wave of emigration that was primed to crest on northern and west coast cities in the 1920s and 1930s.

In the preceding decade, the depression of 1918–22 had already stunted the growth of Montana's agricultural industry by the time the Great Depression fully bore down on Montana's extractive resource economy. By 1931 prices for copper and timber had dropped significantly, and western production was substantially curtailed.[48] With the election of Roosevelt and the implementation of New Deal programs like the Civilian Conservation Corps and the Works Projects Administration, Montana launched into a period of increased federal involvement in the development of national parks, national forests, and other public lands. While jobs building trails and paving highways as well as and other infrastructure projects provided labor for tens of thousands of workers, a majority of the state's New Deal funds went to rebuild Montana's agriculture.[49] With dust bowl conditions gripping the middle of the continent, most monies designated for Montana aimed to take advantage of wetter weather and better growing conditions by the mid-1930s.[50]

Farms and old homesteads were, of course, almost exclusively in the hands of white settlers. Black Montanans who stayed through the 1920s and 1930s would have seen Montana's New Deal programs as insufficient at best. Civilian Conservation Corps (CCC) fire crews hired hundreds of Black workers, though only a handful hailed from Montana. One CCC forester recalled the Black workers as hardworking and friendly, but somewhat unused to "roughing it" in the mountains and forests, as they were all from crews stationed in Tennessee and other southern states, places to which their conscription would return eventually them.[51] While federal money attempted to stimulate the stagnant economy, more Black Montanans, along with African Americans from the East, increasingly moved to western cities where the New Deal fed leftist politics, which greatly benefited Black residents.

Quintard Taylor notes that African Americans in other parts of the country, especially Texas, found gaining access to WPA or CCC jobs fraught with racism. In some cases the endeavor was completely hopeless.[52] However, western cities from Denver to Seattle to Los Angeles were a boon to the Black community during the New Deal era. Much of the success seen by these western states came directly from a dynamic that had already been suffocated in Montana: the cooperation between Blacks and leftist labor unions.[53] Black Montanans had tried and failed for decades to align their politics with labor, to carve out a political niche for themselves. By the 1930s, when many Black westerners turned to Roosevelt's new Democratic Party for representation, too few African Americans remained in Montana to forge that relationship, and too many of those bridges already had been burnt. The situation in states like Washington and Oregon was almost the opposite. The Washington and Oregon Commonwealth Federations (the WCF and OCF), representing the leftist arm of the Democratic Party, openly embraced and aided Black political organizations and the NAACP while pushing to abolish discriminatory pay scales and other racist policies in those states.[54] Compare this to Montana, where the most politically active Black group, the Montana State Federation of Colored Women Clubs, received only marginal support from liberals.[55] In many ways the successful activism of African Americans in other western states played a role in attracting Black Montanans away from a society that at every turn made it clear they were not welcome.

Anti-Black conditions continued after the New Deal had made its unequivocal mark on Montana and its economy. Missoula, the westernmost city with a relatively large Black population in the early twentieth century, tells a story of colonial erosion somewhat different from the rest of the state. In 1930, before the timber industry weathered a sustained period of turmoil, the Black population there had decreased little compared to the decimated communities in Butte, Helena, Havre, and Miles City.[56] Throughout the next two or three decades, Missoula—and western Montana at large—would be profoundly remade by the increased role of the federal government in the management of the public lands and forests that comprised most of the western third of the state.

An argument could be made that the increased scope of federal oversight and the cultural ties that formed between Montanans and their public lands is one of the defining factors in the development of Montana. As this process only truly began in the early 1900s, in many ways Montana is the standard for twentieth-century state development; it is the century in which Montanans formed their identities through many trials. Between the world wars, Montana was the only state to experience a population loss. The people who toughed it out (or "stickers," as Stegner referred to them) formed intense kinship networks with their fellow Montanans and sought to reshape the future of their state. Perhaps the best example of this force was the constitutional convention of 1972, in which the 1889 constitution was thrown out, and a new governing document was written and ratified in June of that year.[57] Among the document's many remarkable qualities, one garners the most attention and relays a singular Montana character: article 2, section 3 states that "all persons are born free and have certain inalienable rights," which "includes the right to a clean and healthful environment."[58]

Though the opening lines of article 2, section 3 state that all men are born free, referring back to both the Thirteenth Amendment as well as the West's place in the mid-nineteenth-century "free land, free men" ideology of the Republican party during the end of the Civil War and the founding of Montana Territory in 1864, the origins of environmental protection were steeped in colonial history. The right to a clean and healthful environment stems from different chapters in Montana's past. It comes in part from earliest days of exploration and settlement, when the territory was the great wilderness that promised to remake the sickly city dweller into the individualistic and democratic American man. It refers to the environmental damage that extractive mining and industrial capitalism wreaked on the state for almost a century with little to no accountability. It derives from the increased role in the federal and state governments to manage and protect, in the words of the 1972 preamble, "the quiet beauty of our state and the grandeur of our mountains."[59] And it grows out of the dedication of Montanans to that conservation ethic, born a half century before those words were written. As this book has shown, sometimes even the most laudable historical developments are inextricably tangled with issues of race, whiteness, and belonging. To be clear, all this is not to say that we should not celebrate the altruism and forward-thinking at work in the democratic process. After all, it was not malicious persons who penned such an expression of hope for their future on this planet, but average Montanans called to write their own laws. Yet even Montana's new constitution, viewed from a long historical perspective, is a colonial document, bearing witness to the past and present sedimentation of the settler state. These words from the preamble of the Montana state constitution speak to a latent understanding of land ownership, thanking God not for the grandeur of *the* mountains, but of *our* mountains. More than just the possessive inflection of the phrasing, the refrain is meant to recall the words of various national anthems—"America, the Beautiful," most notably. African Americans—especially after emancipation—also cultivated and sang national anthems. However, whereas white anthems are often laden with the imagery of land ownership and conquest, Black anthems like "Lift Every Voice and Sing" only reference conquest as the conquest over the foes of liberty. Instead, the environment, as Mark Fiege argues, is a place that offers "redemption in an awesome providential landscape," rather than somewhere to be settled.[60]

In Missoula, a city that would become a hub for state and federal land management work, the profusion of new jobs in conservation gave little to no help to a Black community that was already weighing its options and considering a future elsewhere. Of the thousands of state and federal employees hired to run the expanded vision of government, only one known person was Black. Raymond Johnson, who grew up in Missoula in the early 1900s, when the Black community there was at its zenith, became the first Black Montanan to work for the Forest Service. The precedent of Black federal soldiers manning posts and operations in the early days of Glacier and Yellowstone National Parks had been all but forgotten. When he was interviewed by Quintard Taylor in 1979, Johnson recalled no other Black Forest Service workers in the state.[61] Even new movements in state history are subject to designs of imperial formation and are necessarily born among the sediments of Montana's racial past. In the case of the management of federal and state lands, conservation ideologies that would dominate those professions were forged in part by racist beliefs espoused by the conservationists of the early twentieth century. In spite of the fact that men like Raymond Johnson could tie the Black conservation and wilderness ethic all the way back to earliest days of non-Indigenous peoples in the area via York, mountain man Jim Beckwourth, or the Buffalo Soldiers, the management of Montana's natural resources continued apace as an almost unflinchingly white movement in the twentieth century.

Colonial Ghosts

When the Montana legislative session of 1953 commenced in January, lawmakers were as forward-looking as perhaps they had been since the early decades of the century. New economies of scale infused the state with much-needed economic growth. The oil and gas industries expanded in the east, timber markets in the West were ripe in the postwar suburban housing boom of the 1950s, and the coming years would see an end to underground mining in Butte, as the city shifted toward open-pit operations in the now infamous Berkeley Pit. Despite a turn to what state historians have called an era of consensus conservatism, a number of mid-century progressive reforms also managed to pass through the chambers of the Montana Capitol.[62] Among them was HB 8, which repealed the language of the 1909 law banning "miscegenous" marriages. In the years immediately leading up to 1953 a number of court cases in the American West—notably *Perez v. Sharp*, ruled on by the California Supreme court in 1949—suggested that the constitutionality of marriage bans was very much in doubt. Though the 4–3 ruling that California's ban was unconstitutional marked a discernable turn, Peggy Pascoe notes that the narrow victory "fell far short of establishing a judicial consensus."[63] Thus U.S. Supreme Court rulings and federal legislation would lag behind as eleven western states removed legislative bans before *Loving v. Virginia*.[64]

Despite Montana's Supreme Court upholding the state ban as late as 1942, a decade of social thaw following the war ultimately led to little being made of the issue when it came before the House in January 1953. One newspaper only briefly digressed into the issue of repeal as part of its standard reporting on session proceedings on January 20: "Four measures got 'do pass' recommendations from the House committee of the whole this morning without apparent opposition." In addition to the fact that there were no objections, it is also curious, if only for readers of this book, to note the other measure in the batch that accompanied HB 8, which "included bills to permit miscegenous marriages in Montana, to give the fish and game commission power to set the Park county special elk season rather than doing it by statute, and to ask congress to come to the assistance of Montana's landless Indians."[65] Though these bills were separately drafted, introduced, and passed, their grouping at this time serves as a useful reminder that colonial logics continued to press upon the daily lives of Montanans in the mid-twentieth century.

In this conspicuous grouping can be found signposts of a history that direct our attention to other elements of the settler project that continued unabated. Perhaps no group of Indigenous people in Montana have so long suffered the full force of nineteenth-century eliminatory logics as those that came to be known as the "landless Indians."[66] Arriving in Montana as Indigenous refugees in the late nineteenth century, the Little Shell Chippewa, Cree, and Métis Indians settled in various locations around the state, as they had no formal treaty with the federal government, no reservation, and no welfare or assistance from the Bureau of Indian Affairs. Even after the Rocky Boy Reservation was established in 1916, due to its remarkably small size urban Indian poverty among those known as the "landless Indians" persisted.

In particular, "Hill 57" in Great Falls, a name given to a part of town where hundreds of individuals lived in abhorrent conditions, continued to represent a daily reminder of the state's woeful neglect and general lack of empathy for its residents for decades after 1916. The measure that passed in 1953 alongside the repeal of HB 8 called upon the federal government to provide assistance to the residents of Hill 57, as state funds had either run out or been appropriated elsewhere in the new era of consensus conservatism.[67] In the mid-1950s the public push for federal action may have come from equal parts contempt for the way that the Chippewa, Cree, and Métis continued to be ignored, and from the growing perception that Indian affairs should not be a burden to the state government and taxpayers, who passed the buck, as it were. By 1955 federal legislation was proposed to mitigate "one of the most difficult and pathetic situations in the United States" by channeling funds through the Department of the Interior. At that time nearly two hundred Indigenous peoples lived in "deplorable" conditions in Great Falls without "proper sanitation and health facilities, and [were] continuously faced with a shortage of food, and proper clothing."[68] For all the increased attention to their condition, what the Chippewa, Cree, and Métis people really needed—land and federal recognition—was not forthcoming. In the 1980s the state finally recognized the Little Shell Chippewa Tribe of Montana. At the time of this writing, legislation has passed, and the Little Shell are finally a federally recognized tribe, if a century too late.[69]

In similar ways, redress concerning racist legislation that had stood for half a century, undermining the stability of many interracial couples and Black family networks, was also too late. As the short excerpt included above suggests, the repeal of the 1909 law prompted remarkably little discussion, akin to the buried references to the marriage bans that appeared sparsely in white newspapers from 1909.[70] Only passing references to HB 8 were made as the bill was introduced, discussed in committee hearings, voted on, and signed in a matter of only a few weeks. Legislative coverage in the Helena paper noted, for example, that Governor Aronson had signed a bill "permitting miscegenous marriages" before moving on to the more hotly contested proposals dealing with extended oil leases and pay raises for state workers.[71]

Perhaps meaning might be read into both the bill's lack of newspaper coverage as well as its framing as almost the reluctant permission of "deviant" practices. Though laws changed, readers of state papers would not have sensed any shift in social norms. So, while it may have seemed that the old erosive racial logics that went by familiar names had in 1953 at last been vanquished, it could still prove otherwise. For over 120 years and more than three generations, the Driver family of Anaconda withstood all manners of this colonial erosion. When John Driver was born in 1941, it was in no small part thanks to his father's ability to secure membership in the United Steelworkers union a few years prior, giving him steady work at the Anaconda Smelter. Before John's father, Woodrow, likely became the first Black man in Montana to secure that protection, his grandfather Lee Pleasant Driver had shrewdly worked and saved to acquire a ranch east of town that sustained his family when the hard times hit in 1917.[72]

In 1962, sixty-seven years after Lee and Pearl Driver arrived in the Deer Lodge Valley of southwest Montana, fifty-three years after the state passed its ban on interracial marriages, and nine years after that law was finally repealed, John Driver and Marilynn Ryan drove across the state line into Idaho, where a justice of the peace in Lemhi County pronounced them husband and wife.⁷³ The couple had both grown up attending Catholic Mass in Anaconda. John's mother, Mary Mundy Driver, was an engaged, devout member of St. Peter's in town. She sent John and his siblings to Catholic grade schools and ensured their participation in the church as well. "You *will* be an altar boy," John recalled his mother saying. The Drivers attended mass with such frequency, he recollected, that "you'd think my mother was the priest or the bishop!" The church stood out as the most significant part of his early life in Anaconda. "They had a five o'clock. mass in the summertime for the fisherman," he said, noting the early hour at which his mother would wake him and tell him to "get on down there." John could vividly recall his mother speaking with the priest after the first service, at which point Mary would quickly volunteer him and his brothers for the next mass. After hourly services from five to eleven, he laughed, "your whole Sunday's shot."⁷⁴ Marilynn Ryan's Irish background placed her firmly within the largest ethnic and religious group in the Smelter City, but, despite his upbringing, it was a world of which John was decidedly on the outside.

When Driver and Ryan approached the priest to perform the sacramental mass, the father informed them that their marriage would not be possible in Anaconda. The Roman Catholic Church held that marriage was central to the lives of their followers, and, as such, it did not prohibit interracial marriages. On the ground, however, numerous avenues for impeding a union were open to priests who may have personally objected. "She's Irish and I'm not, I'm black," John explained matter-of-factly.⁷⁵ The refusal of the Anaconda clergy on such grounds so angered John and Marilynn that they left town, and the Church, and were married in Idaho, where they did not have to wait on any cumbersome paperwork or file applications. The Drivers moved to Helena in 1966, where John eventually went on to have a successful career as a sales- and serviceman for a small company named IBM. When asked if he ever thought of leaving Montana after what had occurred, he quickly shot back, "No. I'd never take my family outta here."⁷⁶ Though elements within Montana had rejected, hurt, and certainly angered the couple deeply, John and Marilynn held tightly to their home for their own sake and so that their children could call it home as well.

Conclusion: Imperial Debris

This final chapter has taken a wider view of colonial logics at work in the twentieth century after 1917. In doing so it retreads some terrain covered earlier in this book. Around the turn of the century, the threads of settler colonial formations were clear enough. To take them up again at mid-century, though, is to pull on them as if they were ropes that had long been on the ground, overgrown by and partially buried in sediment. This task also insists upon a reckoning of the connectedness of lives within settler society and a deeper reflection on the narrowness of the exclusion of Black settlers. This narrowness can be seen beyond the history of Montana as well. All across the West, the diversity of the region's cities is, in part, evidence of the successes of Indigenous communities and people of color in their ability to resist and make home, even though urban Black communities continue to face odious new forces of erosion. In much of the West, Native elimination and racial domination to this day remains, thankfully, an unrealized goal. The settler project, as one scholar has noted, is merely an imperial formation that has failed to secure its own permanence.[77]

The impermanence of settler forms was evident in 1917, and it remains so over a century later. Reformers of the 1910s back east and boosters out west who sought to pair "landless men" with "man-less land" saw immigrants like Sven Bauste of Norway better suited to the "frontier" of Montana and the West than an urban life in New York.[78] They would have been doubly pleased to learn that the homesteading bubble they helped create played a central role in sending thousands of white settlers into Montana's cities, where they competed with Blacks already fighting against the forces of colonial erosion. At nearly the same moment, the famous painter Charlie Russell put his final touches on his masterpiece, a soaring eulogy to a fantasy time when Montana was a "man-less land." *When the Land Belonged to God* depicts a dawn crossing of a bison herd on the Upper Missouri River in present-day Choteau County, not far from Bauste's homestead. The central figure, the leading bull, crests the hill at daybreak followed by a thunderous force of nature. The buffalo's gaze meets the viewer's. It is defiant, almost contemptuous.[79]

When the Land Belonged to God now hangs in the Charlie Russell Gallery of the Montana Historical Society Museum in Helena. It is my favorite painting. This is partly because I spent many hours looking at it whenever I could steal a moment away from my research back in 2016. It is also because I cannot help but think about the place it depicts, the time when it was painted, in 1914, and individuals like Sven Bauste and their turbulent history on that land. My mind moves to how that history intersects with the lives of Black Montanans like Sergeant Jefferson Harrison. I imagine that he was able to steal some moments with the painting while it hung in the Montana Club for years before he lost his job and was forced to leave his home of two decades. I cannot help but think of what impression, if any, it might have made on the former Buffalo Soldier. It is my favorite painting also because, beneath the accumulation of pigment and beyond the pangs of loss that Russell imbued in the scene, I can see a tangled history of real people: of rapacious settler conquest, of uncertain futures, and of broken and reformulated communities. To be sure, it is an exquisite painting, made with a master's control of color and form, but it is also a piece of imperial debris. Though occluded on the canvas's surface, the entanglements of race and region lie beneath. Another famous Montana painter once said that *When the Land Belonged to God* was his favorite Russell piece because "it *is* Montana."[80] In a way, he is right.

Epilogue *The Endurance of Black Montana*

It is my hope that, through this book, a certain conceptualization of "Black Montana" has emerged as an idea that future historians will situate within the broader narrative of western African American history. To be sure, the lived experiences of African Americans in Montana cannot be lumped together into a single, monolithic category. However, the group of individuals and families I have set out to study here built and shared various networks that connected them in small but meaningful ways across the vast distances of the state. Many people arrived in the years following the end of Reconstruction. They lived in an era of both palpable anxiety and hope about the future of Black people in America. Together they witnessed and propelled momentous changes in western history as their new home rapidly shifted from a world geographically and demographically dominated by Indigenous peoples into a landscape imbued with eerie shadows of violence and dispossession. They formed and joined Black fraternal lodges and women's auxiliaries, literary societies, sports teams, and political clubs. They printed their own newspapers, which connected readers in various towns across the state. From the pages of the Black press we also know that Black Montanans themselves traveled frequently to visit one another in towns and cities often over a hundred miles away. These connections, sometimes by necessity, fostered new and enduring networks of kinship, tying together individuals living in Anaconda or Missoula to those in Butte, or Great Falls, or Billings. Chapter 6 showed how the vibrancy, promise, and communal bonds of Montana's African American community were almost entirely broken by the events of the late 1910s, 1920s, and 1930s.

Yet the history of Black Montanans does not end with the migration of the majority of the population to other states. Rather, this study is a focused attempt to unearth the relevant factors that led to Montana being the least Black state in America by the early decades of the twenty-first century. The history of Black Montana, which continued to form and to struggle with the society and culture of the "Last Best Place," is bound to the afterlife of U.S. colonialism, the theft of Native lands, and the attempted elimination of the region's Indigenous people. That history began as York first saw Montana's mountains and plains—and the people who lived in that landscape. In a migration that has become all but invisible to present day observers, Black Montanans became entangled with the project of settlement. As they moved into the West, Black settlers built railroads, calmed and inflamed the anxieties of the white settlers who presided over the twilight of the Western Indian Wars, panned for precious metals in its rivers, felled its forests, and supported growing communities that included their own. All these developments occurred in accordance with the initial goal of the settler state. However, the creation of that state and the expansion of its settlements had long operated as a racially defined project—one that would be complicated and undermined by the sovereignty of Black settlers.

Once physically established in Montana, African Americans sought to carve out a better life for themselves, culturally, socially, and politically. By the 1880s many newcomers championed home ownership and steady employment, as well as access to integrated public education, as the surest way to secure racial equality. Unlike other U.S. regions after the sabotage of Reconstruction, Montana at first appeared willing to embrace a Black community. Black men peacefully enjoyed the right of suffrage and voted en masse; several even won office with the support of white Republicans. Moreover, their ability to politically engage both their particular community as well as the society at large led to a unique push to establish a real western Black political agenda that did more than toe the Republican Party line. The early settler state, in this fashion, became a laboratory of Black settler ideology in Montana. However, even as new and exciting steps were being taken by Black settlers, the colonial regime's standard of whiteness weighed heavily against them as they sought recognition as members of the body politic as well as the body of the state.

Culturally, even when Black Montanans possessed "legitimate," historical ties to a founding piece of Montanans' collective identity and the state's relationship with the land and environment, the movement championing that ideology excluded African Americans both from their leadership and from their cultural memory. The views held by many conservationists in early twentieth-century Montana, as well as across the country, were undeniably informed by racist understandings of the body, the environment, the "nation," and the anticipated beneficiaries of conservation itself. In Montana settler logics of elimination and anti-Blackness bolstered conservationist approaches about which resources should be preserved and why. Though Black Montanans in many cases pioneered the region's first outdoor exploits and continued to cultivate and maintain the Black wilderness ethic well into the twentieth century, their exclusion from our cultural memory of that aspect of Montana's past is testament to the effectiveness of colonial erosion.

Those effects, as well as the sediments of colonial violence and dispossession, reach well beyond the way we remember certain eras or events. Montanans after the turn of the century contended with a variety of compounding racist policies implemented by the state and upheld by the federal government. Few extended as far from the very heart of colonial power to affect the everyday lives of Black Montanans as did the 1909 ban on interracial marriage. At a moment when young, single African Americans represented the largest group of Black Montanans to leave the state between 1910 and 1930, those who remained were made painfully aware of the degree to which white Montanans believed they were unfit for integration into their networks of kinship and community. Black Montanans already married to whites left the state in startling numbers. A future in Montana for interracial couples or their children was in question, and those doubts now carried with it the weight of law.

By 1998, when historian Quintard Taylor wrote the first comprehensive survey of Black western history, the richness and vibrancy of Black communities that he found reflected in so many dusty archival boxes persisted in only a handful of western cities; many more Black towns, neighborhoods, and enclaves have not survived. In many ways Taylor set out to rescue western Black history, a project he very appropriately titled *In Search of the Racial Frontier*. On the surface the title alludes to the action of historic Black westerners themselves, who set out in search of new beginnings in new lands where they saw the potential for unprecedented racial equality. But, on another level, the title also references the process of the historian uncovering this past. Once found in the archive and in the lives and landscapes of the West, the next logical step is to understand why the racial frontier needed to be searched for in the first place. What made it difficult to find?

The paradox of westward expansion was that, in the process of settling the region and dispossessing Native peoples of their lands, the settler state was incapable of preventing communities of color from exercising their right to forge a self-determinate path that might lead to peace and freedom on a new racial frontier. The colonial sediments that this study seeks to uncover attest to the entanglements of race and region. The origins of Montana—as both a state and the place that informed the identity of millions of Montanans of all races since 1889—are rooted in the goals of U.S. expansionism. Its founding myths are based on individuals or events that conformed to the standard of whiteness implicit in the settler project. These origins and myths, along with the overall sense of one's self as a Montanan, proliferates cultural memory even today because and in spite of the events that took place in the state's past. Examining Montana in this way unearths the racial dynamic that runs deep through its history: how racist individuals and societal structures sought to displace communities of color, and how that history is manifested in the erosion of racial frontier.

Linda Gordon has reminded us that whether or not a story has a "happy" conclusion has much to do with where and when the chronicler decides to end the narrative.[1] To be sure, Montana's Black history did not end in the interwar period, and the many lives of Black Montanans who lived after that era cannot be reduced to a scholarly footnote or postscript. Arguments could be made for various later conclusions, up to and including the present moment. For instance, the profound impact that the Montana Federation of Colored Women's Clubs had on Montana as result of its tireless pursuit of social change and progressive reform continued long past 1930; indeed, the club did not disband until the 1970s.[2] Likewise, in Great Falls, the doors of the Union Bethel AME church remain open. That religious and social institution has shaped the lives of the community through members such as Alma Jacobs, whose dedication to education in her tenure as the state librarian accomplished untold good for the people of Montana.

Perhaps the most uplifting of the many possible satisfactory endings would be the election of Wilmot Collins as the mayor of Helena in 2017. As I finished a (very) early draft of this book in the form of my master's thesis at Montana State University during that time, I was tempted to narrate the election of Montana's first Black mayor as some kind of triumphant conclusion that settler anti-Black racism can and would be vanquished. Certainly, Collins's election will stand as monumental in state history, especially given that it took place immediately following the 2016 election and the rising national vitriol against immigrants and refugees that accompanied a rebirth of white nationalism. As a Liberian-born refugee himself, Collins's election to the highest municipal office in the capital city of a "red state" (only a few months after the terrorist attack on protesters at Charlottesville, Virginia) drew national attention. Yet even the media buzz around his elevation to office at times reinscribed certain settler logics—namely, the novelty of a Black politician in a "white" state. "Can you even imagine?!" Indeed, much of the initial fanfare trumpeted the election of the "first" Black mayor in Montana, an assumption by many despite it not being entirely true. In 1873, before Helena even incorporated as a town, a Black barber and mayoral candidate named E. T. Johnson won the election over two other challengers, having secured his majority with only fifty-three votes. It does not appear that he served in any official capacity, since Helena lacked a city government at the time. Nevertheless, it is much easier to assume that nothing like the election of E. T. Johnson could have taken place before our own "enlightened" era than it is to contemplate the presence of Black settlers at the social and political founding of Montana. The 1873 election only came to the attention of the community after public historians at the Montana Historical Society who worked on the African American Heritage Places Project insisted that Montana's early Black history be taken into account.[3]

More relevant to the arguments presented in this book about colonial occlusions, I have opted for a different type of end point. As this book began with the life of Rose Gordon, I would suggest that her subversion of the settler state continues with us despite noticeable attempts to ensure our forgetting. The land we call Montana changed drastically from the 1880s—when Rose Gordon was born as the first settler in an isolated mining camp still populated mostly by Indigenous peoples—to 1971, when her personal papers arrived in Helena and were placed in the collections of the Montana Historical Society. Her parents, Annie and John, began their lives as enslaved people in Alabama and Missouri before coming to the mountains of Montana as part of the first wave of Black settlers. The other settler-miners and their families did not hide their bemusement when the Crow midwife who delivered Rose Gordon declared her to be the first white child, as all other children that had been born into their world had been Indians.[4] In Gordon's retelling, their tongue-in-cheek response give us a momentary flash of insight into the kind of world many early white settlers imagined the American West to be. It was, in their estimation, a place where an Indigenous population of racialized others would, by way of "natural law," forfeit their homelands by transfer (violent or otherwise, but usually violent) to those whose hard work and tenacity had secured their own civilization, which they would now plant in the very soil and that would bring about a golden age of settler modernity. But if it had been simple and unproblematic enough merely to call a new Black child "white" and thus bestow upon her the mantle of "settler" and all that that entailed, then the history of Rose Gordon and Black Montana would in all probability have played out very differently indeed.

Rather than represent "color-blind" acceptance, the symbolism contained within the curious birth of Rose Gordon ultimately proved to be profoundly subversive to the society into which she was born. It bears mentioning that this story is, of course, from the writings of an individual produced later in her life about her own birth. Her account, then, would have relied upon others' remembrances, or perhaps it did not. The historicity of the event is not important. What matters is the way the tale of Gordon's birth calls to our attention the types of stories we tell about ourselves and asks what kind of political work they might be doing. In Gordon's case her birth was a claim of belonging, one that grew more potent as she became one of the only Black people living in her community. The Indigenous people and settlers who witnessed her birth related differently to the world into which Rose Gordon was born, and each in their own way contested the legitimacy of her origins. Her own frequent retellings of the story may reflect the necessity she must have felt to challenge those beliefs and to assert her own "rootedness." Though her personal papers suggest she had a number of friends and acquaintances as she grew older, her younger years are variously characterized later on as a time she felt prone to wander. This wandering included a brief move to Washington State when she decided to seek training toward a career as a physiotherapist. Her brother's globe-trotting during the peak of the Harlem Renaissance with the most elite members of Black and white social and literary circles must also have fueled her restlessness. Within her own memoir, these years—the chapters after her youth in White Sulphur Springs—turn away from her own story and instead focus on various moments relevant to the settling of the area and tales of early pioneer life. What drew her back and rooted her in the land she called home is for her to know. She may have left clues, from her love of nature and the wild high meadows, to the value she placed on her own place in the origin stories of central Montana. Whatever it was, we now know that the world around her took many steps to uproot Rose Gordon.

More directly, though, the story of Rose Gordon's birth is exemplary of a tension that runs through the history of Montana like a vein of copper ore, hidden until someone ventures to dig a little deeper. Gordon's voice is among the rare few who commented directly and eloquently on the concepts of "home" and "belonging" that have threaded through the arguments of this book. As she recalled childhood adventures and church picnics among the meadows and rocky outcroppings in the hills above White Sulphur Springs—the same hills where the Montana novelist Ivan Doig set his acclaimed elegy to the meaning of home, *This House of Sky*—Rose Gordon forcefully defined "home" for herself.

These are the stories Rose Gordon told about herself, and we can only begin to imagine the meaning they held for her. There are also those stories we tell about ourselves. Perhaps the most important thing I learned from my beginnings in public history is that the cultural landscape of our present reveals a great deal about what we value in our past. If you were to drive north from I-90 just east of Livingston, Montana, along Highway 89, you would eventually come to White Sulphur Springs. It was here where Gordon and her family moved when she was a child, and where she lived out the rest of her life. It is where she wrote stories of her mother's life under slavery in the South. It is where she fell in love with the mountains and saw in the different flowers the equality of all people—somewhat fitting for a woman named Rose. And it was in this little town where she fed her friends and neighbors from the kitchen of Rose's Café. But if you parked your car along main street and walked through town looking for the building that once housed her café, you would not find it. If you wandered up the hill to the location where the Gordon home once stood, over a century ago, again, you would not find it. Like many of the buildings and houses that were once home to the Black communities of Helena, Butte, or Billings, the cultural resources that might attest to the Black history of White Sulphur Springs are both physically absent and largely eroded from memory.

Trying to redress even a fraction of that erosion has been the purpose of this project. An overwhelming amount of the research conducted for this book began with a name and an address. Stories of individuals, families, and communities flowed first from the census, then to city directories, and then to newspapers. At times the archive reluctantly yielded the names of relatives, and on to surviving descendants, some of whom provided photo albums along with their stories that held the names of more people and where they lived, and on, and on, and on. This project came to uncover the lives and stories of thousands of Black Montanans—histories that were buried beneath a century of colonial sediment. The goal of Montana's African American Heritage Places Project was to find and preserve the remaining places of significance to the historic Black community and to use those places to tell the stories of their lives in Montana. But what of the nearly 80 percent of Black homes and business that no longer remain? What of their stories?

We might rightly fear for what will become of the history associated with the multitude of leveled buildings. Yet a great deal is still known about the life of Rose Gordon; she is one of the most remarkable people in Montana's rich history. Why? She lived in a remote pocket of the state, where the Black community quickly faded around her. She never married. She did not scandalize her fellow Montanans as a Black businesswoman. Nor is she remarkable for any of her other many professional or literary exploits. Indeed, she is not even remarkable for her famous brother, Taylor Gordon, whose singing career and best-selling novel made him Montana's best-known African American "native." Rose Gordon is remarkable precisely because she is Rose Gordon, and historians are able to remark about her. Prior to when the substantial papers of the Bridgewater Family of Helena were gifted to the Smithsonian Institute in 2016, more boxes of documents, letters, books, drafts, finances, recipes, and poetry had been preserved and archived around the life of this one single woman than (very nearly) all other Black Montanans combined. Rose Gordon saved everything. Even as her home and café were eventually leveled, she preserved the record of her life in the place where she was home and in doing so subverted a foundational goal of the settler state in which she lived: to erode the memory of Black Montana.

Appendix

Montana Homesteader Displacement Data following 1917

The following data set was compiled by the author using the following methodology: GLO Homestead patents, listed at https://glorecords.blm.gov/details/patent/default.aspx?accession=566771&docClass=SER&sid=py1ptgm4.glg (accessed October 13, 2020), were compiled into a data set that listed the names of individuals awarded homestead patents in the early months of 1917. Patent holders were taken from the list alphabetically by last name, offering a diversity of homesteads across Montana with no preference or distinction by county. All 287 patents were analyzed. The owners of the homesteads awarded in 1917 were traced via 1920 and 1930 censuses, relevant Polk City Directories, and historic newspapers accessed at http://www.chroniclingamerica.loc.gov and http://www.ancestry.com. Data was compiled based on the following resulting criteria: the county or city of residence (in Montana) listed for 1920, 1930, or any available Polk City Directories in years following, as well as the listed profession of the individual listed on the patent.

The information table below notes the percentage of individuals who remained on the homestead through the next census year, the percentage of individuals who appear in new locations, and their new occupations (if listed), and the percentage of individuals who no longer appear in Montana's residential records or archive after 1917.

n.b. Each individual patent holder or homesteader potentially represents more than one individual (i.e., families or cohabitants)

Total individuals surveyed	110
Total patents surveyed	287
Individuals remaining on homestead after 1920	37
Individuals living elsewhere in Montana after 1920	28
Individuals no longer living in Montana after 1920	45
Total individuals living elsewhere	73
Total percentage of homesteaders that left Montana after 1920	66.3%
Total percentage of individuals who left homesteads and who moved residences within Montana	38.4%

Notes

Preface

1. Data from 1892 yielded the closest year in which a Sanborn map was rendered to the buildings that were represented in the African American community. Structures built after 1892 were redrawn to what was represented on the 1930 Helena Sanborn, a version not available to our office due to the post 1924 copyright standards.

Introduction

1. Gordon, "Gone Are the Days," MHS, 1.
2. Rose's mother's full maiden name was Mary Anna Goodall. Some other scholars who have worked with her papers refer to her as "Mary." I use "Annie" because this is how Rose referenced her in this particular account. Gordon, "Gone Are the Days," MHS.
3. Gordon, "Gone Are the Days," MHS.
4. In one draft of the autobiography, Gordon claims "the distinction of being the first White child born there. All the rest of the babies were Indian babies" ("Gone Are the Days," MHS, 2). In the more complete edition, she claims the Indian midwife makes that distinction, drawing laughs from the white settlers who "knew better" (4). She omits this as well in an article: "My Mother Was a Slave," *Meagher County News* (White Sulphur Springs), May 25, 1955, 1.
5. The most succinct work on settler colonial theory is Veracini, *Settler Colonialism*. For the most comprehensive work on the subject, see Wolfe, *Traces of History*. In the American context, a useful synthesis is Hixon, *American Settler Colonialism*. For an excellent account of settlers in the Anglophone world, particularly Australia and New Zealand, see Belich, *Replenishing the Earth*.
6. Stoler, *Duress*, 61.
7. Wolfe, *Traces of History*, 32–33, 271.

8. Here I am referring to the ignorance of white settlers themselves; Native peoples are more than aware of their colonial condition and the violence it has perpetrated on their communities.
9. There are various critiques to Wolfe's materialist structuralism; among the most productive are Kelley, "Rest of Us"; and Day, "Being or Nothingness."
10. Wolfe, "Elimination of the Native," 387.
11. Iyko Day has argued that "racial dynamics are internal rather than external to the logic of settler colonialism in North America" ("Being or Nothingness," 107). For other works on the intimacy of race and imperial forms, see Stoler, *Duress*; Stoler, *Haunted by Empire*; Lowe, *Intimacies of Four Continents*; Wolfe, *Settler Colonialism*; and Wolfe, *Traces of History*.
12. For a critique of "white settler colonial studies," see King, *Black Shoals*, especially 62–65. King asserts that white settler colonial studies disavows the violence of conquest, both toward Indigenous peoples and on Black bodies, even as it displaces Indigenous and Black studies as the "legitimate" mode of critique; in this sense, she comments directly on the work of Wolfe, Cavanaugh, and Veracini. King aptly recognizes many enduring gaps in the field, but, to my reading, she presents the field as far less pliable and responsive than it often is. Nor do I think Veracini or others attempt to avoid the discussion of Native genocide or ongoing settler violence through discourses of "elimination" or "dispossession," or of land and territoriality. On the contrary, this theorizing has produced a number of major works in the U.S. context that take such violence as their primary subject. See Ostler, *Surviving Genocide*; and Madley, *American Genocide*.
13. Kelley, "Rest of Us."
14. Wolfe, *Traces of History*, 5.
15. Among the notable exceptions to the binary of white and Indigenous are Fujikane and Okamura, *Asian Settler Colonialism*; and Day, *Alien Capital*. Chicano/a studies and scholars of the Southwest also complicate the settler binary by struggling with the role of Mexican Americans in the United States as both colonized and colonizer. For a succinct overview of recent scholarship, see Pulido, "Geographies of Race and Ethnicity."
16. The best examples thus far are Miles, *Ties That Bind*; Hernandez, *City of Inmates*; Leroy, "Black History in Occupied Territory"; and Field, *Growing up with the Country*. Tiffany Lethabo King has written one of the first sustained theoretical texts on the intimacy of Black and Indigenous studies; she provides some compelling reasons for lack of intersectionality. See King, *Black Shoals*.

17. On "settler ambivalences" and "third spaces," see Hixon, *American Settler Colonialism*, 1–3.
18. Hernandez, *City of Inmates*.
19. Iyko Day has suggested that, compared to conversations of "Asian settler colonialism," a lack of economic and political power within African Americans' settler identity has led to the dearth of theorizing on "black settler colonialism" (*Alien Capital*, 22).
20. See Day, "Being or Nothingness"; Byrd, *Transit of Empire*; Mamdani, "Beyond Settler and Native," 657; Tuck and Yang, "Decolonization Is Not a Metaphor"; and, for a reading from Afro-pessimism, see Sexton, "Social Life of Social Death," 18.
21. Miles, "Beyond a Boundary," 417.
22. Wolfe, *Traces of History*, 27, my emphasis.
23. Iyko Day's salient critique of Wolfe that "folding [racialized immigrants, former slaves, and refugees] into a generalized settler position through voluntaristic assumptions constrains our ability to understand how their racialized vulnerability and disposability supports a settler colonial project" is a fair and generative position to take on this issue ("Being or Nothingness," 107).
24. Miles, "Beyond a Boundary," 421.
25. These claims can be reduced down to which form of violence—Native elimination, appropriation, or slavery—is the historic structure that most informs the violence of modernity. The usefulness of settler colonialism to Black studies requires the primacy of the logic of enslavement within that conceptual framework. Conversely, Indigenous/settler colonial studies demand that slavery be a secondary consideration to the logic of Native elimination. Leroy suggests that neither theory alone can account for the variations and messiness of the archive while maintaining such disciplinary separation. Instead, he suggests that the expansion of the United States and other settler states relies upon both "anti-blackness and a logic of settlement." This more nuanced consideration allows us to conceptualize settler colonial processes in places that may "lack a clear indigenous population or a history of slavery" and "account for the particular history of blackness within settler societies." See Leroy, "Black History in Occupied Territory," 2–7. In terms of multiculturalism, some Indigenous scholars have argued that our modern settler state has been forced to react to the unprecedented racial diversity that it was wholly unable to keep at bay. While holding real power largely out of reach of racialized Others, our

society now loudly praises its own diversity and liberal multiculturalism as a testament that things have changed, even while the injustices of racial and colonial regimes continue to sediment around us. The crisis of access to clean water that has been inflicted upon the Native and Black residents of Standing Rock Reservation, Flint, and Detroit alike is only one of many symptoms pointing to our current colonial condition. We might also ask ourselves why the same adulation of neoliberal multiculturalism has not as of yet taken root in more rural, "unsettled" states like Montana at the same scale as elsewhere, in the more populated parts of the country. The most sustained critique of American multiculturalism is Byrd, *Transit of Empire*; on the primacy of Black fungibility in the emerging theory of Afro-pessimism, see Sexton, "*Vel* of Slavery."

26. I see my formulation here to be in productive tension with Day's critique of Wolfe's totalizing definition of "settler." See Day, "Being or Nothingness," 107.
27. White, "Race Relations," 404–5; Ruffin II, "Bibliographic Essay," 364.
28. Logan, *Betrayal of the Negro*.
29. Edlie L. Wong examines the "dialectic" of Black inclusion and Chinese exclusion in America during Reconstruction. Her book *Racial Reconstruction* is an excellent example of a study whose primary focus is the politics of racialization occurring between two groups even while many others are significant to the history she examines. She claims, "As a rhetorical figure, the dialectical configuration of black inclusion/Chinese exclusion is significant for what it both hides *and* reveals about U.S. racial formations in the era of emancipation. Dialectic designates 'a relationship that simultaneously embodies antagonism and interdependence'" (3). In a somewhat related fashion, though the dialectical tension between Black and white settler colonialism hides certain facts, it also reveals some important subtleties about racial formation. See Wong, *Racial Reconstruction*.
30. Strictly within the context of the American West of the nineteenth and twentieth centuries, there is a sense in which this subversion of the white settler project is somewhat narrow (though, I would argue, still critical). As Lorenzo Veracini rightfully argues, all settler societies by virtue of the relationship between colony and metropole are framed by the transnational. As such I would also put forth the possibility that the tension of Black settler colonialism is *not* defined solely by Black settlers' lack of whiteness (read, Europeanness). Rather, following Robin D. G. Kelley, we could argue that the fundamental subversion of Black settlers to European settler colonialism was their African-ness. On African indigeneity in settler

colonial studies, see Kelley, "Rest of Us," 268. For settler colonialism as transnational, see Veracini, "Career of a Concept," 314.

31. There are an expanding number of studies on settler colonialism in the American West. While they do not often or sufficiently address nonwhite and Indigenous histories, they nevertheless provide the foundation for conceptualizing how other groups fit into the settler project. For a sample of studies on U.S. colonial expansion and Indigenous peoples, see Ostler, *Plains Sioux and U.S. Colonialism*. For an Indigenous studies perspective, see Dunbar-Ortiz, *Indigenous Peoples' History*. For a study of western genocide, see Madley, *American Genocide*. For a comparative study of settler colonial legal structures, see Banner, *Possessing the Pacific*. For a study of gender and the family, see Jacobs, *White Mother to a Dark Race*.
32. Here, "racial regimes" and "regimes of race" draw meaning from both Patrick Wolfe's scholarship of the last decade as well as from Cedric Robinson, who employed the idea of racial regimes most clearly in his 2007 book, *Forgeries of Memory and Meaning*.
33. Wolfe, "Elimination of the Native," 387. For a study dealing specifically with whiteness and the American West, see Pierce, *Making the White Man's West*.
34. Jason Pierce makes a compelling argument that the West was conceived of and shaped by visions of white racial hegemony; see *Making the White Man's West*.
35. Nash, *American West*; and Taylor, "People of Color."
36. For 2018 estimates, see "The African American Population," Black Demographics, accessed May 1, 2018, https://blackdemographics.com/population/black-state-population/.
37. We are often tempted to wrap ourselves in comfortable terms such as "legacy" when speaking of such things. Though legacies no doubt abound in western spaces, settler colonial historians argue that it is not simply the *legacy* of settler conquest with which we now contend, but its ongoing reality. These scholars have turned away from terms like "legacy" precisely because it can suggest that colonialisms are past, and that we now only deal with post-colonialisms. Terms such as "afterlife" therefore function as a more active form of legacy and one more reflective on the ongoing nature of things that are often difficult to perceive. As such, the effects of such hauntings are just as likely to be immaterial (such as a belief that the protection of wilderness in Montana came only from the efforts of white settlers) as they are to be more concrete (such as an empty lot that

once held a boarding house for Black laborers). Stoler, *Duress*, 4, 25, 33, 352; Gregory, *Colonial Present*; Good et al., *Postcolonial Disorders*.

38. How I understand the definitions and usefulness of the terms "erosion" and "sedimentation" is largely indebted to the scholarship of historical anthropologist Ann Laura Stoler. Her conceptual work in *Imperial Debris* articulates the durabilities of imperial forms across the globe by reanimating the ruin (noun) caused by colonial invaders into its active form, ruination (both verb and noun). In a Foucauldian sense, imperial debris becomes a lasting apparatus—a *dispositif*—of social control that outlives the physical presence of a colonizing force. Certainly the American West is replete with its own colonial ruins: military forts outfitted as museums; national parks whose early histories tell of the violent expulsion of Indigenous peoples; sites of massacres still referred to as "battlefields"; massive open pit copper mines; and, quite personally for myself, towering smelter chimneys that stand as a monument to the reign of extractive industrial capitalism. Indeed, westerners have fallen in love with many of these ruins, the totems of our settler identity; I am as guilty of this as anyone. For a deeper dive into the geological metaphor of "erosion," as well as colonial ruins, see Wood, "Colonial Erosion."

39. As the intentionally similar subtitle of this book eludes, attending to eroded histories of Black westerners should be read as complementary to Taylor's superb scholarship.

40. De Graaf, "Race, Sex, and Region."

41. *In Search of the Racial Frontier* remains a foundational piece of scholarship for its focused commitment to presenting the experiences of African Americans in the West. The scope of Taylor's study, however, did not provide for close considerations in many parts of the country. His approach to western Black history in the twentieth century as primarily an urban study continues to inspire numerous scholars to explore various local African American histories. Likewise, Albert Broussard focused his survey *Expectations of Equality* on the foundation of Black western identity in the nineteenth century as it influenced the struggle for civil rights from World War II onward. However, much of the region is neglected for the rich stories of places like Texas, California, and Kansas.

42. Some examples of major works in urban Black western history are Taylor, *Forging of a Black Community*; Broussard, *Black San Francisco*; and Self, *American Babylon*. Both Taylor and Broussard have written extensively on Black history beyond urban studies, but not as state or community

histories. See Taylor and Moore, *African American Women*; and Broussard, *Expectations of Equality*.

43. Dwayne Mack's excellent book *Black Spokane* is emblematic of this tradition. Black communities in places like Butte and Pocatello were home to modest but significant populations. Cheyenne, which has no existing scholarship (that I have found), was home to an astonishing seven hundred Black residents. 1910 U.S. Federal Census, Cheyenne, Laramie, Wyoming, Enumeration Districts: 0077; 0078; 0079; 0080; 0081; 0082; 0083; 0084, accessed October 9, 2020, http://www.ancestry.com.

44. Aiding historians in this task is an emerging body of interdisciplinary scholarship from the fields of Black and Native critique. Tiffany Lethabo King's recent articulation of the "shoals" as a theoretical and methodological intervention in current white settler colonial studies posits that, like the offshore geological and oceanic formation, the Black shoals arrest the colonial logics that work to sever the relationship between Indigenous genocide and Black slavery: "As an accumulation of Black thought, aesthetics, and politics," King writes, "the shoals . . . halt the all too smooth logics of White settler colonial studies." King and other scholars engaged in this disruption of settler epistemologies are rightly focused on the present and call for sustained critique of the ongoing recuperation of the settler state through "Indigenous genocide and Black social death" (*Black Shoals*, 10).

45. For an excellent discussion of colonial occlusions, see Stoler, *Duress*, 10–13.

46. Hämäläinen, *Lakota America*, 324–25.

47. On the history of Progressivism, Marylin Lake reminds us that settler logics imbue the development of the U.S. state well into the twentieth century. See her superb study on the shaping of American reform in the early twentieth century, *Progressive New World*. In terms of citizenship, most Native Americans were not recognized as U.S. citizens until 1924. Chinese residents in the United States became eligible for naturalization in 1943, Filipino and Asian Indian naturalization passed in 1946, and not until the McCarren-Walter Act in 1952 could Japanese residents become naturalized as citizens. All Asian groups faced exclusion in immigration policy until 1965. And, as Linda Gordon, Katherine Benton-Cohen, and Anthony Mora have shown us, Mexican and Mexican American communities in the Southwest continued to face political and social exclusion despite a treaty attesting to both their citizenship and "whiteness." See Gordon, *Great Arizona Orphan Abduction*; Benton-Cohen, *Borderline*

Americans; Mora, *Border Dilemmas*; and, for a broader account, see Chan et al., *Peoples of Color*.
48. Wolfe, *Traces of History*, 3, 18.
49. Berardi and Segady, "Development of African-American Newspapers," 100.
50. This statue remained officially in place until 1926. See Limerick, *Legacy of Conquest*, 278.
51. McLagan, *Peculiar Paradise*, 79.
52. Limerick, *Legacy of Conquest*, 280.
53. Madley, *American Genocide*, 42–66; see also Smith, *Freedom's Frontier*.
54. *Californian*, March 15, 1842, 2. See also Aarim-Heriot, *Chinese Immigrants, African Americans*; and Smith, *Freedom's Frontier*.
55. Kornel Chang has written on the networks of Asian immigrant labor that simultaneously bolstered American imperial expansion in the Pacific Northwest and Pacific even as that same process became the impetus for growing racial anxieties of white settlers in the region. See Chang, *Pacific Connections*; on race and settler colonial capitalism, see Day, *Alien Capital*.
56. Edlie L. Wong's excellent book *Racial Reconstruction* presents the formation of American identity and citizenship by attending to the complexities of differential racialization in California during Reconstruction. By using writings of Black westerners like James Williams and William Newby as well as white and Chinese sources, Wong shows how race functioned as the arena in which the ambiguities of citizenship were negotiated. For our purposes, replacing the legal category of "citizen" with the more capacious domain of "settler colonist" is helpful in thinking how the Chinese experience speaks to settler histories. For more studies of the Chinese exclusion in the American West, see Shah, *Stranger Intimacies*; Pfaelzer, *Driven Out*; and Merritt, *Coming Man from Canton*.
57. Wong, *Racial Reconstruction*, 72.
58. For a discussion of free African Americans prior to the Civil War challenging exclusionary ideas around citizenship and national belonging, Jones, *Birthright Citizens*.
59. The connections between the logics of Black settler colonialism, therefore, might bear similarities to those of "Black orientalism." Both concepts present, in their negative articulation, an observation that Wong brilliantly makes in her own work. Using the writings of nineteenth-century Black and Chinese westerners, Wong proposes that if we can "disarticulate this complex structure of state violence and white supremacy," then we can

better conceive of how the ongoing processes of Indigenous appropriation, Chinese exclusion, and the struggle for Black equality became intertwined. See *Racial Reconstruction*, 69–123.

60. Limerick, *Legacy of Conquest*, 280. Additionally, Martha Jones has argued that free Blacks before the Civil War consistently made claims to citizenship through the discourse of nativity and national belonging. Conversely, the racist calls for Black colonization to Africa, against Black citizenship, and, later, against Black enfranchisement were fundamentally white rejection of Black claims to national belonging. We might productively read western states like California and Oregon declining to ratify the amendment through the established discourses of Black belonging as well as citizenship. See Jones, *Birthright Citizens*.

61. See Arnesen, *Brotherhoods of Color*, 25–26; and Arneson, "Specter of the Black Strikebreaker."

62. Taylor, *In Search of the Racial Frontier*, 187–89.

63. Robin Kelley has argued forcefully that scholars should not neglect the wide variations of resistance that African Americans engaged in to subvert white supremacy during Jim Crow. Elevating the importance of these hidden transcripts of resistance necessarily means broadening our definitions of resistance. White settlers laid claim to the land not just through the overt reign of violence against Indigenous peoples, but through the establishment of their institutions of government, education, and industry, as well as through the molding of cultural and regional identities. Thus, trespassing into these "white spaces" by Indians, Blacks, Asians, Latinos, and those poor whites deemed not "fit" to be settlers amount to a vast archive of hidden resistance to the settler state. Kelly Lytle Hernandez also has described a "rebel archive" formed from the voices of men and women in their struggle against a capacious, carceral settler regime. See Hernandez, *City of Inmates*; and Kelley, "We Are Not What We Seem."

64. Veracini, *Settler Colonialism*, 3; Ostler, *Surviving Genocide*.

65. Despite such sovereignty, the history of the "Black towns" of Oklahoma, Kansas, and Colorado, tellingly, is abounding with prolonged, and often unsuccessful, struggles on the part of Black residents to maintain political autonomy. Black settler sovereignty does not preclude continued racist oppression; see Painter, *Exodusters*. Greg Dowd has also written on the multiple valences of settler sovereignties and offered a useful critique the field's tendency to flatten and generalize colonial and Indigenous legal histories. See Dowd, "Indigenous Peoples without the Republic."

66. "An Act to Provide for the Allotment of Lands in Severalty to Indians on the Various Reservations (General Allotment Act or Dawes Act)," Statutes at Large 24, 388–91, NADP Document A1887, February 8, 1887; see also Genetin-Pilawa, *Crooked Paths to Allotment*.
67. Allotment reduced the Native land holdings in the United States by over ninety million acres, which is roughly the same size as the state of Montana. See Lake, *Progressive New World*, 15.
68. "Views of the Great Northwest," *Chicago Defender*, March 22, 1913, 1–2.
69. That exception was the Helena Election Riots of 1867, where officials sought to experiment with Black suffrage. It led to the murder of Sammy Hayes, a Black man who tried to exercise his right to vote under the Territorial Suffrage Act of that year. For this account, see Smurr, "Jim Crow Out West," 161–62.
70. The notable exceptions to this in Montana were the cities of Great Falls and Billings.
71. Spence, *Dispossessing the Wilderness*.
72. Ann Laura Stoler asserts that insofar as colonial states are by their nature racial, then the issue of interracial sex and sexuality between both colonizers and colonized is *the* central concern of those structures. See Stoler, *Race and the Education of Desire*.
73. See Miles, *Ties That Bind*; Miles, "Long Arm of the South?"; Pascoe, *What Comes Naturally*; and Perez, *Colonial Intimacies*.
74. For statistics on census records, populations, and ethnic demographics see "Montana—Race and Hispanic Origin: 1870 to 1990: Research of the Montana Historical Society," MHPRF, accessed August 31, 2020, http://mhs.mt.gov/Portals/11/shpo/AfricanAmerican/CensusData/MontanaRace_HispanicOrigin1870_1990.pdf. Hereafter referenced as: "Montana—Race and Hispanic Origin: 1870 to 1990." For overall Montana populations, 1900–1950, see U.S. Census Information, "Number of Inhabitants: Montana," accessed May 1, 2018, https://www2.census.gov/prod2/decennial/documents/15276180v2p26ch1.pdf.
75. Stoler, *Duress*, 5–7.

1. The Golden West

1. The Indigenous peoples of the Northern Rockies share versions of the story of *natisqelix*, the "people eater," and his death at the hands of Coyote. My sources come from Montana's American Indian tribes, who each offer their history to the people and students of Montana as part of the state's Indian Education for All initiative. Though lack of funding at times

limits the efficacy of the program, the curriculum and sources produced by the tribes themselves offer a wealth of Montana's Indigenous history. See "Montana Indians: Their History and Location," Montana Office of Public Instruction Division of Indian Education, accessed February 10, 2019, http://opi.mt.gov/Portals/182/Page%20Files/Indian%20Education/Indian%20Education%20101/Montana%20Indians%20Their%20History%20and%20Location.pdf, 23. See also John Fahey, "Flathead Life before the Horse," in Chan et al., *Peoples of Color*, 49–59.

2. On the expanding Horse and Gun frontiers, see Hämäläinen, *Lakota America*, 50–84; on those frontiers in Montana, see West, *Last Indian War*, 3–19.
3. "Montana Indians," Montana Office of Public Instruction Division of Indian Education, 8.
4. West, *Last Indian War*, xxvii.
5. Malone, Roeder, and Lang, *Montana*, 11–21.
6. Hämäläinen, *Lakota America*, 5–8.
7. Malone, Roeder, and Lang, *Montana*, 34.
8. DeVoto, *Journals of Lewis and Clark*, 167–69, 448–49.
9. Montana's Indian history has tended to emphasize the "late arrival" of many eastern tribes. Even some of the Indians encountered by the Corps of Discovery, as Malone, Roeder, and Lang note, had lived in the region for less than a few centuries. Both Indigenous political rivalries and European pressures compounded this (*Montana*, 16–17.)
10. Until recently, locals frequently made analogies to Switzerland when discussing the Indian history of the Gallatin Valley; local historians have begun the arduous task of undoing this misconception. For a conceptual study of terra nullius, see Banner, *Possessing the Pacific*.
11. Though many scholars have serious reservations about his life story, one element that perhaps deserves more attention is the ubiquity of violence in Beckwourth's writings. Ned Blackhawk contends that, as the region's first settlers, "mountain men" like Beckwourth became the principle harbingers of American imperialism and were profoundly enmeshed in the deepening cycles of violence that engulfed the Indian peoples of the Great Basin and Northern Rockies. Beckwourth's recounting of a massacre on the Bear River in the mid-1820s that claimed to have ended the lives of 488 Bannocks illustrates the central role of violence in these early narratives. See Blackhawk, *Violence over the Land*, 169–72; For more on Beckwourth's time in Montana, see Taylor, *In Search of the Racial Frontier*, 49–52.

12. Taylor, *In Search of the Racial Frontier*, 28–29, 48–50.
13. Candace Fujikane and Jonathan Y. Okamura argue that Japanese settlers in Hawaii entered the white power structure, appropriated Hawaiians' land, and thus became settler colonists within the larger U.S. settler society. Though seemingly similar to African Americans as settlers, Asian settlers continued to appropriate and profit off Indigenous land, and thus conformed to the state of "whiteness" in ways that the overwhelming majority of Black westerners never could. See Fujikane and Okamura, eds., *Asian Settler Colonialism*.
14. Ostler, *Plains Sioux and U.S. Colonialism*, 358.
15. "Montana—Race and Hispanic Origin: 1870 to 1990."
16. Critical race theorist David Goldberg and historian David Roediger were among the first scholars to argue that settler states aspire to whiteness. In his seminal work *The Wages of Whiteness*, Roediger provides a succinct, compelling explanation of the settler colonial model: "After the failure of early attempts to 'reduce the savages to civility' by enslaving them, it became clear that the drama of the white-Indian contact outside the fur trade would turn on land and conquest, not on labor" (22). Likewise, in *Racial State*, critical race theorist David Theo Goldberg conceived of settler states as such: "Racially conceived states are invariably molded in the image of whiteness, to reflect the interest of whites" (162). See Roediger, *Wages of Whiteness*, 21–22. Beyond theory, the reality of these aspirational impasses as they played out on the ground are chronicled in many early histories of both Black slavery and Black migration in the West. See Berwanger, *West and Reconstruction*; Lapp, *Blacks in Gold Rush California*; Painter, *Exodusters*; and McLagan, *Peculiar Paradise*.
17. For the deployment of Black regulars, see Glasrud and Searles, *Buffalo Soldiers in the West*.
18. Alegria, "Last Will and Testament." For Jefferson Harrison, see Delia Hagen, "African American Heritage Places in Helena, MT," National Register of Historic Places Multiple Property Documentation Form, MHPRF, accessed October 1, 2019, https://mhs.mt.gov/Portals/11/shpo/AfricanAmerican/Helena_Af_Am_MPD.pdf; Wood, "After the West Was Won," 49–50; and "Walker Browning Obituary," *Billings Gazette*, February 8, 1925, n.p.
19. Studies on the Great Migration consider the intensification of the Jim Crow regime in the early twentieth century as the main causes of the migrations to northern cities in the 1910s and 1920s. Other diasporic narratives, such

as Nell Irvin Painter's *Exodusters*, follow the roots of Black migrations out of the Deep South immediately after radical Republicans abandoned Reconstruction and acquiesced to the political demands of the southern planter class in 1877. Ira Berlin's work *The Making of African America* also constructs a new framework for how we should understand the movement of African Americans, by examining four great migrations, beginning with the middle passage and ending with African immigration after the 1965 Immigration bill that coincided with the Civil Rights Act. Likewise, historian James Gregory argues that the Great Migration should itself be understood within a dual lens of both Black and white social developments. Such works illustrate that African American diaspora cannot be reduced to the Middle Passage and Great Migration alone. See Painter, *Exodusters*; Berlin, *Making of African America*; and Gregory, *Southern Diaspora*.

20. Veracini, *Settler Colonialism*, 3. It is also worth noting that Patrick Wolfe challenges Veracini's inference here that migrants who merely join a political form already established by settler colonists are somehow distinct from their predecessors. I am inclined to Wolfe's position, that there is no necessary tension between being a settler and being a refuge, which he articulates in "Recuperating Binarism."
21. Kendra Field's pathbreaking work on Black-Indian freedmen and freed southern Blacks who settled in Indian Territory before the Exoduster migration and the biracial kinship networks that emerged does not shy away from the complexities of Black settlers seeking citizenship and liberty through the expansion of American empire. See Field, *Growing up with the Country*.
22. See Mitchell, *Righteous Propagation*, 16–50.
23. Field, *Growing up with the Country*, 3.
24. Du Bois, *Darkwater*, 18.
25. For statistics on census records, populations, and ethnic demographics, see "Montana—Race and Hispanic Origin: 1870 to 1990."
26. Generally, I wish to warn readers against an urban or eastern bias that might immediately compare the Black populations of major cities like Chicago or Los Angeles to small towns in the West. For statistics on census records, populations, and ethnic demographics, see "Montana—Race and Hispanic Origin: 1870 to 1990."
27. Berardi and Segady, "Development of African-American Newspapers," 100.
28. William Knott, interview by Quintard Taylor, April 2, 1974, WAUL, 2002. For more on Great Falls's African American history, see Kenneth Rob-

ison, "Early Black American Settlers, Great Falls MT," Historical Black Americans in Northern Montana, May 2, 2009, http://blackamericansmt.blogspot.com/2009/05/early-black-american-settlers-great.html.
29. Union Bethel African Methodist Episcopal Church, National Register Nomination Form, section 8, 2, MSHPO.
30. "The Golden West," *Kansas City Sun*, February 26, 1916, 1.
31. Quoted in Taylor, *In Search of the Racial Frontier*, 147.
32. Taylor, *In Search of the Racial Frontier*, 144.
33. "Boosterism" was a robust form of media advertisement that frequently played fast and loose with the truth; it varied widely in both scope and effectiveness. Black westerners likewise saw the pairing of "landless men with man-less land" as a potential economic and social boon. For a very enlightening examination of racial boosterism, see Deverell and Flamming, "Race, Rhetoric, and Regional Identity."
34. "Interesting News Concerning the Race," *Denver Star*, April 27, 1918, 1.
35. "Open Coeur d'Alene Indian Reservation," *Montana Plaindealer*, March 16, 1906, 3.
36. Cotroneo and Dozier, "Time of Disintegration," 410.
37. "How to Register," *Montana Plaindealer*, June 18, 1909, 2.
38. "How to Register."
39. It is possible that some African Americans took advantage and either purchased land for themselves or cashed out on timber rights, the outcome of Black success in the lottery is unknown. However, geographically the story centers on a truly interesting place and feature of Black migration to the region. See Cotroneo and Dozier, "Time of Disintegration."
40. "Where the Negro Fails," *Chicago Defender*, March 19, 1910, 1.
41. "The Places Are Pine Ridge and Rosebud Reservations in South Dakota," *Chicago Defender*, September 30, 1911, 4.
42. A discussion of white nativism would be very helpful in the scholarship of settler colonialism as a whole. Becoming "native" to North America is an organizing element of white settler ontology. Yet, for this book, a sustained engagement with nativism risks hiding as much as it reveals. The scholarship on nativism has long centered on immigration, Chinese exclusion, the National Origins Act of 1924, and the "assimilation" of white and not-quite-white ethnic groups. As such, the terms of this debate pitted the white native against the white or suspect foreigner, as Matthew Frye Jacobson and Matthew Wray have argued. As we saw in the case of the *Defender*, African Americans were more than capable

of claiming the same ground as white nativists. Because of the generally uncontested claim to citizenship on the grounds of the Fifteenth Amendment, white nativism became an exclusionary ideology that dismissed Black Americans. At the same time, white nativists could also be the same individuals seeking to make a "white man's West" to the exclusion of Blacks. For this project, different categories of legitimacy were needed, and the distinction between settler and citizen fell along different discursive fault lines.

43. A useful overview of the history of Fort Peck Reservation can be found on the tribes' official website. See fortpecktribes.org/tribal_history.html (accessed February 10, 2019).
44. "To Give Away Many Farms, Government Will Throw Open Reservation in Montana Soon," *Chicago Defender*, September 27, 1913, 8.
45. "Go West Young Man," *Chicago Defender*, July 14, 1928, 2; "Montana Offers Farmers a Chance," *Chicago Defender*, May 31, 1930, 6.
46. Chapter 3 discusses Duncan, a Black labor Democrat in 1902, and his journal the *New Age* at length.
47. Robinson, *Black Marxism*, 185–95; Franklin, *George Washington Williams*.
48. See Kelley, *Hammer and Hoe*, 84.
49. Robinson, *Black Marxism*, 191.
50. "Helena Colored Citizens in Line Organize a Local Business League," *Montana Plaindealer*, August 9, 1907, 1.
51. Kelley, "We Are Not What We Seem."
52. Kelly Lytle Hernandez also has described a "rebel archive" formed from the voices of men and women in their struggle against a capacious, carceral settler regime. See Hernandez, *City of Inmates*.
53. Kuletz, *Tainted Desert*; Smith, *Fight for Red Power*.
54. U.S. Census, 1910, Billings, Yellowstone, Montana; Roll: T624_837; Page: 3A; Enumeration District: 0251; FHL microfilm: 1374850 1910.
55. "Walker Browning Obituary," *Billings Gazette*, February 8, 1925, 1.
56. Historian Crystal Alegria made a deep archival dive to uncover the life of Elizabeth Williams in Bozeman, Montana. Amid her pointed analysis of Williams was the postulation that Black women and men who fled the South before or after Reconstruction might best be characterized as refugees, rather than as settlers or pioneers. Nevertheless, William's life in Montana after finding refuge continued to be marked by the structures and means of appropriation of a settler society. Alegria, "Last Will and Testament."

57. B. Derek Strahn, National Register of Historic Places Nomination Form for Samuel Lewis House, Helena, Montana, 1999, MHS.
58. See entries on Sarah Bickford and Mattie Castner in Taylor and Wilson Moore, *African American Women Confront the West*, 128–30, 142–43; and in Riley, "American Daughters." On Castner, see also Miles, "Long Arm of the South?" Numerous histories have been written on the famous Mary Fields, including popular books, chapters in academic books, and even a children's book. For the best examination of fact and fiction in the life of Mary Fields, see Garceau-Hagen, "Finding Mary Fields," in *Portraits of Women*, 121–55. For the most comprehensive assessment of Sarah Bickford, see Arata, *Race and the Wild West*.
59. Jacobs, *White Mother to a Dark Race*.
60. "Montana—Race and Hispanic Origin: 1870 to 1990."
61. Taylor and Wilson Moore, *African American Women Confront the West*, 128–30.
62. Libbie Custer wrote about Davidson in both *Boots and Saddles* and *Tenting on the Plains*. In the latter she noted that after Eliza came to visit her in New York in 1886, she returned to Ohio, not Montana (*Tenting on the Plains*; "*Boots and Saddles*"). See also Allen, "Standing up for Liberty."
63. Taylor and Wilson Moore, *African American Women Confront the West*, 142–43.
64. "Four Survivors of Custer's Cook Are Anaconda Residents," *Montana Standard*, June 26, 1960, 10B. The article does not contest that Custer's cook was named Eliza, only saying that Eliza's real name was Susan Tinsley Mundy, and that her only child Thaddeus had lived as a rancher outside Helena.
65. The history of Buffalo Soldiers as complicated historical actors and agents of American colonialism is still underdeveloped. Some very contentious public debates were waged in the 1990s and 2000s regarding the commemoration of Buffalo Soldiers. See Vernon Bellecourt, "The Glorification of Buffalo Soldiers Raises Racial Divisions between Blacks, Indians," *Indian Country Today (Lakota Times)*, May 4, 1994, A5; and M. Dion Thompson, "Visiting the World of the Buffalo Soldiers," *Baltimore Sun*, April 21, 1996, travel section, 1. After these debates, some scholars—namely, Quintard Taylor—forcefully challenged reductionist and totalizing characterizations of Black soldiers as "Indian killers." Taylor pointed to the historical record to show that "Indian fighting" constituted very little of the activities of Black soldiers in the West. He also emphasized the role that the Ninth and Tenth Cavalries played in protecting certain Native peoples from

raids by the Comanches, Kiowas, and even the Texas Rangers ("Native Americans and African Americans"). That debate highlighted an acute need for historians to portray historical actors as the complicated and often contradictory human beings they were and to avoid wrongheaded valorization or demonization. However, the emergence of settler colonialism as a frame of analysis has complicated the discussion yet again. If "settler invasion is a structure, not an event," as Wolfe asserts, then Native elimination is not something confined to the violent acts of murder, massacre, or war. Totalizing arguments return as some scholars either completely absolve individuals of the structural violence or fully implicate all participants. Striking the right balance becomes exceedingly difficult. Though not attending to settler forms directly, a good history that address this issue head on is Leiker, *Racial Borders*.

66. Born in Lewiston, Tennessee, in 1865, Lee Pleasant Driver grew up a lover of music and education. In his early twenties he chose to pursue both by attending Fisk College, near Nashville. Though he never completed his degree, he was enrolled at Fisk for several semesters, teaching at a Black school while attending to his own studies. During his last year there, 1888, he likely shared classes with one of the great emerging thinkers of his day, W. E. B. Du Bois. Driver's birth: U.S. Census, 1880 (District 1, Marshall, Tennessee; Roll: 1269; Family History Film: 1255269; Page: 310C; Enumeration District: 132). Driver's family history: "Lee Pleasant Driver Obituary," *Anaconda Standard*, January 12, 1935, 6; Polk, *Anaconda City Directory*, 1902, 126. Military service: "Headstone Applications for Military Veterans, 1925–1963," accessed October 9, 2020, http://www.ancestry.com; Fisk College history: "History of Fisk College," Fisk College, accessed June 6, 2015, http://www.fisk.edu/about/history.

67. "Lee Pleasant Driver Obituary," *Anaconda Standard*, January 12, 1935, 6; Polk, *Anaconda City Directory*, 1902, 126; "Headstone Applications for Military Veterans."

68. Glasrud and Searles, *Buffalo Soldiers in the West*.

69. There is a wealth of sources detailing the lives and history of the Buffalo Soldiers. Analysis, surveys, and primary sources are all included in the vast and ever-expanding scholarship of the military and Black soldiers. See Glasrud and Searles. *Buffalo Soldiers in the West*; Fowler, *Black Infantry in the West*; Harris, *Negro Frontiersman*; Koelle, "Pedaling on the Periphery"; Lane, *Brownsville Affair*; Leiker, *Racial Borders*; Schubert, *Trail of the Buffalo Soldier*; and Wood, "After the West Was Won."

70. Koelle, "Pedaling on the Periphery," 305–26.
71. For a review of Black perspectives on the War in the Philippines, see San Juan Jr., "African American Internationalism and Solidarity."
72. Wood, "After the West Was Won."
73. "Locals," *Montana Plaindealer*, June 29, 1906, 4.
74. Wood, "After the West Was Won," 42–43.
75. Dunbar-Ortiz argues that "the explicit purpose of the buffalo soldiers and the army of the West as a whole was to invade Indigenous lands and ethnically cleanse them for Anglo settlement and commerce." However, she also contends that, in the tradition of European colonial management, the Buffalo Soldiers were "a specially organized colonial military unit" that the United States could direct as it saw fit, even to foster interethnic resentment so as to avoid oppressed peoples allying against their white oppressors (*Indigenous Peoples' History*, 146–48).
76. See Gregory, *Southern Diaspora*, 11–41.
77. Isabel Wilkerson depicts the new world of the Great Migration in vivid detail in her excellent book *The Warmth of Other Suns*.
78. Gregory, *Southern Diaspora*, 47–48.
79. Montana's local and state newspapers at this time were somewhat indicative of other early publications. Towns often printed a Republican and a Democratic paper, and various other periodicals with political affiliations. In addition, Montana cities like Butte, Anaconda, and Great Falls published papers that fell along pro-union or pro-company lines as well. Montana's two Black news outlets, the *Butte New Age* (1901–2), and the *Montana Plaindealer* (1906–12), represented largely Republican views, yet both occasionally broke from white Republicans to voice the dissent of the Black community on a number of issues. For information on early Montana newspapers, see Berardi and Segady, "Development of African-American Newspapers"; Meyers, "Montana's Negro Newspapers." Also, information about many early Montana papers are available online at Chronicling America, accessed August 31, 2020, http://www.chroniclingamerica.loc.gov.
80. "Fading of Negro Race," *Anaconda Standard*, November 19, 1899, 8.
81. The concept of "race extinction" existed as a major concern in both white and Black communities in the 1890s. Fredrick Hoffman, a German social scientist hired by the U.S. government to analyze the new census in 1890, printed his *Vital Statistics of the Negro* in 1892, a cold pronouncement of African Americans' future racial prospects. Historian Michele Mitchell notes that Hoffman's analysis of "racial deterioration" largely grew

from his condemnation of Black women, who had a high level of early motherhood, and stillbirths. His disdain for Black femininity along with "general intemperance" led to Hoffman's proclamation that the Negro race would vanish. The response of the Black community to this assertion of their erasure focused on the policies of uplift, often including civic and industrial participation. See Mitchell, *Righteous Propagation*, 81–84.
82. Warren, *God's Red Son*, 27.
83. Du Bois, *Philadelphia Negro*, 387.
84. Mitchell, *Righteous Propagation*, 92–93.
85. Mitchell, *Righteous Propagation*, 93.
86. "Montana—Race and Hispanic Origin: 1870 to 1990."
87. "Southern Race Wars," *Butte Inter-Mountain*, November 5, 1901, 6.
88. For other articles on the "race question" in Montana, see "No Drink and No Shine: The Experiences of a Colored Citizen of Billings in Helena," *Anaconda Standard*, September 23, 1894, 7; "Negro Conference at Tuskegee: The Present Meeting Shows the Good Results of Educating the Black Man on Practical Lines," *Anaconda Standard*, February 19, 1899, 19; "Must Educate or Kill Them: Booker T. Washington a Freak," *Kalispell Bee*, September 25, 1903, 5; "The Negro Problem," *Daily Missoulian*, February, 1909, 2; and "The Value of Wool," *Montana Post*, September 2, 1865, 1.
89. For some examples of reporting on "negro crime," see "Henry Salzner the Wife Murderer Is Lynched," *Billings Gazette*, November 12, 1909, 1; "Was Burned at the Stake: Negro Murderer Paid a Frightful Penalty for a Most Horrible Crime," *Anaconda Standard*, April 24, 1899, 1; "It Is Not Because They Are Negros That They Are Lynched, But Because They Are Fiends," *Rosebud County News*, July 16, 1903, 4.
90. Khalil Muhammad, *Condemnation of Blackness*.
91. "Colored Children in Public Schools," *Helena Independent*, February 4, 1882, 2.
92. Not all white Montanans recoiled in fear at the prospect of sharing settler space with Blacks, though an overwhelming portion of the white press's commentary on African Americans during the time when most Black settlers migrated to the state was negative. However, factions of more progressively minded Montanans also utilized local papers to speak out against overt racism. More specifically, they voiced their commitment to civil rights as members of the Republican Party. A prime example of this position appears in the more progressive paper, the *Daily Missoulian*. See "The Negro Problem," *Daily Missoulian*, February 8, 1909, 2.

93. Even as late as 1911, the federal agent refers to his white audience as "settlers," despite the Flathead valley being "settled" a generation earlier. "An Indian Problem Being Solved," *Daily Missoulian*, December 2, 1911, 7.
94. "An Indian Problem Being Solved."
95. "An Indian Problem Being Solved."
96. Wolfe, *Traces of History*, 182–88.
97. This topic is discussed further in chapter 5.
98. Mahmood Mamandi, "When Does a Settler Become a Native? Reflections of the Colonial Roots of Citizenship in Equatorial and South Africa," lecture, University of Cape Town, May 13, 1998.
99. Malone, Roeder, and Lang, *Montana*, 117.
100. Graybill, *Red and the White*; Wylie, *Blood on the Marias*; Malone, Roeder, and Lang, *Montana*, 120.
101. Malone, Roeder, and Lang, *Montana*, 121.
102. Malone, Roeder, and Lang, *Montana*, 143.
103. Malone, Roeder, and Lang, *Montana*, 141.
104. Mitchell, *Righteous Propagation*, 144.
105. Roediger, *Wages of Whiteness*, 21, 22; Goldberg, *Racial State*, 162.
106. See Reeve, *Religion of a Different Color*; Wray, *Not Quite White*; and Pierce, *Making the White Man's West*, 123–49.
107. See Limerick, *Legacy of Conquest*, 257–92; and Pfaelzer, *Driven Out*.
108. Field, *Growing up with the Country*, 3.
109. "Montana—Race and Hispanic Origin: 1870 to 1990."

2. Making Black Settler Space

1. For a number of reasons, many of which are elaborated in this and the next chapter, the center of Black politics in Montana around the turn of the century arose in the famous mining town of Butte, rather than in the state capital of Helena, which at the time was home to the largest Black community. Most substantially, Butte played host to state's largest and most politically powerful entities, the copper kings.
2. "The Two Colors of the Chop House Affair," *Butte Weekly Miner*, December 20, 1881, 5.
3. "Two Colors of the Chop House Affair."
4. "Two Colors of the Chop House Affair"; see also Smurr's account in "Jim Crow Out West," 175–76.
5. Smurr, "Jim Crow Out West," 175–76.

6. The chapter in which Smurr retold the story of William Woodcock was emblematically titled "Jim Crow out West" and was printed in *Historical Essays on Montana and the Northwest* in 1957. Smurr's chapter revolved around the short tenure of public school segregation in Montana that lasted only a few years into statehood, but it also touched on various moments of race relations throughout early state history. Even today Smurr's analysis and treatment of race has aged far better than most histories from mid-century. Smurr, "Jim Crow Out West," 149–203.
7. Du Bois, *Souls of Black Folk*, 9.
8. Stoler, *Duress*; Stoler, *Imperial Debris*.
9. On the issue of settler and Native space, geographers can offer historians many compelling insights. For a most useful study, see Harris, *Making Native Space*.
10. For a sampling of scholarship on Jim Crow, see Kelley and Lewis, *To Make Our World Anew*; Litwack, *Trouble in Mind*; Woodward, *Strange Career of Jim Crow*; Packard, *American Nightmare*; Gilmore, *Gender and Jim Crow*; and Oshinsky, *Worse Than Slavery*.
11. "Local and Personal," *Colored Citizen*, September 24, 1894, 3.
12. It is impossible to know how much control J. P. Ball had over the paper and its future. He was a photographer, not a newspaper man, and so perhaps he had no intention of continuing it. His vociferous admonishments of Marcus Daly and Anaconda also come across as somewhat scripted. Clark, his benefactor, was a known racist, and his feud with Daly might even have begun when he purportedly called Daly's partner, James Ben Ali Haggin, a "n——." (He was Turkish.) Though it was more or less true, as Ball claimed, that the Anaconda Company did not employ any Black smeltermen (it did at least by 1900), no Black miners worked in Clark's mines either. Of course, both of these conditions had more to do with labor union's racially discriminatory membership requirements. See "About the Colored Citizen," Chronicling America, accessed August 31, 2020, https://chroniclingamerica.loc.gov/lccn/sn84036198/; for Clark-Daly feud and racial slur, see Malone, Roeder, and Lang, *Montana*, 211.
13. "Peace! Prosperity! Union!!!," *Montana Plaindealer*, March 5, 1909, 1.
14. "Obituary," *California Eagle*, November 9, 1934, 2.
15. Historian Delia Hagen has written the best account of Bass and Helena's Black community as part of Montana's African American Heritage Places Project. See "African American Heritage Places in Helena, MT,"

National Register of Historic Places Multiple Property Documentation Form, MHPRF, accessed August 31, 2020, https://mhs.mt.gov/Portals/11/shpo/AfricanAmerican/Helena_Af_Am_mpd.pdf.

16. A useful volume on the mirrored racial regimes of the American North and South is Lassiter and Crespino, *Myth of Southern Exceptionalism*.
17. Kelley, "We Are Not What We Seem," 79.
18. For more on Montana's Black churches, see Anthony Wood, "African American Churches of Montana," MHPRF, accessed August 31, 2020, https://mhs.mt.gov/Shpo/AfricanAmericans/History/AfricanAmericanChurches; see also individual church histories at "Montana's Churches," MHPRF, accessed August 31, 2020, https://mhs.mt.gov/Shpo/AfricanAmericanChurches/MontanasChurches.
19. Muhammad, *Condemnation of Blackness*, 58.
20. Numerous studies on Booker T. Washington have been published. His own autobiography, *Up from Slavery*, remains an important insight to the origins of the "great educator." Scholars generally follow two lines of analysis, the first being one of understanding, the second being more critical of his positions. For more, see Norrell, *Up From History*; Harlan, *Booker T. Washington*; Washington, *Up from Slavery*; Washington, *Future of the American Negro*; Litwack, *Been in the Storm So Long*; and Litwack, *Trouble in Mind*.
21. Bernadette Pruitt, "Beautiful People," 45.
22. Pruitt writes, "This notion of inadequacy and paranoia had its roots in African American Slavery, when many African cultural mandates disappeared and white American cultural and social constructs were embraced, even at the emotional and spiritual expense of Blackness" ("Beautiful People," 53).
23. King, *Black Shoals*, xi.
24. Like Washington, Du Bois has garnered a mountain of scholarship dedicated to understanding the complexities of his life. Perhaps more than most scholars, his own work reveals a great deal how Du Bois thought and interacted with others, especially Washington. For a small sampling, see Du Bois, *Souls of Black Folk*; *Darkwater*; and *Black Reconstruction in America*. The authoritative biography is David Levering Lewis, *W. E. B. Du Bois*. See also Wolters, *Du Bois and His Rivals*; Litwack, *Trouble in Mind*; and Muhammad, *Condemnation of Blackness*.
25. Wells, *Southern Horrors*, 14–45; see also Schechter, *Ida B. Wells-Barnett and American Reform*.

26. Schechter, *Ida Wells-Barnett and American Reform*, 23–26.
27. Schechter, *Ida Wells-Barnett and American Reform*, 37–38.
28. Schechter, *Ida Wells-Barnett and American Reform*, 37.
29. Du Bois, "Damnation of Women," in *Darkwater*, 96.
30. See also Cooper, *Beyond Respectability*.
31. Greenidge, *Black Radical*; "William Monroe Trotter (1872–1934)," Black Past, accessed August 31, 2020, https://www.blackpast.org/african-american-history/trotter-william-monroe-1872-1934.
32. "William Monroe Trotter (1872–1934)."
33. Raymond Wolter's chapter "Du Bois and Booker T. Washington" in *Du Bois and His Rivals* is a useful introduction to their relationship.
34. Du Bois, *Souls of Black Folk*, 31.
35. Du Bois, *Souls of Black Folk*, 31.
36. A helpful entry into Du Bois and Washington is Miller, "Annotated Bibliography."
37. Litwack, *Trouble in Mind*, 370.
38. Du Bois, *Souls of Black Folk*, 26.
39. Robinson, *Black Marxism*, 185–95; see also Frazier, *Black Bourgeoisie*.
40. It must also be noted that, while Republicans relied on Black voters in many local elections to carry the office, when promises of civil rights advancements were broken or egregious acts of racism carried out by those officials, Black Montanans protested with scathing opinion pieces, and quite possibly with a retaliation at the ballot box.
41. Du Bois, *Autobiography of W. E. B. Du Bois*, 236–37. See also Robinson, *Black Marxism*, 189–94.
42. Their different geography and small population may also have deterred the growth of what Maceo Dailey Jr. has called "constructionalism," a method of resistance that used public deference to whites as a tool to subversively build up Black institutions for the benefit of Black people. While middle- and upper-class Blacks in cities like Houston or Memphis may have argued that acquiescing to whites was a necessary price to pay for the security it offered and the benefits it promised to both Black and white southerners, the small population in Montana and other Western cities of the era were never really in the same position. Thus the elements of Washington's accommodationist program they opted for were often materialist and self-serving in nature rather than self-deprecating. See Dailey Jr., "Neither 'Uncle Tom' nor 'Accommodationist.'"

43. See appendices on home ownership; for Black businesses see "Montana—Race and Hispanic Origin: 1870 to 1990."
44. Smurr, "Jim Crow Out West," 167.
45. Smurr, "Jim Crow Out West," 179.
46. "Montana—Race and Hispanic Origin: 1870 to 1990."
47. Smurr, "Jim Crow Out West," 184–85.
48. "Montana—Race and Hispanic Origin: 1870 to 1990."
49. Smurr, "Jim Crow Out West," 184.
50. It is important to note that Smurr's essay was written and printed very much as part of the national discourse on segregation following the decision of Brown v. Board in 1954.
51. A number of wonderful oral interviews with members of this community or their children were conducted in the 1970s by Quintard Taylor. Several contain accounts of their childhood and school-age years. See Raymond Johnson, interview by Quintard Taylor, March 3, 1974, WSUL; Walter Duncan, interview by Quintard Taylor, April 3, 1974, WSUL.
52. Gordon, "Gone Are the Days," MHS.
53. "Helena Notes," *New Age*, June 6, 1902, 1.
54. "Helena Notes."
55. "Helena Notes."
56. For several reasons, I think we should approach the issue of authorial intent or sincerity with caution. The very fact that Gordon's speech was nearly a word-for-word representation of the broader dialogue as presented by many of Washington's white sympathizers might suggest that the school administration had some hand in controlling the tone of the address—or this could very well have been Gordon's opinion, stark and unpolished as it was. However, that the *New Age*, a political newspaper devoted to the struggle for political equality reprinted the speech, is even more interesting still.
57. The *Plaindealer* frequently reprinted one such article while Bass was away. The paper reran portions of that front-page column "Mrs. A. J. Walton Writes on Problems Which Confront the Race" every week that year. For instance, the first time the piece appeared for readers, Bass also commented that "Dr. Washington has the confidence of the great masses of all people and they will stand by him loyally." It also appeared with a frequent column, "Five New Rights, White and Black," extolling Du Bois's five common human rights. *Montana Plaindealer*, March 24, 1911, 1.
58. The *New Age* notes that the other Black graduate was a Jessie Woodcock, but did not reference her father or his identity. Census records confirm that

it is the same William Woodcock who had taken residence in Helena working as a steam carpet cleaner for some time. Search for "Jessie Woodcock, William Woodcock," U.S. Census, 1900, Helena Ward 4, Lewis and Clark, Montana; Page: 12; Enumeration District: 0173; FHL microfilm: 1240912.

59. Data on homeownership rates is taken from the 1910 and 1930 Federal Census reports. African American specific census spread sheets are available online at "Resources and Research," MHPRF, accessed August 31, 2020. http://mhs.mt.gov/Shpo/AfricanAmericans/ResourcesResearch.
60. Washington put it succinctly: "The general political agitation [during Reconstruction] drew the attention of our people away from the more fundamental matters of perfecting themselves in the industries at their doors and in securing property" (*Up from Slavery*, 40).
61. "Helena Is Highly Praised by Masonic Visitors," *Montana Plaindealer*, May 27, 1910, 1.
62. "Jefferson Harrison," U.S. Bureau of the Census, 1910, Helena, Lewis and Clark, Montana, Roll T624_833, 13B.
63. "Mrs. A. J. Walton Writes on Problems."
64. Ken Robison has written an excellent article on this type of social reliance and reciprocity in the history of the Ozark Club. See Robison, "Breaking Racial Barriers."
65. "Views of the Great Northwest," *Chicago Defender*, March 22, 1913, 2.
66. Wood, "After the West Was Won," 42.
67. For a history of the *Colored Citizen*, see "About the Colored Citizen," Chronicling America, accessed August 31, 2020, http://chroniclingamerica.loc.gov/lccn/sn84036198/.
68. Taylor, *In Search of the Racial Frontier*, 211; "Walker Browning Obituary," *Billings Gazette*, February 8, 1925, 1.
69. Svingen, "Jim Crow, Indian Style."
70. Molina, *How Race Is Made in America*.
71. Svingen, "Jim Crow, Indian Style," 283.
72. Molina, *How Race Is Made in America*, 7.
73. "Race Problem in the West," *Montana Plaindealer*, May 27, 1910, 1.
74. "Race Problem in the West."
75. On Jess Lee Brooks's early college career, see the *Montana Plaindealer*, February 24, 1911, 1. On his acting career, see "Obituary," *California Eagle*, December 14, 1944, 1.
76. For a study on the perception of African Americans in westerns, see Johnson, *Hoo-Doo Cowboys and Bronze Buckaroos*.

77. "Views of the Great Northwest," *Chicago Defender*, March 22, 1913, 1–2.
78. "Views of the Great Northwest," 2.
79. Mercier, *Anaconda*, 14.
80. Frank Zogart, interview by Laurie Mercier, November 18, 1982, OH 411, tape 2, side A, 89–117, MHS.
81. A number of excellent works touch on the violence that was engendered against politically active Black southerners. For more, see Litwack, *Been in the Storm So Long*; Litwack, *Trouble in Mind*; Packard, *American Nightmare*; Ayers, *Promise of the New South*; Woodward, *Strange Career of Jim Crow*; Curtain, *Black Prisoners and Their World*; Goldsby, *Spectacular Secret*; and Jaspin, *Buried in the Bitter Waters*.
82. "Republican Candidates for Aldermen," *Montana Plaindealer*, March 30, 1906, 1.
83. Report of the Inspector General of the Army, "The Brownsville Affray," in Carroll, *Black Military Experience*, 471–97.
84. "Brownsville Affray."
85. "Sentiment So Strong against Dismissal," *Montana Plaindealer*, November 23, 1906, 1.
86. "Sentiment So Strong against Dismissal."
87. Lang, "Tempest on Clore Street," 12–13.
88. "The Famous Zanzibar-Pekin Is No More," *Montana Plaindealer*, January 4, 1907, 4.
89. Wood, "After the West Was Won," 42.
90. Bass stated that Graye "was the object of admiration" of white prostitutes. It is unclear if this is simply referring to Graye's personal or sexual relations with white women, or, as it later appears, he actually has business dealings with them. Regardless, it is clear that, like most establishments that rented rooms in western mining towns, prostitutes operated out of Graye's establishment in some capacity. For Bass's quotation, see "Famous Zanzibar-Pekin Is No More."
91. "Eagle's Week at the Zanzibar," *Montana Plaindealer*, June 15, 1906, 1.
92. Lang, "Tempest on Clore Street," 12–13. For articles by Joseph Bass in the *Montana Plaindealer*, see "Famous Zanzibar-Pekin Is No More"; and "Tillman Methods Prevaileth Not," *Montana Plaindealer*, June 29, 1906, 1.
93. "Tillman Methods Prevaileth Not."
94. This was in the estimation of Bass, who rested his assessment on the fact that Graye had become a pimp to white prostitutes and that they worked

for him because he was an "object of [the women's] desire." See "Famous Zanzibar-Pekin Is No More."
95. Lang, "Tempest on Clore Street," 12–13.
96. "Tillman Methods Prevaileth Not."
97. It is difficult to put the remarkable nature of such a charge in context for 1907 Helena. No doubt it was intended to be as snide and demeaning as possible.
98. "Famous Zanzibar-Pekin Is No More."
99. "Famous Zanzibar-Pekin Is No More."
100. "Famous Zanzibar-Pekin Is No More."
101. Lang, "Tempest on Clore Street," 14.
102. A. E. Banks and Elenorah Bank, July 21, 1973, interview by Quintard Taylor, WAUL.
103. Stoler, *Imperial Debris*, 29.

3. Great Debates

1. Armeta Duncan, interview by Quintard Taylor, April 4, 1974, WAUL.
2. Armeta Duncan, interview.
3. As stated in earlier chapters, the *Colored Citizen*, published in Helena during the state capital campaign of 1894, cannot truly qualify for this distinction; it was owned and funded by copper baron William Clark. Though its editor, J. P. Ball, did an excellent job shaping the paper, too much of what it contained would be understood by modern audiences as "sponsored content." Articles that at first appeared to be about issues pertaining to the Black community often turned into boosterism for Helena and denigration of the rival city, Anaconda. See "About the *Colored Citizen*," Chronicling America, accessed August 31, 2020, https://chroniclingamerica.loc.gov/lccn/sn84036198/; and "About the *New Age*," Chronicling America, accessed August 31, 2020, https://chroniclingamerica.loc.gov/lccn/sn84036148/.
4. Those two occupations paired as well together in Montana as they did in the upper South, where socially and politically active barbershops had been a staple of local cultures for over a century. See Bristol Jr., "From Outposts to Enclaves."
5. Armeta Duncan, interview.
6. Armeta Duncan, interview; Anthony Wood, "John and Armeta Duncan Residence (24SB0990)," Montana Historic Property Record Form, MHPRF,

accessed August 31, 2020, https://mhs.mt.gov/Shpo/AfricanAmericans/Places/PropertyRecords.

7. See "Mapping Historic Places," MHPRF, accessed August 31, 2020, https://mhs.mt.gov/Shpo/AfricanAmericans/Places/Sanborns.

8. "Booker T. Washington Pays Butte a Visit," *Anaconda Standard*, Anaconda, Montana, March 7, 1913, 10. When Quintard Taylor interviewed Duncan, then eighty-nine years old, in 1974, she mentioned several prominent Black figures, noting that "Du Bois and all of them [had come to] Butte and that she had met them." Dr. Taylor asked her to clarify, and she responded that they had "been in this very house." This is actually quite likely, as Armeta Duncan had served as the president of the Colored Women's Club in Butte and as the founder of the State Federation of Colored Women's Clubs, the most socially and politically active Black organizations in most Montanan cities. Women's clubs and literary societies were often the groups that invited famous speakers to visit. It makes a great deal of sense that her position in the community, together with John's stature—especially later, when he became a doctor—would place the young couple in the company of visiting Black dignitaries. For Washington's brief account of the visit see the *Chicago Defender*, "Views of the Great Northwest," March 22, 1913, 1–2; and "Race Makes Progress in Montana," *Chicago Defender*, April 5, 1913, 2.

9. Armeta Duncan, interview.

10. "Race Makes Progress in Montana."

11. The political movement of the editors of the *New Age*, as well as the later formation of the Colored Democrats Club, can be seen as a "grassroots" phenomenon, as neither the paper nor the club were instituted by political patrons and sponsors or formal party organization; its mobilization came from within the Black community. For a useful synthesis of African American political movements and ideology, see Dawson, *Black Visions*.

12. For some insightful western regional studies of race and African American political exclusion, see Aarim-Heriot, *Chinese Immigrants*; Smith, *Freedom's Frontier*; and Berwanger, *Frontier Against Slavery*.

13. Quoted in Murphy, *Mining Cultures*, 1.

14. For a sampling of Butte's mining, political, social, and labor history, see Calvert, *Gibraltar*; Emmons, *Butte Irish*; Glasscock, *War of the Copper Kings*; Hyde, *Copper for America*; McNelis, *Copper King at War*; Malone, *Battle for Butte*; Mercier, *Anaconda*; and Murphy, *Mining Cultures*.

15. Chadwick, "Montana's Silver Mining Era."

16. Historian Michael Witgen has shown that throughout the North American interior Indigenous peoples remained more or less autonomous and demographically dominant well into the nineteenth century. The myth that fringe settlements constitute the exercise of sovereignty over surrounding Native peoples loses all credibility in the face of Witgen's exhaustive analysis. See Witgen, *Infinity of Nations*.
17. Richard White argues that violence of the Seven Years' War undid the uneasy alliances and fragile contingencies that nurtured the creation of a middle ground in the Great Lakes region. See White, *Middle Ground*.
18. West, *Contested Plains*.
19. Most of the physical space of Montana remained "unsettled" until at least the era of the second homesteading boom from 1900 to 1917. Especially the eastern two-thirds of the state, where vast prairies dominate, homesteaders were the only Euro-Americans who claimed and lived the land beyond cities and well-watered river bottoms. See "Homestead Boom, 1900–1918," in Malone, Roeder, and Lang, *Montana*, 232–53.
20. For works on several massacres of Native peoples in Montana, see West, *Last Indian War*; Graybill, *Red and the White*; and Wylie, *Blood on the Marias*.
21. Alegria and Fulton, "Fraud at Fort Parker."
22. Malone, Roeder, and Lang, *Montana*, 84.
23. "Population: Montana, Number of Inhabitants by Counties and Minor Civil Divisions," Fourteenth Census of the United States: 1920 Bulletin, U.S. Census Bureau, accessed May 1, 2018, ftp://ftp2.census.gov/library/publications/decennial/1920/bulletins/demographics/population-mt-number-of-inhabitants.pdf.
24. See Emmons, *Butte Irish*, 13–19.
25. This saga has been exhaustively detailed first by C. B. Glasscock, in his study *The War of the Copper Kings* (1935), as well as by Sarah McNelis, in her biography of Augustus Heinze (1968). More recently Michael Malone's *The Battle of Butte* (1981) revisits this critical time in light of developments in the fields of both social and labor history. Malone's argument is neatly summarized in his chapter "Copper and Politics, 1880–1910," appearing in Malone, Roeder, and Lang, *Montana*. I rely on Malone's truncated account here to summarize this political moment.
26. Malone, Roeder, and Lang, *Montana*, 202.
27. See Emmons, "Orange and the Green"; and Malone, Roeder, and Lang, *Montana*, 209–14.

28. Malone, Roeder, and Lang, *Montana*, 204.
29. Daly labored behind the scenes to ensure the election went to the Republican Thomas Carter in 1889. The move made political sense for Daly—a Democrat in need of a sympathetic ear and a conduit to the Republican president, Benjamin Harrison, which Clark would certainly not be. When Clark finally managed to gain a seat following the 1899 Montana legislature, after doling out bribes purportedly to the tune of as much as $400,000, Daly again worked in Washington, presenting the evidence of Clark's wrongdoing to a Senate committee called to investigate. When it was clear that Daly had been victorious yet again, Clark resigned in disgrace. Malone, Roeder, and Lang, *Montana*, 220.
30. Malone, Roeder, and Lang, *Montana*, 222–23.
31. Malone, Roeder, and Lang, *Montana*, 223.
32. Armeta Duncan, interview.
33. "Women's Club Notes"; "Booker T. Washington and His New Home"; and "Danish West Indies," *New Age*, May 30, 1902, 1.
34. "Women's Club Notes," *New Age*, May 30, 1902, 1.
35. "Pertinent Facts Regarding Our Position," *New Age*, May 30, 1902, 2.
36. "Pertinent Facts Regarding Our Position."
37. "Local Notes," *New Age*, July 4, 1902, 4; "Local Notes," *New Age*, August 24, 1902, 4; "Our Dope Book," *New Age*, September 6, 1902, 1.
38. Literacy rates recorded in the U.S. census. See "Montana—Race and Hispanic Origin: 1870 to 1990."
39. From our short window in Black life in Butte during 1902, it seems that the community members not only read the *New Age*, but also supplemented their media diet with Black journals from places like Kansas City, Chicago, and Atlanta. When Quintard Taylor interviewed Black Montanans from this era, as well as their children in the 1970s, they affirmed that periodicals such as the *Chicago Defender* and W. E. B. Du Bois's the *Crisis* were very much part of the intellectual landscape of Black Montana—of course all these national publications began circulation years after 1902. Armeta Duncan, interview.
40. *New Age*, November 15, 1902, 2.
41. *New Age*, November 15, 1902, 2.
42. *New Age*, November 15, 1902, 2.
43. Armeta Duncan, interview. Most notable might be C. F. Jones, who was the president of the African American Mining and Development Company. Jones operated several claims in the mountains outside of Butte. Many of

his exploits appear in the *New Age*; for a more detailed column, see "We Are Rising," *New Age*, Butte, Montana, June 20, 1902, 4. Colonel Jim Collins of Butte, who later served as secretary of the Colored Democrats Club, also owned a copper mine near the city; as of 1902, he was still waiting for it to pay out. See "Col. Jim Collins," *New Age*, Butte, Montana, September 20, 1902, 1. Millie Ringold was also a prominent prospector who managed claims near Lewistown. See entry for "Millie Ringold," Black Past, accessed August 31, 2020, https://www.blackpast.org/?s=Millie+Ringold.
44. Walter Duncan, interview, April 5, 1974.
45. *New Age*, November 15, 1902, 2.
46. *New Age*, November 15, 1902, 2.
47. "Local Notes," *New Age*, December 6, 1902, 4.
48. "Local Notes."
49. "Women's Club Notes," *New Age*, May 30, 1902, 1.
50. Bacon, *Negro and the Atlanta Exposition*, 12–16.
51. Here Dorsey is clearly referencing C. F. Jones, a Black man from Butte who campaigned for Republican candidates in the city. Calling him "a candidate for the doorkeeper of the Legislature," Dorsey claimed that Party officials promised Jones that they "would show the appreciation of his services by giving him something to do in the Legislature." "Local Notes," *New Age*, January 3, 1903, 4.
52. Taylor, *In Search of the Racial Frontier*, 211.
53. Malone, Roeder, and Lang, *Montana*, 221.
54. "The Dope Book," *New Age*, June 27, 1902, 2.
55. "Heinze Changes Front," *New Age*, July 12, 1902, 4.
56. "Alaska Notes," *New Age*, August 9, 1902, 1.
57. "Heinze Changes Front."
58. "Heinze Changes Front."
59. "True Democracy," *New Age*, October 25, 1902, 1.
60. Malone, Roeder, and Lang, *Montana*, 226–27.
61. "African Methodist Church Almost Ready for Use," *Butte Inter-Mountain*, October 25, 1901, 18; Armeta Duncan, interview.
62. Mercier, *Anaconda*, 14.
63. Walter Duncan, interview.
64. A report on September 20 noted: "Editor Chris Dorsey and Manager John Duncan of *The New Age* . . . will leave for Bozeman Monday." By October 11, Dorsey had left the paper. See "Editor Chris Dorsey," *New Age*, September 20, 1902, 1; and *New Age*, October 11, 1902, 1.

65. *New Age*, October 11, 1902, 1.
66. "Our Candidates Who Are the Friends of the Negro," *New Age*, October 4, 1902, 2.
67. "Political Rally," *New Age*, October 18, 1902, 1.
68. "Political Rally."
69. "For an Untampered Judiciary," *New Age*, October 11, 1902, 2.
70. "Our Candidates."
71. "The Inter Mountain," *New Age*, September 6, 1902, 2; quoted sections from "Our Candidates."
72. "Didn't Want Potatoes," *Butte Inter Mountain*, January 24, 1902, 3.
73. For a history of Butte Inter Mountain, see "About the Butte Inter Mountain (Butte, Mont.) 1901–1912," Chronicling America, accessed August 31, 2020, https://chroniclingamerica.loc.gov/lccn/sn83025294/.
74. "May Be a Double Tragedy," *Butte Inter Mountain*, November 4, 1902, 9; "Colored Songbird Held for Shooting to Kill Entertains Other Prisoners," *New Age*, July 11, 7; and "Divine Woman is Hardly Heavenly," *New Age*, July 11, 7.
75. "A Rousing Meeting," *New Age*, October 25, 1902, 1.
76. Walter Duncan, interview.
77. Taylor, *In Search of the Racial Frontier*, 231.
78. Armeta Duncan, interview; Walter Duncan, interview.
79. "The Turning of the Lane," *New Age*, July 4, 1902, 2. For information on the Portland *New Age* (1896–1905), another Black newspaper in the Northwest, see "About the *New Age*," Chronicling America, accessed August 31, 2020, https://oregonnews.uoregon.edu/lccn/sn83025107/.
80. "John W. Duncan Obituary," *Montana Standard*, February 24, 1958, 15; Polk, *Butte City Directory*, 1904, 237.
81. "Local Notes," *New Age*, December 6, 1902, 4.
82. "Local Notes."
83. Armeta Duncan, interview; Walter Duncan, interview.
84. The August 4 "Emancipation Day" commemorated the day when the Loyal Creek Council formally declared that African Creeks would be considered full citizens of the Creek Nation. Why the Black community of Butte almost forty years later continued to recognize the holiday is one of the more intriguing mysteries in Montana history. It is possible that some residents were themselves African Creeks or Black Indians. The census is unhelpful here, and it is also likely that some Black citizens of Butte were recent transplants from Indian Territory and Oklahoma, where most

August 4 celebrations took place. At least one other account of an August 4 celebration appears in the Black paper of Helena in 1908: "All Readiness for the Big Doing's At Central Park on Aug. 4th," *Montana Plaindealer*, July 31, 1908, 1. See entry for "Emancipation Day (August 4th)," Black Past, accessed October 9, 2020, https://www.blackpast.org/african-american-history/emancipation-day-august-4th/. See also Zellar, *African Creeks*.
85. "Great Emancipation Day Celebration at Basin on the Fourth," *New Age*, August 9, 1902, 2.
86. "Views of the Great Northwest," *Chicago Defender*, March 22, 1913, 2.

4. Thinking with Magpies

1. Berry, "Magpies versus Livestock," 13–17.
2. Here Berry also draws our attention to the fact that colonial spaces are always defined in part by their potentiality. By recognizing that the land has certain native species living on it, Berry underscores what must be removed or changed so that land can meet its "potential." This discussion touches on issues explored by Frieda Knobloch in her study *The Culture of Wilderness: Agriculture as Colonization in the American West*. Knobloch focuses keenly on the genealogy of both "agriculture" and "colony," arguing that the two terms share deep ideological roots. Knobloch "presents components of western American agriculture with an eye to the colonial purposes that inform them." Magpies in a material sense, and Black westerners in a social sense, do not adhere to the imagined potential of the colony. Knobloch's chapter on weeds is especially pointed to this dynamic and suggests that Raymond Williams's assertion that the natural and social worlds inhabit one another is a useful frame for this history. See Knobloch, *Culture of Wilderness*.
3. Berry, "Magpies versus Livestock," 13.
4. The drought of 1917 in Montana had widespread environmental and social repercussions. The boom of the homesteading economy proliferated the number of occupants on Montana's prairies. As Sherlin Stillman Berry so keenly suggested in 1922, such an expansion had inevitable consequences on the ecosystem. He made his observations at a time when the state was reeling from mass population loss and homestead failures. Even as Berry recognized the biological realities of intensive farming on a natural landscape, he maintained that aggressive magpie behaviors like attacking sheep was likely the result of individual birds' violent proclivities, rather than being the natural of all magpies.

5. Veracini, *Settler Colonialism*; Wolfe, *Traces of History*.
6. Wolfe, "Settler Colonialism and the Elimination of the Native," 387.
7. Banner, *Possessing the Pacific*.
8. This is a deceptively simple observation insisted upon by many environmental historians whose work and methods I rely upon throughout this chapter. For the discussion here, it pushes us to the point at which we must acknowledge that the historical figures are not just talking about birds; people are never just talking about birds. Indeed, we often do not possess the skills necessary to "just talk about birds" even when we mean to. Magpies are just as numerous in Montana today as they were in 1910. Ask any person in the state their opinion of the birds, and they will likely go into a long-winded rant so thoroughly couched in the language of the human world that one wonders what, *exactly*, they are talking about. Montanans today, like Berry, who was an amateur ornithologist and professional scientist, still do not understand magpies enough to talk about them in any other way than as social metaphors. Magpies "harass" pets; "steal" food; "kill" animals, including other, more docile birds; and they "raid" and sometimes "destroy" crops. So we call them "bad." But even this most simple and universal characterization takes magpies—"the animals"—and transfers them into a moral, human universe where they commit "violent" acts and other "depredations." See also note 14 in this chapter.
9. Jon Coleman discusses a very similar relationship in his work on wolves. In *Vicious: Wolves and Men in America*, Coleman argues that colonization played a significant role in how humans and wolves interacted. As humans relied upon livestock to succeed in both extractive and settler colonizing projects, wolves' understandable adaptation to the new environment human created a circumstance in which "wolves symbolized the frustration and anxieties of colonization, and the canines paid in blood for their utility as metaphors." I suggest that magpies also represent the complexity, frustration, and anxiety of settler colonial processes. See Coleman, *Vicious*, 11.
10. Berry, "Magpies versus Livestock," 13.
11. Quoted in Pratt, "Advantages of Mingling Indians with Whites," 261.
12. Williams, *Problems in Materialism and Culture*, 67.
13. See Jacoby, *Crimes Against Nature*; Warren, *Hunter's Game*; Taylor, *Rise of the American Conservation Movement*; Tyrell, *Crisis of a Wasteful Nation*; Stern, *Eugenic Nation*; and Allen, "Culling the Herd."

14. Claude Leví-Strauss famously suggested that any number of things are "good to think with." William Cronon, speaking of Marsha Weisiger's *Dreaming of Sheep in Navajo Country*, wrote that sheep, too, were good to think with. Using Strauss's axiom, he said, "A rock is never just a rock, a tree a tree, a cow a cow." None of these objects or animals stands on its own; each weigh heavy with the meaning humans heap upon it. See Cronon, "Sheep Are Good to Think With," ix.
15. Myron Carpenter, the editor of the *Three Forks News* and *Belgrade Journal*, came up among a generation of conservationists that leaned heavily upon the belief that species like the magpie could be controlled and selected for extermination to ensure the survival of others. This species-centered approach would in time give way to an ecosystem-centered understanding, but it remained prevalent in the early twentieth century. Stout, *Montana*; see also Tyrell, *Crisis of the Wasteful Nation*, 173–88.
16. "Carpenter Makes Plea for Wild Lands in Our Mountains," *Powder River County Examiner*, April 29, 1921, n.p.
17. For a similar argument regarding the cultivation of the Great Plains region, see Cunfer, *On the Great Plains*, 16.
18. Leroy, "Black History in Occupied Territory," 2.
19. Taylor, *Rise of the American Conservation Movement*, 211.
20. For an important synthesis of racial regimes and Black portrayal in film, see Robinson, *Forgeries of Memory and Meaning*; on blackface minstrelsy and the "Jim Crow routine," see Berrey, *Jim Crow Routine*.
21. "West Indian Negroes," *Western News*, October 23, 1907, 7.
22. Warren, *Hunter's Game*.
23. Tyrell, *Crisis of a Wasteful Nation*.
24. See Tyrell, *Crisis of a Wasteful Nation*, 3–36.
25. Wolfe, *Traces of History*, 23.
26. Berry, "Magpies versus Livestock," 13.
27. See review of literature, note 13.
28. White, "Are You an Environmentalist?," 176.
29. In 1910 64.5 percent of Montana's population was rural, or living in a town of 2,500 people or less. Following the drought of 1917–18, the crash of the homesteading boom, and the subsequent state-wide depression in the 1920s and 1930s, the rural population dropped to 56.3 percent after World War II. For census information on Montana Populations 1900–1950, see "Number of Inhabitants: Montana," U.S. Census Bureau, accessed

May 1, 2018, https://www2.census.gov/prod2/decennial/documents/15276180v2p26ch1.pdf.

30. Just because many prominent environmental and conservationist movements or activist groups were formed and influenced by white racist ideologies does not mean that alternatives did not emerge from other racial communities. Black urban and suburban studies could be further extended to consider the environmental concerns that animated Black westerners both within and beyond the confines of city neighborhoods.
31. White, "Are You an Environmentalist?," 176.
32. Grant, *Early History of Glacier National Park*, 6.
33. White notes that figures such as York or Métis trappers are passed by in favor of Lewis and Clark and Daniel Boone as the historic white men whose labor comes to be mimicked by the leisure of the modern environmentalist ("Are You an Environmentalist?").
34. Taylor, *In Search of the Racial Frontier*, 50–52.
35. See Beckwourth, *Life and Adventures of James T. Beckwourth*; and Ravage, *Black Pioneers*.
36. In the creation of Montana's Glacier National Park, the governing logic for setting aside what George Bird Grinnell famously called the "Crown of the Continent" was first and foremost a project in Native land appropriation. In the *Early History of Glacier National Park*, written by the conservationist and eugenicist Madison Grant, the author tells how Grinnell first suggested that the federal government set aside the western forested range of the Blackfeet reservation for future resource management and a possible national park, arguing that the tribe "did not use that land" (5). In *Dispossessing the Wilderness* Mark Spence shows that the primary concern of the military control of both Yellowstone and Glacier National Parks—in which Buffalo Soldiers participated—was focused on the frictions of Indian inhabitants, leading to their eventual removal. Likewise, Pacific and settler colonial scholars have also explored this relationship. See Mar, "Carving Wilderness."
37. See Glasrud and Searles, *Buffalo Soldiers in the West*; Fowler, *Black Infantry in the West*; Koelle, "Pedaling on the Periphery"; Schubert, *On the Trail of the Buffalo Soldier*; and Wood, "After the West Was Won."
38. Photographic print of African-American Tenth Cavalry escorts to General Merritt's party, St. Mary's, 1894, 957-93, photo archives, Montana Historical Society Research Center, accessed August 31, 2020, http://mhs.mt.gov/Shpo/AfricanAmericans/ResourcesResearch/MHSCollections.

39. Photographic print of African American Ninth Cavalry members and other W. S. Webb excursion members at "Beaver Dick's" tepee, 1896, H-3715, photo archives, Montana Historical Society Research Center, accessed August 31, 2020, http://mhs.mt.gov/Shpo/AfricanAmericans/ResourcesResearch/MHSCollections.
40. "Walker Browning Obituary," *Billings Gazette*, February 8, 1925, 1.
41. "Local Notes," *New Age*, July 4, 1902, 4.
42. For examples of newspaper notes on African Americans in nature, see "Local Notes," *New Age*, July 4, 1902, 4; "Local Notes," *New Age*, August 9, 1902, 4; "Local Notes," *New Age*, August 24, 1902, 4; and "How the National Forests Serve the Public," *Montana Plaindealer*, July 12, 1907, 1.
43. "Local Notes," *New Age*, August 2, 1902, 4.
44. "The Dope Book," *New Age*, August 2, 1902, 4.
45. "Our Dope Book," *New Age*, September 6, 1902, 1.
46. Group photographs of the Pleasant Hour Club picnic, Colorado Gulch, 1926, PAC 2002-36.10–11, Photo Archives, Montana Historical Society Research Center, accessed August 31, 2020, http://mhs.mt.gov/Shpo/AfricanAmericans/ResourcesResearch/MHSCollections.
47. Allen, "Culling the Herd," 59; see also Stern, *Eugenic Nation*, 139–72.
48. Though these movements may seem to have existed on opposite ends of the political spectrum, several factors led to a small group of progressives embracing both. Historian and biologist Garland Allen noted that, for such individuals, "eugenics and conservation were intertwined by both vision and methodology" ("Culling the Herd," 59).
49. Allen, "Culling the Herd," 65.
50. Allen, "Culling the Herd," 65.
51. Stern, *Eugenic Nation*, 145–51.
52. A wealth of sources explore the intersection of preservation and eugenics, with specific attention being paid to Charles Goethe and Madison Grant. Early works such as Susan Schrepfer's *The Fight to Save the Redwoods: A History of Environmental Reform, 1917–1978* spends much of the early chapters addressing the impact that eugenicist ideology might have had on the nation's leading conservationists. Alexandria Stern's work *Eugenic Nation*, on the rise of eugenics in the sociopolitical climate of California in the early twentieth century could almost double as a history of early conservationists.
53. After founding and presiding over various state and national eugenics organizations, these wealthy elites likewise established various con-

servation groups, most notably the Save-the-Redwoods League (Stern, *Eugenic Nation*, 145–51). The history of racial animalization is an interesting corner of race studies. Nineteenth- and twentieth-century racist culture animalized many racial and ethnic groups. A useful study that lays out an excellent sampling of recent literature is Peterson, *Bestial Traces*; Peter Coates traces the parallels between the immigration of plants and animals—namely, birds—and the human immigration in the United States especially from 1880–1920 in *Strangers on the Land*.

54. Du Bois has a great deal to say on this issue in his 1897 essay "The Conservation of Races." In it Du Bois examines the scientific consensus of the turn of the century, with regards to biological race, and finds it wanting. He rejects the notion that races exist in any physical, scientific sense beyond that of melatonin and instead argues for race classification based on sociohistorical qualifications. The acclaimed philosopher and historian Kwame Anthony Appiah notes that Du Bois presents a dialectic between the claim to equality and a simultaneous claim to a unique contribution that only the "negro race" could offer. In this sense, Appiah claims, "the white race and its racial Other are not related as superior to inferior but as complementarians." With this understood, Du Bois stands in the midst of eugenicists like Grant and Pinchot, asserting that a common ancestry—derived from the very Darwinian science those same progressives applied to society—meant that whites and Blacks were equal. Where Grant saw African Americans as the dangerous, weed-like masses, choking out the life from redwoods, the white race, Du Bois allowed for no such distinction to be made. African Americans, too, were as the threatened redwoods, in danger of regressing to a state in which they would be unable to offer humanity their unique gift. See Du Bois, "Conservation of Races"; and Appiah, "Uncompleted Argument," 25.

55. "How the National Forests Serve the Public," *Montana Plaindealer*, July 12, 1907, 1.

56. Jefferson was perhaps misled on the elevation of Butte, which sits roughly a mile above sea level. "Reverend D. A. Jefferson of Butte to the Dallas Express," *Montana Plaindealer*, July 12, 1907, 1.

57. A review of the recent scholarship pertaining to African Americans and the environmental and conservation movements reveals the extent to which this history is seen as a national concern. Carolyn Finney, Dorceta Taylor, Mark Stoll, and others all consider the broader role and purpose that conservation played in racial politics. The scholarly scaffolding erected

around concepts of national vitality and social justice is very much akin to the underlying concerns of the 1964 Wilderness and Civil Rights Acts. Indeed, Finney argues that the two should not be so easily separated from one another, and thus that theories in environmental and social justice retain common epistemological moorings. Likewise, Taylor contextualizes issues of race and class within the national arena of early conservation movements in America, where stereotypes of southern Blacks affected the ways that white, middle-class conservationists constructed myths of Black nature experiences. See Finney, *Black Faces, White Spaces*; and Taylor, *Rise of the American Conservation Movement*.
58. Stoll, "Religion and Environmental Activism," 160.
59. Stoll, "Religion and Environmental Activism," 160.
60. Stoll, "Religion and Environmental Activism," 160.
61. Fiege, *Republic of Nature*, 492.
62. For whiteness as ownership, see Du Bois, *Darkwater*, 18; see also "The Man Child," in Baldwin, *Going to Meet the Man*, 64, cited in Japtok, "Gospel of Whiteness," 489.
63. See Lipsitz, "Possessive Investment in Whiteness"; and Harris, "Whiteness as Property."
64. Yet we must also ask ourselves, how could such substantial racial monuments have been erected in Montana's cultural memory without being overtly stated and constantly scrutinized? Martin Japtok, in his essay "The Gospel of Whiteness: Whiteness in African American Literature," makes the important distinction that whiteness never considers itself as "white"; rather, it establishes itself as the standard and norm against which all others are measured. George Lipsitz states that "as the unmarked category against which difference is constructed, whiteness never has to speak its name, never has to acknowledge its role as an organizing principle in social and cultural relations" (quoted in Japtok, "Gospel of Whiteness," 489).
65. Du Bois, *Darkwater*, 2.
66. "Great Emancipation Day Celebration at Basin on the Fourth," *New Age*, August 9, 1902, 2.
67. See "Emancipation Day (August 4th)"; and Zellar, *African Creeks*.
68. "Emancipation Day," *Montana Plaindealer*, July 29, 1910, 1.
69. The geography of the valley in relation to Gordon's home is significant to understand to what ends many African Americans went to commune with nature. While Rose Gordon's lifelong home in the small town of White Sulphur Springs lay near the south end of what is known as the Smith

River Valley, the famous river and its stunning canyon walls, adjacent meadows, and dense forests were actually found many miles to the north.
70. Gordon, "Gone Are the Days," MHS.
71. Du Bois, *Darkwater*, 2.
72. The best work on Taylor Gordon is Johnson, *Can't Stand Still*, especially 15–25.
73. Gordon, "Gone Are the Days," MHS.
74. Stoll, "Religion and Environmental Activism," 160.
75. Coeditor of the *New Age* Chis Dorsey wrote eloquently of the mountains and rivers of Alaska while on a trip there with his employer, copper magnate Augustus Heinze: "We started on a trip up the channel of the Alaskan coast . . . the grandeur of the scenery and the remarkable incidents of which are almost impossible to describe in a limited newspaper article." Dorsey continued to describe his adventure in terms such as "the grandeur and sublimity of the mountain scenery . . . which one never tires of." See Dorsey, "Alaska Notes," *New Age*, August 9, 1902, 1.
76. Berry, "Magpies versus Livestock," 13.

5. Colonial Kinships

1. "Peace! Prosperity! Union!!," *Montana Plaindealer*, March 5, 1909, 1.
2. "Peace! Prosperity! Union!!"
3. "Los Angeles in History Making First Inter-Racial Marriage," *California Eagle*, November 25, 1948, n.p.
4. Molina, *How Race Is Made in America*, 120.
5. *Senate Journal of the Legislature of the State of Montana*, 1909, 11th sess., 386.
6. Michele Mitchell notes that the 1890s was a time of intense Afrocentric examination and self-examination when it came to matters of sexuality and the family. Many early reformers saw intermarriage as part of the slow degradation of the Black race, or as an attempt to separate one's self from the Black community by marrying "out" (11). Here Bass may be giving voice to this particular sentiment. See Mitchell, *Righteous Propagation*, 11, 32, 43.
7. See tables 3 and 4, in this book; 1910–30 individual city data on marriage status derived from census enumerations, Research of the Montana Historical Society, accessed August 31, 2020, http://mhs.mt.gov/Shpo/AfricanAmericans/ResourcesResearch.
8. On relational "racial scripts" see Molina, *How Race Is Made in America*.

9. Malone, Roeder, and Lang, *Montana*, 211–13.
10. Stoler's argument is laid out thoroughly in *Carnal Knowledge and Imperial Power*, 79–111. Even though her analysis focuses on the French Indochina colonies and Netherland Indies, she nevertheless manages to speak to structures of colonial writ large. Operating under the Foucauldian principle of biopower, Stoler probes the relationship between the Métissage and the white colonials to show the connection between race, sex, and colonial rule. Mirroring the argument of this chapter, Stoler addresses intermarriage and its prohibition in colonial spaces as well (16, 43).
11. For a useful introduction to blood quantum, see Spruhan, "Legal History of Blood Quantum"; Villazor, "Blood Quantum Land Laws"; Berger, "Red," 591; and Ellinghaus, "Benefits of Being Indian."
12. This has been especially documented among the five nations in Indian Territory. Among the Creek, for instance, David Chang notes that Blacks as well as whites took advantage of marriage customs to gain access to kinship networks and clan membership. See, Chang, *Color of the Land*, 21–22; see also Field, *Growing up with the Country*; and Miles, *Ties That Bind*. This was not the case for many Métis and even the Little Shell and Chippewa Tribes of central Montana, who until 1917 moved from town to town across the state, earning them the moniker of wandering tribes. See Roeder, Malone, and Lang, *Montana*, 17.
13. See Shah, *Stranger Intimacies*.
14. For a Montana example of the effects of Allotment, see Smith, "Politics of Allotment."
15. West, *Contested Plains*, 185–89.
16. "An act prohibiting marriage between white persons and negroes, or persons of negro blood, and between white persons and Indians, Chinese, and Japanese, and making such marriages void, and prescribing punishment for solemnizing such unions" (Senate bill no. 71, 1907 SJ 140, 206).
17. It would be wrong to assume that Muffly was himself a southerner; he was actually born in Montana to Irish immigrant parents. This touches on misconceptions of region and ideology that often occur in Montana's history, especially around the supposedly southern roots of the mostly northern "Vigilantes." Joseph Bass did not think that Muffly was a southerner; rather, he saw the influences of southern racial ideology in Muffly's actions. 1910 U.S. Federal Census, Beaver Creek, Broadwater, Montana; Roll: T624_829; Page: 4B; Enumeration District: 0002; FHL microfilm: 1374842.

18. Patrick Wolfe discusses, if imperfectly, the connection between Indianness and Blackness within a settler colonial structure in his landmark article "Settler Colonialism and the Elimination of the Native," 387–88.
19. Jacobs, *White Mother to a Dark Race*, 69–70.
20. Search for "Marriage License for Prof. Z. A. Coleman and Mary A. Laughlin," Ancestry.com, accessed October 12, 2020, http://www.ancestry.com.
21. Coleman carried the honorific "professor," often a title given to pianists.
22. The 1890 Montana census, which would have provided the most information about their lives, was lost in a Washington DC, fire in 1920.
23. Here, descriptors like "fair" and "white" can better be understood as a reference to skin pigment or biology rather than racial comportment. See "A Case of Miscegenation," *Helena Independent*, January 16, 1891, 5.
24. "Case of Miscegenation."
25. "Case of Miscegenation."
26. "Case of Miscegenation."
27. Identifying her as Mary Leonard rather than with the common Irish surname Laughlin may be read in several different ways. It may just be that the reporter got the name wrong on accident, or that Laughlin had chosen to go by Leonard around Helena rather than her legal name. It might also have been that the paper changed her name to make their story of the couple fooling the minister more believable. Montana had a very large Irish population in its cities, and any reader—including the minister, for that matter—would have readily questioned a woman with a prominent Irish name claiming that she was Black. Unlike in Chicago, New York, or Boston, there was significantly less debate in Montana as to whether Irish were considered white or not.
28. Miscegenation and its governing laws in the American West and Montana is an especially rich field for scholarship. The seminal work in this subfield is Peggy Pascoe's sublime book *What Comes Naturally: Miscegenation and the Making of Race in America*. Pascoe succeeds to place the unique history of race in the American West within a larger, national context; in many ways, she places the West at the center of the creation of racial categories in twentieth-century America. Historian Anne Hyde also provides important temporal perspective to the field in her study *Empires, Nations, and Families: A New History of the North American West, 1800–1860*. By placing intermarriage with Indigenous peoples rooted in the history of the fur trade in the West, Hyde provides the starting point to understanding race and sexuality later in the nineteenth and twentieth

centuries. Specific to settler colonialism, Margaret Jacobs shows the devastating connections between sexuality and colonial policies of erasure and cultural genocide in her book *White Mother to a Dark Race*. Though not specific to the American West, Michele Mitchell's study *Righteous Propagation* analyzes the discourse about sex and race within the African American community at the end of the nineteenth and early twentieth centuries. Tellingly, Mitchell also makes the connections between the tightening of bodily control and the expansionist, imperial project of the United States in the Pacific (67–78). Another useful collection is Hodes, *Sex, Love, and Race*.

29. "Case of Miscegenation."
30. Miles, "Long Arm of the South?"; see also Taylor and Moore, *African American Women Confront the West*, 128–30.
31. I am so much indebted to the archival work and scholarship of Ken Robison, who has kept the light burning, so to speak, for Black history in Montana for many decades. See Robison, "On Being a Black American in Territorial Fort Benton, Parts 1 and 2," Historical Black Americans in Northern Montana, accessed January 1, 2018, http://blackamericansmt.blogspot.com/2009/05on-being-black-american-in-territorial.html.
32. Pascoe, *What Comes Naturally*, 85–93.
33. See note 23.
34. The Colemans disappear from the historical record after the *Independent* runs its piece. The census that would tell us the most about ZA and Mary, the 1890 federal enumeration, was infamously destroyed in a fire in Washington DC. Montana's census was among the most completely destroyed. They are not listed in Great Falls or elsewhere in Montana by 1900, nor are they listed in city directories across the state, suggesting they left Montana sometime before the end of the century.
35. "May Be a Double Tragedy," *Butte Inter Mountain*, Tuesday, November 4, 1902, 9.
36. "May Be a Double Tragedy."
37. "May Be a Double Tragedy."
38. "Two Victims to Their Sins," *Butte Inter Mountain*, Thursday, November 6, 1902, 6.
39. "The Famous Zanzibar-Pekin Is No More," *Montana Plaindealer*, January 4, 1907, 4; Lang, "Tempest on Clore Street."
40. "Butte in Brief," *Butte Inter Mountain*, Saturday, June 7, 1902, 3.
41. "Butte in Brief," 3.

42. *Treasure State*, February 20, 1909; quoted in Lang, "Helena, Montana's Black Community," 212–14.
43. Senate Journal of the Legislature of the State of Montana, 1909, 11th sess., 386; see also "Whipping Post Bill Is Passed by the House," *Daily Missoulian*, February 19, 1909, 1.
44. This is one point where I find Peggy Pascoe's analysis somewhat lacking. While I agree that miscegenation law reinforced racialist thinking and led to the continued structuring of racial categories in America, Pascoe shies away from making any claims about the social effect of marriage bans had on African Americans at the level of community experiences, specifically in states like Pascoe's home state of Montana, where the community was already precariously positioned. For Pascoe's discussions about Montana, see *What Comes Naturally*, 10, 91, 136.
45. Gullickson, "Black/White Interracial Marriage Trends."
46. The Columbia study names the 1910 data set as an outlier because the small sample size of only 0.4 percent. Gullickson, "Black/White Interracial Marriage Trends," 303.
47. This drop from twenty couples to only eight must be taken into consideration with the drop of the overall Black population during the same time by nearly 50 percent, close to the same as the decrease in interracial marriages. See tables 3 and 4.
48. I by no means wish to downplay the importance and role of symbolism in racial analysis.
49. Both Ian Tyrell and Peggy Pascoe make the argument that the rise of the eugenics movement played a significant role in the wave of anti-miscegenation laws that were passed in the early twentieth century. See Tyrell, *Crisis of the Wasteful Nation*, 181, 182, 184–85; and, Pascoe, *What Comes Naturally*, 7, 115–18.
50. Ian Tyrell focuses on the impact of eugenicists in Roosevelt's administration and various conservation bodies in *Crisis of the Wasteful Nation*, 173–88.
51. Scheper-Hughes and Lock, "Mindful Body," 6.
52. It is important to place this discourse within a settler colonial frame; otherwise, western miscegenation laws are too easily construed as reactionary to rest of the nation. This of course implies that somehow the West is not part of the nation, or in any way contributes to these broader historical discussions. I suggest that we also consider the regional factors at play in conjunction with national debates. Montana, North Dakota, and South

Dakota all instituted their first marriage bans in 1909, following other western states like Idaho, Colorado, Wyoming, Oregon, and California, which had implemented bans in the late nineteenth century. Pascoe, *What Comes Naturally*, 29, 30, 118.

53. Wong, *Racial Reconstruction*; Molina, *How Race Is Made in America*.
54. Stern, *Eugenic Nation*.
55. Chang, *Pacific Connections*.
56. It follows that the security and legitimacy of the nation-state as a political form is reliant upon the settler-state as stable and imminent project. The challenge for the nation-state has always been the instability of the settler-state. This is why the some of the most cutting critiques of the nation-state have come from thinkers engaged in settler colonial studies and Indigenous critique. See Kelley, "What Is Racial Capitalism?"; King, *Black Shoals*; and Moten, "Blackness and Nothingness."
57. Pascoe, *What Comes Naturally*, 133; see also Scott, *Seeing Like a State*.
58. Ann Stoler's "concept work" is particularly insightful here. She argues that concepts and their genealogies accrue force and meaning as they interact with other ideas and are never static. Stoler's powerful critique of "historical forgetting" leads her to formulate the more productive language of "colonial aphasia," a concept that works with and between occlusions and recursivity, both of which are at play here. In practice colonial aphasia tends to those histories that do not get taken up by colonial epistemologies and thus become inoperative in such societies. See Stoler, *Duress*, 123–35.
59. Much has been written about the impacts of Turner's frontier thesis. Kerwin Kline's massive historiographical study *Frontiers of Historical Imagination: Narrating the European Conquest of Native America, 1890–1990* stands as the most complete excursion through the afterlife of Turner's 1893 declarations.
60. Quoted in Washington, "African American History and the Frontier Thesis," 239.
61. Wood, *Black Majority*.
62. Though I fear that it causes more problems than it solves, Patrick Wolfe held rather tightly to the idea of passing frontiers, and to Turner himself, when describing the "progression" of settler societies. Partly because Wolfe was not a historian of the U.S. West, he really saw no issue with grafting settler colonial theory onto Turners frontier. Aside from naming no less than four possible dates for the "end" of the frontier in America, I fear that Wolfe risks isolating the many important insights his work

offers from western historians who would view his model as both overly structuralist and somewhat anachronistic. For Wolfe on the frontier, see *Traces of History*, 41, 142, 173–74.

63. 1910 U.S. Federal Census, Anaconda Ward 1, Deer Lodge, Montana; Roll: T624_831; Page: 14B; Enumeration District: 0012; FHL microfilm.

64. 1910 U.S. Federal Census, Anaconda Ward 1, Deer Lodge, Montana; Roll: T624_831; Page: 14B; Enumeration District: 0012; FHL microfilm.

65. Death records indicate that the Roys eventually moved to King County, Washington. The 1909 Anaconda city directory listed Roy as "removed to Salmon City, Idaho." The family also appears to have lived in Utah during the 1920 census. It is notable that Joseph listed himself as Black in that document, despite appearing in all others before and after as white. Utah did not repeal its marriage ban until 1963. Only Washington and New Mexico counted as western states that passed and repealed such laws before the twentieth century. 1920 U.S. Federal Census, Ogden Ward 3, Weber, Utah; Roll: T625_1869; Page: 16A; Enumeration District: 159. See also "Death Certificate for Joseph Walker Roy," Washington Death Certificates, 1907–1960, Ancestry.com, accessed October 12, 2020, http://www.ancestry.com; and 1909 R. L. Polk & Co. City Directory for Anaconda, Montana, 192.

66. Miles, "Long Arm of the South?"

67. See tables 3 and 4.

68. See tables 3 and 4.

69. 1910 U.S. Federal Census, Missoula Ward 4, Missoula, Montana; Roll: T624_834; Page: 2A; Enumeration District: 0070; FHL microfilm: 1374847. 1930 U.S. Federal Census, Missoula, Montana; Roll: 1259; Page: 3A; Enumeration District: 0014; FHL microfilm: 2340994.

70. Data on singles 15–40 derived from the 1910 and 1930 U.S. Federal Censuses, African American populations, "Montana—Race and Hispanic Origin: 1870 to 1990."

71. "Marriage Certificate for Richard Fisher and Belle Ward" (August 15, 1925), Ancestry.com, accessed August 31, 2020, https://www.ancestry.com/imageviewer/collections/61478/images/47792_554304-01593?treeid=&personid=&hintid=&queryId=1de356cf6a07a6069d0859544f79f806&usePUB=true&_phsrc=YIX25&_phstart=successSource&usePUBJs=true&pId=900043831.

72. "Marriage License for Woodrow Driver and Mary Mundy" (January 3, 1940), Ancestry.com, accessed August 31, 2020, https://www.ancestry.com/imageviewer/collections/61578/images/48279_555323-00413?treeid

=&personid=&hintid=&queryId=4f885789fa963abf4817b3c65aa7af2d&usePUB=true&_phsrc=YIX27&_phstart=successSource&usePUBJs=true&pId=90233325; "Marriage License for Felix Driver and Ruth Mundy" (January 20, 1942), Ancestry.com, accessed August 31, 2020, https://www.ancestry.com/imageviewer/collections/61578/images/48279_555260-00665?treeid=&personid=&hintid=&queryId=0cc2e2dd852b8de7acd815e67b2319f7&usePUB=true&_phsrc=YIX30&_phstart=successSource&usePUBJs=true&pId=95350.

73. Data on singles 15–40 derived from the 1910 and 1930 U.S. Federal Censuses, African American populations, "Montana—Race and Hispanic Origin: 1870 to 1990."
74. Pascoe, *What Comes Naturally*, 243.
75. Gordon, "Gone Are the Days," MHS, 83, 132.
76. "Women's Club Notes," *New Age*, May 30, 1902, 1.
77. "Death Certificate for James Jackson" (August 15, 1960), Montana: State Deaths, 1907–2016, Ancestry.com, accessed August 31, 2020, https://www.ancestry.com/imageviewer/collections/5437/images/47791_1220706333_0534-00260?treeid=&personid=&hintid=&queryId=58e0c81b7f10fb60cb6b0feebad8158e&usePUB=true&_phsrc=YIX31&_phstart=successSource&usePUBJs=true&pId=919561.
78. Pascoe, *What Comes Naturally*, 133.
79. "World War I Draft Registration Card for Fred U. Harris," U.S. World War I Draft Registration Cards, 1917–1918, Ancestry.com, accessed October 12, 2020, http://www.ancestry.com; "Death Certificate for Emily Harris," May 15, 1924, Washington Death Certificates, 1907–1960, Ancestry.com, accessed October 12, 2020, http://www.ancestry.com.
80. Bozeman was still a small town at this point. Though several Black women lived in town, they were all either elderly or married. The once-large Chinese population, which had consisted mostly of men, was also negligible. It is unclear if any Native women lived in Bozeman. Some may have worked around the nearby Fort Parker. Regardless, for Black men looking for partners, Bozeman offered none. 1910 U.S. Federal Census, Bozeman Ward 3, Gallatin, Montana; Roll: T624_832; Page: 8B; Enumeration District: 0139; FHL microfilm: 1374845. 1930 U.S. Federal Census, Tacoma, Pierce, Washington; Roll: 2510; Page: 8A; Enumeration District: 0125; FHL microfilm: 2342244.
81. See Bozeman census data, 1910–1930, "Montana—Race and Hispanic Origin: 1870 to 1990."

6. History among the Sediments

1. Federal Land Patents, State Volumes, Bureau of Land Management, General Land Office Records, Washington DC, accessed August 31, 2020, https://glorecords.blm.gov/details/patent/default.aspx?accession=566771&docClass=SER&sid=py1ptgm4.glg. See also National Archives and Records Administration (NARA); Washington DC, NARA Series: Passport Applications, January 2, 1906—March 31, 1925; Roll #: 2440; Volume #: Roll 2440—Certificates: 377350–377849, March 8, 1924–March 10, 1924.
2. Bottomly-O'Looney and Lambert, *Montana's Charlie Russell*.
3. Federal Land Patents, State Volumes, Bureau of Land Management, General Land Office Records, Washington DC. See also National Archives and Records Administration (NARA); Washington DC, NARA Series: Passport Applications, January 2, 1906—March 31, 1925; Roll #: 2440; Volume #: Roll 2440—Certificates: 377350–377849, March 8, 1924–March 10, 1924.
4. Malone, Roeder, and Lang, *Montana*, 280.
5. In 1910 64.5 percent of Montana's population was rural, or living in a town of 2,500 people or less. Following the drought of 1917–18, the crash of the homesteading boom, and the statewide depression in the 1920s and 1930s, the rural population dropped to 56.3 percent by 1945. During this time the six largest cities in Montana grew at a rate of 16 percent from 1910 to 1920. Decreases in rural populations and the decrease of urbanites in the six largest cities by percentage from 1910 to 1930 reflect that urban population increases occurred in medium-sized towns across the state, typically closer to ranching and agricultural areas. Bozeman, Havre, Miles City, Kalispell, Lewistown, and Livingston saw steady increases, representing 5 percent of the population in 1910 and doubling to 10 percent by 1950. While African American communities in the six largest cities fell by 27.5 percent from 1910 to 1920 (while those cities experienced an overall growth rate of +16 percent), the Black population of medium-sized towns dropped from 216 to 142 individuals (-34 percent), further accentuating the impact of urbanization on Black Montanans. For census information on Montana populations from 1900 to 1950, see U.S. Census Information, "Number of Inhabitants: Montana," accessed October 12, 2020, https://www2.census.gov/prod2/decennial/documents/15276180v2p26ch1.pdf. For census information for African Americans in Montana, see "Resources and Research," Montana African American Heritage Resources, accessed August 31, 2020, http://mhs.mt.gov/Shpo/AfricanAmericans/ResourcesResearch. See also tables 1 and 2.

6. See the appendix.
7. National Archives and Records Administration (NARA), Washington DC, NARA Series, passport applications, January 2, 1906–March 31, 1925; Roll #: 2440; Volume #: Roll 2440—Certificates: 377350–377849, March 1924–March 10, 1924.
8. Malone, Roeder, and Lang, *Montana*, 297.
9. Polk, *Helena City Directory*, 1908, 227; Harrison listed as porter at Eddy Hotel, in Polk, *Helena City Directory*, 1914, 207.
10. Bottomly-O'Looney and Lambert, *Montana's Charlie Russell*.
11. Polk, *Tacoma City Directory*, 1914, 371.
12. Stegner, *Where the Bluebird Sings*.
13. Intellectual historians might see such a task as this last chapter as one that seeks to (very) loosely establish a genealogy of settler colonial *dispositif* in Montana's history. Colonial sedimentation—or, at the very least, its conceptual scaffolding—shares epistemological roots with Stoler's "ruination" and "debris," and thus Foucault's *dispositif* as well.
14. Taylor, *In Search of the Racial Frontier*, 212.
15. Anna Lowenhaupt Tsing observes that when writing about a history where the defining characteristic is one of "ruination," one must be diligent in pursuing new "arts of noticing." Tsing argues that one such art of noticing requires the historian to think through "precarity." Precarity (interchangeable with precariousness) "is the condition of being vulnerable to others." More than just a relationship of unequal standing, precarity is also a force that shapes historical development. She continues, "Unpredictable encounters transform us; we are not in control, even of ourselves. Unable to rely on a stable structure of community, we are thrown into shifting assemblages, which remake us as well as our others." A world thrust into a state of precarity no longer adheres to the designs one has made for it; moreover, according to Tsing, "thinking through precarity changes social analysis. A precarious world is a world without teleology." In many ways Tsing's precarity thesis is a useful lens through which we might read the history of Montana in the 1920s and 1930s: events shattered the status quo, and sent the ecological, economic, and cultural stability of Montana into flux. See Tsing, *Mushroom at the End of the World*, 20.
16. Montana historians Malone, Roeder, and Lang discuss the extractive economy at length in their chapters "The Mining Frontier," and "Copper and Politics, 1880–1910," in Malone, Roeder, and Lang, *Montana*, 201–31.

17. For a helpful introduction to unions, reformers, and constructions of the "body," see Poovey, *Making a Social Body*.
18. Mercier, *Anaconda*, 14.
19. Mercier, *Anaconda*, 14.
20. Mercier, *Anaconda*, 235n63.
21. For occupation statistics for Anaconda, 1910–30, see "Montana—Race and Hispanic Origin: 1870 to 1990."
22. Frank Zogart, interview by Laurie Mercier, November 18, 1982, tape 2, side A (89–117), OH-411, MHS.
23. This is also a feeling that Frank Zogart alludes to in his 1982 interview (see note 22).
24. Mercier, *Anaconda*, 108.
25. John Driver, a Black man from Anaconda who worked at the smelter during his high school and early college years, recalled that the only jobs Black smeltermen could get on the hill were places of extreme physical danger, such as being exposed to arsenic up near the smelter furnaces, feeding the fires, or working in sections where dangerous trains and cars were always a threat. Interview by Kate Hampton, Anaconda, Montana, May 15, 2008, audio file, Montana Historical Society Research Center, Helena, Montana.
26. For neighborhood and geographic information see "Mapping Historic Neighborhoods," MHPRF, accessed August 31, 2020, http://mhs.mt.gov/Shpo/AfricanAmericans/Places/Sanborns.
27. Anthony Wood, "Mrs. Browning's Furnished Rooms," MHPRF, accessed May 1, 2018, https://mhs.mt.gov/Shpo/AfricanAmericans/Places/PropertyRecords.
28. Limerick, *Legacy of Conquest*, 61–62.
29. For neighborhood and geographic information see "Mapping Historic Neighborhoods," MHPRF, accessed August 31, 2020, http://mhs.mt.gov/Shpo/AfricanAmericans/Places/Sanborns.
30. For more information on African American Churches in Montana, see Anthony Wood, "African American Churches of Montana," MHPRF, accessed August 31, 2020, http://mhs.mt.gov/Shpo/AfricanAmericans/History/AfricanAmericanChurches.
31. "Noted Bishop to Dedicate Church," *Billings Gazette*, July 23, 1909, 3; see also Susan Olp, "Wayman Chapel's Roots Go Way Back," *Billings Gazette*, September 8, 2006, https://billingsgazette.com/lifestyles/wayman-chapel-s-roots-go-way-back/article_2695ff4e-5496-5dad-9acd-b340563133dd.html.

32. Anthony Wood, "Wayman Chapel," MHPRF, accessed May 1, 2018, http://mhs.mt.gov/Portals/11/shpo/AfricanAmerican/PropertyRecords/24yl2047.pdf.
33. "Projects Get Consideration, Plan to Call Meeting to Sound out Opinions," *Billings Gazette*, July 12, 1935, 1; "City Projects Are Discussed," *Billings Gazette*, August 31, 1938, 5; "Municipal Building Programs Highlights Review of City's Affairs for Last 12 Months," *Billings Gazette*, January 1, 1939, 6.
34. For several examples of Billings papers tying crime with the Southside neighborhood and minorities, see "Mexican Charged with Annoying Girl, Dismissed," *Billings Gazette*, January 13, 1914, 2. This article states that while attempting to hold up three Black men in the Southside neighborhood, one man, Otto Mason, shot the "Mexican, wounding him," then goes on to note that the Black man served one year in prison. See also "Charge Vagrancy," *Billings Gazette*, February 9, 1924, 2; and "Chink 'Doctor' is Caught in Dope Dragnet," *Billings Gazette*, March 23, 1924, 10.
35. On the matter of sensationalized crime reporting during the late 1930s, readers may note similar patterns of increased surveillance and policing that characterize turn-of-the-century urban spaces. Khalil Muhammed has tracked the rise of the overpolicing of racial minorities and Black neighborhoods during roughly this same era. To whatever extent Southside residents were criminalized is unknown, but the different demographic realities between eastern cities and Billings suggest that its effects were not nearly as pronounced. Still, the Southside was increasingly viewed as "degraded" in various ways, economically and environmentally, after mid-century. See Muhammed, *Condemnation of Blackness*.
36. Ashely, "Montana's Refining Industry," 22.
37. "Yale Oil of South Dakota-Billings Facility," Montana Department of Environmental Quality, Data and Resources, accessed April 10, 2018, http://deq.mt.gov/Land/statesuperfund/yaleoilsd.
38. Sturdevant, "White Hoods under the Big Sky."
39. Erickson, "'Come Join the KKK in the Old Town Tonight': The Ku Klux Klan in Harlowton, Montana, during the 1920s," *Montana: The Magazine of Western History* 64, no. 3 (Autumn 2014): 51.
40. *Laurel Outlook*, September 16, 1925, quoted in Sturdevant, "White Hoods under the Big Sky," 317.
41. Sturdevant, "White Hoods under the Big Sky," 318–19.
42. "Montana Indians Lynch Man," *Chicago Defender*, November 6, 1926, 1.
43. "U.S. Government Dishonest, Violated Its Indian Treaties," *Chicago Defender*, October 31, 1925, 1; "Recognizing Indians," *Chicago Defender*, May 31, 1924, A14.

44. "Civilized!," *Chicago Defender*, November 13, 1926, A2.
45. For Black populations of Livingston and Lewiston, see "Montana—Race and Hispanic Origin: 1870 to 1990."
46. *Anaconda Standard*, February 6, 1923, quoted in Sturdevant, "White Hoods under the Big Sky," 317.
47. Taylor, *In Search of the Racial Frontier*, 223.
48. Malone, Roeder, and Lang, *Montana*, 293.
49. Ober, "CCC Experience in Glacier National Park."
50. Malone, Roeder, and Lang, *Montana*, 297.
51. Charles McDonald, interview by Laurie Mercier, November 18, 1982, tape 2, side B (50–60), OH-262, MHS.
52. Taylor, *In Search of the Racial Frontier*, 228–29.
53. Taylor, *In Search of the Racial Frontier*, 231.
54. Taylor, *In Search of the Racial Frontier*, 231.
55. The Montana Federation of Colored Women's Clubs (MSFCWC) is one of the most consistently studied topics in the state's Black history. The archive of this fascinating organization is held at the Montana Historical Society. Historians there have written on the MSFCWC extensively, for an overview of that scholarship, see "'Lifting as We Climb': The Activism of the Montana Federation of Colored Women's Clubs," Women's History Matters, July 1, 2014, http://montanawomenshistory.org/lifting-as-we-climb-the-activism-of-the-montana-federation-of-colored-womens-clubs/.
56. See tables 1.1 and 1.2 in chapter 1.
57. This document is also remarkable for the nature in which it was written. Beyond the plain-language approach, committees consisted of people of many backgrounds, with relatively few having experience in constitutional law or backgrounds as lifetime politicians. The result is a document that many have noted represents a distinct character of Montana and its cultural memory. Historian Cody Ferguson examines this moment in Montana's history in "Beyond Oro Y Plata."
58. Montana State Constitution, article 2, section 3, Montana Judicial Branch, accessed March 27, 2018, https://courts.mt.gov/portals/189/library/docs/72constit.pdf.
59. Montana State Constitution, article 2, section 3.
60. Perry, *We May Forever Stand*. See also Fiege, *Republic of Nature*, 331.
61. Raymond Johnson, interview by Quintard Taylor, March 3, 1974, Manuscripts, Archives, and Special Collections, Washington State University Libraries, Spokane, Washington, 2002.

62. Malone, Roeder, and Lang, *Montana*, 390–93.
63. Pascoe, *What Comes Naturally*, 220.
64. Pascoe, *What Comes Naturally*, 243.
65. "Four Measures Pass," *Independent Record*, January 20, 1953, 1.
66. For a history of the tribe now recognized as the Little Shell Chippewa, see Dusenberry, "Waiting for a Day"; Eder, "Question of Recognition."
67. Higgins, "House Joint Memorial No. 1," 44.
68. Quoted in "Providing Assistance for Certain Landless Indians in the State of Montana," report submitted by Committee on Interior and Insular Affairs, to accompany S. 2556, July 27, 1955, ProQuest U.S. Serial Set Digital Collection, accessed May 9, 2019, https://congressional-proquest-com.proxy.lib.umich.edu/congressional/result/congressional/congdocumentview?accountid=14667&groupid=95663&parmId=173AB445798.
69. "Montana Indians: Their History and Location," 55–56.
70. "Whipping Post Bill Is Passed By the House," *Daily Missoulian*, February 19, 1909, 1.
71. *Helena Independent*, February 3, 1953, 2–3.
72. "Lee Pleasant Driver Obituary," *Anaconda Standard*, January 12, 1935, 6.
73. Marriage license for John Driver and Marilyn Ryan, marriage index for years 1947–64, Idaho Department of Health and Welfare, Bureau of Vital Records and Health Statistics, Boise, Idaho, Ancestry.com, accessed October 12, 2020, http://www.ancestry.com.
74. John Driver, interview.
75. John Driver, interview.
76. John Driver, interview.
77. Stoler, *Duress*, 61.
78. Quoted in Pisani, *Water and American Government*, 123–53.
79. We might read some of that raw emotion into Russell's own contempt for modern white settler society. Scholars have noted that he drew more from his own idealized memories in 1880s and 1890s and his time living among the Blood in Canada, rather than any stated remorse for the violence of settler invasion, a narrative that his paintings recast in the quiet glory of numerous sunsets casting golden light on the lives mounted cowboys and Montana's "noble Indians." See Bottomly-O'Looney and Lambert, *Montana's Charlie Russell*.
80. Lambert and Bottomly-O'Looney, "Bob and Charlie," 50.

Epilogue

1. Gordon, *Great Arizona Orphan Abduction*.

2. "'Lifting as We Climb': The Activism of the Montana Federation of Colored Women's Clubs," Women's History Matters, July 1, 2014, http://montanawomenshistory.org/lifting-as-we-climb-the-activism-of-the-montana-federation-of-colored-womens-clubs/.
3. "Will Helena's Wilmot Collins Be Montana's First Black Mayor? Not Exactly, Historians Say," *Independent Record*, November 8, 2017, https://helenair.com/news/local/will-helenas-wilmot-collins-be-montanas-first-black-mayor-not-exactly-historians-say/article_aeb6ff03-98f2-56c3-b8c3-3aec7de62af5.html.
4. Gordon, "Gone Are the Days," MHS.

Bibliography

Archival Materials
Montana's African American Heritage Resources (MHPRF)
Montana Historical Society Collections, Helena, Montana (MHS)
   Manuscript Collections
      Charles Benton Power Papers. MC55a box 8–9.
      Emmanuel Taylor Gordon Papers, 1881–1980. MC150.
      Martha Edgerton Plassmann Papers. MC78.
      Rose Gordon, "Gone Are the Days" (unpublished manuscript), MC150, 11-2.
   Oral History Collections
      Alan M. Thompson Public Presentation. OH177.
      Albert J. Clark Interview. OH412.
      Charles D. McDonald Interview. OH262.
      Eugene Cox Interview. OH934.
      Frank Zogarts Interview. OH411.
      Mary Duncan Colley Interview. OH1812.
      Walter Duncan, Perdita Duncan, Elmo Fortune, William Fenter Interviews. OH483.
   Special Collections
      Dutrieuille Family Papers. SC785.
      Edwin W. Knight Letters. SC946.
Montana State Historic Preservation Office, Helena, Montana (MSHPO)
   National Record of Historic Places Documentation
      Delia Hagen, "African-American Heritage Places in Helena, MT," NRHP Multiple Properties Documentation Form. September 2016.
      Belt Commercial Historic District, NRHP Registration Form. 24CA826.
      Crump-Howard House, NRHP Registration Form. 24LC2450.
      Dorsey Grocery and Residence, NRHP Registration Form. 24LC2433.
      Haight-Bridgwater House, NRHP Registration Form. 24LC2272.
      Morgan-Case Homestead, NRHP Registration Form. 24GN0195.
      Samuel Lewis House, NRHP Registration Form. 24GA1502.

Union Bethel African Methodist Episcopal Church, NRHP Registration Form. 24CA0970.

Historic Property Record Forms

Allsup Family Home, Montana Historic Property Record Form. 24HL1623.

Armstrong Apartments, Montana Historic Property Record Form. 24SB1053.

Barnes Residence, Montana Historic Property Record Form. 24HL1624.

Conley Residence, Montana Historic Property Record Form. 24HL1626.

Dan Hurt Residence, Montana Historic Property Record Form. 24CR1340.

David and Katie Knott Residence, Montana Historic Property Record Form. 24CA1747.

Dorsey House, Montana Historic Property Record Form. 24MO1681.

Frank and Sarah Q. Walker Residence, Montana Historic Property Record Form. 24DL0822.

John and Armeta Duncan Residence, Montana Historic Property Record Form. 24SB0990.

Lee Pleasant Driver's Saloon and Club Rooms, Montana Historic Property Record Form. 24DL0821.

McDonald House, Montana Historic Property Record Form. 24FA1919.

Mrs. Browning's Furnished Rooms, Montana Historic Property Record Form. 24YL2046.

Oswald and Ada Smith House, Montana Historic Property Record Form. 24GA1953.

Shaffer's Chapel, Montana Historic Property Record Form. 24SB0991.

Taylor-Reed House, Montana Historic Property Record Form. 24CA1748.

Walter and Alyce Duncan Residence, Montana Historic Property Record Form. 24SB1054.

Wayman Chapel, Montana Historic Property Record Form. 24YL2047.

William and Gertrude Johnson Residence, Montana Historic Property Record Form. 24MO1682.

National Archives and Records Administration (NARA)

Washington DC, NARA Series: *Passport Applications, January 2, 1906–March 31, 1925.*

U.S. Federal Census

U.S. Federal Census, 1870, 1880, 1900, 1910, 1920, 1930. Federal Census Collection.

Washington State University Libraries, Pullman, Washington (WAUL)

Black Oral History Interviews, 1972–1974. Accession No.: 78-3 Manuscripts, Archives, and Special Collections.

A. E. Banks, John Driver, Armeta Duncan, Walter Duncan, Raymond Johnson, William Knott, Ethel Monroe, Thomas Walker, Ophelia Walker Interviews.

Published Works

Aarim-Heriot, Najia. *Chinese Immigrants, African Americans, and Racial Anxiety in the United States, 1848–82*. Urbana: University of Illinois Press, 2003.

Albright, Robert Edwin. "The American Civil War as a Factor in Montana Territorial Politics." *Pacific Historical Review* 6, no. 1 (March 1937): 36–46.

Alegria, Crystal. "The Last Will and Testament of Lizzie Williams: An African American Entrepreneur in 1870s Bozeman." Extreme History Project Lecture Series, Museum of the Rockies, Bozeman, Montana, February 16, 2017.

Alegria, Crystal, and Marsha Fulton. "Fraud at Fort Parker: How Corruption and Contracting Built Early Bozeman." *Montana: The Magazine of Western History* 66, no. 3 (Autumn 2016): 51–67.

Allen, Gerald. "'Culling the Herd': Eugenics and the Conservation Movement in the United States, 1900–1940." *Journal of the History of Biology* 46, no. 1 (Spring 2013): 31–72.

Allen, Nancy P. "Standing up for Liberty: Eliza Brown Davidson and the Custers." *Research Review: The Journal of the Little Bighorn Associates* 17, no. 1 (Winter 2003): 2–12.

Allmendinger, Blake. *Imagining the African American West*. Lincoln: University of Nebraska Press, 2005.

Anderson, Warwick. *The Cultivation of Whiteness: Science, Health, and Racial Destiny in Australia*. Durham NC: Duke University Press, 2006.

Appiah, Anthony. "The Uncompleted Argument: Du Bois and the Illusion of Race." *Critical Inquiry* 12, no. 1 (Autumn 1985): 21–37.

Arata, Laura J. *Race and the Wild West: Sarah Bickford, The Montana Vigilantes, and the Tourism of Decline, 1870–1930*. Norman: University of Oklahoma Press, 2020.

Arnesen, Eric. *Brotherhoods of Color: Black Railroad Workers and the Struggle for Equality*. Cambridge MA: Harvard University Press, 2001.

———. "Specter of the Black Strikebreaker: Race, Employment, and Labor Activism in the Industrial Era." *Labor History* 44, no. 3 (2003): 319–35.

Ayers, Edward L. *The Promise of the New South: Life after Reconstruction*. New York: Oxford University Press, 1992.

Bacon, Alice M. *The Negro and the Atlanta Exposition*. Baltimore: Trustees, 1896.

Bakken, Gordon Morris, and Brenda Farrington. *Racial Encounters in the Multi-Cultural West.* New York: Garland, 2000.

Baldwin, James. *Going to Meet the Man.* New York: Dial, 1965.

Banner, Stuart. *How the Indians Lost Their Land: Law and Power of the Frontier.* Cambridge MA: Harvard University Press, 2007.

———. *Possessing the Pacific: Land, Settlers, and Indigenous People from Australia to Alaska.* Cambridge MA: Harvard University Press, 2007.

Barker, Joanne, ed. *Sovereignty Matters: Locations of Contestation and Possibility in Indigenous Struggles for Self-Determination.* Lincoln: University of Nebraska Press, 2002.

Basso, Matthew L. *Meet Joe Copper: Masculinity and Race on Montana's World War II Home Front.* Chicago: University of Chicago Press, 2013.

Beckwourth, James P. *The Life and Adventures of James T. Beckwourth: Mountaineer, Scout and Pioneer.* Edited by T. D. Bonner. New York: Harper & Brothers, 1856.

Behan, Barbara Carol. "Forgotten Heritage: African Americans in the Montana Territory, 1864–1889." *Journal of African American History* 91, no. 1 (2006): 23–40.

Belich, James. *Replenishing the Earth: The Settler Revolution and the Rise of the Anglophone World, 1783–1939.* Oxford: Oxford University Press, 2009.

Benton-Cohen, Katherine. *Borderline Americans: Racial Division and Labor War in the Arizona Borderlands.* Cambridge MA: Harvard University Press, 2009.

Berardi, Gayle K., and Thomas W Segady. "The Development of African-American Newspapers in the American West: A Sociohistorical Perspective." *Journal of Negro History* 75, nos. 3–4 (1990): 96–111.

Berger, Bethany R. "Red: Racism and the American Indian." *UCLA Law Review* 56 (2008): 72–92.

Berlin, Ira, ed. *The Black Military Experience.* New York: Cambridge University Press, 1982.

———. *The Making of African America: The Four Great Migrations.* New York: Penguin, 2010.

Berrey, Stephen. *The Jim Crow Routine: Everyday Performances of Race, Civil Rights, and Segregation in Mississippi.* Chapel Hill: University of North Carolina Press, 2015.

Berry, S. Stillmen. "Magpies versus Livestock: An Unfortunate New Chapter in Avian Depredations." *Condor* 24, no. 1 (January–February 1922): 13–17.

Berwanger, Eugene. *The Frontier against Slavery: Western Anti-Negro Prejudice and the Slavery Extension Controversy.* Urbana: University of Illinois Press, 1967.

———. "Hardin and Langston: Western Black Spokesmen of the Reconstruction Era." *Journal of Negro History* 64, no. 2 (Spring 1979): 101–14.
———. *The West and Reconstruction*. Urbana: University of Illinois Press. 1981.
———. "Willian J. Hardin: Colorado Spokesman for Racial Justice, 1863–1873." *Colorado Magazine* 52, no. 1 (Winter 1975): 52–65.
Billington, Monroe. *New Mexico's Buffalo Soldiers, 1866–1900*. Niwot: University Press of Colorado, 1991.
Billington, Monroe Lee, and Roger D. Hardaway. *African Americans on the Western Frontier*. Boulder: University Press of Colorado, 1998.
Blackhawk, Ned. *Violence over the Land: Indians and Empires in the Early American West*. Cambridge MA: Harvard University Press, 2006.
Brady, Marilyn Dell. "Kansas Federation of Colored Women's Clubs, 1900–1930." *Kansas History* 9, no. 1 (Spring 1986): 19–30.
Bristol, Douglas, Jr. "From Outposts to Enclaves: A History of Black Barbers from 1715–1915." *Enterprise and Society* 5, no. 4 (December 2004): 594–606.
Bottomly-O'Looney, Jennifer, and Kirby Lambert. *Montana's Charlie Russell: Art in the Collection of the Montana Historical Society*. Helena: Montana Historical Society, 2014.
Brooks, James F., ed. *Confounding the Color Line: The Indian-Black Experience in North America*. Lincoln: University of Nebraska Press, 2002.
Broussard, Albert S. *Black San Francisco: The Struggle for Racial Equality in the West, 1900–1954*. Lawrence: University Press of Kansas, 1993.
———. *Expectations of Equality: A History of Black Westerners*. New York: Wiley-Blackwell, 2012.
Byrd, James W. "Afro-American Writers in the West." In *A Literary History of the American West*, edited by J. Golden Taylor, 1139–47. Fort Worth: Texas Christian University Press, 1987.
Byrd, Jodi. *The Transit of Empire: Indigenous Critiques of Colonialism*. Minneapolis: University of Minnesota Press, 2011.
Calvert, Jerry. *The Gibraltar: Socialism and Labor in Butte, Montana, 1895–1920*. Helena: Montana Historical Society, 1988.
Carper, James C. "The Popular Ideology of Segregated Schooling: Attitudes toward the Education of the Blacks in Kansas, 1854–1900." *Kansas History* 1, no. 4 (Winter 1978): 254–65.
Carroll, John M., ed. *The Black Military Experience in the American West*. New York: Liveright, 1971.
Chadwick, Robert. "Montana's Silver Mining Era: Great Boom and Great Bust." *Montana: The Magazine of Western History* 32, no. 2 (Spring 1982): 16–31.

Champion, Laurie, and Bruce Glasrud, eds. *The African American West: A Century of Short Stories*. Boulder: University Press of Colorado, 2000.

Chan, Sucheng, Douglas Daniels, Mario Garcia, and Terry Wilson, eds. *Peoples of Color in the American West*. Lexington MA: D. C. Heath, 1994.

Chang, David. *The Color of the Land: Race, Nation, and the Politics of Landownership in Oklahoma, 1832–1929*. Chapel Hill: University of North Carolina Press, 2010.

Chang, Kornel. *Pacific Connections: The Making of the U.S.-Canadian Borderlands*. Berkeley: University of California Press, 2012.

Chaudhuri, Nupur. "'We All Seem Like Brothers and Sisters': The African-American Community in Manhattan, Kansas, 1865–1940." *Kansas History* 14, no. 4 (Winter 1991): 270–88.

Christian, Garna L. *Black Soldiers in Jim Crow Texas, 1899–1917*. College Station: Texas A&M University Press, 1995.

Coates, Peter. *Strangers on the Land: American Perceptions of Immigrant and Invasive Species*. Berkeley: University of California Press, 2006.

Coleman, Jon. *Vicious: Wolves and Men in America*. New Haven CT: Yale University Press, 2004.

Coleman, Ronald. "A History of Blacks in Utah, 1825–1910." PhD diss., University of Utah, 1980.

Cooper, Brittney. *Beyond Respectability: The Intellectual Thought of Race Women*. Champaign: University of Illinois Press, 2017.

Cotroneo, Ross R., and Jack Dozier. "A Time of Disintegration: The Coeur d'Alene and the Dawes Act." *Western Historical Quarterly* 5, no. 4 (October 1974): 405–19.

Cox, Thomas C. *Blacks in Topeka: A Social History*. Baton Rouge: Louisiana State University Press, 1982.

Crockett, Norman L. *The Black Towns*. Lawrence: Regents Press of Kansas, 1979.

Cronon, William. *Nature's Metropolis: Chicago and the Great West*. New York: W. W. Norton, 1991.

———. "Sheep Are Good to Think With." In *Dreaming of Sheep in Navajo Country*, by Marsha Weisiger, ix–xiv. Seattle: University of Washington Press, 2009.

Cronon, William, ed. *Uncommon Ground: Rethinking the Human Place in Nature*. New York: W. W. Norton, 1996.

Cross, Gary. "Labor in Settler State Democracies: Comparative Perspectives on Australia and the U.S., 1860–1920." *Labor History*, 70 (May 1996): 1–24.

Cunfer, Geoff. *On the Great Plains: Agriculture and Environment*. College Station: Texas A&M Press, 2006.

Curtain, Mary Ellen. *Black Prisoners and Their World: Alabama, 1865–1900*. Charlottesville: University Press of Virginia, 2000.

Custer, Elizabeth. *"Boots and Saddles," or Life in Dakota with General Custer*. New York: Harper & Brothers, 1885.

———. *Tenting on the Plains*. New York: Harper & Brothers, 1887.

Dailey, Maceo C., Jr. "Neither 'Uncle Tom' nor 'Accommodationist': Booker T. Washington, Emmett Jay Scott, and Constructionalism." *Atlanta History: The History of Georgia and the South* 38, no. 4 (January 1995): 20–33.

Dann, Martin E. "From Sodom to the Promised Land: E. P. McCabe and the Movement for Oklahoma Colonization." *Kansas Historical Quarterly* 40, no.3 (Autumn 1974): 370–78.

Davenport, Loralee, and Thos. W Eva. *A Journey Toward Sovereignty and Security: The African American Community of Butte, Montana from 1885–1955*. Housed at Butte-Silver Bow Public Archives and the Montana Historical Society, n.p., 2001.

Dawson, Michael C. *Black Visions: The Roots of Contemporary African-American Political Ideologies*. Chicago: University of Chicago Press, 2001.

Day, Iyko. *Alien Capital: Asian Racialization and the Logic of Settler Colonial Capitalism*. Durham NC: Duke University Press, 2016.

———. "Being or Nothingness: Indigeneity, Antiblackness, and Settler Colonial Critique." *Critical Ethnic Studies* 1, no.2 (Fall 2015): 102–21.

de Graaf, Lawrence B. "Race, Sex, and Region: Black Women in the American West, 1850–1920." *Pacific Historical Review* 49, no. 1 (February 1980): 285–314.

———. "Recognition, Racism, and Reflections on the Writing of Western Black History." *Pacific Historical Review* 44, no. 1 (February 1975): 22–51.

Deverell, William, and Douglas Flamming. "Race, Rhetoric, and Regional Identity: Boosting Los Angeles, 1880–1930." In *Power and Place in the North American West*, edited by John M. Findley and Richard White, 117–43. Seattle: University of Washington Press, 1999.

DeVoto, Bernard, ed. *The Journals of Lewis and Clark*. Boston: Houghton Mifflin, 1953.

Dowd, Gregory. "Indigenous Peoples without the Republic." *Journal of American History* 104, no. 1 (June 2017): 19–41.

Du Bois, W. E. B. *Black Reconstruction in America: An Essay toward a History of the Part Which Black Folk Played in the Attempt to Reconstruct Democracy in America, 1860–1880*. New York: Harcourt, Brace, 1935.

———. *Darkwater: Voices from within the Veil*. New York: Harcourt, Brace, 1920.

———. *The Philadelphia Negro: A Social Study*. New York: Shocken, [1899] 1967.

———. *The Souls of Black Folk: Essays and Sketches*. Chicago: A. C. McClurg, 1903.

Dunbar-Ortiz, Roxanne. *An Indigenous Peoples' History of the United States*. Boston: Beacon, 2014.

Dusenberry, Verne. "Waiting for a Day That Never Comes." *Montana: Magazine of Western History* 8, no. 2 (Spring 1958): 26–39.

Eder, Marie Oyawin. "Chief Little Shell's Tribe of Landless Chippewa Indians of Montana: A Question of Recognition." *Master's Thesis*. Montana State University, 1983.

Egan, Ken Jr. *Montana 1864: Indians, Emigrants, and Gold in the Territorial Year*. Helena MT: Riverbend, 2014.

Ellinghaus, Katherine. "The Benefits of Being Indian: Blood Quanta, Intermarriage, and Allotment Policy on the White Earth Reservation, 1889–1920." *Frontiers: A Journal of Women Studies* 29, nos. 2–3 (2008): 81–105.

Emmons, David. *The Butte Irish: Class and Ethnicity in an American Mining Town, 1875–1925*. Urbana: University of Illinois Press, 1989.

———. "The Orange and the Green in Montana: A Reconsideration of the Clark-Daly Feud." *Arizona and the West* 28, no. 3 (Autumn 1986): 225–45.

Erickson, Christine. "'Come Join the KKK in the Old Town Tonight': The Ku Klux Klan in Harlowton, Montana, during the 1920s." *Montana: The Magazine of Western History* 64, no. 3 (Autumn 2014): 49–64.

Eruteya, Glenda Rose Spearman. "Racial Legislation in Montana: 1864–1955." Master's thesis, University of Montana, Missoula, 1981.

Ferguson, Cody. "Beyond Oro Y Plata: The 1972 Montana State Constitution." Honors thesis, Carroll College, 2001.

Fiege, Mark. *The Republic of Nature: An Environmental History of the United States*. Seattle: University of Washington Press, 2012.

Field, Kendra Taira. *Growing up with the Country: Family, Race, and Nation after the Civil War*. New Haven CT: Yale University Press, 2018.

Finney, Carolyn. *Black Faces, White Spaces: Reimaging the African American Relationship with the Great Outdoors*. Chapel Hill: University of North Carolina Press, 2016.

Foley, Jodie, and John Axline, eds. *Speaking Ill of the Dead: Jerks in Montana History*. Helena MT: Morris, 2005.

Fowler, Arlen L. *The Black Infantry in the West, 1869–1891*. Westport CT: Greenwood, 1971.

Franklin, John Hope. *George Washington Williams: A Biography*. Chicago: University of Chicago Press, 1985.

Franklin, Joseph. *All through the Night: The History of Spokane's Black Americans*. Fairfield WA: Ye Galleon, 1989.
Frazier, E. Franklin. *Black Bourgeoisie*. New York: Free Press, 1957.
Fujikane, Candace, and Jonathan Okamura, eds. *Asian Settler Colonialism: From Local Governance to the Habits of Everyday Life in Hawaii*. Honolulu: University of Hawaii Press, 2008.
Garceau-Hagen, Dee, ed. *Portraits of Women in the American West*. New York: Routledge, 2005.
Gatewood, Willard B. *Aristocrats of Color: The Black Elite, 1880–1920*. Bloomington: Indiana University Press, 1990.
Genetin-Pilawa, Joseph. *The Crooked Paths to Allotment: The Fight over Federal Indian Policy after the Civil War*. Chapel Hill: University of North Carolina Press, 2012.
Gilmore, Glenda Elizabeth. *Gender and Jim Crow: Women and the Politics of White Supremacy in North Carolina, 1896–1920*. Chapel Hill: University of North Carolina Press, 1996.
Glasrud, Bruce A., and Charles A. Braithwaite. *African Americans on the Great Plains: An Anthology*. Lincoln: University of Nebraska Press, 2009.
Glasrud, Bruce A., and Michael N. Searles. *Buffalo Soldiers in the West a Black Soldiers Anthology*. College Station: Texas A&M University Press, 2007.
Glasscock, C. B. *The War of the Copper Kings: Builders of Butte and Wolves of Wall Street*. New York: Grosset & Dunlap, 1935.
Graybill, Andrew. *The Red and the White: A Family Saga of the American West*. New York: Liveright, 2013.
Greenridge, Kerri. *Black Radical: The Life and Times of William Monroe Trotter*. New York: Liveright, 2020.
Goldberg, David Theo. *The Racial State*. Malden MA: Blackwell, 2002.
———. *Racist Culture: Philosophy and the Politics of Meaning*. Malden MA: Blackwell, 1993.
Goldsby, Jacqueline. *A Spectacular Secret: Lynching in American Life and Literature*. Chicago: University of Chicago Press, 2006.
Good, Mary Jo, Sandra Teresa Hyde, Sarah Pinto, Byron J. Good, eds. *Postcolonial Disorders*. Berkeley: University of California Press, 2008.
Gordon, Linda. *The Great Arizona Orphan Abduction*. Cambridge MA: Harvard University Press, 1999.
Gordon, Taylor. *Born to Be*. Lincoln: University of Nebraska Press, 1995.
Grant, Madison. *Early History of Glacier National Park, Montana*. Washington DC: Washington Government Printing Office, 1919.

Gregory, Derek. *The Colonial Present: Afghanistan, Palestine, Iraq*. Malden MA: Blackwell, 2004.

Gregory, James N. *The Southern Diaspora: How the Great Migrations of Black and White Southerners Transformed America*. Chapel Hill: University of North Carolina Press, 2005.

Grinde, Donald, and Quintard Taylor. "Red vs. Black: Conflict and Accommodation in the Post-Civil War Indian Territory, 1865-1907." *American Indian Quarterly* 8, no. 3 (Summer 1984): 211-29.

Guenther, Todd. "At Home on the Range: Black Settlement in Rural Wyoming, 1850-1950." Master's thesis, University of Wyoming, 1988.

Gullickson, Aaron. "Black/White Interracial Marriage Trends, 1850-2000." *Journal of Family History* 31, no. 3 (2006): 289-312.

Hämäläinen, Pekka. *Lakota America: A New History of Indigenous Power*. New Haven CT: Yale University Press, 2019.

Hansen, Moya. "Entitled to Full and Equal Enjoyment: Leisure and Entertainment in the Denver Black Community, 1900 to 1930." *University of Colorado at Denver Historical Studies Journal* 10, no. 1 (Spring 1993): 57-71.

Hardaway, Roger D. *A Narrative Bibliography of the African-American Frontier: Blacks in the Rocky Mountain West, 1535-1912*. Lewiston NY: Edwin Mellen, 1995.

Harlan, Louis R. *Booker T. Washington: The Wizard of Tuskegee, 1901-1915*. New York: Oxford University Press, 1983.

Harris, Cheryl. "Whiteness as Property." *Harvard Law Review* 106, no. 8 (June 1993): 1707-91.

Harris, Cole. *Making Native Space: Colonialism, Resistance, and Reserves in British Columbia*. Vancouver: University of British Columbia Press, 2002.

Harris, Theodore, ed. *Negro Frontiersman: The Western Memoirs of Henry O. Flipper, First Negro Graduate of West Point*. El Paso: Texas Western College Press, 1963.

Hernandez, Kelly Lytle. *City of Inmates: Conquest, Rebellion, and the Rise of Human Caging in Los Angeles*. Chapel Hill: University of North Carolina Press, 2017.

Higgins, J. "House Joint Memorial No. 1." In *Juvenile Delinquency (Indians): Hearings Before the Subcommittee to Investigate Juvenile Delinquency on the Committee of the Judiciary, United States Senate, Eighty-Fourth Congress, First Session, Pursuant to S. Res. 62, March 11, April 28, 29, and 30*. Washington DC: United States Government Printing Office, 1955.

Hixon, Walter. *American Settler Colonialism, A History*. New York: Palgrave Macmillan, 2013.

Hodes, Martha, ed. *Sex, Love, and Race: Crossing Boundaries in North American History*. New York: New York University Press, 1999.

Hyde, Anne F. *Empires, Nations, and Families: A New History of the North American West, 1800–1860*. Lincoln: University of Nebraska Press, 2011.

Hyde, Charles K. *Copper for America: The U.S. Copper Industry from Colonial Times to the 1990s*. Tucson: University of Arizona Press, 1998.

Jacobs, Margaret D. *White Mother to a Dark Race: Settler Colonialism, Maternalism, and the Removal of Indigenous Children in the American West and Australia, 1880–1940*. Lincoln: University of Nebraska Press, 2009.

Jacoby, Karl. *Crimes against Nature: Squatters, Poachers, Thieves, and the Hidden History of Conservation*. Berkeley: University of California Press, 2001.

Japtok, Martin. "The Gospel of Whiteness: Whiteness in African American Literature." *Amerikastudien/American Studies* 49, no. 4 (Winter 2004): 483–98.

Jaspin, Elliott. *Buried in the Bitter Waters: The Hidden History of Racial Cleansing in America*. New York: Basic Books, 2007.

Johnson, Jeffrey Alan. "Border Patrols, Buffalo Soldiers, and Boredom: Fort Assiniboine, Montana, 1879–1911." Master's thesis, Washington State University, 2000.

Johnson, Michael K. *Can't Stand Still: Emmanuel Taylor Gordon and the Harlem Renaissance*. Jackson: University of Mississippi Press, 2018.

———. "Essay Review, 'The Like of Which Is Found Nowhere Else in All the World': Placing and Imagining an African American West." *Western American Literature* 41, no. 3 (2006): 336–44.

———. *Hoo-Doo Cowboys and Bronze Buckaroos: Conceptions of the African American West*. Jackson: University Press of Mississippi, 2014.

Jones, Martha S. *Birthright Citizens: The History of Race and Rights in Antebellum America*. Cambridge: Cambridge University Press, 2018.

Kelley, Robin D. G. *Hammer and Hoe: Alabama Communists during the Great Depression*. Chapel Hill: University of North Carolina Press, 1990.

———. "The Rest of Us: Rethinking Settler and Native." *American Quarterly* 69, no. 2 (June 2017): 267–76.

———. "'We Are Not What We Seem': Rethinking Black Working-Class Opposition in the Jim Crow South." *Journal of American History* 80, no. 1 (June 1993): 75–112.

Kelley, Robin D. G., and Earl Lewis, eds. *To Make Our World Anew: A History of African Americans*. Oxford: Oxford University Press, 2000.

King, Tiffany Lethabo. *The Black Shoals: Offshore Formations of Black and Native Studies*. Durham NC: Duke University Press, 2019.

Klassen, Teresa C., and Owen V. Johnson. "Sharpening of the *Blade*: Black Consciousness in Kansas, 1892–97." *Journalism Quarterly* 63, no. 2 (Summer 1986): 298–304.

Klein, Kerwin Lee. *Frontiers of Historical Imagination: Narrating the European Conquest of Native America, 1890–1990*. Berkeley: University of California Press, 1999.

———. "Reclaiming the 'F' Word, Or Being and Becoming Postwestern." *Pacific Historical Review* 65, no. 2 (May 1996): 179–215.

Knoblock, Frieda. *The Culture of Wilderness: Agriculture as Colonization in the American West*. Chapel Hill: University of North Carolina Press, 1996.

Koelle, Alexandra V. "Pedaling on the Periphery: The African American Twenty-Fifth Infantry Bicycle Corps and the Roads of American Expansion." *Western Historical Quarterly* 41, no. 3 (2010): 305–26.

Kuletz, Valerie L. *The Tainted Desert: Environmental and Social Ruin in the American West*. London: Routledge, 1998.

Lake, Marylin. *Progressive New World: How Settler Colonialism and Transpacific Exchange Shaped American Reform*. Cambridge MA: Harvard University Press, 2019.

Lambert, Kirby, and Jennifer Bottomly-O'Looney. "Bob and Charlie: A Pair to Draw To." *Montana: The Magazine of Western History* 65, no. 1 (Winter 2015): 40–96.

Lane, Ann J. *The Brownsville Affair: National Crisis and Black Reaction*. Port Washington NY: Kennikat, 1971.

Lang, William. "Helena, Montana's Black Community, 1900–1912." In *African Americans on the Western Frontier*, edited by Monroe Lee Billington and Roger D. Hardaway, 212–14. Niwot: University of Colorado Press, 1998.

———. "The Nearly Forgotten Blacks on Last Chance Gulch, 1900–1912." *Pacific Northwest Quarterly* 70, no. 2 (April 1979): 50–57.

———. "Tempest on Lore Street: Race and Politics in Helena, Montana, 1906." *Scratchgravel Hills* 3 (Summer 1980): 9–14.

Lapp, Rudolph. *Blacks in Gold Rush California*. New Haven CT: Yale University Press, 1977.

Larsen, Lawrence H. *The Urban West at the End of the Frontier*. Lawrence: Regents Press of Kansas, 1978.

Lassiter, Matthew, and Joseph Crespino, eds. *The Myth of Southern Exceptionalism*. Oxford: Oxford University Press, 2010.

Laurie, Clayton D. "The United States Army and the Labor Radical of the Coeur d'Alenes: Federal Military Intervention in the Mining Wars of 1892–1899." *Idaho Yesterdays* 37, no. 2 (Summer 1993): 12–29.

Leiker, James. *Racial Borders: Black Soldiers along the Rio Grande*. College Station: Texas A&M University Press, 2002.

Leroy, Justin. "Black History in Occupied Territory: On the Entanglements of Slavery and Settler Colonialism." *Theory and Event* 19, no. 4 (2016): 1–12.

Lewis, David Levering. *W. E. B. Du Bois: Biography of a Race, 1868–1919*. New York: Henry Holt, 1993.

Limerick, Patricia Nelson. *The Legacy of Conquest: The Unbroken Past of the American West*. New York: W. W. Norton, 1987.

Limerick, Patricia Nelson, Andrew Cowell, and Sharon K. Collinge, eds. *Remedies for a New West: Healing Landscapes, Histories, and Cultures*. Tucson: University of Arizona Press, 2009.

Lipsitz, George. "The Possessive Investment in Whiteness: Racialized Social Democracy and the 'White' Problem in American Studies." *American Quarterly* 47, no. 3 (1995): 369–87.

Litwack, Leon. *Been in the Storm So Long: The Aftermath of Slavery*. New York: Vintage, 1979.

———. *North of Slavery: The Negro in the Free States, 1790–1860*. Chicago: University of Chicago Press, 1961.

———. *Trouble in Mind: Black Southerners in the Age of Jim Crow*. New York: Vintage, 1998.

Liwack, Leon, and August Meirer, eds. *Black Leaders of the 19th Century*. New York: Vintage, 1988.

Loewen, James. *Sundown Towns: A Hidden Dimension of American Racism*. New York: New Press, 2005.

Logan, Rayford. *The Betrayal of the Negro: From Rutherford B. Hayes to Woodrow Wilson*. New York: De Capo, 1965.

Lowe, Lisa. *The Intimacy of Four Continents*. Durham NC: Duke University Press, 2015.

Lyles, Lionel Dean. "An Historical-Urban Geographical Analysis of Black Neighborhood Development in Denver, 1860–1970." PhD diss., University of Colorado, 1977.

Mack, Dwayne. *Black Spokane: The Civil Rights Struggle in the Inland Northwest*. Norman: University of Oklahoma Press, 2014.

———. "May the Work I've Done Speak for Me: African American CCC Enrollees in MT, 1933–34." *Western Journal of Black Studies* 27, no. 4 (Winter 2003): 236–45.

Madley, Benjamin. *An American Genocide: The United States and the California Indian Catastrophe*. New Haven CT: Yale University Press, 2016.

Malone, Michael P. *The Battle for Butte: Mining and Politics on the Northern Frontier, 1864–1906.* Seattle: University of Washington Press, 1981.

———. "Beyond the Last Frontier: Towards a New Approach to Western American History." *Western Historical Quarterly* 20, no. 4 (November 1989): 409–27.

Malone, Michael P., Richard B. Roeder, and William L. Lang. *Montana: A History of Two Centuries.* Seattle: University of Washington Press, 1991.

Mamdani, Mahmoud. "Beyond Settler and Native as Political Identities: Overcoming the Political Legacy of Colonialism." *Comparative Studies in Society and History* 43, no. 4 (October 2001): 651–64.

Mar, Tracey Banivanua. "Carving Wilderness: Queensland's National Parks and the Unsettling of Emptied Lands, 1890–1910." In *Making Settler Colonial Space: Perspectives on Race, Place, and Identity*, edited by Tracey Banivanua Mar and Penelope Edmonds, 73–94. London: Palgrave Macmillan, 2010.

Mar, Tracey Banivanua, and Penelope Edmonds, eds. *Making Settler Colonial Space: Perspectives on Race, Place, and Identity.* New York: Palgrave Macmillan, 2010.

Marx, Anthony W. *Making Race and Nation: A Comparison of South Africa, the United States, and Brazil.* Cambridge: Cambridge University Press, 1998.

McGowen, Tom. *African-Americans in the Old West.* New York: Children's Press, 1998.

McLagan, Elizabeth. *A Peculiar Paradise: A History of Blacks in Oregon, 1788–1940.* Portland OR: Georgian, 1980.

McMillen, Christian. "Border State Terror and the Genesis of the African American Community in Deer Lodge and Chouteau Counties, Montana, 1870–1890." *Journal of Negro History* 79, no. 2 (Spring 1994): 212–14.

McNelis, Sarah. *Copper King at War: The Biography of F. Augustus Heinze.* Missoula: University of Montana Press, 1968.

Mercier, Laurie. *Anaconda: Labor, Community, and Culture in Montana's Smelter City.* Urbana: University of Illinois Press, 2001.

———. "Reworking Race, Class, and Gender into Pacific Northwest History." *Frontiers: A Journal of Women Studies* 22, no. 3 (2001): 61–74.

Merritt, Christopher W. *The Coming Man from Canton: The Chinese Experience in Montana, 1862–1943.* Lincoln: University of Nebraska Press, 2017.

Meyers, Rex C. "Montana's Negro Newspapers, 1894–1911." *Montana Journalism Review* 16 (Fall 1973): 17–22.

Miles, Tiya. "Beyond a Boundary: Black Lives and the Settler-Native Divide." *William and Mary Quarterly* 76, no. 3 (July 2019): 417–26.

———. *The House on Diamond Hill: A Cherokee Plantation Story*. Chapel Hill: University of North Carolina Press, 2010.

———. "The Long Arm of the South?" *Western Historical Quarterly* 43 (Autumn, 2012): 274–81.

———. *Ties That Bind: The Story of an Afro-Cherokee Family in Slavery and Freedom*. Berkeley: University of California Press, 2015.

Miller, Jan. "An Annotated Bibliography of the Washington-Du Bois Controversy." *Journal of Black Studies* 25, no. 2 (December 1994): 250–72.

Mitchell, Michele. *Righteous Propagation: African Americans and the Politics of Racial Destiny after Reconstruction*. Chapel Hill: University of North Carolina Press, 2004.

Molina, Natalia. *How Race Is Made in America: Immigration, Citizenship, and the Historical Power of Racial Scripts*. Berkeley: University of California Press, 2014.

Mora, Anthony. *Border Dilemmas: Racial and National Uncertainties in New Mexico, 1848–1912*. Durham NC: Duke University Press, 2010.

Moten, Fred. "Blackness and Nothingness (Mysticism in the Flesh)." *South Atlantic Quarterly* 112, no. 4 (2013): 737–81.

Muhammad, Khalil. *The Condemnation of Blackness: Race, Crime, and the Making of Modern Urban America*. Cambridge MA: Harvard University Press, 2010.

Mukenge, Ida Rousseau. *The Black Church in Urban America: A Case Study in Political Economy*. Lanham MD: University Press of America, 1983.

Murphy, Mary. *Mining Cultures: Men, Women, and Leisure in Butte, 1914–1941*. Urbana: University of Illinois Press, 1997.

Nash, Gerald. *The American West in the Twentieth Century: A Short History of an Urban Oasis*. Englewood Cliffs NJ: Prentice Hall, 1973.

Norrell, Robert. *Up From History: The Life of Booker T. Washington*. Cambridge MA: Harvard University Press, 2011.

Norris, Melvin Edward, Jr. "Dearfield, Colorado–The Evolution of a Rural Black Settlement: A Historical Geography of Black Colonization on the Great Plains." PhD diss., University of Colorado, Boulder, 1980.

Ober, Michael J. "The CCC Experience in Glacier National Park." In *The Montana Heritage: An Anthology of Historical Essays*, edited by Robert Swartout Jr. and Harry W. Fritz, 199–211. Helena: Montana Historical Society, 1992.

O'Brien, Claire, "'With One Mighty Pull': Interracial Town Boosting in Nicodemus, Kansas." *Great Plains Quarterly* 61, no. 2 (Spring 1996): 117–30.

Oliver, Mamie O. *Idaho Ebony: The Afro-American Presence in Idaho State History*. Boise: Idaho State Historical Society, 1990.

Organ, David Joseph. "The Historical Geography of African American Frontier Settlement." PhD diss., University of California, Berkeley, 1995.

Oshinsky, David. *Worse Than Slavery: Parchman Farm and the Ordeal of Jim Crow Justice*. New York: Free Press, 1997.

Ostler, Jeffery. *The Plains Sioux and U.S. Colonialism from Lewis and Clark to Wounded Knee*. Cambridge: Cambridge University Press, 2004.

———. *Surviving Genocide: Native Nations and the United States from the American Revolution to Bleeding Kansas*. New Haven CT: Yale University Press, 2019.

Packard, Jerrold M. *American Nightmare: The History of Jim Crow*. New York: St. Martin's, 2002.

Painter, Nell Irvin. *Exodusters: Black Migration to Kansas after Reconstruction*. Topeka: University Press of Kansas, 1986.

———. *The History of White People*. New York: W. W. Norton, 2010.

———. *Standing at Armageddon: The United States, 1877–1919*. New York: W. W. Norton, 1987.

Pascoe, Peggy. *What Comes Naturally: Miscegenation Law and the Making of Race in America*. Oxford: Oxford University Press, 2009.

Peterson, Christopher. *Bestial Traces: Race, Sexuality, Animality*. New York: Fordham University Press, 2013.

Perez, Erika. *Colonial Intimacies: Interethnic Kinship, Sexuality, and Marriage in Southern California, 1769–1885*. Norman: University of Oklahoma Press, 2018.

Perry, Imani. *We May Forever Stand: The History of The Black National Anthem*. Chapel Hill: University of North Carolina Press, 2018.

Pfaelzer, Jean. *Driven Out: The Forgotten War against Chinese Americans*. New York: Random House, 2007.

Pierce, Jason E. *Making the White Man's West: Whiteness and the Creation of the American West*. Boulder: University Press of Colorado, 2016.

Pisani, Donald. *Water and American Government: The Reclamation Bureau, National Water Policy, and the West*. Berkeley: University of California Press, 2002.

Poovey, Mary. *Making a Social Body: British Cultural Formation, 1830–1864*. Chicago: University of Chicago Press, 1995.

Pratt, Richard H. "The Advantages of Mingling Indians with Whites" (1892). In *Americanizing the American Indians: Writings by the "Friends of the*

Indian,"*1880–1900*, edited by Francis P. Prucha, 260–71. Cambridge MA: Harvard University Press, 1973.

Pulido, Laura. "Geographies of Race and Ethnicity III: Settler Colonialism and Nonnative People of Color." *Progress in Human Geography* 42, no. 2 (2018): 309–18.

Ravage, John W. *Black Pioneers: Images of the Black Experience on the North American Frontier*. Salt Lake City: University of Utah Press, 1997.

Reeve, W. Paul. *Religion of a Different Color: Race and the Mormon Struggle for Whiteness*. Oxford: Oxford University Press, 2015.

Richard, K. Keith. "Unwelcome Settlers: Black and Mulatto Oregon Pioneers," Part 1. *Oregon Historical Quarterly* 84, no. 1 (Spring 1983): 35–36.

Rico, Monica. *Nature's Noblemen: Transatlantic Masculinities and the Nineteenth-Century American West*. New Haven CT: Yale University Press, 2013.

Riley, Glenda. "American Daughters: Black Women in the West." *Montana: The Magazine of Western History* 38, no.2 (Spring 1988): 14–27.

R. L. Polk. *Anaconda (Deer Lodge, Mont.) City Directory*. Salt Lake City UT: R. L. Polk, 1902, 1905, 1906, 1909, 1910, 1912, 1915, 1915, 1916, 1917, 1918, 1925, 1928, 1930, 1936, and 1939.

———. *Billings (Yellowstone County, Mont.) City Directory*. Salt Lake City UT: R. L. Polk, 1901, 1903, 1905, 1909, 1912, 1913, 1916, 1917, 1918, 1919, 1921, 1922, 1925, 1927, 1929, 1930, 1932, 1933, 1935, 1937, and 1944.

———. *Butte (Silver Bow, Mont.) City Directory*. Salt Lake City UT: R. L. Polk, 1884, 1890, 1893, 1896, 1898, 1899, 1900, 1904, 1905, 1906, 1907, 1908, 1909, 1910, 1911, 1912, 1913, 1914, 1915, 1916, 1917, 1918, 1923, 1925, 1926, 1927, 1928, 1929, and 1930.

———. *Bozeman (Gallatin, Mont.) City Directory*. Salt Lake City UT: R. L. Polk, 1902, 1903, 1904, 1906, 1908, 1910, 1912, 1914, 1916, 1918, 1922, 1925, 1927, 1929, 1931, 1933, and 1935.

———. *Great Falls (Cascade, Mont.) City Directory*. Salt Lake City UT: R. L. Polk, 1903, 1904, 1906, 1908, 1910, 1911, 1913, 1914, 1915, 1916, 1918, 1919, 1923, 1925, 1927, 1928, 1929, 1930, 1931, 1932, 1934, 1935, 1937, and 1940.

———. *Helena (Lewis and Clark, Mont.) City Directory*. Salt Lake City UT: R. L. Polk, 1889, 1890, 1891, 1892, 1894, 1895, 1896, 1897, 1898, 1899, 1900, 1901, 1902, 1903, 1904, 1905, 1906, 1907, 1908, 1909, 1910, 1911, 1912, 1913, 1914, 1915, 1916, 1917, 1918, 1920, 1922, 1927, 1931, 1933, 1935, and 1941.

———. *Miles City (Custer, Mont.) City Directory*. Salt Lake City UT: R. L. Polk, 1909, 1912, 1914, 1916, 1923, 1927, and 1930.

——. *Missoula (Missoula, Mont.) City Directory*. Salt Lake City UT: R. L. Polk, 1901, 1903, 1905, 1907, 1909, 1911, 1913, 1925, 1917, 1922, 1925, 1927, 1929, 1930, 1932, 1934, 1938, and 1940.

Pruitt, Bernadette. "'Beautiful People': Community Formation in Houston, 1900–1941." In *Freedom's Racial Frontier: African Americans in the Twentieth-Century West*, edited by Herbert Ruffin II and Dwyane A. Mack, 45–86. Norman: University of Oklahoma Press, 2018.

Robinson, Cedric. *Black Marxism: The Making of the Black Radical Tradition*. 2nd ed. Chapel Hill: University of North Carolina Press, 2000.

——. *Forgeries of Memory and Meaning: Blacks and the Regimes of Race in American Theater and Film before World War II*. Chapel Hill: University of North Carolina Press, 2007.

Robison, Ken. "Breaking Racial Barriers: 'Everyone's Welcome' at the Ozark Club Great Falls, Montana's African American Nightclub." *Montana: The Magazine of Western History* 62, no. 2 (Summer 2012): 44–58.

Roediger, David R. *The Wages of Whiteness: Race and the Making of the American Working Class*. London: Verso, 1991.

Ruffin, Herbert, II, and Dwyane A. Mack, eds. *Freedom's Racial Frontier: African Americans in the Twentieth-Century West*. Norman: University of Oklahoma Press, 2018.

Rydall, E. H. "California for Colored Folk." *Colored American Magazine* 12, no. 5 (May 1907): 386–88.

San Juan, E., Jr. "African American Internationalism and Solidarity with the Philippine Revolution." *Socialism and Democracy* 24, no. 2 (2010): 32–65.

Schechter, Patricia. *Ida B. Wells-Barnett and American Reform, 1880–1930*. Chapel Hill: University of North Carolina Press, 2001.

Scheper-Hughes, Nancy, and Margaret M. Lock. "The Mindful Body: A Prolegomenon to Future Work in Medical Anthropology." *Medical Anthropology Quarterly* 1, no. 1 (March 1987): 6–41.

Schubert, Frank, ed. *On the Trail of the Buffalo Soldier: Biographies of African Americans in the U.S. Army, 1866–1917*. Wilmington DE: Scholarly Resources, 1995.

Scott, James C. *Seeing Like a State: How Certain Schemes to Improve the Human Condition Have Failed*. New Haven CT: Yale University Press, 1998.

Self, Robert O. *American Babylon: Race and the Struggle for Post-War Oakland*. Princeton NJ: Princeton University Press, 2003.

Sexton, Jared. "The *Vel* of Slavery: Tracking the Figure of the Unsovereign." *Critical Sociology* 42, nos. 4–5 (December 2014): 583–97.

Shah, Nayan. *Stranger Intimacies: Contesting Race, Sexuality, and Law in the North American West*. Berkeley: University of California Press, 2012.

Smith, Burton M. "The Politics of Allotment: The Flathead Indian Reservation as a Test Case." *Pacific Northwest Quarterly* 70, no. 3 (1979): 131–40.

Smith, Stacey L. *Freedom's Frontier: California and the Struggle over Unfree Labor, Emancipation, and Reconstruction*. Chapel Hill: University of North Carolina Press, 2013.

Smurr, J. W. "Jim Crow Out West." In *Historical Essays on Montana and the Northwest: In Honor of Paul C. Phillips*, edited by J. W. Smurr and K. Ross Toole, 149–203. Helena MT: Western Press/Historical Society of Montana, 1957.

Smythe, Donald, SJ. "John J. Pershing at Fort Assiniboine." *Montana: The Magazine of Western History* 18, no. 1 (Winter 1968): 19–23.

Spence, Mark. *Dispossessing the Wilderness: Indian Removal and the Making of National Parks*. Oxford: Oxford University Press, 1999.

Spiro, Jonathan Peter. *Defending the Master Race: Conservation, Eugenics, and the Legacy of Madison Grant*. Burlington: University of Vermont Press, 2009.

Spruhan, Paul. "A Legal History of Blood Quantum in Federal Indian Law to 1935." SDL *Law Review* 55, no. 1 (2006): 1–50.

Stegner, Wallace. *Where the Bluebird Sings to the Lemonade Springs*. New York: Knopf, 1992.

———. *Wolf Willow*. New York: Viking, 1962.

Stern, Alexandria. *Eugenic Nation: Faults and Frontiers of Better Breeding in Modern America*. 2nd ed. Berkeley: University of California Press, 2015.

Steward, T. G. *The Colored Regulars in the United States Army*. Philadelphia: AME Book Concern, 1904.

Stoler, Ann Laura. *Carnal Knowledge and Imperial Power: Race and the Intimate in Colonial Rule*. Berkeley: University of California Press, 2002.

———. *Duress: Imperial Durabilities in Our Times*. Durham NC: Duke University Press, 2016.

———. *Race and the Education of Desire: Foucault's* History of Sexuality *and the Colonial Order of Things*. Durham NC: Duke University Press, 1995.

Stoler, Ann Laura, ed. *Haunted by Empire: Geographies of Intimacy in North American History*. Durham NC: Duke University Press, 2006.

———, ed. *Imperial Debris: On Ruins and Ruination*. Durham NC: Duke University Press, 2013.

Stoll, Mark. "Religion and Environmental Activism." In *"To Love the Wind and the Rain": African Americans and Environmental History*, edited by Dianne D. Glave and Mark Stoll, 150–63. Pittsburg: University of Pittsburg Press, 2006.

Stoll, Mark, and Dianne D. Glave, eds. *"To Love the Wind and the Rain": African Americans and Environmental History*. Pittsburg: University of Pittsburg Press, 2006.

Stout, Tom, ed. *Montana, Its Story and Biography: A History of Aboriginal and Territorial Montana and Three Decades of Statehood*. Vol 2. Chicago: American Historical Society, 1921.

Sturdevant, Anne Marie. "White Hoods Under the Big Sky: Montanans Embrace the Ku Klux Klan, 1920s." In *Speaking Ill of the Dead: Jerks in Montana History*, 311–27. 2nd. ed. Guilford CT: Globe Pequot, 2011.

Svingen, Orlan J. "Jim Crow, Indian Style." *American Indian Quarterly* 11, no. 4 (Autumn 1987): 275–86.

Swartout, Robert, Jr. *Montana: A Cultural Medley*. Helena MT: Farcountry, 2015.

Swartout, Robert, Jr., and Harry W. Fritz, eds. *The Montana Heritage: An Anthology of Historical Essays*. Helena MT: Montana Historical Society Press, 1992.

Taylor, Dorceta. *The Rise of the American Conservation Movement: Power, Privilege, and Environmental Protection*. Durham NC: Duke University Press, 2016.

Taylor, Quintard. "Black Urban Development–Another View: Seattle's Central District, 1910–1940." *Pacific Historical Review* 58, no. 4 (November 1989): 429–48.

———. "The Emergence of the Afro-American Communities in the Pacific Northwest, 1865–1910." *Journal of Negro History* 64, no. 4 (Fall 1979): 342–51.

———. *The Forging of a Black Community: Seattle's Central District from 1870 through the Civil Rights Era*. Seattle: University of Washington Press, 1994.

———. "From Esteban to Rodney King: Five Centuries of African American History in the West." *Montana: The Magazine of Western History* 46, no. 4 (Winter 1996): 2–23.

———. "The Great Migration: The Afro-American Communities of Seattle and Portland during the 1940s." *Arizona and the West* 23, no. 2 (Summer 1981): 109–26.

———. *In Search of the Racial Frontier: African Americans in the American West, 1528–1990*. New York: W. W. Norton, 1998.

———. "Native Americans and African Americans: Intersections across Time and Space in the West." Shifting Borders of Race and Identity: A Research and Teaching Workshop on the First Nations and African American Experience, University of Washington, Seattle, February 23, 2004.

———. "People of Color in the West: A Half Century of Scholarship." *Western History Quarterly* 42, no. 3 (Autumn 2011): 313–18.

———. "Slaves and Free Men: Blacks in the Oregon Country, 1840–1860." *Oregon Historical Quarterly* 83, no. 2 (Summer 1982): 165–69.

Taylor, Quintard, and Shirley Ann Wilson Moore. *African American Women Confront the West: 1600–2000*. Norman: University of Oklahoma Press, 2003.

Tsing, Anna Lowenhaupt. *The Mushroom at the End of the World: On the Possibility of Life in Capitalist Ruins*. New Haven CT: Princeton University Press, 2015.

Tuck, Eve, and K. Wayne Yang. "Decolonization Is Not a Metaphor." *Decolonization, Indigeneity, Education & Society* 1, no. 1 (2012): 1–40.

Tyrrell, Ian. *Crisis of a Wasteful Nation: Empire and Conservation in Theodore Roosevelt's America*. Chicago: University of Chicago Press, 2015.

Veracini, Lorenzo. *Settler Colonialism: A Theoretical Overview*. New York: Palgrave Macmillan, 2010.

Villazor, Rose Cuison. "Blood Quantum Land Laws and the Race Versus Identity Dilemma." *California Law Review* 96, no. 3 (June 2008): 801–37.

———. "'Settler Colonialism': Career of a Concept." *Journal of Imperial and Commonwealth History* 41, no. 2 (2013): 313–33.

Warren, Louis. *God's Red Son: The Ghost Dance Religion and the Making of Modern America*. New York: Basic Books, 2017.

———. *The Hunter's Game: Poachers and Conservationists in Twentieth-Century America*. New Haven CT: Yale University Press, 1997.

Washington, Booker T. *The Future of the American Negro*. New York: Haskell House, 1899.

———. *Up from Slavery: An Autobiography*. New York: Doubleday, 1901.

Washington, Margaret. "African American History and the Frontier Thesis." *Journal of the Early Republic* 13, no. 2 (Summer 1993): 230–41.

Wayne, George H. "Negro Migration and Colonization in Colorado." *Journal of the West* 15, no. 1 (January 1976): 102–20.

Weisiger, Marsha. *Dreaming of Sheep in Navajo Country*. Seattle: University of Washington Press, 2009.

Weiss, Nancy J. *The National Urban League, 1910–1940*. New York: Oxford University Press, 1974.

Wells, Ida B. *Southern Horrors: Lynch Law in All its Phases in Selected Works of Ida B. Wells-Barnett*. Compiled by Trudier Harris. New York: Oxford University Press, 1991.

Wesley, Charles H. *The History of the National Association of Colored Women's Clubs, Inc.: A Legacy of Service*. Washington: Associated Publishers, 1984.

West, Elliott. *The Contested Plains: Indians, Goldseekers, and the Rush to Colorado*. Lawrence: University Press of Kansas, 1998.

———. *The Last Indian War: The Nez Perce Story*. Oxford: Oxford University Press, 2009.

Wilkerson, Isabel. *The Warmth of Other Suns: The Epic Story of America's Great Migration*. New York: Vintage, 2010.

Williams, Raymond. *Problems in Materialism and Culture*. London: Verso, 1980.

Willis, Deborah, ed. *J. P. Ball, Daguerrean and Studio Photographer*. New York: Garland, 1993.

Witgen, Michael. *An Infinity of Nations: How the Native New World Shaped Early North America*. Philadelphia: University of Pennsylvania Press, 2012.

White, Richard. "Are You an Environmentalist, or Do You Work for a Living?" In *Uncommon Ground: Rethinking the Human Place in Nature*, edited by William Cronon, 171–85. New York: W. W. Norton, 1996.

———. *"It's Your Misfortune and None of My Own": A New History of the American West*. Norman: University of Oklahoma Press, 1991.

———. *The Middle Ground: Indians, Empires, and Republics in the Great Lakes Region, 1650–1815*. Cambridge: Cambridge University Press, 1991.

———. "Race Relations in the American West." *American Quarterly* 38, no. 3 (1986): 394–416.

Wolfe, Patrick. "Recuperating Binarism: A Heretical Introduction." *Settler Colonial Studies* 3, nos. 3–4 (2013): 257–79.

———. "Settler Colonialism and the Elimination of the Native." *Journal of Genocide Research* 8, no. 4 (December 2006): 387–409.

———. *Settler Colonialism and the Transformation of Anthropology: Politics and Poetics of an Ethnographic Event*. London: Cassell, 1999.

———. *Traces of History: Elementary Structures of Race*. London: Verso, 2016.

Wolters, Raymond. *Du Bois and His Rivals*. Columbia: University of Missouri Press, 2002.

Wong, Edlie L. *Racial Reconstruction: Black Inclusion, Chinese Exclusion, and the Fictions of Citizenship*. New York: New York University Press, 2015.

Wood, Anthony. "After the West Was Won: How African American Buffalo Soldiers Invigorated the Helena Community in Early Twentieth-Century Montana." *Montana: The Magazine of Western History* 66, no. 3 (Autumn 2016): 36–50.

———. "Colonial Erosion: Unearthing African American History in the Settler Colonial West." *Settler Colonial Studies* 9, no. 3 (Summer, 2019): 396–417.

Wood, Peter H. *Black Majority: Negroes in Colonial South Carolina from 1670 through the Stono Rebellion*. New York: W. W. Norton, 1974.

Woodward, C. Vann. *The Strange Career of Jim Crow*. London: Oxford University Press, 1955.

Wray, Matt. *Not Quite White: White Trash and the Boundaries of Whiteness.* Durham NC: Duke University Press, 2006.
Wylie, Paul. *Blood on the Marias: The Baker Massacre.* Norman: University of Oklahoma Press, 2016.
Zellar, Gary. *African Creeks: Estelvste and the Creek Nation.* Norman: University of Oklahoma Press, 2007.

Index

Adams, Mary, 53
African Americans: as Black Indians, 5, 40, 134, 160–62; and the Black press, 9, 21, 22, 38, 42, 64, 73–75, 76, 80, 85, 95–96, 97, 116–35, 155–56, 161, 186, 212–13, 225; and business ownership, 32, 51, 80, 81, 86–90, 106–7, 194; and community formation, xv, 21, 22, 37, 51, 64–65, 81–90, 226; education of, 22, 79, 80–86, 93–94, 118–20; as government officials, 22, 90–91, 122, 226; and home ownership, 22, 80, 81, 86–90, 106–7, 226; and homesteading, 30, 40, 42–44; and Montana politics, 9, 22, 45, 80, 90–92, 95, 106–9, 116–35, 226; racialization of, 17–19, 62; religious communities of, 38, 75, 99, 208–9, 222, 258n18; violence against, 13, 30, 61–62, 73, 77, 80, 164, 179, 190–91, 211–13; women, 51–53, 77–78, 116–17, 120, 121, 153. See *Buffalo Soldiers*; Black Settler colonialism
African Methodist Episcopal Church (AME), 38, 87, 99, 102, 125, 208–9, 213; Shaffer's Chapel, 106, 112, 125, 134, 160; St. James AME, 87, 99, 102; Union Bethel, 38, 229

Allen, Jordan, 134, 160–62
Allotment: Black participation in process of, 9, 21, 39–45; and the Dawes Act, 21, 39–40, 161, 172, 173, 187; and Indian Territory, 40, 161; and Montana reservations, 9, 21, 39–45, 63
Anaconda Company, 61, 114, 125, 189, 206–7
Anaconda MT, 35, 36, 54, 61, 81, 86–87, 90, 95, 121, 131, 178–79, 189–91, 206–7, 213, 221–23
Anderson, Julian, 201
anti-miscegenation law, 23–24, 62, 75, 169–71, 174–75, 177, 180–85, 186–87, 189–96; Montana 1907 Bill and, 173–74, 277n16; Montana 1909 Bill and, 22, 24, 169–71, 174–75, 177, 179–85, 189–96; repeal of, 194, 219–21

Baker Massacre, 65, 111
Ball, J. P., 73–74, 257n12
Bass, Charlotta, 169–70
Bass, Joseph, xv, xix, 42, 44, 50, 74–75, 87–89, 93, 95–103, 156, 161, 169–70, 174, 175, 205
Bauste, Sven, 199–203, 223–24
Beckwourth, James, 29, 50, 148, 152, 218, 247n11

315

Belden, James, 212
"belonging," 7, 9, 18, 20, 23, 66, 135, 141, 146, 157, 161, 203, 217, 232–33
Berry, Sherlin Stillman, 137–40, 142, 164
Bickford, Sarah Gammon, 51–53
Billings MT, 35, 36, 50, 65–66, 81, 86, 151–52, 188, 207–10
Bivins, Horace, 151, 208
Blackfeet, 28–29, 65, 111, 148
Black settler colonialism, 2–3, 8–11
Black settler space, 8, 11, 21, 59, 67, 71–103; and Black settler sovereignty, 19–20, 30, 34, 64, 226, 245n65; and Black womanhood, 51–53; challenges of, 6–9, 30, 35, 65–66; ideology of, 8–9, 22, 67, 71, 76–81, 85, 93, 102, 108, 133, 226; and violence, 9, 10, 44
Black towns, 11, 20, 34, 39, 40
Black West, in scholarship, xix, 5, 7, 8, 14–15, 147, 203, 221–28
Botkin, Alexander C., 69–71
Bozeman MT, 36, 50–51, 86, 90, 124, 126, 153, 196–97, 200
Bridger, Jim, 148, 152
Brooks, Jess Lee, 92–94, 102
Browning, Ruth, 50
Browning, Walker, xix, 33, 50, 65, 150, 152, 208–9
Brownsville Affair, 96–97, 156
Buffalo Soldiers, 9, 19, 30, 32, 42, 44, 52, 54, 59, 66, 89–90, 96–97, 150–51, 152, 188, 201, 218, 262n65; 9th Cavalry, 30, 55, 150, 156; 10th Cavalry, 55, 56, 150; 24th Infantry, 19, 24, 55, 58, 156, 201; 25th Infantry, 54, 55, 56, 96–97

Bureau of Indian Affairs, 111, 211
Butte MT, 35, 36, 43, 61, 69–71, 81, 84, 86, 90, 95, 105–35, 152, 156, 159–62, 179–80, 188, 200, 206, 219

capitalism, 167, 174–75, 187–88, 205, 206; Black, 8–9, 45–46, 76–77, 80
Carpenter, Myron S., 142, 164
Castner, Mattie Bell, 51, 177, 190
Cheyenne, Wyoming, 11, 14, 243n43
Chicago Defender, 43, 44, 94, 212–13
citizenship: of African Americans, 16, 18–19; of Chinese, 16, 18–19, 31; of Native Americans, 31; of Mexican Americans, 16
Civil War, 7, 16, 50, 55, 65
Clark, William. *See* Corps of Discovery
Clark, William A., 74, 113–16, 123–30
class: Black bourgeoisie, 39, 45–49, 77, 80; and Black middle-class, 45, 77, 80, 81, 88; and Black working-class, 16, 19, 29, 32, 46–49, 77, 80, 81, 128, 131, 143, 156, 188; white settler elite, 16, 31–32, 39, 72–73, 80, 125, 143, 146; and white working-class, 18–19, 35, 109, 128, 131, 195
Clements, M. A., 213
Coleman, Z. A., 175–77, 179
Collins, Wilmot, 229
colonial erosion, xix, 12–15, 23, 25, 164, 191, 195, 203, 204, 221, 223–24; and occlusions, xiii, xvii, 14, 15, 25, 142, 157, 203, 224
color line: in the North, 75; and settler colonialism, 71–76, 86, 102; in the South, 24, 33, 70, 72–76, 95; in the West, 71, 72–76, 86

The Colored Citizen, 45, 73–74, 126, 257n12
Conservationism, 23, 140–47, 154–56, 159, 165–66, 216–18, 226; Black participation in, 23, 141–42, 146, 147, 156, 164; colonial ideology of, 23, 146, 147, 148, 156, 165–66, 226; during the Great Depression, 214–16; federal oversite of, 156, 214–16, 218; origins of, 145–47, 154–56; racism of, 23, 141–46, 154–57, 158, 164–66, 226
Corps of Discovery, 28–29, 152
Creek Nation, 5, 16, 40, 41, 134, 160–61
Crow Indians, 1, 28, 29, 65, 211–12, 230
Custer, George Armstrong, 53, 110
Cuba, 16, 56, 145, 201

Daly, Marcus, 74, 106, 113–16, 123, 126
Day, Iyko, 4, 239n23
Democratic Party, 22, 73–74, 80, 90, 107, 115–16, 120–32, 215; Black Democrats, 107–9, 126–30; Colored Democrats Club, Butte, 127–28, 130
differential racialization, 11, 18
Doig, Ivan, 232
Dorsey, Chris, xix, 93, 108, 116–35
Dorsey, Sarah, 192
Dorsey, Solomon, 192
Driver, Felix, 193
Driver, Lee Pleasant, 54, 90, 221
Driver, John, 221–23
Driver, Marilynn Ryan, 221–23
Driver, Mary Mundy, 53, 193, 222
Driver, Pearl, 221
Driver, Ruth Mundy, 53, 193

Driver, Woodrow, 193, 221
drought, 24, 38, 66, 200–201, 211, 269n4
Du Bois, W. E. B., 35, 60, 72, 76–81, 90, 158–59, 160, 163, 185, 274n54
Duncan, Armeta, 105–6, 133
Duncan, John, xix, 45, 93, 105–9, 116–35
Duncan, Perdita, 133
Duncan, Walter, 126, 131, 133

1875 Civil Right Act, 70
Emancipation Day, August 4th, 134–35, 159–62
empire: as an "Americanizing" project, 37, 46, 66; expansion of, 8, 12, 14, 16, 64, 196; imperialism, 2, 16, 46, 145; imperial political forms, 3, 46, 117
exclusion, 14, 15, 16, 18–19, 22, 25, 145, 157, 170–72, 173, 176, 182, 186, 205–6, 223; of Blacks, 10, 11, 12, 15, 17, 18–19, 25, 67, 71, 92–93, 109, 157, 170, 206, 223; of Asians, 17–19, 67, 170, 186, 206; of Indians 17, 18–19, 170, 173; of Latinos, 17, 18–19, 169–70

Fiege, Mark, 157–58, 218
Field, Kendra, 6, 34–35, 67
Field, Mary, 51–53
Flathead Indians, 65, 148
Fort Benton MT, 1, 37, 82, 177
frontier, 46, 52, 187–89, 196, 223
fur trade, 28, 29, 111

genocide, 17, 58–59, 188, 238n12
Glacier National Park, 148, 150, 159, 218
"Golden West," as potential for Black settlers, 30, 31–39, 43–44, 64–65, 67, 80

Gordon, Aaron, 97, 101
Gordon, Annie, 1, 230, 237n2
Gordon, Emmanuel Taylor, 84, 162, 233
Gordon, Rose, 1–2, 10, 12, 15, 51, 84, 90, 162–64, 194–95, 230–33
Gordon, William, 84–86
Grant, Madison, 155, 159, 185
Gray, Lloyd Vernon, 97–103, 179
Great Depression, 131, 211
Great Falls MT, 35, 36, 37–38, 50, 52, 81, 86, 92–93, 95, 131, 176, 188, 200–201, 210, 220
Greater Reconstruction, 11, 15, 33
Greely, Horace, 37–38

Haggin, James Ben Ali, 114, 257n12
Harding, Sam, 179–80
Harris, Emily, 196–97
Harris, Fred, 196–97
Harris, Fred, Jr., 196–97
Harrison, Jefferson, 33, 87–88, 201–3, 224
Harrison, Louise, xix, 202
Havre MT, 36, 66, 82, 84, 90
Heinze, Augustus, 113–16, 123–30, 132
Helena Independent, 62, 175–77
Helena MT, xi–xvi, 35, 36, 41, 42, 58, 73–75, 81, 84–89, 96–102, 107, 119, 122–24, 131, 153, 175–77, 179, 188, 193–94, 195, 201–3, 205, 229–30
Hernandez, Kelly Lytle, 6
"home," 7, 9, 20, 23, 49, 108, 141, 161, 174, 203, 223, 231–33
homesteading, 35, 200–203, 215, 223, 235
hunting, 27, 29, 118, 143, 144, 148, 150, 153, 219–20

identity: creation of, xx, 2, 25, 49, 72, 99–102, 216; and region, 2, 25, 49, 118; and place, 2, 72, 99–102, 135
Indian Territory, 35, 40–41, 160–61
Indigenous peoples, 11, 13, 27–31, 41–44, 49, 62–66, 91–92, 110–12, 148, 160–62, 172–74, 211–13, 219, 225, 230; dispossession of, 2, 8, 9, 12, 14, 16, 20–21, 22, 32, 33, 37, 41–42, 45, 59, 65, 111, 138, 159–62, 172–74, 225; of Montana, 1–2, 21, 27–29, 211–19; sovereignty of, 3, 10, 41, 49, 65–66, 92, 138, 172, 173; violence against, 9, 10, 12, 13, 30–31, 44, 49, 52, 54, 55, 59, 65, 111, 140, 188, 225; voting rights of, 91–92
interracial marriage, 24, 62, 111, 169–97, 219, 221–23, 227; of Black men to white women, 175–82; of Black women to white men, 189–91; rates of, 170, 182–84
Irving, William, 101

Jackson, Jim, 195
Jacobs, Alma, 229
Jim Crow, 13, 16, 21, 49, 55, 67, 71, 72–76, 83, 90, 143–44, 159, 169, 170–71, 176, 180, 214
Johnson, E. T., 229–30
Johnson, Raymond, 218

Kelley, Robin D. G., 4, 49, 75, 240n30
King, Tiffany Lethabo, 4, 77, 238n12, 243n44
Ku Klux Klan, 210–13

labor unions: exclusion of African Americans from, 19, 22, 93–95,

108, 130–31, 205–7, 215; membership of African Americans in, 215, 221; political power of, 22, 108, 113–16, 130, 213; United Steelworkers Union, 221; Western Federation of Miners, 19
Lakota Sioux, 15–16, 28, 30, 65, 187
landless Indians of Montana. *See* Little Shell Chippewa Tribe
Lang, William, 98–99
Laughlin, Mary, 175–77, 278n27
Lewis and Clark. *See* Corps of Discovery
Lewis, Samuel, 51
Lewistown MT, 36–37, 65, 213
Little Shell Chippewa Tribe, 219–21
Livingston MT, 36–37, 65, 213

Madison, Jennie, 178–79
Madison, Robert, 178–79
magpies, 137–46, 155, 166–68; extermination of, 142–45, 166–68; racialization of, 140, 142–46, 155, 166; as a social metaphor, 138–40, 145, 155, 270n8
memory: as "colonial aphasia," 281n58; loss of memory about Black history, xv, xvi–xvii, 11, 13–14, 51, 141, 145, 157, 165, 213, 232; as public memory, xvi, 13–14, 51, 157, 232; as settler memory, 9, 13–14, 15, 162
middle ground, 110–11
migration, 28, 59–60, 64; of African Americans to Montana, 20–21, 30, 32–46, 62, 64–65, 144; of African Americans out of Montana, 24, 204, 213–16, 225, 227; of African Americans to the West, 7, 20, 37, 52, 59–60, 64; Exoduster migration, 32, 34, 59–60, 64, 157; as a form of political dissent, 45–47; and the Great Migration, 32, 59–60, 213–16
Miles, Tiya, 6, 24, 190–91
Miles City MT, 30, 36–37, 58, 66, 90
mining, 50, 52, 90, 106, 109–16, 118–20, 125, 131, 171, 201, 205–7, 219
Missoula MT, 35, 36–37, 54, 81, 86, 191–92, 216, 218
Montana: African American population, 25, 35, 52, 62, 81–82, 145, 167, 182, 211, 216; massacres in, 13, 65, 111; 1972 constitution, 216–8; political climate of, 70–71, 113–35, 171, 216–18; territory of, 2, 16, 20–21, 35, 50, 52, 70–71, 81–82, 85, 110
Montana African American Heritage Places Project (MAAHPP), xi, xiii, 230, 233
Montana Club, 201, 224
The Montana Plaindealer, 41–42, 45, 58, 74–75, 87–89, 95–103, 122
Montana State Federation of Colored Women's Clubs, 106, 229, 288n55
Montana State Sportsmen Association, 142, 167–68
Morgan, Annie, 53
Muffly, Charles, 169, 170, 173–74, 189, 192, 277n17
Muir, John, 145, 158

National Conservation Commission, 185
Native Americans. *See* Indigenous peoples

Nature, 140–68; writings about, 146, 158–59, 162–64
"Negro problem," 59–64, 109
The New Age, 45, 84–85, 93, 105–9, 116–35, 153, 159–62
New Deal, 131, 214–16
newspapers, 38, 41–43, 45, 59–64, 95–97, 128–29, 131, 144, 177, 180, 209, 254n79
Nez Perce, 28, 30, 65, 111
1924 Indian Citizenship Act, 91, 212
1924 National Origins Act, 186
Northern Cheyenne, 28, 65, 173

oil production, 207–10

Parsons, Roy, 134
Pascoe, Peggy, 24, 177, 187, 195, 219
the Philippines, 16, 42, 56, 58, 145, 201
Pleasant Hour Club, Helena, 153
Plessy v. Ferguson, 70–71
populism, 115, 124
prostitution, 98–99, 179–80

Racial Frontier, 25, 203–4, 228; concept in scholarship, 14, 25, 204, 228
racial regimes, 4, 7, 10, 12, 13, 15–19, 21, 22, 23, 35, 49, 62, 67, 71, 73–75, 162, 165, 171
racial scripts, 91–92, 171
racism: in hiring, 22, 92–94, 126, 150, 215–16; in housing, 22, 207–10; in legislation, 21–22, 70–71, 91–92, 221. *See* school segregation
railroads, 32, 38, 50, 51, 65, 171, 207–8
Reconstruction, 7, 11, 32, 45, 60, 62, 70, 77, 133, 225; amendments, 16, 19, 91, 217
Republican Party, 22, 74–75, 80, 90, 95, 103, 115–6, 121–30, 152, 217, 226

Robinson, Cedric, 4, 45–46, 80
Rocky Mountains, 27–29, 51, 108, 110, 133–34, 138, 148, 150–51, 199
Roosevelt, Franklin, 122, 131, 214
Roosevelt, Theodore, 56, 96–97, 116, 145, 156, 185
Roy, Joseph, 189–91
Roy, Lillie, 189–91
Russell, Charlie, 199–203, 223–24

school segregation, 62, 63, 81–86
settler colonialism: as a binary, 1, 4, 5, 6, 11, 138; decolonization of, 3, 4, 9; as incomplete, 3, 11, 16, 223; individuals' participation in, 6, 33, 37, 44, 46, 71; logic of anti-blackness, 13, 71–72, 92, 108, 143, 156, 204, 227; logic of assimilation, 3, 13, 63–64, 140; logic of elimination, 3–4, 5, 6, 9, 10, 12–13, 22–23, 33, 44, 63–64, 71–72, 91, 140, 143, 161, 166, 174, 204, 223, 227; logic of native land appropriation, 13, 16, 20, 33, 37, 41–42, 66; logic of white supremacy, 10, 13, 20, 22, 108, 166; and maternalism, 52–53; relation to franchise colonialism, 2–3; as a structure, 4, 6, 8, 9, 13, 138–39; violence of, 3, 4, 7, 8, 12, 13, 15; as a white racial project, 10, 11, 12, 13, 18, 20, 157, 159, 167, 171, 189, 226, 248n16
settler colonial studies, 3–5, 7–8, 10–11, 49; afropessimist critique of, 4, 238n12; and Black studies, 4–5, 7–8, 239n25; and ethnic studies, 4, 6; and Indigenous studies, 4–5, 7–8
settler colonists, as an analytical category, 7, 8, 11; legitimacy of, 3, 6, 10, 11, 12, 19, 49, 52, 140, 167; as an

ontological condition, 4, 25, 138–39; origin myths of, 29–30, 53, 146, 228; and total settler sovereignty, 20
Silver Bow Literary Society, 119
Simington, Geo, 134
Simms, Ed, 37–38, 50
slavery, 5, 6, 11, 15, 20, 24, 29, 38, 77, 188; of Indians, 17
Small, Gail, 91–92
Smurr, J. W., 71, 83
Spanish American War, 42, 56, 58
Steger, Wallace, 202
Stoler, Ann Laura, 25, 172, 242n38
Stoll, Mark, 156–57, 163
Svingen, Orlan, 91–92

Taylor, Quintard, xix, 14, 25, 39–40, 147, 205, 215, 218, 227–28
terra nullius, 29, 138
Thoreau, Henry David, 145, 158
Trotter, William Monroe, 78–80, 185
Tsing, Anna, 205, 285n15
Turner, America, 82
Turner, Fredrick Jackson, 187–89

uplift ideology, 21, 45–49, 67, 76–81, 84–91, 102, 117; and accommodationists, 76–81
U.S. Federal Censuses: 1870 Federal Census, 60; 1890 Federal Census, 60–61, 184; 1910 Federal Census, xv–xvi, xviii
U.S. military forts: Fort Assiniboine, 55, 58, 150; Fort Custer, 55; Fort Harrison, 55, 58, 98, 201; Fort Keogh, 30, 55, 58; Fort Laramie, Wyoming, 50, 150; Fort Maginnis, 55; Fort Missoula, 54, 55; Fort Shaw, 55

U.S. West: Black population of, 13; diversity of, 12, 13, 17–19; historical narratives of, 14, 16, 147, 155

Walton, Mahala Ann, 88–89
Ward, Belle, 192–93
Washington, Booker T., 21, 46–49, 67, 76–81, 84–90, 94–95, 102–3, 106–8, 116, 117, 121, 134
Webb, Aaron, 127, 130
Wells, Ida B., 76–81, 185
westward expansion, 12, 30, 34, 46, 66, 138, 167, 225, 228; paradoxes of, 23, 30, 32, 228
White Sulphur Springs MT, 51, 65, 82, 84, 90, 163, 194–95, 231–33
whiteness: as ownership, 17, 23, 35, 158, 159; and the settler binary, 4, 12; the West as the locus of, 17, 31; "whitening the West," 12
wilderness, 23, 135, 141, 145–48, 152, 154–59, 161, 162, 165–66, 227
Williams, Annie, 191–92
Williams, Elizabeth, 33, 50–51, 90
Williams, John, 191–92
Willis, Ida, 134
Wolfe, Patrick, 3–4, 6–7, 10, 138, 145
Wong, Edlie L., 18–19, 240n29
Wood, Peter, 188–89
Woodcock, William, 69–71, 85–86, 102, 128

Yellowstone National Park, 33, 50, 150, 218
York, 28–29, 50, 148, 152, 218, 225

Zanzibar Club, 89, 97–102, 179

www.ingramcontent.com/pod-product-compliance
Lightning Source LLC
Chambersburg PA
CBHW031849220426
43663CB00006B/546